FAITH IN THE WILDERNESS

The Story of the Catholic Indian Missions

FAITH IN THE WILDERNESS

MARGARET & STEPHEN BUNSON
Illustrated by Margaret Bunson

Our Sunday Visitor Publishing Division
Our Sunday Visitor, Inc.
Huntington, Indiana 46750

ISBN: 0-87973-745-X
LCCCN: 00-130352

The drawings that appear in this book are by author Margaret Bunson
and were inspired by portraits and photographs from a variety of sources.

Cover design by Monica Haneline
PRINTED IN THE UNITED STATES OF AMERICA

*For the Native American residents
of the islands of Hawaii*

ACKNOWLEDGMENTS

There are many individuals to whom a debt of gratitude is owed for their kind assistance in the creation of this book. Among them are: the staffs of a number of libraries including Marquette University, the Catholic University of America, and the Sahara West library; Kim Clanton-Green; Mark Thiel of the University of Marquette Library; Lisa Grote; Father Ted Zuern, S.J.; and Patricia O'Rourke of the Bureau of Catholic Indian Missions; Henry O'Brien, managing editor of Religious Books at Our Sunday Visitor; Greg Erlandson, editor in chief of Our Sunday Visitor; and Robert Lockwood, former publisher of Our Sunday Visitor. Special thanks are owed to: His Excellency, Most Reverend Donald Pelotte, S.S.S., Ph.D., Bishop of Gallup; His Excellency, Most Reverend Charles J. Chaput, O.F.M. Cap., Archbishop of Denver; and Monsignor Paul Lenz, head of the Bureau of Catholic Indian Missions, without whose assistance this book would not have been possible. Finally, we would like to express our deepest thanks to His Eminence, John Cardinal O'Connor, Archbishop of New York, who passed away shortly after contributing the Preface to this work.

TABLE OF CONTENTS

Preface

FATHER Andrew White, S.J., was the superior of the tiny Jesuit community in colonial Maryland, having arrived there in 1634. He lived among the Piscataway and other Indian tribes in Kittamaquindi, during which time he baptized many of the Native Americans, including Chitomachon, the "Emperor of the Piscataway," as the principal chief was called. I remember reading a marvelous account of Father White's work in an annual report sent to the Jesuit provincial in 1640. Allow me to share a portion of this account with you as I introduce this work by the Bunsons:

> Not long ago, when he [Chitomachon] held a council of the tribe, in a crowded assembly of the chiefs and the people, with Father White and some of the English present, he publicly attested that it was his advice, together with his wife and children, that they should forsake their native superstition and give themselves to Christ; for there was no other true God but that of the Christians, nor could men in any other way save their immortal souls. . . . For the greatest hope is that, when the family [of kings] is baptized, the conversion of the whole empire will speedily take place.

As you read *Faith in the Wilderness: The Story of the Catholic Indian Missions*, I know you will deeply appreciate the legacy that the Bureau of Catholic Indian Missions has given to the Church in America. The dedication, faith, and zeal of countless men and women, religious and laity, who have labored in Christ's vineyard since the earliest days of this place we call America, is a sign of hope and inspiration to carry on in a spirit of missionary service.

I am particularly proud of the work of the Bureau of Catholic Indian Missions, because since 1874 it has been motivated by one very fundamental truth: wherever life is being created, saved, and sanctified, God is present as the ultimate author of that activity. The pages of this book are filled with historical and religious accounts of men and women dedicated to proclaiming that truth to a people worthy to hear it and open to embrace it.

✠ *JOHN CARDINAL O'CONNOR*
ARCHBISHOP OF NEW YORK
(1920-2000, R.I.P.)

Foreword

This book is distinguished by its focus on early missionary ministry that led to the development of the Bureau of Catholic Indian Missions, which is the oldest agency of the Church in the United States. Today, the United States Catholic Conference-National Conference of Catholic Bishops is the official agency of the Church in the United States; but, back in 1874, Archbishop James Roosevelt Bayley (a convert to Catholicism and the nephew of St. Elizabeth Ann Seton) was approached by Archbishop Francis Norbert Blanchet to start an office on Indian affairs in the western area of the United States.

Archbishop Bayley called on Charles Ewing, a Union general and Civil War veteran, to become the first head of the Bureau of Catholic Indian Missions. He became the fund-raiser of the organization as well as its dedicated lobbyist. While most of America was trying to push Indians farther west, he argued with the White House and Congress to allow the Indians to have some of their land as a base for their existence. Indians were never popular in this land, and at the time after the Civil War they suffered more than at probably any time in history. In 1890, the first census in which they were counted listed fewer than 250,000 Native Americans, although they were not legally citizens of the United States. From a population of millions they had been decimated to some quarter million Indians. They were called "the vanishing Americans" because they were expected to disappear from this land.

In 1874, when the Bureau of Catholic Indian Missions came into existence, the immediate challenge to Ewing was President Ulysses S. Grant's Peace Policy. It was a program that was to give religious leadership to the Indian reservations. Grant found that "no branch of the National government is so spotted with fraud, so tainted with corruption, so utterly unworthy of a free and enlightened government, as this Indian department." The program did not work. Although religious leaders were recommended to head Indian reservations, they failed to do their jobs. As usual, Catholics were denied due representation on Indian reservations. They were given control of only eight reservations, whereas, according to the number of Catholic Indians, they should have had thirty-eight reservations.

General Ewing recommended that his successor be a Catholic priest. Today, Monsignor Paul A. Lenz of the diocese of Altoona-Johnstown in Pennsylvania is the sixth priest to head the bureau as executive director.

The story of the Bureau of Catholic Indian Missions is set in a wide-ranging account of mission ministry to the American Indians by the Catholic Church. Father Pierre De Smet, S.J., is only one of the many missionary leaders portrayed in this book. It is a challenging account that will fascinate all who read it.

✠ DONALD E. PELOTTE, SSS, PH.D.
BISHOP OF GALLUP, NEW MEXICO

Introduction

God gives each of us a great many gifts in the course of a lifetime, and among those I hold most dear are two: my vocation as a Catholic priest, and my roots as a member of the Potawátomi people. Reading this wonderful book by the Bunsons reminded me of just how blessed I am.

It was common in the years immediately after the Second Vatican Council to reexamine and criticize much of the Church's traditional missionary effort. Purifying memory and confessing past sins is a good thing, as Pope John Paul II has so eloquently preached throughout his pontificate, especially in preparing for the Great Jubilee. History has certainly been marred by those missionaries who failed to live up to the dignity of their calling.

But focusing on the errors of history can lead to its own strange kind of forgetfulness. It can also be a form of *injustice* when the great achievements of missionaries on behalf of native peoples are ignored. The story of the Catholic Indian missions in North America is woven together from hundreds of smaller but very moving stories of missionary women and men who lived and died, preached and taught, century after century, to bring Jesus Christ to the native peoples. And in witnessing the Gospel, it was missionaries, above all, who spoke up in defense of native peoples' rights.

Jesus Christ is the meaning of history — the Redeemer of all peoples and all nations in every age. My family owes our faith, and I owe my priesthood, to missionaries who loved the Potawátomi people enough to commit their own lives to service in a strange land among foreign people. Was their sacrifice worthwhile? Beyond any doubt, it was. The Church is, by her nature, missionary — and for every missionary who stumbles, ten or twenty others succeed in living the Gospel authentically and leading others to Jesus Christ. So the kingdom is built. Margaret and Stephen Bunson deserve the gratitude of all American Catholics for helping us remember the past . . . and for telling the history of the Catholic Indian missions with compassion and truth.

✠ *Charles J. Chaput, O.F.M. Cap.*
Archbishop of Denver

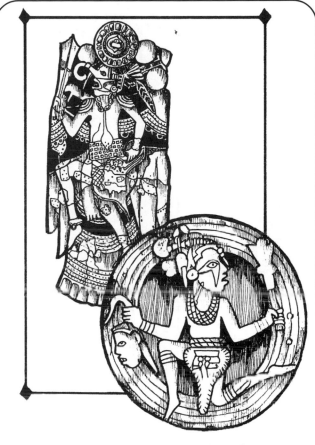

Copper breastplate from Safety Harbor Culture, Florida, and a shell gorget from the Temple Mound

CHAPTER 1

The New World

land overflowing with wealth and exotic splendors ignited their ambitions and served their imperial designs.

Christopher Columbus, seeking the "Indies" — the fabled lands of silks, gems, and fragrant spices — sailed into the waters of a new geographic entity and communicated his discoveries to his patrons in the royal court of Spain. Columbus's voyage did nothing to enhance his career, since he had not fulfilled his promise of finding the "Indies," though his account of the land masses rising out of the azure sea drew considerable interest. This report, along with the oft-repeated, fascinating tales of sailors and lesser explorers, spurred Europeans to venture into uncharted waters in Columbus's wake. Such men did not understand that they were about to confront a wilderness so immense and compelling that few of them could hope to envision the realities of the continent that awaited them.

No legends or logs of voyages could describe in truth this product of geological, volcanic, and tectonic processes over eons. The American continent, molded and shaped by ages of planetary upheaval, was a pan-

More than four centuries ago, the splendor of North America beckoned to the great powers of Europe. The distant continent took on the legendary charms of Atlantis as mystic tales of Cíbola (the Seven Cities of Gold) and the Lost Empire found their way across the Atlantic Ocean. The rulers of the European nations, with their ancient traditions and competitions, had depleted many of the natural resources of the Old World by engaging in endless wars and explorations for trade and conquest. America was described as a vast domain of natural wonders — a place where silver and gold gushed out of the earth as emblems of nature's generosity. The tales the Europeans heard of this new

orama of mountains and plains, fertile farmlands and haunting bayous. The Canadian Shield, or Laurentian Plateau, allowed the continent to rise above sea level and to begin the great march toward its present formation. Continuing natural processes brought the Shield into prominence, followed by southern elevations in the East and West.

The Great Plains of America, called the Interior Lowlands, emerged as did the sweeping coastal plains so treasured today. In the East, the Appalachians began their towering ascent, as did the Cordilleros in the West. Volcanic peaks, mementos of the wilder geological eras, emerged on the Pacific coast as part of the "rim of fire." There were also the four great "slope" regions in which land and water moved in one particular direction. One slope led to the Atlantic Ocean, one to the Hudson Bay and the Arctic Ocean. The third slope moved toward the Gulf of Mexico, while the last headed steadily toward the Pacific Ocean. Lesser slopes can be seen around the Great Lakes, emptying into the St. Lawrence River and then into the Atlantic.

The vast mountain ranges in the eastern and western sectors of the continent rise as splendid barriers or sentinels — some snow-crested, some covered with dense forests and vegetation. These mountains, towering over the continent, are the result of violent upheavals, but their splendors add a luster to the landscape, a majesty of natural creation. The Great Lakes, actually inland seas, nurture fields and plains. The Mississippi River

Cree-Ojibwa pouch

and the other powerful waterways that move southward across the North American continent enrich the earth and provide access to untold areas. In the Southwest, the wind-blown seas of sand and scrub demonstrate the climactic variations formed over the centuries.

The withdrawal of the glaciers and the warming of the continental climate allowed the New World to assume the diverse splendors that greeted the first Europeans who appeared on the horizon. Yet they were not the first human beings to step foot on American soil. When Christopher Columbus sailed into the waters of the continent, he discovered native populations. He termed these natives "Indians," because he was still convinced that he had made his way to the fabled East. The men who followed Columbus found vast native populations as well. These people have been called "Amerinds" or "Native Americans" over the centuries, but the name given to them by Christopher Columbus, "Indians," remains the popular designation, the traditional one still in use.

The "Indians" of the New World did come out of Asia, sustained by their own customs and with individual and group survival skills. Their arrival on the North American continent has been dated to the close of the last glacier era or perhaps earlier. Scholars provide varying dates, ranging from twelve thousand to thirty-five thousand years ago, but it is known that the first Indians followed migrating herds across the Bering Strait, at the time a solid mass of ice. From there they trekked across the continent, in all directions, seeking their own territories and opportunities. Some of these nomads may have used small vessels to voyage along the coastal regions from north to south.

The Indians had to confront the land formations of the continent, which required demonstrating considerable abilities to adapt and devise new ways of coping with natural forces and wildlife. They discovered clearly distinct environments in their realms as well, all of which offered unique challenges and priorities. These American landforms have been designated:

Subarctic
Northwest Coast
California
Western Plateau
Western Great Basin
Southwest
Plains
Eastern Woodlands
Southeast

About two hundred fifty recorded Indian cultures inhabited these geographical regions when the first Europeans entered the continental limits. Each one of these cultures reflected the geographic and climatic imperatives of their particular environments, as their artistic endeavors mirrored the natural splendors and available materials for expression of their spiritual and metaphysical traditions.

Chumash rock painting design

The Subarctic population of the North American continent was relatively small when the Europeans encountered the land and the people; unusual, considering the vastness of this particular territory and yet realistic considering the climatic impacts. The Native Americans resided in distinct, recognized cultures that spanned the region from Alaska to Labrador. The cultures included Abitibi, Ahtena, Aleut, Algonkin (Algonquin), Angmágsalik, Beaver, Beothuk, Carrier, Chippewa, Cree, Dogrib, and Inuit (Eskimo) groups (including Baffinland, Copper, Igulik, and Netsilik). Other Eskimo groups were the Caribou Eskimo, Eastern Eskimo, Labrador Eskimo, Pacific Coast Eskimo, Polar Eskimo, Western Eskimo, and the Eyak, Han, Hare, Ingalik, Inupiat, Koyukon (also Kayukum), Kutchin, Montagnais, Mountain, Naskapi, Ojibwa (Chippewa), Sekani, Slave, Tagish, Tanaina, Tanana, Têtes de Boule, Tsetsaut, Tutchone, Yellowknife, and Yup'ik. These were sturdy peoples, prepared to wrest survival out of the harsh environment and to maintain their ancestral wisdom even in the face of change. The nations of this area were particularly gifted as artists.

The native populations of the Pacific Northwest in the sixteenth century had the benefit of proximity to the ocean and to diverse natural resources. The Native Americans residing in that environment actually inhabited a long, narrow territory along the coast and on the offshore islands. The area stretched from Yakutat Bay in Alaska to Cape Mendocino in modern California, and many thousands of Indians flourished there by using the resources available and by improving their own survival skills to meet challenges. These recorded Indian peoples included the Alsea, Bella Bella, Bella Coola, Chilkat, Chinook, Coos,

Eyak, Gitksan, Haida, Haisla, Heiltsuk, Hupa, Kalapuya, Karok, Kwalhioqua, Kwakiutl, Makah, Nootka, and Quileute-Chimakum. Salish groupings include Comox, Cowlish, Duwamish, Klallam, Nesqually, Puyallup, Sechett, Snoqualmi, Siuslaw, Tillamook, Tlingit, Tolowa, Tsimshian, Tututni, Umpqua, Wiyot, Yakutat, and Yurok.

When the Europeans arrived in California, the Indians they met had survived centuries of diverse landscapes and climatic variations. They survived by maintaining small groups that relied upon their own languages, customs, and traditions as cohesive forces. These were hunter-gatherers for the most part, although agricultural settlements were established along the banks of the local rivers. Most relied upon sea products, local animals, and vegetation, and the social and educational traditions of these groups were complex and long-standing. The cultures in California included the Achomawi, Alsea, Akwa'ala, Athapaskan (which included the Koto, Lassik-Wailaki, Mattole, Nongatl, and Sinkyone), the Achomawi, Atsugewi, Cahuilla (Kawia), Chimariko, Chumash, Cócopa, Costanoan, Copehan, Cupeño, Diequeño, Esselen, Fernandano, Gabrielino, Guaiacura, Halchidhoma, Hupa, Juaneño, Kamia, Karok, Kawaiisu, Kawailsu, Kitanemuk, Luiseño, Maidu, Mariposan, Mission, Miwok, Mono, Moquelumman, Murietta, Patwin, Pericú, Perris, Pomo, Soboba Serrano, Salinan, Serrano, Seri, Shasta, Tabatulabal, Temecula, Wintun, Wiyot, Yahi, Yakut, Yana, Yuma, Yukian, and Yurok.

The Indians who confronted the Europeans in the Western Plateau of the North American continent resided in a vast area surrounded by mountain chains. The Western Plateau is bounded by the Rocky Mountains and the Coast and Cascade ranges. The region stretches from modern British Columbia to Washington state, including part of Montana and the northern areas of Oregon. Two large river systems drained the Western Plateau, and there was a plentiful supply of game and wild vegetation. The tribes there developed into sophisticated social hierarchies and supported governments and well-established arts and traditions. The four linguistic families of the area were the Salish, Kutenai, Sahaptin, and the Klamath-Modoc, or Lutuami. The recorded peoples using these languages were the Achomawi, Cayuse, Chilcotin, Coeur d'Alene, Columbia, Cowlitz, Flathead, Kalispel, Klamath, Klickitat, Kutenai, Lake, Lillovet, Lummi, Modoc, Molala, Muckleshoot, Nespelen, Nez Percé, Okanagon, Palus, Pend d'Oreille, Puget Sound, Sahaptin, Salish, Sanpoil, Shushwop, Siletz, Sinkaieth, Snake, Snohomish, Spokan, Suquamish, Swinomish, Tenino, Thompson, Umatilla, Walla Walla, Wenatchee, Wishram, and Yakima.

When the Europeans arrived in the Great Basin of the North American continent, they discovered a vast area that included the interior mountain and basin region of southeastern modern California, as well as Nevada, southeastern Oregon, and western Utah. This is a region that is dominated by harsh terrains, wildly beautiful panoramas, and a climate that ranges from arid to semiarid. Unique Indian cultures adapted to the natural realities by developing nomadic lifestyles that enabled them to take advantage of seasonal resources in a somewhat hostile environment. Small family bands of hunters and gatherers crossed the area and survived by honing their collective skills. The peoples of the Great Basin included the Bannock, Chemehuevi, Gosiute,

Kawaiisu, Koso, Las Vegas, Lemhi, Moapa, Mono, Paiute, Paviotso, Shivwit, Shoshone, Tumpanogat, Uinkaret, Ute, and Washo.

The Southwest area of the North American continent comprises modern Arizona and New Mexico as well as parts of Colorado, Texas, Utah, and Mexico. Four river systems nurture the area, but there is also an unstable climatic presence that can be hostile. The Indians residing in the Southwest when the Europeans arrived had flourishing art forms and remarkable settlements, including multiple apartment houses. Besides the Navajo in the north, several distinct nations shared the southwestern territories. They were the Yuma, Pima, Papago, Pueblo, Hopi, and Hano. The tribes included the Acoma, Apache (including the Chiricahua, Jicarilla, Mescalero, San Carlos, and White Mountain), Arivaca, Calabasas, Coahuiltec, Cochíti, Cócopa, Cora, Hano, Havasupai, Hopi (including the Hano Mishóngovi, Oraibi, Shipáulovi, Shongópovi, Sichómovi, and Walpi), Hualapai, Huichol, Isleta, Jemez, Keres (Queres), Laguna, Maricopa, Mishóngnovi, Mohave (or Mojave), Moquis, Nambé, Navajo, O'odham, Opata, Oraibi, Papago, Pecos, Picuris, Pima, Pojoaque, Pueblo, Sandia, San Felipe, San Ildefonso, San Juan, Santa Ana, Santa Clara, Santo Domingo, Shipáulovi, Shongópovi, Sia (Zia), Sichómovi, Sobaipura, Tanoan Pueblos (including Tewa, Tiwa, and Towa), Taos, Tarahumara, Tepehuan, Tesuque, Tubac, Tumacacuri, Yaqui, Yavapai, Yuma, and Zuñi.

The native populations of the Great Plains of the continent stunned the Europeans with their vigor, lush attire, and military skills. These tribes became the symbols of the American Indian in time, depicted and idealized in European works. There were several linguistic families present in the

Chief Wolf Robe and
Cheyenne parfleche (carrying pouch)

Great Plains, which is the area between the Mississippi and the Rocky Mountains and the modern Canadian territories. The Great Plains extend from northern Alberta and Saskatchewan in Canada to the Rio Grande in Texas. The Indian peoples who shared this vast and fertile area were the Apache, Arapaho, Arikara, Assiniboin, Atsina, Bax, Blackfoot (including the Siksika and Sihasapa), Blood (Kaina), Caddo, Cheyenne, Chicoutimi, Comanche, Cree (Plains), Crow, Dakota Sioux (including the Santee and Teton, composed of Bruté, Hunkpapa, Miniconjou, Oglala, Sans Arc, Sihasapa, and Two Kettles), Hidatsa (Gros Ventres of the River), Iowa, Karánkawa, Kansa, Kiowa,

Osceola, Seminole chief, with a regional
stone symbol and silver tribal buckle

Lipán, Mandan, Mascouten, Missouri, Nip-issing, Ojibwa (Bungi), Omaha, Osage, Ota, Ottawa, Pawnee (including the Chaui, Kit-kehahki, Piegan, Pitahauret, and Skidi), Ponca, Quapaw, Sarsi, Sept-iles (Seven Isles), Shoshone, Sinsinawa, Sisseton, Sutaio, Tawákoni, Tónkawa, and Wichita. The arrival of the horse had a remarkable impact upon these tribes, although there are references to a smaller equine available ear-lier. Adaptable and agile, they altered their lifestyles and accepted with skill the new form of transportation, the horse, introduced to the continent by the Spanish.

In the Eastern Woodlands, the territory stretching from Lake Superior to the Atlan-tic coast, three distinct language groups of Indians were in residence at the time of dis-covery of the North American continent. The three language groups were the Iroquoian, Algonkian, and the Siouan. The tribes of the region include the Abenaki, Cayuga, Conestoga (Susquehanna), Delaware, Erie, Fox, Huron, Illinois (including Peoria, Michigamea, Cahokia, and Kaskaskia), Iroquois League (including the Mohawk, Oneida, Onondaga, Seneca, and later the Tuscarora), Iroquois Laurentian, Kickapoo, Mahican, Malisit, Mascouten, Massachuset, Menóminee (or Menómini), Miami, Micmac, Mingo, Mohawk, Mohegan, Mohican, Montauk, Narragansett, Nauset, Neutral, Niantic, Nipmuc, Ojibwa (Chippewa), Passamaquoddy, Patuxent, Pennacook, Penobscot, Pequot, Piankashaw (Piankeshaw), Piscataway, Pocomtuc, Potomac, Potawátomi, Powhatan (including Chickahominy, Mattapony, Pamunkey, and Rappahannock), Santee Dakota (including Mdewakanton, Santee, Wahpekute, Wahpeton, Yankton, and Yantonai), Sauk (Sac), Secotan (including Pamlico and Weampemeoc), Seneca, Shawnee, Timucua, Tionontati, Tuscarora, Tútila, Wampanoag, Wappinger, Wenrohronon, Winnebago, Wyandotte, and Yaocomoco. These groups maintained stable villages, sophisticated governments, and hereditary rights. They also nurtured confederacies and militarily unified campaigns. The Eastern Woodlands Indians, like their counterparts across the entire continent, had a strong sense of territorial and community rights and obligations. As a result, they took a dim view of the European compulsion for land grabbing and considered the practice a violation of the natural circle of harmony provided for all creatures on the earth. The Iroquois, dedicated to military prowess and fearlessness in battle, quickly taught the Europeans that tribal peoples deemed primitive by the newcomers could exact a fearful price for intrusion and injustice in land matters.

In the Southeast region of the North American continent, Europeans encountered one of the most densely populated areas of the New World. This landform is bounded by the Atlantic Ocean and the Gulf of Mexico, although some scholars distinguish southern Florida as part of the circum-Caribbean culture. A coastal lowland belt, the Southeast includes a diversity of landscapes and cultures. It is a region that boasts warm climates, scrub forests, savanna grasslands, alluvial flood plains, rolling hills, rivers, forests, and even some of the southern Appalachians. The Seminoles are well known in the area today, but the name came into use around the time the United States was seeking independence, not before.

When the Europeans arrived, the recorded tribes in residence in the Southeast included the Acolapissa, Acuera, Adai, Ais, Akokisa, Alabama, Alibamon, Anacostan, Apalachee, Arkansas, Asinais, Atakapa, Avoyel, Bayougoula, Biloxi, Caddo, Calusa, Catawba, Cenis, Chackchiuma, Chapitoula, Chatot, Cheraw, Cherokee, Chiaha, Chickasaw, Chitimacha, Choctaw, Congaree, Coosa, Coweta, Creek, Cusabo, Eno, Eufaula, Fresh Water, Guacata, Guale, Hasinai, Hitchiti, Houma, Icaful, Jeaga, Karánkawa, Kashita, Koasati, Manahoac, Mobile, Mococo, Monacan, Muskogee, Nahyssan, Naniaba, Natchez, Natchitoches, Ocale, Occaneechi, Ofo, Onathesqua, Pamlico, Pascagoula, Pedee, Pensacola, Pohoy, Potano, Quapaw, Santee, Saponi, Saturiwa, Secotan, Seminole (circa 1780s), Sisseton, Sugeree, Surrque, Tacatucuru, Taensa, Tamaroa, Tamathli, Tekesta, Timucua, Tocobaga, Tohome, Tunica, Tuskegee, Tutelo, Utina, Waccamaw, Wateree, Waxhau, Winyaw, Woccon, Yamasee, Yazoo, Yuchi, Yui, and Yustaga.

The tribes listed in various anthropological and social studies represent the present Native American tribes or their ancestors. The impact of European settlements on the continent should not be underestimated: the Europeans' presence dispersed the tribes even in the earliest stages or brought about tribal decimation. As the Indian nations moved westward, further disruptions resulted in tribal consolidations or the division of some nations. The names of some of the smaller tribes have been lost over the centuries as a result of the chaos.

Thus, the New World was not a desolate landscape but the homeland of a vast native population. Tribes and Indian nations interacted in certain regions and followed their individual destinies in territories claimed by their ancestors. The arrival of the white Europeans signaled the end of the Native American lifestyles and tribal aspirations in many regions. Explorers, adventurers, military expeditions, and colonists swarmed over the land. In time, a different breed of men and women followed — human beings who envisioned America with eternal connotations that had nothing to do with metallic treasures or hoarded estates.

The Catholic missionaries who followed the explorers and conquerors into the New World discovered a continent that would serve as an arena of the "Good Work" of evangelization for centuries. Actually, America remained a mission territory in Vatican designation until the beginning of the twentieth century, despite the burgeoning populations, exuberance, and energies displayed. The missionaries coming to the continent carried the faith to far-flung outposts before and after the Revolutionary War, and remain still at their posts in modern times. It must also be remembered that such evangelists were entering *terra incognita*, the "unknown land." Unlike the natives, these Europeans did not understand the vast domain or the seasonal demands and challenges of survival in the harsher environment. They were strangers entering a wild and alien world that seemed to go beyond the horizon. Still, they conducted their apostolates in these wilds with devotion and stamina, often enduring even death to bring the Good News to America.

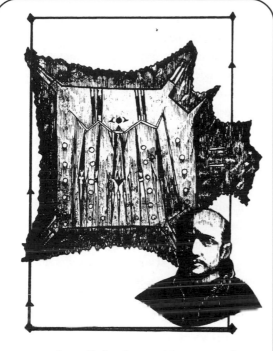

*Jesuit Father Jacques Marquette and
an early Great Lakes painted bison robe*

CHAPTER 2

The First Missions

The history of the Catholic Indian missions in America is a rich, multilayered, and complex tapestry that reflects the social attitudes of various eras, the changing roles of the peoples of the continent, and the political ramifications of European affairs as they were played out in the New World. The Catholic faith predates all other Christian denominations in North America, arriving soon after Columbus's discovery of the New World.

The exploration of America was actually a Catholic endeavor, in both the north and the south. These Catholic explorers and their accomplishments follow.

1499 — Amerigo Vespucci sails into American waters.

1500 — Gaspar Corte-Real discovers Newfoundland and Labrador.

1509 — Sebastian Cabot explores the North American coast.

1513 — Juan Ponce de León discovers Florida.

1524 — Giovanni da Verrazano discovers New York harbor.

1526 — Lucas Vásquez de Ayllón attempts colony near South Carolina.

1528 — Pánfilo de Narváez explores western coast of Florida.

1534 — Jacques Cartier explores St. Lawrence River and founds Montreal.

1535 — Álvar Núñez Cabeza de Vaca looks for Seven Cities of Gold in the American Southwest.

1539 — Hernando de Soto discovers the Mississippi River.

1540 — Francisco Coronado explores Southwest area. García López de Cardenas discovers the Grand Canyon.

1565 — Pedro Menéndez de Avilés settles St. Augustine in Florida.

1602 — Sebastian Vizcaíno explores the California coast.

1608 — Samuel de Champlain settles Quebec. Étienne Brulé explores the Great Lakes.

1638 — Jean Nicolet explores Great Lakes.

1673 — Jacques Marquette and Louis Joliet navigate the Mississippi River.

In the first eras of exploration, Pope Alexander VI divided the uncharted vastness of America between Spain and Portugal in the famous "Papal Line of Demarcation," which was included in the terms of the Treaty of Tordesillas. Other European nations chafed over such a limited disposition of possible wealth and treasures and set out to claim their own shares of the unspoiled wilderness — with or without papal blessings.

John Cabot, from Genoa, Italy, set sail under English patronage and arrived in Labrador, or Cape Breton Island, in June, 1497. He returned the following year, sailing south along the North American coast, reportedly reaching Chesapeake Bay. The English would substantiate their claims to North America later, using the evidence of Cabot's explorations. The Dutch and the Swedes competed as well, with historical entries into the continent and then with the wholesale occupation of certain regions. By the end of the sixteenth century the European nations had explored a good part of the continent, setting the stage for eventual migrations to the New World and the first settlements that changed forever the lives of Native Americans.

While these explorers were venturing into the unknown wilds of the North American continent in search of treasure or following the legends of cities of gold, the spiritual welfare of the Native Americans was of considerable concern to their Catholic governments in Europe. France and Spain demonstrated this concern in the patents issued for the exploration or settlement from the time of the first contact with North America. The patent granted to Lucas Vásquez de Ayllón in 1532 for exploration along the Florida coasts, for example, reads:

> Whereas our principal intent in the discovery of new lands is that the inhabitants and the natives thereof, who are without the light or knowledge of faith, may be brought to understand the truth of our holy Catholic Faith, that they may come to a knowledge thereof, and become Christians and be saved, and this is the chief motive that you are to bear and hold in this affair, and to this end it is proper that religious persons should accompany you, by these presents I empower you to carry to the said land the religious whom you may judge necessary, and the vestments and other things needful for the observance of Divine worship; and I command that whatever you shall expend in transporting the said religious, as well as maintaining them and giving them what is needful, and in their support, for their vestments and other articles required for Divine worship, shall be paid entirely from the rents and profits which in any manner shall belong to us in the said land.

Because of this religious mandate, few expeditions entered North America without the presence of religious or secular chaplains — priests dedicated to the evangelization of the tribes encountered in their journeys. The first explorers did not come to the New World on holy missions, of course, but the priests they brought with them were dedicated to just such an adventure of the spirit.

It must be remembered that the Spanish explorers in North America were looking for gold, silver, and other treasures. Their experience in South and Central America had forged a compelling avarice and expectation of such wealth. The Incas of Peru in South America could fill one room with gold and two rooms with silver when asked to provide such a ransom. The Aztecs and other Mesoamerican nations used gold and silver freely, along with various gemstones. Hernán Cortés had received a large, ornate mask fashioned out of gold as a gesture of friendship from Montezuma, the Aztec ruler of Tenochtitlan. Such casual displays of wealth did not promote the expected amiability in the Spanish of that era, but roused an overwhelming greed for the glittering metal that led to the view that the North American continent was but an extension of the golden empires conquered in the south. The Spanish had no way of knowing that the North American Indians felt no great compulsion to mine the earth's riches, or to adorn themselves with the golden symbols of the Aztecs or Incas. Conquerors seeking such metals would enter the new continent in vain.

In 1537, five years after Ayllón's patent, Pope Paul III, disturbed by the reports by Father Bartolomeo de las Casas sent him concerning the Spanish treatment of the conquered peoples of Mexico, issued the bull *Sublimus Deus*. In this bull, the pope announced: "The said Indians and all other people who may later be discovered by Christians are by no means to be deprived of their liberty or the possession of their property, even though they may be outside of the faith of Jesus Christ."

Pope Paul III was clearly hoping to stem the lurid cruelty being displayed, and to provide the first missionaries with certain mandates guaranteeing the protection of the native populations. He hoped that his word would infuse an element of evangelization and spiritual awareness into the wholesale enterprise of conquering a New World. His declaration did not halt the avarice or cruelty, but early missionaries in the

company of these explorers displayed a readiness to serve as the bearers of the Good News of Christ. They possessed a willingness to protest behavior contrary to the norms of the faith as a result of this papal decree and their religious tenets.

In time the missionaries entered America from both the north and the south. The first Catholic Mass reportedly celebrated within the present boundaries of the United States was offered by the priests with the expedition of Ponce de León at the southeastern tip of Florida in 1521. The second recorded Mass was celebrated in 1526 by the famous Dominican priest Antonio Montesino (also known as Antonio de Montesinos), the earliest recorded opponent of Indian slavery, at San Miguel de Guandape, north of Charleston, South Carolina. Some eighty years before the much-celebrated Jamestown was founded, San Miguel de Guandape flourished and died.

The region known as Florida in the sixteenth century was not limited to the present boundaries of the modern state. Ponce de León provided the name of the state while conducting his lunatic search for the "fountain of youth." He landed in the area on an Easter Sunday and called it *Pascua Florida*, "The Easter of Flowers," an obvious reference to the lush vegetation visible at his landing site. In time, Florida became the general designation for all of the Spanish interests in the entire southeastern portion of modern America; from Virginia to Alabama and extending to or beyond the Mississippi River.

Fifteen priests lost their lives in Florida while accompanying the expedition of Narváez, including the new bishop of Florida, Bishop Juan Juarez, and Brothers Juan de Palos (1527-1528) and De Soto (1539-1542). Nevertheless, another mission was attempted by Dom Luis Cáncer de Barbastro, the "Apostle of Guatemala," under a royal commission, in 1549. He was slain at Tampa Bay with his faithful Dominican companions.

In 1565, the first permanent settlement within the borders of the modern United States was made on August 28, by Pedro Menéndez de Avilés, a famous Spanish naval commander. He named the site after St. Augustine. Father Francisco López de Mendoza Grajales was with this founding group, and he remained in the area, starting an Indian mission at Santa Lucia, but was threatened by the local tribes. He then sailed to Havana, Cuba, but his ship was blown back to Florida, where it sank off the coast. Rescued by aid from the shore, Father Francisco became the pastor of St. Augustine, the first parish in the United States. The monastery of St. Helena, at St. Augustine, was the Franciscan headquarters.

One year later, Father Pedro Martínez and two Jesuit companions went to Cumberland Island on the coast of modern Georgia to begin a mission for the local tribes, and were slain on the site. Father Martínez was a nobleman from a powerful Spanish family. He had volunteered for the American Indian missions, and before his departure he had received the personal blessings of Pope St. Pius V and St. Francis Borgia. Father Martínez is the Jesuit protomartyr of America.

Undaunted by the terrible losses, other Jesuits pioneered another mission, Santa Catalina de Guale, in that same year, 1566, on St. Catherine's Island near modern Savannah, Georgia. By 1598, there were several such missions stretching from St. Augustine's up the eastern coast. The Jesuits started another mission for the Calusa Indians in southern Florida and in 1568, joined by ten more Jesuits, went to Havana to establish a school to educate young Calusa and other Native American youths.

The arrival of Father Juan Bautista Segura in Florida, soon after, added a new impetus to this mission. Serving as the Jesuit vice-provincial, Father Segura established missions to serve the Calusa, Tegesta, and Tocobaga Indians residing on the coasts. Father Antonio Sedeño and a lay brother went to the Yamasee territory of Georgia. The lay brother, Domingo Baez, wrote a grammar and catechism for the Yamasee in the mission. In 1569, a mission was started in Port Royal, south of Charleston in modern South Carolina, for the Orista Indians by the Jesuits Juan de la Carrera and Juan Rogel. These two missions were abandoned after a few years, but the Indian students joined other Florida Native American youths in the school in Havana to continue their studies. In 1570, Father Segura, with Father Luis de Quiros and novices and lay brothers of the Society of Jesus, went to Virginia to begin a mission for the Powhatan Indians. A chapel was erected, as the mission held promise, but a year later the entire party was martyred for the faith.

In 1577, the Franciscan priest Father Alonso de Reynosa started evangelizing the Timucua Indians at St. Augustine. Other missions followed in the Yamasee and Timucua villages to the north. Devotional books in the languages of the tribes were published and distributed, the first books ever printed in an Indian language in the United States. In 1597, however, the missions were destroyed in a Yamasee uprising, and five of the missionaries were killed.

Franciscan Pedro de Corpa was slain in St. Augustine, targeted first because he had preached against polygamy. At the Topoqui mission, Father Blas de Rodríguez was surrounded by attackers in his chapel. He asked to be allowed to celebrate Mass, and the Yamasee agreed. They sat quietly throughout the liturgy, killing the Franciscan at the closing prayers. At Mission Santa Catalina de Guale, in what is now Georgia, Franciscan Father Miguel de Anón died beside the local chief, a devout Catholic, who had come to try to save him. At Asao Mission, the Indians could not find Franciscan Francisco de Beráscola (Veráscola), and this delayed the revolt for a time. At Ospa, a Franciscan was taken prisoner and tortured. An elder Yamasee woman, however, intervened, and he was released.

The Timucua missions near the lower St. John's River remained intact. There were four such outposts of the faith by 1602, serving twelve hundred Christian Indians. These missions flourished enough to bring the bishop of Cuba to Florida. In 1606, Bishop Juan de las Cabezas Altamirano, O.P., arrived to confirm some fifteen hundred Christian Indians. The Franciscans committed themselves totally to the missions, despite the appalling losses. In 1612, twenty-three Franciscans arrived from Cádiz, Spain. In 1613, Mexican authorities sent eight more priests, and in 1615 another twelve arrived.

The powerful Apalachee in western Florida also asked for missionaries in 1633, and by 1655 the Franciscans operated thirty-five such sites in Florida and Georgia. Two years later, the Apalachee went to war with the Spanish government, and eight missions had to be closed as a result of the hostilities. The Franciscans sailed for Havana to begin again there, but drowned when their vessel sank en route.

In 1674, the abandoned Apalachee missions were reopened, and ten years later the Diocesan Synod of Havana, the ecclesiastical authority for the region, issued regu-

St. Catherine's Island sixteenth-century medal

lations for the protection of all Indians in the missions. Prompted by these regulations and by the aggressive advances being made by the English colony established in Georgia, the Spanish governor of the Florida territory decided to remove the Indians in the northern missions to the safer havens in the south.

The Yamasee revolted as a result of this enforced migration and turned to the English for aid. The tribe was supplied with arms by the colony of Georgia, and they attacked St. Catherine's Island Mission, taking the Christian Indians to sell as slaves in Charleston. The custom of inducing Indian tribes to raid other encampments was a long-standing English policy of the time, used by the slave traders in Carolina annually. These raids produced large numbers of Indian slaves, to be sold in Carolina and in Barbados.

The War of the Spanish Succession (1701-1712), called Queen Anne's War in the New World, prompted the English of Georgia to attack Florida, and in May, 1702, the Lower Creeks (then allied with the En-

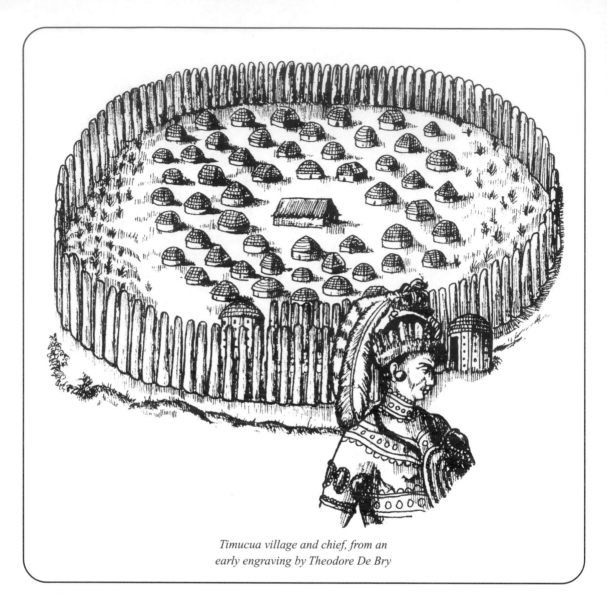

*Timucua village and chief, from an
early engraving by Theodore De Bry*

glish) destroyed the Timucua mission, Santa Fe. In October of that year, English and Indians combined their forces and, using naval ships as well, assaulted the mission towns north of St. Augustine. One by one these missions fell, and the English soon burned St. Augustine itself, destroying one of the finest libraries in the New World. In January, 1704, Governor Moore of Carolina led whites and a vast combined force of Creek, Catawba, and other Indians in attacks on the Apalachee missions, destroying ten such havens and taking fourteen hundred Catholic Indians to be sold as slaves or to be given to the tribes taking part in the campaign. Four Catholic missionaries perished in the attack, two after being tortured and burned at the stake. Spanish military personnel were hacked to pieces. The churches, gardens, school buildings, and orange groves were demolished and the sacred vessels and vestments were carried off as trophies of a Protestant victory. The Florida missions had fallen.

In 1726, there were still more than a thousand Catholic Indians in the region, but they disappeared as the English colony of Georgia gained power. In 1743, two Jesuit priests, Fathers José María Monaco and José Xavier de Alana, started the Florida mission again, with considerable success for a time. The Seminole Wars in the early 1800s put an end to the Catholic Indian apostolate in that region of America for many decades. (For other details on the missions in this area, see the chronological account of the states in Appendix 1.)

* * *

The Society of Jesus was evident in New England, far to the north of the embattled St. Augustine, as early as 1603, when Father Nicholas Aubry offered Mass in the area. The Jesuits founded Saint-Sauveur, the first mission in Maine, in 1613. This outpost of the faith was part of a French post on Mount Desert Island, in the present diocese of Portland, Maine, a hotly contested area, open to English attack at all times. Father Pierre Biard, from Grenoble, France, and three Jesuit companions including Abbé Jesse Fleché opened Saint-Sauveur for the Abenaki Indians, a tribe with an enduring Catholic history in America. Father Biard was a professor of scholastic theology and Hebrew, a true scholar who had been assigned to the Jesuit mission in the New World. Tradition states that he healed a dying Indian baby on Mount Desert Island, winning the respect of the Abenakis.

Within months, the English military units from other New England colonies attacked Saint-Sauveur as a French outpost and killed a Jesuit lay brother, Gilbert du Thet. They then arrested the priests, who were taken to Jamestown and later forced to accompany a second English expedition that completed the destruction of Saint-Sauveur. It was hoped that their assistance, or at least the presence of the priests in this second attack, would discourage the local Native Americans from having any good relations with any French missionaries. Father Biard was sent to England and eventually returned to France. He became a noted military chaplain in his homeland, unable to return to the missions because of the political realities.

Six years later, in 1619, the Recollect Franciscans opened a mission in the area of modern Nova Scotia and New Brunswick after having tried to evangelize the Hurons, Wyandottes, Montagnais, and the Micmacs without success. The Capuchin Franciscans took over the apostolate and labored among the local tribes on the Penobscot River in 1633, until the English again assaulted the mission and destroyed the site. The Jesuits had reentered the North American missions in New England in 1632, and two years later had thirty-five missions in operation. These French missions in America were targeted by the English because of continental rivalries and the political situation in Europe, events always mirrored in the New World. The New England Indians normally sided with the French in disputes because the missionaries who came among them from Canada proved trustworthy and single-minded in their mission vocations. This alliance made such missions distinct targets for the English aggressions.

Micmac design from Maine

Raids continued, and Catholic Indians felt compelled to migrate into Canada to escape English assaults. The Abenakis, for example, had a mission on the Kennebec River as early as 1636, served by the Jesuit Gabriel Druillettes. Some Abenakis remained on their lands after the exodus, served by a remarkable missionary, Father Sebastian Rale (or Rasle), who compiled a dictionary in the Abenaki language.

* * *

The name Abenaki reportedly was bestowed upon the tribe by other Native Americans and can be translated as: "Our ancestors of the East," a sign of respect. Early records include the Lord's Prayer in Abenaki, as follows:

> *Kemitanksena spomkik ayan waiwaielmoguatch ayiliwisian amantai paitriwai witawaikai ketepelta mohanganeck aylikitankonak ketelailtamohangan spomkik tali yo nampikik paitchi kik tankouataitche mamilinai yo paimi ghisgak daitaskiskouai aiponmena yopa katchi anaihail tama wihaikai kaissikakan wihiolaikaipan aliniona kisi anihailtamakokaik kaikauwia kaitaipanik mosak kaita lichi kitawikaik tampamohontchi saghi houeneminamai on lahamistakai saghihousoouaminai mamait chikil, Nialest.*

Father Rale arrived in the Abenaki mission in 1694, serving the settlement of Norridgewock, on the Kennebec River. When the Indians went on hunting or fishing expeditions, Father Rale moved with them. He had devised ways of carrying all that he needed for such trips, and when the tribe camped on the trail, he erected a portable chapel. For almost three decades Father Rale served the Abenakis, despite English threats.

When Father Rale heard that a new, warlike tribe had moved into the mission area, he went to visit them and to conduct a service for their people. At the end of the service he told them: "Let us not separate, that some may go one way and some another. Let us all go to heaven. It is our country, and the place to which we are invited by the sole Master of life, of whom I am but the interpreter." The tribe made no comment at the time, but within the year they were part of Father Rale's mission.

In 1713, the English asked the Abenaki to send Father Rale back to Canada. They would then be provided, in turn, with various gifts and a Puritan minister. The Abenakis were far too devout to even contemplate such an offer and speedily declined. In 1717, the English tried again to rid the area of Father Rale. The local governor sent word to the Abenaki that if they ousted the Jesuit he would give them a Bible and a Protestant minister, a Reverend Baxter. The Abenaki sent back the following message: "All people love their own priests! Your bibles we do not care for, and God has already sent us a teacher." This disturbed the English, who had a certain wariness when dealing with this tribe. The Abenakis could be fearful foes in battle, and the English had to devise another way to rid themselves of the French priest.

On August 23, 1724, attacking Mohawks killed Father Rale and destroyed the mission at Norridgewock. The Mohawks were acting as agents for the English, who had put a price on Rale's head. His Abenaki dictionary disappeared during the raid but is reportedly now at Harvard University and is considered one of the great masterpieces of indigenous language. The Abenaki mourned but stayed in the faith, and the missions continued even as the various Catholic Indian tribes moved north into Canada. When the Revolutionary War began, the Americans had to ask the Abenaki Indians for aid against the English. The Abenakis made a rather startling request in reply — they asked for a chaplain — and George Washington was compelled to honor the request in order to earn their alliance. When the Abenaki dealt with Bishop John Carroll after the Revolutionary War, they did so in the name of Father Rale.

It must be remembered that Massachusetts and other New England colonies were founded by Protestant groups who were truly enemies of the Catholic Church. Bans against Catholic priests, especially Jesuits, were enforced as early as 1647. The intolerance demonstrated was not only based on religion but on nationalities as well, with the Irish and French targeted as enemies of all Puritans. These Puritans held firmly to two distinct and yet connected views of Catholics and Native Americans, and as a result both groups were condemned and eradicated whenever possible.

The Indians were considered temporary intruders in God's "New Kingdom" on earth, the land called America. Believing that the divine plan for the New World could not be completed as long as Indians resided in their midst, the Puritans prayed that such foes would be eliminated. In order to accomplish this act of faith, the Puritans established their own reign of terror on the local Pequot tribe along the Connecticut frontier. In 1637, a force of two hundred fifty colonial militia, aided by almost one thousand warriors from the Narragansett and Mohegan territories, attacked the camp of Chief Sassacus on the Mystic River. More than six hundred

Pequot died in the raid, with women and children trapped and burned to death.

Dr. Cotton Mather, the Puritan leader, is reported to have expressed his personal satisfaction over the affair, rejoicing that "no less than six hundred Pequot souls were brought down to hell" as a result. The Puritans had basic tenets that inspired such actions, but there were far more personal sentiments involved as well. They feared the Catholic missionaries, and they had few delusions about the power of the faith, as members of their own community had succumbed to Indian abductions and conversions.

On August 10, 1683, Esther Wheelright, the daughter of a prominent Puritan leader, was abducted by the Abenaki Indians at Wells, Massachusetts. Held as a captive for six years, Esther was ransomed by a Jesuit missionary and taken to Quebec. There Esther was adopted by Governor Vaudrieul and his family and was converted to the Catholic faith. Esther entered the Ursuline Convent, becoming Marie Joseph of the Infant Jesus in October, 1712. She served as a nursing Sister during the Anglo-French Wars and was elected superior of the Ursulines in 1760.

In 1702, Eunice Williams, the six-year-old daughter of Reverend John Williams of Deerfield, Massachusetts, was captured by the Mohawks. Raised by the tribe, Eunice visited Montreal, became a Catholic, and was given the baptismal name of Margaret. Soon after, Reverend Williams found her and begged her to come home, whereupon the Mohawks threatened war. Margaret had no intention of renouncing her faith or her standing as a Mohawk, and she refused her father's pleas. Married and honored as a wise matron, she died in 1786 in the Mohawk camp.

Another Puritan, John Saywood, lost

his daughters to Indian abductors about the same time. These young women were given to missionaries, who took them to Montreal, where they received the faith. One daughter became Marie Geneviève and the younger was named Marie Joseph. Marie Geneviève entered the religious life and died in 1717. Marie Joseph married Pierre l'Estage, a Montreal merchant. She is buried under the chapel of the Church of Notre Dame in that city.

Yet another Puritan girl who entered religious life was Mary Anne Davis, who was born in Salem, Massachusetts, in 1680. At the age of six she was taken captive by the Abenakis and remained with them until she was seventeen. Then Father Sebastian Rale, who would be slain by the English, ransomed her and took her to Quebec. She was baptized there and entered the Ursulines in 1698 as Sister Mary Benedict. Elected superior in time, Sister Mary Benedict served as a religious for half a century.

The most famous Puritan to turn her back on her family and her Protestant beliefs was Frances Allen, the daughter of the Revolutionary War hero Ethan Allen. Having studied in Montreal, at age twenty-one Frances expressed her desire to be a Catholic and a religious. Her parents made her return home for a year, and then they relented and allowed her to go to Hotel-Dieu in Montreal.

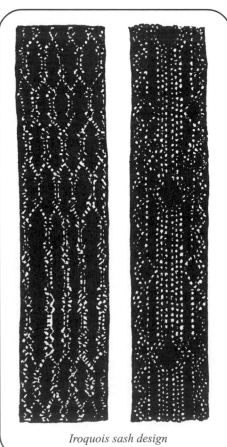
Iroquois sash design

Frances made her religious profession in 1810. She died as a nun on December 10, 1819, from lung complications.

* * *

In New York, the Iroquois confederation ruled a large portion of the territory now comprising that state. This confederation consisted of the Cayuga, Mohawk, Oneida, Onondaga, and Seneca nations — called the Iroquois League, the League of Five Nations, or simply the Five Nations. (When the Tuscarora nation joined the league in 1722, the English referred to them as the Six Nations.) The Iroquois, who could field more than two thousand warriors for a battle, were not friends of the Canadian French. Samuel de Champlain had allied himself with the Iroquois' enemies, the Algonquins, in 1609, an event remembered by the Iroquois League. Catholic French missionaries were not welcomed in New York as a result.

In 1626, a Recollect Franciscan, Joseph de la Roche Daillon, who headed the Huron mission in Ontario, entered the region and founded a mission at Niagara, but did not remain long. In 1642, St. Isaac Jogues and two companions were captured by the Iroquois, along with several Catholic Hurons. The captives were taken to Ossernenon (Caughnawaga), near modern Auriesville, where the Hurons were burned at the stake. St. Isaac

Jogues had his nails torn out, two fingers crushed by cruel bites by the Indians, and one thumb sawed off. St. René Goupil was killed, and the third Frenchman, named Couture, was adopted into the tribe. St. Isaac Jogues remained a captive for fifteen months before being ransomed by a Dutch party in the region. The Dutch also ransomed Father Francisco Giuseppe Bressani, a Jesuit who had been held and tortured for two months in 1644.

St. Isaac Jogues returned to Canada and then to France where everyone, including the French queen, wanted to touch his mangled hands. Ironically, the mutilation of his hands canonically disqualified him from celebrating Mass. A petition was sent to Pope Innocent XI, appealing for a dispensation for St. Isaac. Pope Innocent exclaimed in reply: *Indignum esse Christi martyrem, Christi non bibere sanguinem* ("It would be unjust if a martyr for Christ could not drink the blood of Christ"). The dispensation was readily granted.

St. Isaac did not retreat from his mission apostolate, and in May, 1646, he went with another companion into Mohawk territory to complete a settlement of peace that had been negotiated. With this treaty in place, he set out once again to establish a Mohawk mission. The Mohawks, disregarding the treaty because of recent events and new perspectives, captured St. Isaac and took him and his party, including St. Jean Lalande, once again to Ossernenon. There they endured endless tortures and were slain on October 18 and 19, 1646. The head of St. Isaac was displayed on the palisades, and his body was thrown into the river.

Five years later, Father Joseph Poncet, another Jesuit, was captured by the Mohawks, tortured, and sent to Montreal with overtures for another treaty of peace. The Onondaga, Oneida, and Cayuga members of the Iroquois confederation joined the Mohawks in seeking this peace. Father Simon Le Moyne went to Onondaga in 1654 to ratify a treaty, and he founded a mission at Indian Hill, near Manlius, New York. Father Le Moyne was the one who discovered the vast salt deposits of the region that led to settlement. He did not remain at Indian Hill, but three years later was working with tribes in the northern part of modern New York.

Three other Jesuits — Fathers Pierre-Joseph Chaumont, René Menard, and Claude Dablon — also established a mission in Indian Hill, called Fort St. Marie de Gannentaha. Father Dablon, born in Dieppe, France, became the superior of the Jesuit Indian missions of North America in time. He had recorded and published the journeys of Father Jacques Marquette on the Mississippi River, and the records and maps of his own mission explorations provided rich historical details for later generations. On November 14, 1655, St. Mary's Church was erected in a single day at present-day Syracuse. It was abandoned in March, 1658, but an entire band of Jesuits would soon enter the area to reclaim the missions.

In 1655, a group of French colonists made a settlement at Onondaga, and Father Le Moyne returned. Raids on the mission started again three years later, and Onondaga was abandoned until Garaconthié (Garakontié), the Onondaga chief and orator, supported the faith in 1667. Garaconthié persuaded his people to welcome the "Blackrobes," as the priests were called by the local Native Americans. Chief Garaconthié was a respected Iroquois, born at Onondaga and the nephew of Tododho, the famed Iroquois sachem. He listened to the Jesuits and watched them but said little until the French and Iroquois War, at which time he made himself personally responsible for the protection of the missionaries and their converts.

In 1669, Garaconthié and other chiefs were invited to Quebec to confer with Blessed François de Montmorency Laval, the first bishop of Canada. Blessed François was well known in his own land and in the colonies. Native Americans and whites alike announced, "His heart is always with us," when speaking of the saintly prelate.

At this conference, after many Native Americans and missionaries had made speeches concerning the unity required to promote the mission apostolate, Chief Garaconthié rose in his place and announced that he wished to be baptized. Blessed François administered the sacrament in the cathedral. Other chiefs, hearing of Garaconthié's conversion, were baptized as well.

Daniel Garaconthié's life was a living testament of the faith. One contemporary stated that the chief "never committed a willful fault." He walked two miles to Mass with his wife for the rest of his life. At Christmas Eve Mass in 1675, Garaconthié caught cold and began to weaken. Calling his people together, praying and receiving the last rites, he calmly announced: *Onne onage che ca* — "Behold I die."

Other Jesuits, including Fathers Jacques Fremin, Jacques Bruyas, René Menard, Julian Garnier, Pierre Millet (or Milet), and Jacques de Lamberville, were at the Iroquois camp in Monroe, Ontario, and Cayuga counties in 1656. In 1668, Father Fremin went to St. Michael's, near modern East Bloomfield. St. Michael's was a unique village, founded by Christian Hurons who had been carried off by the Seneca during raids. Gathering together, these Catholic Indians had formed their own settlement and had requested a priest. The Cayuga received

their own priest, the Jesuit Father Carheil, at St. Joseph's Mission, near Union Springs, Great Gully Brook. Immaculate Conception Mission was also founded in 1668 at Totiakton, New York. Jesuit Pierre Millet, called "the Looker-up-to-Heaven," was at St. John's Mission. Jesuit Julian Garnier composed a dictionary for the Seneca at Immaculate Conception Mission. In 1671, the Jesuit Jean Pierron was at the Seneca mission of St. James at Gannagaro.

Blessed Kateri Tekakwitha, known as "The Lily of the Mohawks," was nurtured by these missions and by the labors of the priests and the example of a Christian Iroquois. In 1702, the Onondaga and the Seneca had missions that lasted until the English authorities dismantled them in 1709. In 1748, Presentation Mission was established at Oswegatchié, now Ogdensburg, New York, by the Sulpician François Picquet. This mission was closed in 1807. In 1756, the Jesuits opened St. Regis at Aquasane.

In New Jersey, a Mass was celebrated as early as 1762, at Macopin, or Echo Lake. A church would replace the mission later. Even earlier, in 1672, the Jesuits had been laboring at Woodbridge, forced out by the

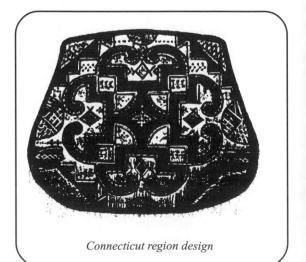

Connecticut region design

1698 ordinance forbidding their presence in the colony. In Delaware, Father Jean Pierron traveled in several areas in 1674. The Jesuits founded Apoquiniminck Mission in New Castle County in 1750, but it did not survive long. No other Indian missions were subsequently opened in the region.

The Puritans of Connecticut had a rare experience with the Jesuits in 1651. Father Gabriel Druillettes arrived in New Haven with diplomatic immunity as the representative of the governor of New France, now Canada. Canadian authorities were hoping to establish a treaty with the New England colonies, a pact that would promote trade but would consist mainly of united efforts against Iroquois attacks. Father Druillettes was well known in the colonies as an Indian authority and as a tireless explorer. He was received with considerable courtesy and good will by the local Puritans. A year earlier he had attended a meeting for the same purpose in Boston, and there he had been the guest of Major General Gibbons, and the leader, John Eliot, had been hospitable. The New Haven meeting proved futile, and Father Druillettes returned to the Abenakis and to Canada.

French missionaries such as Gabriel Druillettes brought a unique approach to their apostolate, one that allowed them to achieve a relative rate of success under difficult circumstances. These missionaries, particularly the Jesuits, went to nomadic Native American camps and moved with them frequently during seasonal migrations. Faced with Indian nations unable to understand French or any other European languages, the missionaries undertook the task of becoming fluent in the local Native American tongues. There was no way of explaining spiritual or theological concepts without a basic awareness of Indian languages, nuances, and spiritual traditions. These missionaries also lived with the Native Americans, enduring hardships that few Europeans could comprehend. If the Jesuits erected a chapel and a mission house, it was a simple wooden cabin in the wilderness. By contrast, the great Spanish missions in California and Texas were economic centers, massive investments that demanded considerable staffing, management, and concern. The French Jesuits could pick up and move unfettered by capital investments or economic considerations. Abandoned missions could be reopened by the simple appearance of a Jesuit. This approach in the missions came probably as a result of the French trappers, who set the pace for living with the various Native American nations, which proved successful. When a missionary abandoned his "European" ways to become part of the Indian lifestyle, he was accepted by the tribes of the region.

In New Hampshire, the Jesuits celebrated Mass on the Oyster River in Durham in 1694, while accompanying a French military expedition, though no mission is recorded in the state. Indian Catholic missions were not cited in Connecticut or Rhode Island either.

Vermont received its name from Samuel de Champlain in 1609, and the Sulpician Dollier de Casson celebrated Mass at Fort Ste. Anne on Isle La Motte in 1666. Two years later Blessed François de Montmorency Laval visited Vermont, and Jesuit Jacques Fremin was laboring among the local tribes. In 1710, the Jesuit missions at Swanton and Ferrisburg opened.

In 1670, several Jesuits entered the Susquehanna region of Pennsylvania, where St. Isaac Jogues had labored in 1643, and were followed by other Jesuits, Recollect Franciscans, and Sulpicians. In 1687, Jesuit

Henry Harrison served in the mission, and in 1720, Jesuits Joseph Greaton and Richard Molyneux visited Pennsylvania tribes. Father Molyneux attended an Indian council in Lancaster in 1744. Ten years later a chapel was erected at Fort Duquesne, called "The Assumption of the Blessed Virgin of the Beautiful River [the Ohio River]." Recollect Franciscans Denys Baron, Gabriel Amheuser, and Luke Collet were at this mission. In 1755, Jesuit Claude François Virot labored among the Delawares, Shawnees, and Mingos at Sawcunk on the Delaware River.

Northern Great Lakes pouch

* * *

Fathers Juan de Gallegos and Louis de Soto accompanied the Hernando de Soto expedition into Tennessee in 1541. In 1673, Jesuit Jacques Marquette was welcomed by the local Chickasaw, and Recollect Franciscans Zenobius Membré and Anastase Douay were in Tennessee with René-Robert Cavelier, Sieur de La Salle, in 1682. No Catholic Indian missions were founded.

The Jesuits were instrumental in Virginia, and the state was visited as early as 1526 by the Dominicans: Antonio Montesino is noted at the settlement of Lucas Vásquez de Ayllón. In 1570, Jesuit Juan Bautista Segura led Father Luis de Quiros and Brothers Solís, Méndez, Linares, Redondo, Gabriel, and Gómez to Axacan near the future site of Jamestown. They were slain there on the Rappahannock River. In 1634, Jesuit John Altham served the local Indians in the area, but within ten years priests were outlawed. In 1689, Capuchin Franciscan Christopher Plunket was arrested and died on a coastal island in exile.

The region of West Virginia recorded no Catholic Indian missions. Kentucky had no recorded permanent Indian missions either.

Maryland, the cradle of Catholicism in the United States, was founded as a Catholic colony but came under Protestant control as a result of political changes in Europe. In 1634, Jesuits Andrew White and John Altham arrived in Maryland and were welcomed by the Yaocomoco Indians. Father White celebrated the first Mass in Maryland on St. Clement's Island on the lower Potomac River upon his arrival. He labored among the Piscataway while other newly arrived Jesuits, including Father Rigby, served the tribes on the Patuxent River. In 1637, Jesuits Thomas Copley and John Knoller entered the area missions as well. Two years later, Father White opened the Kittamaquindi mission for the Piscataway, with stations at Mettapony, Anacostan (in modern-day Washington, D.C.), and at Potopaco. On July 5, 1640, Chitomachon, the "Emperor of the Piscataway," was baptized by Father White. The "emperor" took the baptismal name of Charles and was honored during the ceremony by the attendance of Governor Calvert and other dignitaries. This Piscataway chief and his wife aided the missions throughout the region.

In 1642, secular priests Gilmett and Territt entered the Maryland missions, and in 1673, six Franciscans, led by Masseus Massey, were also in the area, despite attacks by the local English authorities. Priests were arrested and deported, but the faith took hold, nurturing Catholic families who stood firm in the later Penal Period. In 1706, Jesuit Thomas Mansell founded St. Xavier's in Cecil County, but the era of Indian missions was coming to an end in the region.

* * *

In colonial times, the area called the "Northwest Territory" (not to be confused with Canada's "Northwest Territories") was actually the basis for the American modern Midwest region. The original Northwest Territory included the present states of Illinois, Indiana, Michigan, Ohio, Wisconsin, and part of Minnesota. Almost all of the territory, except for Illinois and Indiana, was in the control of the French and served by Jesuits. These priests were serving the Native Americans in Green Bay and Mackinaw in the Great Lakes region as early as 1640. Jesuits St. Isaac Jogues and Father Charles Raymbault visited the area called Sault Ste. Marie and planted a cross on the banks of the St. Mary's River to dedicate the site to God and to the holy cause of evangelization. The Michigan missions were thus opened, and Jesuit René Menard was at Keweenaw Bay by 1660. Eight years later, Jesuit Jacques Marquette established the mission at Sault Ste. Marie, and St. Michael's Mission was started as well. The Jesuit Claude Dablon founded St. Ignace Mission in 1669 and labored as well at Sault Ste. Marie. St. Ignace was moved north one year later. St. Joseph's Mission was opened for the Ottawa by the Jesuit François Dollier, who was aided by the famed Jesuit Gabriel Druillettes.

In 1677, the remains of Father Jacques Marquette were brought to St. Ignace Mission at Mackinaw by Indians from the region now near Ludington. Father Marquette had died while returning from these Native Americans, and they had carefully dried his bones and placed them within a birch-bark casket, which they brought to the mission in procession.

While Jesuit Father Henri Nouvel was laboring at Saginaw and Thunder Bay, Recollect Franciscan Louis Hennepin was also in the area. The missions expanded and prospered until the French-Iroquois War of 1687, when St. Francis Xavier Mission was burned to the ground. Jesuit Jean Enjahan barely escaped the fire with his life, but he remained nearby and rebuilt the mission in the following year. Father Rale, the "Jesuit Martyr of Maine," was at St. Ignace Mission at Mackinac and served the Ottawas and the nearby Illinois Indians. He compiled a detailed history of the Ottawa, including their customs and traditions, and with this work provided critical studies and insights.

In Detroit, the Recollect Franciscans opened St. Anne-de-Detroit chapel at Fort Ponchatrain. Recollect Franciscan Nicholas Delhalle was slain there, but the mission and the settlement flourished. Burt Lake and Harbor Springs (formerly L'arbre Croche, "The Crooked Tree") served as mission sites, and the Jesuits and Recollects worked side by side to serve the local tribes.

In Ohio, Jesuit Joseph Bonnecamps celebrated Mass on the Little Miami River while accompanying the expedition of Pierre-Joseph Céloron de Blainville into the territory in 1749. Father Bonnecamps and his Jesuit companion, Pierre Potier, began labors in the area, and in 1751, Jesuit Armand de la Richardie served the Hurons at Sandusky. He arrived in the Ohio region with a large number of Hurons who left Lake Erie because of increasing problems from other tribes and the American colonists. Father de la Richardie had served the Hurons in Quebec from 1725 to 1727 and had led his American group to safety. The Hurons had long been devout Catholics and had endured much suffering for their steadfast loyalty to the faith. Most of the Hurons lived in Canada, in and around Quebec, in an area called *Huronia*. Some of the finest of the Franciscan and Jesuit missionaries labored among the various settlements of the Huron nation, starting with Father Joseph de la Roche Daillon, the Recollect Franciscan, who was with them in 1626. In Ohio, Father Edmund Burke was at Fort Meigs (modern Toledo), with the Maumee in 1795.

The Indiana missions were opened in 1679 when the Recollect Franciscans Louis Hennepin and Gabriel de la Ribourde visited local tribes and mapped entire areas. Jesuit Jacques Marquette had been in the region in 1675, but had not stayed to start missions. After the Franciscans, the Jesuits arrived, receiving a grant of land near modern-day South Bend for their headquarters.

The "Founder of Catholicity in the West," Jesuit Claude Allouez served as an impetus for regional Indian missions. Father Allouez, who was French, went to Canada and spent two years learning the languages of the Native Americans. He served twenty-three Indian nations in a mission territory covering three thousand miles. In the area called Indiana, Father Claude Allouez resided on the St. Joseph's River, close to the present site of Notre Dame University. The vicar-general of the Jesuit mission in the area, Father Allouez was a tireless founder and evangelizer. In 1671, an alliance of fourteen Indian nations met at Sault Ste. Marie, and Father Allouez gave the main address to the assembled Native Americans. Fluent and elegant in the Indian dialects, he was revered by the tribes and was able to instruct almost a hundred thousand and to baptize as many as ten thousand into the faith. His historical accounts provide considerable details of the past cultures and traditions in many regions of the United States. Father Allouez died in 1689 at St. Joseph River Mission.

Other Jesuits labored in Indiana also, and Fort Vincennes was opened in 1732. Father Stephen Doutreleau served St. Francis Xavier there. In Lafayette, in 1756, Jesuit Pierre de Jounay labored among the Miami.

Illinois was a vast mission, linked to the Louisiana missions as well and evangelized by missionaries from many orders and institutions. In 1673, Jesuit Jacques Marquette was among the Peoria Indians, and he established the famous Kaskaskia mission of the Immaculate Conception near what is now Utica. Other Jesuits, including Father Allouez, sustained Kaskaskia, and the Recollect Franciscans Louis Hennepin, Zenobius Membré, and Gabriel de la Richardie visited as well in 1679.

In 1680, the Kaskaskia mission was moved south to escape Iroquois raids, and Fathers Allouez and Jacques Gravier compiled dictionaries in the Native American languages. In that same year, Jesuit Father Ribourde lost his life in an attack. Father Gravier moved on to found missions at Peoria and Starved Rock, and he composed a Peoria dictionary at Rockford. Father Allouez also opened missions for the Peorias.

The new Kaskaskia mission was in operation on the eastern banks of the Mississippi River by 1689. In that same year, seminary priests of the Foreign Missions of Quebec arrived in the area and founded the Cahokia mission nearby, as part of the Louisiana missions. This Catholic outpost was also called Tamaroa and was dedicated to the Holy Family.

The Chicago mission for the Wea (Miami) opened in 1692. Father Gravier and Sebastian Rale served there, aided in time by the Seminarist Father Jean François de Saint-Cosmé, part of the Quebec contingent at Cahokia. The Jesuits founded Piankashaw Mission near Vincennes in 1702, and three years later Father Gravier was mortally wounded in an assault. He lingered until 1708, but his missionary labors were at an end. Cahokia was the site of another martyrdom in 1730, when Father Gaston was slain. The mission was then served by other seculars and eventually by Sulpicians. In 1768, Father Pierre Gibault became vicar-general of the Illinois territory at Kaskaskia.

Wisconsin missions were started by Jesuits in 1636, who were at Green Bay with the Winnebago. In 1660, Father René Menard, the famed Jesuit, followed Jesuit Gabriel Bruillette, who was with the tribes at Green Bay, and visited the Huron villages on the Chippewa and Black rivers. In 1661, Father Menard set out for Green Bay in Wisconsin with a guide, intending to see the Hurons gathered there. When others tried to discourage him, he replied: "God calls me. I must go, if it costs me my life." He was never seen again after being separated from the guide around the first rapid of the Menominee River. His breviary (book of liturgical prayers) and his cassock were discovered in a Sioux village in the region, leading to all kinds of dire conclusions.

Father Allouez labored in the place of Father Menard, instructing several tribes that had migrated to Wisconsin to escape escalating Iroquois assaults. He erected his main mission in Wisconsin at De Pere, on the eastern shore of Green Bay, in 1665. He then founded Saint-Esprit Mission at Chegoimegon for the Chippewa. By 1670, aided by Jesuits Claude Dablon, Gabriel Druillettes, and Jacques Marquette, Father Allouez had twenty missions in the area. All of these missions endured except Saint Esprit, which was attacked repeatedly by the Sioux and closed in 1671.

In 1701, Father Jean Baptiste Chardon, another Jesuit, arrived at Green Bay to assist Father Henri Nouvel, an aged veteran who had labored in the mission there for four decades. Father Chardon went to the Illinois Indians on St. Joseph River in 1711, but returned to Green Bay. He remained here until 1728, and at times was considered the "only priest west of Lake Michigan." The Miami Indians were served by missionaries in the Illinois area as well as in Indiana, and the Potawátomi had priests among them until

Chippewa quill pouch

the priests were removed in 1820. Jesuit Father Louis André joined a group of Ottawa fleeing from the Sioux and aided them before going to Green Bay, Wisconsin, where he established his headquarters in 1671. For more than a decade he traveled by canoe or on foot on daily tours of the region, using St. Francis Xavier Mission as his base of operations. He also ministered to the Chicoutimi and Sept-iles (Seven Isles) Indians. Father André compiled dictionaries and wrote a catechism for the Algonquins and Ottawas. Father Pierre Bailloquet served the Ottawa Indians also, making his mission rounds in the raw wilderness even at the age of eighty. He died in an Ottawa camp in 1692, exhausted and honored by the Native Americans in his care. The Indian tribes of Michigan and Wisconsin were settled in their permanent homelands.

Mississippi Dallas shell

The early Minnesota missions date to 1655, when Jesuits in the company of the French explorers Médard Chouart des Groseilliers and Pierre Esprit Radisson worked among the Dakota Sioux near present-day Hastings. In 1689, Jesuit Joseph Marest was with the Sioux also. In 1727, Jesuits Nicholas de Gonnor and Michel Guignas erected St. Michael the Archangel for the Sioux on Lake Pepin. Father Louis Hennepin had been in the area about 1680, but his missionary efforts did not lead to the start of settlements. Actually, this Franciscan missionary and explorer arrived in Minnesota as a prisoner of the Sioux. The great French adventurer Daniel Greysolon, Sieur Du Lhut, demanded the release of Father Hennepin and two other Frenchmen and won their freedom at a camp near modern Minneapolis.

In 1732, a Jesuit priest by the name of Charles Messaiger founded St. Charles Mission near the Lake of the Woods. Four years later, the Jesuit Jean-Pierre Aulneau, Father Messaiger's successor, was killed by the Sioux. Jesuit Christian Hoecken served the regional missions in 1737. In the 1800s, Minnesota's missions would thrive as the Jesuits and Benedictines as well as seculars established sites in the area.

* * *

The Louisiana missions were a troubled evangelical assignment because of the political and social rivalries taking place in the region. Both the French and English ruled the area, and the Spanish were present in the earlier eras. The Louisiana missions included the lower Mississippi region of America, the modern states of Alabama, Arkansas, Louisiana, Mississippi, and Missouri. Another portion of the mission was established north in Illinois — the Cahokia (Tamaroa) foundation.

In 1673, Father Marquette journeyed down the Mississippi River as far as the Arkansas River, where the Quapaw maintained villages. Nine years later, Recollect Franciscans Zenobius Membré, Anastase Douay, and Maxime LeClerq entered the area with the expedition of La Salle. Father Membré preached to the Arkansas, Taensa, Natchez, and others at the Arkansas site, and a chapel was included in the buildings of the area. His companion, Father Douay, said the first Mass within the limits of modern Louisiana in 1699.

In 1698, the bishop of Quebec, who had the ecclesiastical authority over this region despite its southern geographic location, decided the priests from the seminary of Quebec would begin labors in the Louisiana missions. The Quebec seminary was associated with the famed Paris Congregation of Foreign Missions and trained priests for such labors. One year later, three such seminary priests were in the region, and they brought enthusiasm and energy to their ministry. Father Jean François de Saint-Cosmé founded the Tamaroa mission at Cahokia, Illinois. Father François de Montigny founded the Natchez mission among the Taensa, and Father Antoine Davion established the Tunica mission at modern-day Fort Adams, Mississippi. This mission had to be abandoned in 1708, when it was threatened by the Chickasaw-English alliance in the area. Father Davion also ministered to the Yazoo and other tribes, joined in time by other priests from the Quebec seminary.

The leader of the Louisiana colony, Pierre Le Moyne, Sieur d'Iberville, had his own mission agenda, and he brought Father Paul du Ru, a Jesuit, to the region to found a mission at Biloxi, Mississippi. Father du Ru founded a second mission at Mobile, Alabama, and with the Bayougoula he built a chapel. The Indians gathered around the French post at Mobile, and the missionary cared for their needs. He also welcomed a band of Apalachee who had migrated from Florida. Father Joseph de Limoges, another Jesuit, started a mission for the Huma and Bayougoula, bands of the Choctaw who lived at the mouth of the Red River in Louisiana.

The Native Americans encountered in this region of America were diverse and unique in their cultural developments. Deeply rooted in their own traditions and increasingly hostile to any whites visiting them, many resisted evangelization. The presence of rival nationals from Europe did not offer the Native Americans encouraging signs either. The entire area was engulfed in rivalries and tribal conflicts that the missionaries could not avert or dispel.

In 1702, Father Nicholas Foucault, one of the Quebec priests (called the Seminarists by that time), was slain with two companions while traveling to Mobile. Four years later, Father de Saint-Cosmé, who had come south to the Natchez mission, was slain while sleeping in a campsite on the Mississippi River. These deaths, and the lack of Native American response to the missionaries' overtures and efforts, doomed the labors in the area.

In time, other missionaries undertook the same field of ministry. The Arkansas mission, vacant since 1702, was reopened by Father Paul du Poisson. Father Alexis de Guyenne labored among the Creek, and Father Mathurin le Petit served the Choctaw in Mississippi. To aid these mission endeavors, the Ursulines began a convent in New Orleans in 1727 and started a school for Native American girls. In 1728, Father Michel Baudoin arrived in Louisiana and started a mission among the Chickasaw. He served this mission territory for decades, first in the field and then as superior general of the local Jesuit missions, from 1749 until 1763. When the Society of Jesus was suppressed by Rome, Father Baudoin did not have to leave the area. Grateful Catholics provided him with a home on a planter's estate and a pension of four hundred francs per year.

The Natchez War of 1729 opened on November 28 with a massacre and almost destroyed the mission territory again. Father du Poisson was the first victim. Father Jean Souel was killed by the Yazoo on December 11, and on New Year's Day, 1730, a Jesuit priest named Stephen Doutreleau was attacked while celebrating Mass. With one arm seriously wounded he managed to escape his attackers by paddling a canoe for miles. When the Natchez faced total extinction at the hands of the white military forces, some tribes people fled to the Chickasaw, sparking another round of battles. The Jesuit missionary Antoine Senat was burned at the stake in this episode.

A newly arrived Seminarist missionary, Father Gaston, was killed at the Cahokia mission, putting an end to Quebec's involvement. The seminary in Quebec stopped sending missionaries to Louisiana in 1754. The Alibamon and Choctaw missions survived until 1764. In time, the American Catholic Church was granted ecclesiastical control over the Louisiana missions. The establishment of a bishopric in New Orleans soon involved the French, Spanish, and American-

cans and became an issue for the Secretary of State in the administration of President George Washington.

* * *

In the early 1500s, when Spanish explorers mounted campaigns of discovery, they found the "Province of Quiveria," which stretched from Minnesota and the Wisconsin border to the Rockies. Named after the Wichita-based Native American tribe, this vast area is the Northern and Central Plains. The nomadic tribes that roamed the Plains in seasonal migrations and hunting expeditions were admired for their splendid adornments and feared for their fierce military skills.

The first recorded missionary priest in the "Province of Quiveria" was Father Juan de Padilla, a Franciscan who had been on the expedition of Nuño de Guzman in 1528 and had then joined the forces of Francisco Vásquez de Coronado, who was seeking the Seven Cities of Gold in 1540. The Spanish reached Kansas some months later, and there Coronado decided to return to Mexico because of the harsh barren countryside and the constant confrontations with local tribes. Father Padilla, however, had been laboring among the Wichita in the area and wanted to remain with them, believing that he was needed.

Father Juan de la Cruz, Brother Luis, two Franciscan tertiaries, Lucas and Sebastian, a soldier named da Campo, and three Mexicans elected to remain as well. They watched Coronado and his forces depart and then started a mission for the Wichita. The apostolate was received so warmly and showed such promise that Father Padilla hoped to introduce the faith to nearby Indian settlements as well. He took some of the mission party with him into the wilderness and was slain in their company, presumably by enemies of the Wichita. Father Juan de Padilla is the protomartyr of the nation, the first priest to die for the faith in North America. By 1745, other Franciscans were with the local Potawátomi and Osage. The great missions of Kansas would begin during the 1800s.

In Missouri, priests visited the area in 1542 with the De Soto expedition. The Jesuits opened St. Geneviève Mission in 1659 on the west bank of the Mississippi River, and visited the St. Louis region as well. In 1700, Jesuit Gabriel Marest opened another mission at the present site of St. Louis. By 1734, St. Geneviève and the Old Mines settlements were served by missionaries from the Cahokia mission in Illinois.

In 1760, Recollect Franciscan Luke Collet and Jesuit Sebastian Meurin were laboring at St. Geneviève and at St. Louis. Two years later, a mission was opened at St. Charles, followed by the Carondolet mission in 1767. Father Pierre Gibault was also serving tribes in the area.

In 1673, Jesuit Jacques Marquette visited the Nebraska Native Americans while traveling with Joliet. The two intrepid explorers set out on May 17, 1673, on Lake Michigan, paddling their canoes to Green Bay. From there they went on the Fox River to a portage that crossed to the Wisconsin River and entered the Mississippi River south to the Arkansas River. They turned around and went north again after discovering the Spanish had control of the lower regions of the mighty river. Both mapped the areas visited. Joliet soon lost his map, which made Father Marquette's copy all the more valuable. This missionary appears in the chronological records of many American states as a result of this amazing journey.

By 1682, Nebraska was under the jurisdiction of the bishop of Quebec, Blessed François de Montmorency Laval, although no permanent mission sites are recorded. In 1720, the Franciscan Juan Mingües was put to death near Columbus on the Platte River. No other missionaries are recorded in the area until after the Revolutionary War.

The Coronado expedition entered the present state of Colorado in 1540, with Franciscans as escorts. In 1682, the area was claimed for France by La Salle, but in 1700 became part of the Spanish vicariate apostolic of Leavenworth, Kansas. Unidentified missions were opened in that area but did not survive.

Idaho's missions would not open until after 1812, when Old Ignace, a famed Iroquois Christian, entered the area. What became Iowa was visited by Jesuit Jacques Marquette in 1673, as he was welcomed by the Peoria settlements. Recollect Franciscans Louis Hennepin and Gabriel de la Ribourde labored in the area in 1679, but the great mission era began in 1832.

Nevada's Franciscan mission efforts took place between 1774 and 1776, but no permanent chapels were recorded. North Dakota was visited by Jesuits Jean-Pierre Aulneau and Claude Coquart in 1742, but the vast Catholic mission apostolate in the area opened in 1818. Oklahoma was visited by Father Juan de Padilla in 1541. Franciscans led by Juan de Sales began missions in the area in 1630, but the main mission activity began in 1820. South Dakota's mission eras opened at the same time.

* * *

In the vast territory that became the Lone Star State (Texas), the Spanish early on tried to subdue the small bands that roamed the wilderness, and the missions of Texas were under the authority of Church officials in Querétaro and Zacatecas, Mexico. The Caddo, Hasinai, Tejas, Lipán,

Karánkawa, Tónkawa, Wichita, and Pakawá had formed loose confederacies with language affiliations. The Caddo group extended into western Louisiana, and the Wichita confederation extended north into Kansas. An estimated Indian population at the time of the primary mission efforts was approximately forty thousand.

The Franciscan priest Andrés de Olmos crossed the Rio Grande River into Texas in 1544, and found local Indians receptive to the Good News of the Gospel. Converting many, and seeing firsthand the inhospitable climate and aggressive neighboring bands, Father Olmos led his flock back across the Rio Grande to the province of Tamaulipas, Mexico, where they established a new Catholic settlement called Olives.

In 1553, the Dominicans Diego de la Cruz, Hernando Méndez, Juan Ferrer, and Brother Juan de Mina were slain in the area. A Spanish expedition into the region ended in failure from the harshness of the natural environment and local Indian aversion to the sudden appearance of white settlers. The Franciscans arrived in 1659 and established Nuestra Señora de Guadalupe Mission. In 1675, Father Juan Larios celebrated High Mass in Texas while on the Basque-Larios expedition. In 1682, another Franciscan mission, Corpus Christi de Isleta, was founded for the Jumanos, near what is now El Paso.

In 1685, the French military commander René-Robert Cavelier, Sieur de La Salle, erected Fort St. Louis on Matagorda Bay, then called Espíritu Santo Bay, in Texas. This fort was staffed by a unit of French soldiers and by three priests, the Recollect Franciscan Fathers Zenobius Membré, Anastase Douay, and Maxime LeClerq, and two Sulpician priests named Chefdeville and Cavelier. Father Membré had accompanied La Salle to Illinois in 1679 and wrote a detailed account of the expedition. In 1681, he descended the Mississippi River with La Salle and reached the Gulf of Mexico. After a brief period in Europe the priest was again at La Salle's side in Texas.

La Salle decided to return to Illinois two years after erecting the Texas fort and left behind a force of twenty soldiers and the priests. What happened after his departure is not known in detail, but the fort was discovered in ruins later. A Spanish unit arrived at the fort intending to oust the French, and the soldiers found remains of a burned structure and unburied bones. Later, chalices and breviaries were also recovered, proving that the priests had perished with La Salle's military personnel.

In 1690, a group of Spanish Franciscans from the Querétaro College joined an expedition with Dom Domingo Terán de los Ríos, and Father Damian Massenet led other Franciscans into the region. The Franciscans were Miguel Fontcubierto, Francisco Casañas, Antonio Borday, and Antonio Pereira. Mission San Francisco de las Tejas was founded for the Hasinai (Asinais) and Cenis. This mission closed three years later when seven thousand Indians died in a virulent epidemic.

On June 13, 1691, Father Massenet celebrated the first Mass within the limits of the modern city of San Antonio. He named the site after St. Anthony of Padua. Eight years later, other Franciscans from the Zacatecas College opened a series of missions on the southern bank of the Rio Grande River for the Pakawá Indians. These Franciscans were Francisco Hidalgo, Nicolás Recío, Miguel Estelles, Pedro Fortuny, Pedro García, Ildefonso Monge, José Saldona, Antonio Miranda, and Juan de Garayuschea. They opened missions on the Red River, the

Venerable Antonio Margil de Jesús and the mission now popularly known as the Alamo

Neches, and Guadalupe, and nine years later more Franciscans entered the area. In 1703, Mission San Francisco de Solano was erected on the Rio Grande but was later moved to San Antonio and renamed San Antonio de Valero, known today as the Alamo.

The spiritual giant of this era was Venerable Antonio Margil de Jesús, an educator and college administrator who undertook mission assignments in Louisiana and Texas in 1720. By 1722, he was called the guardian, or superior, of the missions in the region. He literally walked his way across the wilderness of Texas to establish new enclaves of the faith, all the while displaying heroic virtues and the ideals of his order.

The missions established in Texas were operated by complex systems popularly called *Bajo la Campaña*, or "[life] under the bell." The California missions introduced the same approach to dealing with Indian converts to the faith. "Life under the bell" was adopted for serious and compelling reasons, reflecting the political turmoil of that era. Priest missionaries such as Blessed Junípero Serra in California and Venerable Antonio Margil in Texas knew that local Spanish land barons, miners, ranchers, civil officials, and military commanders had long forgotten the mandate of Emperor Charles V of Spain and the bull of Pope Paul III concerning the spiritual concerns and honorable standards of treatment to be observed when dealing with the Native Americans.

The Spanish preyed ruthlessly on the local Indians in Mexico, and they expected to carry on the same abuse in Texas and California. The missions, protected by the power of the Church, defied such predatory practices, keeping military, civil, and secular forces at bay. At the same time, the missionaries hoped to imprint civilization on the Indians, as no one in that age understood or appreciated the lifestyles of the Native Americans. Keeping the Indians safe from forced labor or slavery, and isolated from those who did not accept the faith, the missions established "life under the bell" to educate the local tribes in European ways, believing such knowledge would improve their lot and their chances for the future. Also, the Europeans could not conceive of any civilization that differed from theirs as having intrinsic value and were unable to honor diversity.

The Texas missions include: San Francisco de las Tejas, 1690; San Francisco de Solano (moved in 1718 and renamed San Antonio de Valero), 1703; Nuestra Señora del Pilar de los Adayes, 1716; San José y San Miguel de Aguayo, 1720; Espíritu Santo and La Bahía Mission, 1722; La Purísima Concepción, San Juan Capistrano, San Francisco de la Espada, 1731; San Saba, 1734; San Francisco Xavier, 1748; La Bahía, moved to Goliad, 1749; Rosario Mission, 1754; San Francisco Xavier de Naxera, 1772; Refugio Mission, 1791; Nuestra Señora del Refugio, 1793.

These missions took a deadly toll of priests. In 1721, the Franciscan lay brother José Pita was slain on his way to this mis-

sion area. In 1752, Father José Ganzabal was put to death, and five years later San Saba Mission was attacked, and Fathers Alonso Terreros and José Santiesteban were slain. Despite these disasters, about fifteen thousand Texas Indians were in mission settings at the time. In 1791, another Karánkawa mission, Refugio, was opened, and the mission at Goliad prospered for a time for the Karánkawa. In 1793, the last mission was opened at Goff Bayou.

The Texas missions reflected in part the European rivalries in America, and many remarkable Catholic priests died because Spain and France elected to battle over uncharted regions. These priests bequeathed the faith to countless generations in Texas. The great city of San Antonio, where Venerable Antonio Margil labored as well, stands today as a monument to the missionaries of the region.

* * *

The first Catholic presence in the New Mexico and Arizona wilderness was a Franciscan, Marcos de Niza, who had been given the task of going north from Mexico to find Cíbola, the Seven Cities of Gold. The Spanish still clung to the hope that the northern Native Americans pursued the same levels of metallic splendor as their Mesoamerican cousins. Father Niza, arriving in the area in 1539, planted a cross in the ground forty miles south of modern Gallup, New Mexico, and declared the site "the new kingdom of St. Francis." Priests accompanying the expedition of Coronado in the region started missions as well, and in 1544, Franciscan Father Juan de la Cruz and Brother Luis de Ubeda were slain. Three other Franciscans died in 1584. The name "New Mexico" dates to 1563 when Francisco de Ibarra, an explorer entered the territory of the present state and called it "New

Mexico," a designation immediately put on contemporary maps.

In 1598, Spanish families followed Don Juan de Oñate into the deserts, going to the area of what is now Santa Fe, New Mexico. He had a patent to settle the tribal lands of the Pueblo, Hopi, Pima, Papago, Mescalero, and Navajo. Don Juan and his settlers arrived with high hopes and little knowledge about the local tribes. The Franciscan missionaries Roderic Durán, Augustín Rodríguez, Juan Santa María López, and others had been slain in the area a few years before.

Franciscan Alonso Martínez led nine companions into New Mexico, settling at San Juan de los Caballeros, north of Santa Fe. San Gabriel Mission and a chapel were also founded, and Franciscan Andrés Corchado labored among the Zuñi. Other Franciscans, led by Martín de Arvide, arrived and opened eleven missions in 1612, and eight years later San Gerónimo de Taos was opened. The Franciscans recorded in 1626 that they were operating 43 churches and 27 missions in New Mexico; by 1632, there were 90 pueblos with 25 missions and 50 Franciscans.

Around 1672, Franciscan Pedro de Ávila y Ayala was killed, and three years later Father Alonso Gil de Ávila lost his life as well. The missions were in jeopardy because of the Spanish settlements and attitudes toward the Native Americans of the region, indicating an arrogant and ignorant disregard for their isolated and vulnerable position. The Spanish settlers, conditioned by their lordly status in Mexico, had reduced the native population of New Mexico to the position of serfs.

Father Francisco de Ayeta of the Franciscans arrived at the settlement in 1678 with a mandate to study the operation in progress. He was appalled by his findings, all of which he reported to mission authorities immediately. Father Ayeta also predicted that the evils committed by the Spanish would provoke a terrible vengeance in time. His prediction was proven accurate on August 10, 1680, when twenty-one missionaries and their aides and four hundred settlers died at the hands of the enraged tribes led by the Pueblo Chief Popay, who had been whipped by the Spanish fifteen years earlier. The surviving Spanish fled across the barren wastes, seeking a safe haven, and Father Ayeta went to El Paso, Texas, to aid these refugees. A group of Christian Indians fled as well from Santa Fe and went to El Paso with the Spanish. At that site they founded a new village called Isleta. The Pueblo fought a 1692 attack by Spanish troops yet were never fully suppressed. Franciscan Francisco Vargas reopened the missions that same year as the mission authorities investigated the entire affair and made abrupt changes in their mission operations. The Jesuits entered the region again in 1732, laboring among the Pima and Papago of Arizona. When the Jesuits had to withdraw in 1767, the Franciscans again took up the apostolate.

Over the decades, the Franciscans had served the New Mexico Pueblos with missions or chapels recorded as Socorro, Keres, San Antonio Senecu, Pilabo, Sevilleta, St. Francis, Isleta, Santa Fe, Hemes, and Acoma. In 1733, a mission for the Apaches was opened at Jicarillas, which did not survive long, and nine years later Jesuit John Menchero labored among the Moquis and Navajos. This combined apostolate between the Jesuits and Franciscans reflected the earlier efforts in the mission fields, such as Maine. The paths of the missionaries crossed frequently in the wilds of America, and they learned to welcome one another and to share their experience and wisdom.

This combined effort was also very much evident in Arizona, another area visited in 1539 by the Franciscan Marcos de Niza. The ever-roaming Franciscan Juan de Padilla was in Arizona also in 1540. Arizona did not see missionaries until 1598, however, when the Franciscans scouted the area. By 1629, they were laboring among the Moqui and Hopi, with chapels at Walpi, Awátovi, Shongópovi, Oraibi, and Mishóngnovi.

In 1632, Franciscan Martín de Arvide was slain at Zipias, and a companion, Father Francisco de Parra, was killed at Awátovi. The Pueblo Revolt in the area claimed the lives of Franciscans José de Espeleta, Augustín de Santa María, José de Figueroa, José de Trujillo, and others in 1680.

In 1687, one of America's outstanding missionaries arrived in the region with other Jesuits. His name was Eusebius Kino, and he is called the "Apostle to the Pima," the "founder of Christianity in the Southwest," and "Arizona's Foremost Pioneer." He was

Jesuit Eusebius Kino and the
restored San Xavier del Bac Mission

born in Italy to a family called Chino or Kuehn, and arrived as a Jesuit missionary in Lower California in 1683. Laboring there for a time, Father Kino was assigned to the mission field called Pimería Alta, the region including northern Sonora in Mexico and southern Arizona. This apostolate endured for almost a quarter of a century and would earn the missionary the title of "Horseback Priest" while he lived. In 1687, Father Kino established a mission on the San Miguel River among the thirty thousand Pima, calling the site Nuestra Señora de los Dolores. Coxi, the chief of the Pima at the time, was baptized in July of that year, aiding Father Kino's apostolate.

Father Kino made more than fifty missionary journeys, averaging a hundred to a thousand miles each time. He also founded the famed San Xavier del Bac Mission near Tucson, and a mission at Tumacacuri, north of Nogales. Traveling to the Colorado River, Father Kino drew up maps of his explorations and made geographic notations. These were published in 1705 and used by others for over a century. More than thirty thousand Indians were served by Father Kino, who personally baptized four thousand of them. He also taught his mission flocks the best methods of stock breeding, farming, irrigation, and ranching, and he introduced the latest European enterprises into southern Arizona. In Baja (in Spanish, "Lower") California, he founded nine missions and was the explorer who determined that Baja California was a peninsula, not an island. Father Kino's travel and historical accounts are highly prized, and he represents the state of Arizona in the National Statuary Hall in Washington, D.C.

Father Kino made friends with most of the tribes in his mission region, including the Apaches, because he did not consider himself superior to the Native Americans but their servant in the Lord. He was criticized by some of his mission contemporaries for not inculcating European ways upon the tribes, but he had little use for such details. He had a vast mission territory, few physical reserves or resources, and too little time. Evangelization was his goal, and he adapted his life to the demands of that apostolate.

Other Jesuit missionaries in Arizona were Jacob Sedelmayer, Ignatz Keller, Caspar Stiger, Adam Gilg, Heinrich Ruhen, Gottfried Middlendorf, Ignatz Pfefferhorn, Juan Garaycoccha, and Joseph Och. They were in the region by 1730 and labored on the Upper Gila and in San Pedro Valley until their suppression in 1767. It must be remembered that the missionaries in the area brought a wealth of European knowledge to the Pueblo nation and others. They taught the local Native Americans carpentry, leatherwork, blacksmithing, farming, and the tending of orchards. The most lasting gift to the Pueblos and the Native Americans was cattle- and sheep-herding, knowledge that remains with these Indian nations today.

Missions established in Arizona between 1687 and 1720 include: San José, Tumacacuri; Santa Gertrudis, Tubac; San Miguel; Santa Ana, Arivaca; and San Cayetano, Calabasas. In 1767, the Franciscans returned to their missions, and one year later, Franciscan Francisco Garcés took up residence at San Xavier del Bac.

* * *

The Catholic missions in Columbia — the region called the "Oregon Country" before it was renamed the "Oregon Territory" after the Americans and British settled their border differences in 1846 — started as late as 1820. This was the vast area populated by the Nez Percé, Flathead, Umatilla,

Warmspring, Yamhill, Coeur d'Alene, Yakima, Wasco, Chinook, Kalispel, Kutenai, Lake, Lummi, Puyallup, Spokan, Siletz, and Tulalip Indian nations.

The faith was brought to the area in 1820, when a band of Iroquois led by Old Ignace visited there as companions of a fur-trading group and described their Catholic missions to the east. A Spokan prophet had also predicted: "Soon there will come from the rising sun a different kind of man from any you have yet seen, who will bring you a book . . . and will teach you everything."

Priests had accompanied Sebastian Vizcaíno in his exploration of the Oregon coast in 1602, and in 1774, Franciscans had been with Juan Perez on his expedition into the area. Bruno Heceta had claimed the entire area for Spain in 1775, accompanied by Franciscans. These travelers were brief interlopers in the region, however. The "different kind" of men did not arrive until 1838. Then evangelization was started in the Columbia River Plateau by earnest, dedicated, enthusiastic priests. These missionaries included Father Pierre Jean De Smet, "Father Kickapoo" (Christian Hoecken), and the Blanchet brothers, who served as bishops in time and who had a tremendous impact on the Catholic missions across America.

* * *

In California, the Carmelite Anthony of the Ascension celebrated Mass in San Diego in 1602. Jesuit Hyacinth Cortés was in the area in 1642, and the missions were opened by Jesuit Father Juan María Salvatierra in San Dionisio Bay, in October, 1697. Jesuit Wenceslaus Link was also in the region, using the maps of Father Eusebius Kino. Jesuits Victorian Arnes and John Joseph Diez founded Nuestra Señora de Loreto, or St. Mary's.

From this initial haven a vast chain of missions was established, facing north in Lower California, and dating from 1699 until 1766. By 1767, epidemics among the local tribes (who were especially vulnerable to the diseases brought by the white man) had caused the closing of all but fourteen of the missions. These Jesuit missions were: Nuestra Señora de Loreto (1697); San Francisco Xavier (1699); San Juan de Ligné (1705); Santa Rosalia de Malegé (1705); San José de Comundú (1708); La Purísima Concepción de Cadegomó (1718); Nuestra Señora del Pilar (1720); Nuestra Señora de Guadalupe (1720); Santiago de las Coras (1721); San Ignacio (1728); San José del Cabo (1730); Santa Rosa or Todos los Santos (1733); San Luis Gonzaga (1737); Santa Gertrudis (1752) San Francisco de Borja (1759); and Santa María de los Ángeles (1766).

In 1768, King Carlos III of Spain, long an opponent of the Society of Jesus, recalled all of the Jesuits in these missions. They were chained, tortured, and taken to Spain, and their apostolate was ended officially. The Franciscans were then called upon to assume the evangelization of America's lower West Coast.

Blessed Junípero Serra, a Franciscan priest, arrived at the California missions in 1769 and began the great line of Catholic outposts along *El Camino Real*, "The Highway." In that era, about one hundred forty-six Franciscans labored among the local tribes who represented a great diversity of languages and traditions. Other missionary work also was conducted in that period in the Baja California region.

The missions of California stand today as memorials of a historical quest for souls on the Pacific coast of America. They symbolize not only the labors of dedicated servants across the United States, but serve as well to remind modern Catholics of hard-won freedoms and the rights purchased with lifelong dedication and with the blood of martyrs. The California mission sites include: San Diego (1769), called Cosay by the Indians, and moved in 1774; San Luis Rey de Francia (1798), called Tacayme; San Juan Capistrano (1776), called Sajirit or Quanis-savit; San Gabriel (1771), called Sibagna or Tobiscagna; San Fernando (Rey de España) (1797), called Pashecgna; San Buenaventura (1782), called Miscanaga; Santa Barbara (1786), called Taynayan; Santa Inés (1804), called Alajulapu; La Purísima Concepción (1787), called Algsacupí; San Luis Obispo (de Tolosa) (1772), called Tishlini; San Miguel (1797), called Vahiá or Cholame; San Antonio (de Padua) (1771), called Teshaya or Sextapay; Nuestra Señora de la Soledad (1791), called Chuttusgelis; San Carlos Borromeo de Monterey (1770), called Eslenes and Carmelo; San Juan Bautista (1797), called Popelout or Popeloutchom; Santa Cruz (1791), called Aulintac; Santa Clara (1777), called Thamien, moved in 1781; San José (1797), called Oroysom; San Francisco (de Asís), also called Dolores (1776); Nuestra Señora de los Ángeles (1781); San Rafael (Arcángel) (1817), called Nanaguami; San Francisco de Solano (Sonoma) (1823), called Sonoma.

While it is fashionable to depict Blessed Junípero and the Franciscans in an unappealing light today, revisionist history cannot dim their achievements. In 1877, a western writer declared:

How great are the changes in the womb of time! On the 27th of June, 1776 . . . San Francisco became known in history. Father Junípero Serra, whose name and deeds in California have secured the proudest niche in its history. . . . Look at that old Presidio and that venerable mission of Dolores, and behold the first house erected! These are his handiwork. San Francisco has this, at least, to boast of — that the first building erected within it was dedicated to God's worship under the patronage of St. Francis.

The men and women who undertook the arduous life of the missionary in early America stand today as truly remarkable examples of sacrifice, courage, and generosity of soul. As guardians and heralds of the faith on the continent, these missionaries fashioned a great tapestry of evangelization over the centuries. The fact that they endured untold hardships, risking all to bring the Good News of Christ to the Native Americans, demonstrated a single, inescapable truth about the missions and their religious orders and congregations.

These religious were among the very best in their own eras. Educated, talented, endowed with vision and pioneering graces, such men and women would have brought honors and recognition to their orders in the gracious settings of Europe. Their religious superiors, however, did not keep such special individuals in safe royal courts or universities. The brightest and best of the religious congregations were sent into the wilds of America without reserve. They were called to serve the native peoples of the continent, and they were sent forward with hope and blessings. Many brilliant, gifted missionaries died in the field, violently cut off from their labors by cruel hands, but other dedicated, talented men and women stepped forward to take their places in the wilderness.

Above all, these missionaries were

willing to pay the ultimate sacrifice for their labors on the continent, achieving martyrdom with a consummate grace. The life was not glamorous, not filled with human comforts, but it was the apostolate to which they were called. As St. Jean de Brébeuf, the martyred missionary to the Indians, declared: "Jesus Christ is our true greatness; it is He and His Cross that should be sought in the pursuit of these people, for if you strive for anything else, you will find naught but bodily and spiritual afflictions. But, having found Jesus Christ in this Cross, you have found the rose in the thorns, sweetness in bitterness, all is nothing."

The following is America's honor roll of the early continental missions — no longer well known, perhaps, but entitled to honor and respect from modern generations of Catholics enjoying religious liberty and a secure and prospering Church.

The American Martyrs

1542 — Juan de Padilla, Franciscan priest, protomartyr of the United States, slain in Kansas in the spring season. Juan de la Cruz, Franciscan priest, slain in New Mexico (date unknown). Luis de Escalona, Franciscan brother, slain in New Mexico (date unknown).

1544 — Luis de Ubeda, Franciscan brother, slain at Pecos, New Mexico, on April 19.

1549 — Luis Cáncer de Barbastro, Dominican priest, slain at Tampa Bay, Florida, on June 26. Diego de Peñalosa, Dominican priest, slain at Tampa Bay, Florida, on June 12. Fuentes, a Dominican Tertiary, slain at Tampa Bay, Florida, on June 12.

1566 — Pedro Martínez, Jesuit priest, slain on Cumberland Island, Georgia, with companions, on October 6.

1571 — Luis de Quiros, Jesuit priest, slain at Ajacan, Virginia, on February 4. Gabriel de Solís, Jesuit scholastic, slain at Ajacan, Virginia, on February 4. Juan Méndez, Jesuit scholastic, slain at Ajacan, Virginia, on February 4. Juan Bautista Segura, Jesuit priest, slain at Ajacan, Virginia, on February 9. Pedro Linares, Jesuit brother, slain at Ajacan, Virginia, on February 9. Gabriel Gómez, Jesuit brother, slain at Ajacan, Virginia, on February 9. Sancho Zeballos, Jesuit brother, slain at Ajacan, Virginia, on February 9. Cristóbal Redondo, Jesuit scholastic, slain at Ajacan, Virginia, on February 9.

1581 — Juan de Santa María, Franciscan priest, slain at Puarray, New Mexico, on September 10. Francisco López, Franciscan priest, slain at Puarray, New Mexico, on September 10.

1582 — Augustín Rodríguez, Franciscan brother, slain at Puarray, New Mexico, on May 20.

1597 — Pedro de Corpa, Franciscan priest, slain in St. Augustine, Florida, on September 13. Francisco de Beráscola, Franciscan priest, slain at Asao, Georgia, on September 15. Blas de Rodríguez, Franciscan priest, slain at Tupique, Georgia, on September 16. Miguel de Anón, Franciscan priest, slain at Mission Santa Catalina de Guale, St. Catherine's Island, Georgia, on September 17. Antonio de Badajoz, Franciscan brother, slain at Asopo, Georgia, on September 17.

1613 — Gilbert du Thet, Jesuit brother, slain at Saint-Sauveur, Maine, on September 30.

1631 — Pedro de Miranda, Franciscan priest, slain at Taos, New Mexico, on December 28.

1632 — Francisco Letrado, Franciscan priest, slain at Hawikuh, New Mexico, on

February 22. Martín de Arvide, Franciscan priest, slain at Zipias, Arizona, with companions, on February 27.

1633 — Francisco de Porras, Franciscan priest, slain at Awátovi, Arizona, on June 28.

1642 — St. René Goupil, Jesuit priest, slain at Auriesville, New York, on September 23.

1646 — St. Isaac Jogues, Jesuit priest, slain at Ossernenon, New York, on October 18. St. Jean Lalande, Jesuit priest, slain at Ossernenon, New York, on October 19.

1661 — Jean Deguerre, Jesuit priest, slain at Peoria, Illinois, on November 10. René Menard, Jesuit priest, slain at Crystal Falls, Wisconsin, on August 14.

1672 — Pedro de Ávila y Ayala, Franciscan priest, slain at Hawikuh, New Mexico, on October 7. Jean Guérin, Jesuit brother, slain at Oshkosh, Wisconsin, on December 23.

1675 — Alonso Gil de Ávila, Franciscan priest, slain at Senecu, New Mexico, on August 5.

1680 — Tomás de Torres, Franciscan priest slain at Nambé, New Mexico, on August 10. Juan Bernal, Franciscan priest, slain at Galisteo, New Mexico, on August 10. Manuel Tinoca, Franciscan, slain at Galisteo, on August 10. Domingo de Vera, Franciscan priest, slain at Galisteo, New Mexico, on August 10. Fernando Velasco, Franciscan priest, slain at Galisteo, New Mexico, on August 10. José de Figueroa, Franciscan priest, slain at Awátovi, Arizona, on August 10. Juan Bautista Pio, Franciscan priest, slain at Tesuque, New Mexico, on August 10. José de Espeleta, Franciscan priest, slain at Oraibi, Arizona, on August 10. Augustín de Santa María, Franciscan priest, slain at Oraibi, Arizona, on August 10. José de Trujillo, Franciscan priest, slain at Shon-

gópovi, Arizona, on August 10. Antonio de Mora, Franciscan priest, slain at Taos, New Mexico, on August 11. Juan de la Pedrosa, Franciscan brother, slain at Taos, New Mexico, on August 11. Matías Rendón, Franciscan priest, slain at Picuris, New Mexico, on August 11. Luis de Morales, Franciscan priest, slain at San Ildefonso, New Mexico, on August 11. Antonio Sánchez, Franciscan brother, slain at San Ildefonso, New Mexico, on August 11. Juan de Jesús, Franciscan priest, slain at Jemez, New Mexico, on August 11. Lucas Maldonado, Franciscan priest, slain at Acoma, New Mexico, on August 11. Juan de Val, Franciscan priest, slain at Halona, New Mexico, on August 11. Francisco de Lorenzana, Franciscan priest, slain at San Domingo, New Mexico, on August 12. Juan de Talabán, Franciscan priest, slain at San Domingo, New Mexico, on August 12. Gabriel de la Ribourde, Franciscan priest, slain at Seneca, Illinois, on September 19.

1687 — Louis Le Boeme, Jesuit brother, slain near De Pere, Wisconsin, on April 20.

1689 — Juan (Manuel) Beltrán, Franciscan priest, slain at San Cristóbal, New Mexico, on January 26. Zenobius Membré, Franciscan priest, slain at Fort St. Louis, Texas, on March 24. Chefdeville, Sulpician priest, slain at Fort St. Louis, Texas, on March 24. Maxime LeClerq, Franciscan priest, slain at Fort St. Louis, Texas, on March 24.

1696 — Luis Sánchez, Franciscan priest, slain at Torroro, Florida, on September 16. José de Arbizu, Franciscan priest, slain at San Cristóbal, New Mexico, on June 4. Antonio Carbonel, Franciscan priest, slain at San Cristóbal, New Mexico, on June 5. Francisco de Jesús María Casañas, Franciscan priest, slain at Jemez, New Mexico, on June 5. Francisco Corvera, Franciscan priest, slain at San Ildefonso, New Mexico, on June 8. Antonio Moreno, Franciscan priest, slain at San Ildefonso, New Mexico, on June 8.

1702 — Nicholas Foucault, secular priest, slain at Koroa, Mississippi, on September 11.

1704 — Juan de Parga, Franciscan priest, slain at Ayubale, Florida, on January 25. Marcos Delgado, Franciscan brother, slain at Ayubale, Florida, on January 25. Manuel de Mendoza, Franciscan priest, slain at Patoli, Florida, on January 25.

1706 — Nicholas Constantin Delhalle, Recollect Franciscan priest, slain at Detroit, Michigan, on June 21. Jean François de Saint-Cosmé, secular priest and companions, slain in Mississippi, on February 2.

1708 — Jacques Gravier, Jesuit priest, slain at Isle Massacre, Louisiana, on April 26.

1720 — Juan Mingües, Franciscan priest, slain near Columbus, Nebraska, on August 12.

1721 — José Pita, Franciscan brother, slain with companions at Carnezeria, Texas, on April 18.

1724 — Sebastian Rale, Jesuit priest, slain at Norridgewock Mission, Maine, on August 23.

1729 — Paul du Poisson, Jesuit priest, slain at Natchez, Mississippi, on November 28. Jean Souel, Jesuit priest, slain near Vicksburg, Mississippi, on December 11.

1730 — Gaston, secular priest, slain at Tamorois Mission, Illinois, on February 2.

1736 — Jean-Pierre Aulneau, Jesuit priest, and twenty companions, slain near Fort Charles, Minnesota, on June 6.

1749 — Francisco X. Silva, Franciscan priest, slain near Presidio del Río Grande, Texas, on July 20.

1752 — Franciscan José Ganzabal and companions slain at Mission La Candelaria, Texas, on May 11.

1757 — Alonso Terreros, Franciscan priest, slain at San Saba, Texas, on March 16. José Santiesteban, Franciscan priest, slain at San Saba, Texas, on March 16. Luis Jayme, Franciscan protomartyr of California and companions, slain at San Diego, California, on November 5.

1781 — Juan Barrenechea, Franciscan priest with companions, slain at La Purísima Concepción Mission. Juan M. Díaz and José M. Moreno, slain at San Pedro y Pablo, California, on July 17. Juan M. Díaz, Franciscan priest, Francisco Garcés, Franciscan priest, slain at La Purísima Concepción Mission, California, on July 19. José Matías Moreno, Franciscan priest, slain at Mission San Pedro y Pablo, California, on July 17.

1812 — Andrés Quintana, Franciscan priest, slain at Mission Santa Cruz, California, on October 12. Antonio Díaz de León, Franciscan priest, slain near San Augustine, Texas, on November 5.

Archbishop John Carroll and a Huron pouch

CHAPTER 3

The Penal Period

The Catholic missionaries to the Native Americans performed their labors of faith despite trials and complications. Tribal traditions and inherited spiritual systems affected the missions in each new territory, bringing hardships, discomforts, sometimes death, but in time the real impact on mission progress resulted from affairs taking place beyond the tribes and the geographical locations of Catholic apostolates. European politics played a paramount role in the early colonies and in the missions of the continent, taking dreadful tolls in established settlements and American wilderness areas alike.

These political imperatives shaped the missions of America and in the process too often destroyed Catholic chapels and schools and the ministries of dedicated priests and brothers. The American colonists heard of such devastation with some uneasiness, de-

spite their religious views, and then they began to realize that their own lives and lands were not immune to such grim products of European rivalries.

King William's War, an expansion of the war in Europe by William III of England and the League of Augsburg against King Louis XIV of France, flared across America from 1689 until 1697. The English and French fought each other for lands and people in the New World, imitating the battles between their armies on the march in Europe. Acadia, in the northeast part of Maine, fell to the English during this conflict, and the participation of Indian nations, recruited as allies, made this episode of colonial history particularly bloody. Queen Anne's War, known as the War of the Spanish Succession in Europe, started in 1702 and continued until 1713. England and France once again turned the American continent into a mirror battleground, endangering the welfare of the settlements on both sides.

King George's War, which raged in the New World from 1744 to 1748, was called the War of the Austrian Succession in England and in France. Many Americans suffered as a result, but, in truth, little was gained by either side. This was followed by the terrible French and Indian War, 1754-1763, a series of campaigns that scarred the colonies and brought about a rather unexpected turn of events — the formation of the United States of America.

The Catholic missions were targeted throughout the French and Indian campaigns, as the English wanted to put an end to French Catholicism, along with French dominance. The missions geographically close to the American colonies suffered the most, and their destruction released a new spirit among the people up and down the eastern coast. While the colonists did not necessarily sympathize with the Catholic missionaries or their beliefs, the wanton cruelty visited upon such dedicated religious brought a certain realization into focus.

The Americans began to resent the prolonged military campaigns that threatened the economic and political stability of their beloved colonies. They learned as well that their hard-won towns, villages, farms, and homes could face similar fates because of the hatred and violence being imported from Europe. The French and Spanish Catholic missions were ravaged by the English during these wars, and the French sought revenge by assailing Protestant holdings in the next war. In some instances the northern colonies had already been harmed because English defenses proved unreliable against the French and their Indian cohorts.

Colonial realists, hardened by their pioneering lifestyles and constant confrontation with raw nature in the wilderness, recognized that they would not survive such lunatic onslaughts if they did not develop a certain vigilance and a willingness to defend themselves against all comers. They were also prepared to assume control over their own destinies and were becoming aware of the rightful role of the individual in human

affairs. Unity was the only solution, a combined effort that could consolidate resources and power, and the colonies were taking the first tentative steps toward such a federation. The disasters visited upon the Acadians spurred many Americans toward this unified response.

In the missions of the Acadia region, located north of Maine, farmers and their families refused to take the oath of allegiance to England during Queen Anne's War. Catholics by tradition and practice, the Acadians defied the British authorities because they recognized England's basic intolerance of their faith. Remaining neutral, the Acadians were classified as hostile and treated as a defeated enemy by British troops. As a result, as many as seven thousand men, women, and children of Acadia saw their homes and livestock destroyed. Taken by forced march to waiting ships, the Acadians were carried southward to the various colonies. Many died in Acadia and on the voyages, including small children, and the survivors were dumped unceremoniously in colonies that openly displayed anti-Catholic sentiments. Families were broken apart, children separated from their parents, and the elderly abandoned as the exile continued. Some Acadians eventually made their way back to their own lands, only to discover that the English had brought in new settlers to populate the region. Others went to Louisiana, which was French in tradition and custom and a welcoming site. These Acadians are the modern "Cajuns" of Louisiana, stalwart and enduring in their own ways and in the faith. The torments of the Acadians were commemorated by Longfellow in his poem *Evangeline*.

The entire episode was considered a harsh and unnecessary demonstration of power, and filled the American colonists

56

with increased uncertainty and unease. When other wars ensued, they began to evaluate their own dependency upon English civil and military agencies as well. Such institutions had devastated Acadia without a qualm, a fact that signaled the truth that all colonists were equally vulnerable in certain circumstances.

It must be remembered that while the American colonies were poised on the edge of a raw and unforgiving wilderness, they were not populated by ignorant laborers or the politically naïve. As early as 1691, the children of the colonies were required in most regions to attend school and to learn the basics of an education. Literate to a great extent, these men and women maintained a constant spirit of vigilance concerning European political affairs and American involvements. As pressures mounted, independence thus became more than an idealist's dream, and the Americans felt no great compulsion to endure additional suffering at the whims of distant masters. The New World was not going to remain a playground for European ambitions and rivalries.

As early as 1754, six American colonies sent representatives to attend a council of the Iroquois League (Six Nations). This complex confederacy was originally composed of five tribes: the Mohawks, called the *Ga-né-a-ga-o-no* (the "Flint Processing People"); the Oneidas, the *O-na-yoté-ka* (the "People of the Stone"); the Onondagas, the *O-nun-da-ga-o-no* (the "People on the Hills"); the Cayugas, the *Gue-u-gweh-o-no* (the "People of the Mucky Lands," that is, the marshes); and the Senecas, the *Nun-da-wa-o-ne* (the "Great Hill People"). As mentioned earlier, the Tuscaroras in 1722 entered the confederation, which controlled the lands from the Hudson River to the shores of Lake Ontario. This was truly a bountiful region,

Mohawk cradle board

with rivers, forests, fields, and plentiful game. Each member tribe of the Six Nations was settled on a lake or a river system.

The American delegation to the Iroquois League included Benjamin Franklin, who went to the meeting to study the benefits of this time-honored unified existence. The Iroquois confederation served many valuable purposes, not the least of which was mutual defense against aggressors. The Indian lands held in common were divided into five vertical strips, or sections, situated side by side. Each strip was called a "longhouse" and averaged about two hundred square miles in area. Tribal customs, ceremonies, councils, and traditions were maintained in each longhouse, and the tribes freely reverenced their own totems.

The Council of the Fifty Sachems ruled over all in a distinctly democratic fashion. These sachems, or chiefs, were elected by the women elders of each tribe. Such matriarchs had raised the warriors eligible for office and knew each man's strengths and weaknesses. The tribes met at the council to discuss current events or needs and to enact appropriate responses. A call to arms pronounced by this council was heeded by every individual in the member tribes. Americans were quite aware of the power of the Iroquois League, as they understood the ferocious consequences of violating the mandates of the confederation. The eastern gateway to the lands held in common by the Iroquois League was guarded by the longhouse of the Mohawks, and woe to the white men who trespassed upon such sacred soil.

The confederation making up the Iroquois League was the dream of the Indian sage Dekanawidah (or Tekanawita). He envisioned peace among the tribes in the region, and in 1570 began to preach about the truth of his dream. The Iroquois League eventually united under the Tree of Peace, the *Kaianerekowa*, joined in true brotherhood, using mutual respect of not only the tribes but the individuals of the confederation to ensure strength. United, the tribes could solve problems of resources, shelter the vulnerable, keep alive traditions and customs, and protect the lands. The Iroquois League could also put more than two thousand warriors into the field in emergencies.

Returning from the meeting with the Iroquois League council, Benjamin Franklin and others talked about what they had witnessed. They urged their fellow colonists to unite in the face of devastation caused by the imported political strife. Slowly the Americans responded, and by 1774, the First Continental Congress met in Philadelphia to determine the future for all concerned. The First and Second Continental congresses, meeting in 1774 in the first session and then from 1775 to 1789, began to address concerns relating to British rule.

Ironically, one of the first activities undertaken by the Continental Congress was to pass a resolution condemning the newly promulgated Quebec Act in Canada. The Quebec Act was a rather remarkable piece of English legislation enacted in 1774. This act not only settled a dispute concerning the lands between the Ohio and Mississippi rivers but also established the Roman Catholic Church as a recognized entity throughout the Quebec province. The residents of that region who professed "the religion of Rome" were allowed to "enjoy the free exercise of the Church of Rome, subject to the King's supremacy."

The Continental Congress labeled the Quebec Act as "intolerable" and demonstrated against the legislation with considerable fury and outrage. This demonstration of anger was mirrored throughout the colonies, in fact, because it openly challenged Protestant supremacy in America and added to the general feeling of unrest. King George III of England was ridiculed in American cities and towns as "a disguised Jesuit," and he was condemned mightily for betraying the Protestant cause. The colonists claimed that the king was providing "a nursery" for the Catholic Church, deemed "America's greatest enemy."

Such rabid pronouncements may come as a surprise to modern Catholics who do not understand the Church's hard-won battles that raged for decades. Religious freedom was not allowed in the colonies, even in the period immediately following the Revolutionary War and the establishment of the Republic. The Continental Congress was reflecting the sentiments of their fellow colonials when they protested the Quebec Act, which mirrored the dominant imperatives of that era.

When the colonies were chartered by the English for settlement, various charges and clauses were inserted into the royal patents, depending upon the prevailing views of the time. Virginia's charter, issued in 1606, named the Anglican Church as the established religion of the colony. This position of preeminence was confirmed by the second charter issued in 1609. Colonists were also commanded to take an oath declaring the English monarch as supreme in all religious matters.

In Maryland, designed as a haven for Catholics loyal to the Holy See, the religious freedom anticipated was short-lived. The Act of Uniformity introduced into the colonies denied papal authority and provided for punishment of stiff fines for Catholics who did not attend Anglican religious services. In 1642, further legislation disenfranchised Catholics to an even greater extent and established a penalty of expulsion for all priests entering the colony. Marriages were declared invalid unless performed by an Anglican minister, and children born in marriages conducted in other religious rites were declared illegitimate.

In Virginia, the anti-Catholic feeling was so intense that an act was passed in 1755 that demanded that all "Papists" were to be disarmed by authorities to prevent them from taking part in the French and Indian wars going on at that time. Actually, a group of Catholics was arrested as a result of this legislation, but the local sheriff refused to imprison them, despite threats and demonstrations of outrage from his neighbors.

The charter for Massachusetts had no provisions concerning religious affairs, thus the Puritans were able to devise their own methods of ensuring the dominance of their beliefs. Only members of the Puritan or Congregationalist faith could practice normal routines of citizenship freely. In 1635, the courts ruled every aspect of the colonists' lives, and in 1656 the first of the laws imposing physical torture was instituted. Christmas, for example, was not to be celebrated as a holiday, and anyone who did so was in danger of whippings or worse. The death penalty was also instituted, an act that led to rebellion in Massachusetts and the appointment of an English governor who favored the Anglican Church. In 1691, the governor issued a decree proclaiming that "forever hereafter there shall be liberty of conscience allowed in the worship of God to all Christians (except Papists)."

In Connecticut, Congregationalism was the only religion allowed officially. Even the Quakers, who had lived in comparative safety, found their communities threatened. In New Hampshire, there was a basic tolerance in the early years, but Massachusetts soon dominated, and the stricter laws came into use. In 1679, when New Hampshire became independent again, there was an effort to establish the Anglican Church — the Congregationalists won out. By 1689, the Toleration Act, used in several New England colonies, demanded that Catholics declare themselves disloyal to the pope and to the doctrines of the Church. In time, all Roman Catholics were suspended "from Command and Places of Trust." This meant that no Catholic could vote or hold any public office. The law passed in 1704 even laid a tax of twenty shillings on every Irish servant imported. The Irish were known to be fiercely loyal to the pope, no matter what they faced. If a Catholic mother married to

59

a Protestant husband became a widow, her children could be taken from her so that she could not teach them the faith.

New Hampshire alternated between Anglican and Congregational rule, depending upon the political conditions in England. Catholics and Quakers did not fare well under either regime. New Jersey and New York followed the other colonies, but with restraint. Catholics were disenfranchised, and priests were not welcome, but these colonies also demonstrated a resistance to the "Established Church," the Anglicans. No official records of persecution of Catholics are evident in New Jersey. In New York, around 1684, a Catholic governor, Thomas Dongan, the Second Earl of Limerick, established religious liberty. In 1689, Dongan was overthrown by the Puritans and hunted as a criminal. The fall of King James II in England and the crowning of William of Orange ensured that harsh penal laws were put into place. Missionaries continued to serve the area, men such as "Father Farmer" — as the Jesuit Father Ferdinand Steinmeyer (or Steenmeyer) was known — who celebrated Mass in a house on Wall Street.

A Catholic settlement was founded in New Jersey as early as 1632, and French saltmakers arrived with others of the faith in the next decade. These Catholics had a certain amount of religious freedom, a fact that aroused Protestants and resulted in the murder of a missionary, Father John Ury, in 1741. Father Farmer was also in New Jersey and is honored as an apostle of the area. These missionaries braved torture and death to serve the few Catholics of the region.

William Penn, the founder of Pennsylvania, believed in his "holy experiment" and allowed freedom of religion. Jesuit missionaries roamed freely in the colony, and the first resident priest in Philadelphia was present in 1720. Certain restrictions were placed on Catholics in time, but Pennsylvania remained a haven for the faithful fleeing the harsh laws of other colonies. By 1757, in fact, Catholics lived in comparative peace in that colony. The Jesuits had even opened a mission, St. Xavier, in Cecil County, Pennsylvania.

Delaware was similarly free of overt Catholic penalization. In 1730, Cornelius Hallahan, an Irish Catholic, founded an estate, maintaining a discreet presence. All Catholic Masses were celebrated in private homes, and the dead were buried on the family plantation. Missions did not flourish, and a 1751 report from Dover states that there were five or six Catholic families, listed as "Papists," who were "attended once a month from Maryland by a priest." The mission for the Apoquiniminck Indians opened by the Jesuits in 1750 escaped the notice of the officials, and Catholics did not appear to suffer severe hardships in Delaware. By 1785, they had gained full rights as citizens.

The Carolinas did not have a recognizable Catholic population until after the Revolutionary War. To the south, Georgia was not only inhospitable to the faithful within its borders but sent out military expeditions to destroy the Catholic Indian strongholds and missions of Florida. James Oglethorpe was governor in 1740, and he became infamous because of his crimes against Catholics, Indians, and the Spanish in Georgia and at St. Augustine, Florida.

The Native American tribes endured a cruel penal period during the colonial age as well. Tragedies took place throughout the colonies as the white settlers craved land and enforced the relocation of the tribes residing on the East Coast of the continent. In 1712, in North Carolina, the Tuscaroras rebelled against their own destruction at the hands of whites. A colonial militia attacked with Indian allies and wiped out the local settlements, sending seven hundred Tuscarora men, women, and children into slavery in Charleston. At Natchez, Mississippi, the white colonists killed more than one thousand Indians and took five hundred as slaves to be sold at public auctions.

The diseases carried into the American wilderness by white settlers proved as deadly a weapon as any used against the Indians. Five major epidemics of smallpox and outbreaks of measles were recorded in Indian encampments between 1660 and 1770. Smallpox was particularly deadly as the disease killed up to ninety percent of the Indian population when it struck an area. Not only did smallpox and measles kill their victims, but they ensured the eventual decimation of the tribe as well. A stricken village had no one available to grow or harvest crops. Warriors could not hunt for vital food resources. In some instances, there wasn't a man or woman left well enough to offer nursing care, thus ensuring the demise of all of the victims.

In the original thirteen colonies, Native Americans suffered exile, enslavement, or destruction of their lands and their ancient lifestyles. The Wampanoags on Massachusetts Bay, for example, numbered more than three thousand in 1642. There were only nine hundred thirteen Wampanoags surviving in 1764. When the colonists began to expand beyond their original land holdings, the tribes residing in contested regions faced similar disasters. An estimated two million Native Americans lived in the southeastern portion of what became the United States before the whites invaded the continent. By 1700, the Indian population in that same region was approximately one hundred thirty thousand.

The Catholic missionaries served these tribes for as long as possible, sometimes going with then into the lands of exile. Actually, when the white Americans began their trek westward, they discovered Catholic missions scattered across the land. They also came face to face with some of the most daring, courageous, and holy men and women who ever walked the continent. In the raw wilderness of the continent, and in former French and Spanish domains, the missionaries labored unceasingly to announce the Good News of Christ.

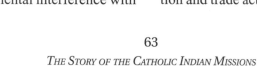

CHAPTER 4

Toward a Perfect Union

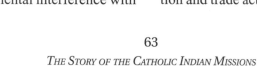

*Mohawk Chief Joseph Brant and a
wampum belt of the Iroquois League*

Throughout the cities, towns, and wilderness areas of the American colonies, news of wars, taxation, legislation, and bureaucratic decisions spread quickly, causing increased resentment about the tragedies being inflicted upon the colonies by faraway nations living in safety. Each new European intervention aroused indignation, and the British dream of an imperial domain in the New World was viewed with disdain. The English, naturally, did not grasp the changes taking place in the colonies and maintained their heavy-handed methods of governing. The English also failed to recognize the homespun resistance being tightly woven with each new law or regulation put into place. Such governmental interference with trade, business, or social aspects of American life was viewed as intolerable and was denounced by leaders in the colonies.

Some colonists responded to continued interventions of the British by simply "moving on" to the beckoning wilderness areas outside of the established perimeters of civilization. Life on such frontiers was perilous at times because of the wild conditions, Indian raids, and the inclement weather. At the same time, such frontiersmen and their families were free of levies, taxes, and British regulations.

By 1765, more than two thousand such families were living along the Ohio River, in an area known today as the city of Pittsburgh. Another thirty-five thousand men, women, and children followed Daniel Boone, a Catholic, into the wild lands of Kentucky and Tennessee. Daniel Boone was an adopted member of the Shawnee, brought into the tribe by Chief Black Fish. He honored Indian customs and ideals and urged other whites to follow him into the wilderness for a new life, not realizing the damage that would be inflicted on the local tribes. Such migrations alarmed the English authorities, of course, who enforced new taxation and trade acts in the colonies in retaliation. The growing tensions led to defiance on the part of the Americans and then to war. Once actual battles started, the colonists rallied to the call, expecting all of their fellow countrymen to march with the same enthusiasm.

It was at this point that saner Americans took the opportunity of cautioning their fellow revolutionaries against the continued intolerance and abusive behavior concerning the Catholics in their ranks. Such warnings were heard throughout the colonies, as the members of the Continental Congress met to consider their own past political errors. Embroiled in a perilous war with Britain, the Continental Congress realized that the prior assault on Catholics over the Quebec Act in Canada was politically reckless and incredibly naïve.

At the same time, the American Army was being mobilized and forged into a cohesive force that would guarantee liberty, and it was recognized that continued demonstrations of anti-Catholicism threatened morale and unity. George Washington, charged with the formidable task of gathering the fighting forces needed, set out to establish unity in the ranks, chiding his countrymen and issuing dire warnings that religious intolerance was a luxury that they could afford no longer. Washington put an end to the "Pope Day" celebrations in military campsites, the mock parades and assaults on the popes, and the burning of Catholic symbols, announcing his surprise that "there should be officers and soldiers in this army so devoid of common sense as not to see the impropriety of such a step at this juncture."

Whether they were tolerated by their fellow rebels or not, the Catholics of the colonies responded to the call to arms, and many distinguished themselves in battle.

These Catholics had no love for England, and they were Americans, as patriotic as their neighbors. Catholics also realized that political liberty would result in religious liberty in time if they defended their countrymen and their land.

These Catholics and their fellow countrymen were underestimated by the British, who seemed unable to view the colonies in a rational manner, thereby condemning their own imperial cause with lethal arrogance. The men and women of the colonies were not ignorant, irate peasants storming the castles of their aristocratic betters. The leaders of the American Revolution were educated men, many with London law degrees. They used their skilled minds and literary talents to rouse their fellow colonials to rebellion and fostered methods of communication and meetings that were sophisticated and successful. Some of the most erudite and stirring essays on human liberties and ideals ever assembled came from the pens of Benjamin Franklin, Thomas Paine, Samuel Adams, Patrick Henry, and John Hancock.

Meanwhile, the American Indians responded to the onset of the war with varying emotions. Envoys arrived in the Native American lands, bearing promises, treaties, and pleas for support in the coming battles. The French and Indian War had alerted the colonies to the military prowess of the tribes, and the American colonists wanted these warriors as allies in their cause. If the Indians did not want to fight for the American rebels, the envoys tried to make sure that they would not be turned loose against them. Many of the tribes listened to the white envoys and then decided to be neutral and avoid taking part in the fray. As the Oneidas declared in Connecticut: "We cannot become involved in this dispute between two brothers. This quarrel seems unnatural. If the great king of England applies to us for aid, we shall deny him; if the colonies apply, we shall refuse."

This neutrality, however, was not widespread. The Five-Nation Iroquois Confederation was split by the American Revolution, as the member nations assumed differing views concerning the fray. The Oneidas (despite their declaration of 1775) supported the colonies, alongside the Tuscaroras. The Mohawks, Onondaga, Seneca, and Cayuga nations were on the side of England in the war.

The Abenakis who remained in the American territory were asked by George Washington to aid the colonial cause as well. The Abenakis agreed, on the condition that the Americans provided the tribe with a Catholic priest chaplain. There were few such missionaries available because of the penal laws of the prior decades, and Washington was hard pressed to secure the services of such a priest. He went to the French naval forces when they arrived in American harbors as allies and asked the admiral for a priest missionary to the Abenakis. A French Catholic chaplain was assigned to the tribe, and the Abenakis joined the cause of the revolution.

The Revolutionary War, of course, was not confined to the coastal region of America. Military engagements raged in the north and south, and the Midwestern and Great Lakes regions were embroiled as well. The Ohio Valley was the scene of many conflicts, as the local Indian tribes declared their own allegiances. The arrival of the French added complications for the Indians because the French missionaries were remembered with esteem and reverence. The arrival of

A ceremonial Seneca headdress

the French as American allies produced an even more pronounced effect on the colonial revolutionaries as a whole. These were devout Catholics, men who were unashamed of being "Papists." At the same time, they brought military discipline, tested strategies, and a profound attitude of culture and courtesy to battlefronts.

The Comte de Rochambeau, the Comte de Barras, Louis Berthier, the Chevalier de Cambray-Digne, the Comte d'Estaing, the Comte de Grasse, the Marquis de Lafayette, Chevalier de Laumay, Louis Le Beque de Prelse Duportail — along with their military associates, Thaddeus Kosciuszko, Count Casimir Pulaski, and others — made a profound impression on the Americans. It was difficult for the Protestants in the ranks to rally against Catholicism when French and Polish Catholics were strengthening the cause of the revolution and ensuring the American victory.

At the same time, the Americans watched a similar spirit of service and distinction among the Catholic colonists who had spent their lives as disenfranchised citizens. Many Catholics dedicated themselves to the point that they earned the praise and respect of their countrymen. Included among these was Charles Carroll, a signer of the Declaration of Independence. He wrote his name as "Charles Carroll of Carrollton," explaining that there were so many Carrolls in Maryland that he had made the distinction "so that King George would know which Carroll to hunt down for treason."

Cornwallis formally surrendered on October 19, 1781, and the task of building a new nation on the continent began in earnest. When the war was declared officially over, a *Te Deum*, the traditional ceremony of thanksgiving and praise, was celebrated at St. Joseph's Church in Philadelphia. The Marquis de la Luzerne, the French ambassador, scheduled the service, which was attended by George Washington and other military and government leaders of all faiths. For Catholics it was a time of consolidation and an end to the dreaded penal age. As the Constitutions of the various states and the Articles of Confederation were drawn up, more and more Catholics received rights of citizenship. The Church, so ably represented by the Europeans during the war, received due recognition.

It had taken years of debate and negotiations to produce "The Articles of Confederation and Perpetual Union" adopted in 1781 by a nation that was now free of European control. The battle for equality was not won easily, however, as the various states had to bequeath such a status by putting an end to the terrible penal laws against Catholics and the faith within their own borders. The Catholic Church, having served faithfully in the Revolutionary War, was beginning to look toward the future with a renewed vigor.

The Church was thus eventually able to begin the necessary administrative operations in order to ensure its survival in the emerging cities and in the missions to the Native Americans. The focus on such a beginning was Maryland, a colony originally intended as a Catholic haven. On June 6, 1784, a former Jesuit priest was named Superior of the Missions of the United States. There were no dioceses, no sees in charge of the Catholics in the young land. America was a mission territory, still struggling to survive in a political as well as in a natural wilderness.

The Superior of the Missions of the United States was Father John Carroll, a remarkable man who was equipped by devotion, temperament, and education to assume such a burden. He was born in Upper Marlborough, Maryland, on January 8, 1735, the third child of Daniel and Eleanor (Darnall) Carroll. His family was wealthy and distinguished, popular at Marlborough and Annapolis, and related to other clans in Maryland and Virginia. Devoutly Catholic, the Carrolls and their relatives maintained cordial relations with the Protestants and took discreet measures concerning the practices of their faith. Their Catholic ceremonies were held on their own estates and plantations, causing no furor in other circles. Protestant neighbors were well aware of the Catholicity of the Carrolls but admired the family and were awed by the cultural and social standing of their related clans.

John Carroll's brother was Daniel Carroll of Marlborough, and his cousin was Charles Carroll of Carrollton. John attended school with Charles at Bohemia Manor, a

Catholic institution eventually closed by the Protestant authorities because of its fame for excellence. John and Charles then left the colony to study at St. Omer's, a college and seminary originally founded by Father Robert Persons, a companion of St. Edmund Campion, the English martyr. St. Omer's was started in France and reestablished in Brugge, Belgium. The Carroll cousins graduated from the school, and Charles went elsewhere to pursue an extensive education in law.

John, however, had a religious vocation and, parting from Charles, entered the Jesuit novitiate near St. Omer's. He was ordained a priest and professed in the Society of Jesus in 1771. Two years later the Jesuits were suppressed by the pope, and the priests and religious found themselves facing arrest, hardships, and exile from their homelands. Father Carroll returned to America as a result, residing at Rock Creek, his mother's home, when he arrived back in Maryland in 1774.

It was a turbulent era, as the colonies were moving toward rebellion, and the Catholics of Maryland welcomed Father Carroll's ministry. Using the time-honored, discreet approach that had served his family well, Father Carroll built a comfortable chapel on his mother's estate and began his apostolate. This chapel at Rock Creek, Maryland, has been designated as the "Bethlehem of the American Church, as truly as Baltimore is its Jerusalem."

Father Carroll lived quietly and frugally, engaged in serving the neighboring Catholics and praying for his troubled homeland. In 1776, he was asked by the Continental Congress to accompany Charles Carroll, Samuel Chase, and Benjamin Franklin on a special mission. The members of the Continental Congress hoped that Canada would aid their cause in the coming revolution and enlisted the services of the Carrolls because of their Catholic connections. It was hoped that Father Carroll and his cousin could allay Canadian resentment about the American uproar over the Quebec Act. As the Canadians were enjoying the benefits of official toleration and the full rights of citizenship, they saw little reason to join with the Protestant bigots in the American colonies in a revolution. The mission was doomed from the start, but during the long journey, Father Carroll demonstrated a genuine concern for Benjamin Franklin, who was ailing at the time and grateful for the courtesies and care that he received from the priest.

The friendship between Benjamin Franklin and Father Carroll endured for decades, and in time it would benefit the Church. Father Carroll assumed the role of Superior of the Missions in the United States and was consecrated the first bishop on September 17, 1789, so declared by Pope Pius VI. Benjamin Franklin took some credit for this appointment. An entry in Franklin's diary confirms his involvement in Bishop Carroll's elevation to the episcopacy. Dated July 1, the entry reads: "The pope's nuncio called and acquainted me that the pope, on my recommendation, appointed Mr. John Carroll superior of the Catholic clergy of America, with many of the powers of a bishop, and that, probably, he would be made a bishop . . . before the end of the year."

As the bishop and then archbishop of Baltimore, America's primary see, John Carroll was the administrator of the parishes and missions of the settled areas in the East and Midwest. He was also the guardian of the Indian missions in lands that would be opened by the American trek West. Bishop Carroll had some awareness of the need and accomplishments in the areas beyond the control of the United States. He started sending missionaries to such distant sites as early as 1795. The great tapestry of the faith being woven in the wilderness, however, was often located in lands still held by foreign nations. Competition for such vast holdings continued, but Spain and France, as Catholic nations, maintained the same evangelical priorities that Bishop Carroll adopted in his ministry. In time, of course, these regions would become American territories and these missions would be Bishop Carroll's concerns or the obligations of his many episcopal successors.

Fox Chief Black Hawk and a tribal quill pouch

The Emerging Church

had not yet impacted on the West or on the routines of the missions.

In the eastern regions of America, affairs of the day were anything but usual or routine. The victory of the American forces and their French allies in the Revolutionary War not only severed the New World's ties with the British crown but also opened a new historical era on the continent. The independent Americans celebrated their hard-won freedom for a time, but they also came face to face with the enormous challenges of shaping a new country and a new government. Suddenly, they realized, the nation's destiny rested uniquely in their own hands. The British monarch and Parliament were irrelevant. America stood alone, and for good or ill, the coming years would depend upon the industriousness, courage, honor, and dedication of its citizens. Americans had dared to seize their destiny. Now they would have the daunting task of forging a union dedicated to the monumental virtues enunciated in the Declaration of Independence.

In time, of course, these young Americans became a radiant symbol of human daring for men and women around the world. As a result, refugees from lands ravaged by

As Americans in the eastern portion of the continent were winning independence and freedom from British rule, two Franciscans, Silvestre Vélez de Escalante and Atanasio Domínguez, were blazing a trail of discovery from Santa Fe, New Mexico, to Utah. In 1776, these monks discovered Utah Lake and were welcomed by the Laguna Indians. The priests remained with the Lagunas until September 25, when they went to the Grand Canyon of the Colorado. They then returned to Santa Fe, reaching that settlement in January, 1777. The Catholic missionaries knew of events taking place on the East Coast, but whatever was happening in the colonies, or the newly founded states,

69

THE STORY OF THE CATHOLIC INDIAN MISSIONS

ancient feuds and rivalries packed their belongings and set sail to the new republic. These immigrants came from far and wide to be part of the great adventure in democracy, and their arrival in vast numbers set in motion new imperatives, especially for the Catholic Church in the United States.

The original thirteen states rejoiced over their independence and then started their legislative compacts with their free citizens. These legislative enactments involved community meetings and debates throughout the land, as Americans demanded a visible role in the process of government. At the same time, the compilation of new laws and regulations left many Americans unsettled. They began to experience a distinct longing, a profound yearning, compounded by the arrival of the hordes of European immigrants. The free citizens of the United States had always been conscious of the vast wilderness awaiting them beyond their established state boundaries. Almost immediately after the war these wild lands took on new luster.

The original states were relatively small and bustling with towns and cities. When the Revolutionary War ended, the city of New York boasted a population of about 33,000 men, women, and children; Philadelphia had more than 28,000 residents; Boston some 18,000; Charleston more than 16,000; and Baltimore about 13,500 inhabitants. By 1790, approximately 3,900,000 Americans lived within 50 miles of the Atlantic Ocean, from north to south, and within 40 short years that number rose to

Chief Ouray and a Ute hide design

13,000,000. The burgeoning population prompted many families to follow what would become a time-honored American custom. They paid their debts, sold their lands, packed up, and started "moving on." Americans turned their faces to the West.

The Catholics of America joined their neighbors in the treks West, set on opening new lands. There were few priests in the original states because of the penal laws, and those serving in parishes were alone, working themselves into early graves. Bishop John Carroll assumed his vast episcopal duties in 1789, aware of the prevailing political and social attitudes and the problems facing both urban parishes and the far-flung outposts of the faith. The Catholics numbered around twenty-five thousand at the time, not counting the mission populations in the outposts.

Bishop Carroll took steps to consolidate the Church and to provide an adequate clergy. In 1791, he was able to bring four Sulpicians to America to begin a seminary. Caught in the French Revolution in their homeland, these Sulpicians came to Baltimore and established St. Mary's Seminary. In that same year, Georgetown College opened for Catholic students. Five years later, the Dominicans, led by Father Edward Fenwick, established a novitiate in Kentucky. The Trappists were nearby in Missouri, and Bishop Carroll sent a Sulpician, Father François Ciquard, to reopen the mission for the faithful Abenakis. In time Father Fenwick would become the bishop of Cincinnati and an outspoken, eloquent supporter of the Native Americans. Establishing educational programs for both Indian children and adults, Bishop Fenwick demonstrated so much concern for Indian rights and welfare that the noted Protestant Lyman Beecher wrote a plea for unity among Protestant groups in the face of such dedication and fervor. Beecher used Bishop Fenwick's defense of the Indians as evidence of a planned Catholic takeover of the American West. Bishop Fenwick was known nationwide for loving the Native Americans "above all others."

The American Indian nations, of course, were embroiled in even more serious situations as a result of the westward migration and the nation's disdain for the Indian lifestyle and aspirations. Catholics had been singled out for public praise by George Washington during the victory celebrations following the Revolutionary War; the Indian allies of the Americans received no such gratitude for their aid during the struggle for independence. Actually, these Indian allies fared little better than the tribes who had fought on the English side during the war. The Constitution of the United States, hailed as a model throughout the world in that era, decreed equal justice for all. Slaves and Indians, however, were not given consideration in that exalted document. Indians were not mentioned in the Declaration of Independence and certainly were not called by name in the Bill of Rights.

As prolonged debates raged about all aspects of life in the new young land, Native Americans had few defenders or friends. Some wiser leaders did plead for a national conscience concerning the Indian lands and rights, but they were ignored. Henry Knox, the Secretary of War during the George Washington administration (1789-1797), announced: "The Indians, being the prior occupants, possess the rights to the soil." The great Tecumseh gave the Native American viewpoint to the American invasion of their lands in the process of "moving on." He declared: "Sell off a country? Why not sell the air, the sea, or the earth? Did not the Great Spirit create all of these for the use of all of his children?"

Both Knox and Tecumseh were deemed naïve by the general public. The Indians viewed themselves as guardians of the lands, not the owners, but if they started claiming such territories by the right of prior occupancy, Americans would be barred from them forever. The lands of the continent were open and inviting, and the men and women of the United States intended to take possession of them, no matter what the "Great Spirit" had intended originally.

George Washington's Farewell Address in 1797 stirred Americans as they watched their great hero retire as a living legend. John Adams followed Washington, and Thomas Jefferson followed Adams. During this era the spirit of "moving on" was inflamed by the explorations undertaken by Lewis and Clark from 1804 to 1806. Sacagawea, the Shoshone woman who had been captured by

Mandans in a raid on her village and was subsequently bought by a fur trader named Toussaint Charbeneau, proved invaluable to Lewis and Clark. Traveling 7,689 miles in just over two years, the explorers and their Shoshone guide witnessed the splendors of the continent, the untamed wilds, and the fertile regions that offered such promise to the young Americans. Lewis and Clark returned to Washington, D.C., where they enthralled the nation with accounts of vastness and splendor. Countless families heard of the wonders and the wilderness; many packed up their belongings and started "moving on" again.

The Louisiana Purchase in 1803 opened the lands all the way to the Rocky Mountains. That negotiation with France also doubled the size of America and added countless numbers of Catholics to the population. Two years after the Louisiana Purchase, Rome appointed Bishop John Carroll administrator of Louisiana and the Florida territories. Aware of the sentiments of the French and Spanish Catholics who suddenly found themselves citizens of the United States, Bishop Carroll knew that he had to provide a suitable spiritual leader for Louisiana, especially. With these concerns in mind, he met with James Madison, the Secretary of State at the time, to discuss the necessity of appointing a French priest as the bishop of the diocese of Louisiana. Madison, a bit taken aback and confused about the inner workings of the Catholic episcopacy, could offer no immediate advice. The discussion, however, brought Madison to the conclusion that Bishop Carroll was not only a brilliant administrator of the Church but also a patriot who had concerns about American sensitivities. Later, Bishop Carroll sent Father Louis Dubourg to Louisiana, elevating him to the rank of bishop soon after.

The Catholic population continued to rise as slave revolts in the Caribbean region brought other white Catholics to the United States. The former masters of estates and plantations on these islands, these Catholics found themselves exiled from their domains. One of the slaves brought to America in this fashion was Pierre Toussaint. In 1807, when his mistress, Madame Bérard, died, he was set free. Toussaint was a gifted hairdresser who had supported Madame Bérard and had made friends throughout New York City. He educated seminarians and slaves, cared for orphans, and displayed heroism during an outbreak of yellow fever; his charity was legendary.

Bishop Carroll continued organizing the Church, establishing hierarchical disciplines, unifying liturgical observances, regulating lay authority, and instituting a firm episcopal tradition in the country. He was also responsible for the Catholic missions in America and aware of what was happening in the territories still ruled by foreign governments. The great missions of Texas had been secularized by the Mexican government in 1794, a great loss to the Church on the continent. A year later, the Miami Indians lost all of their lands in Ohio, opening that region to white settlers.

People across the country were hearing about the "Patriot Priest," Father Pierre Gibault, who had served as a missionary in Indiana and Illinois. Father Gibault had swung the settlers of the region to the American cause at considerable risk to his own safety at the hands of the British. Father Gibault, working with Colonel George Rogers Clark and his aide, Colonel Vigo, had secured the allegiance of Vincennes, Fort Chartres, and other settlements in the present Midwest, thus defeating British hopes there. The Native Americans, so advised by Father Gibault, did not respond to the English offers and remained neutral, thus holding the line. Americans spoke of him and his devotion to his adopted mission land, and once again a Catholic received praise. Other priests and the Catholic Indians of the nation were not recognized at the same time for their valor and faith. The Catholic Indians and their missionaries were beginning to face the harshest and most relentless enemy of all, American bureaucracy. President Washington and his standards of courtesy and honor were all in the past. The new generation of government bureaucrats used legislative activities as weapons against the Native Americans and their priests, demonstrating a remarkable ability to devise words and policies that sounded noble, even as they cut the Indian world into pieces.

The Indian Trade and Intercourse Act of 1802 was the first shot in the undeclared war for Indian lands. In this legislation, the tribal entities disappeared, giving way to federal jurisdictions. Tribal governments, customs, and traditions were dismissed as irrelevant and archaic. If the Native Americans wished to maintain such governments and the historical values handed down to them by their ancestors, they had to relocate outside of federal jurisdictions. Even there they could face new harassment, but in the meantime they could retain their own identities. The Native Americans reluctantly imitated the whites of the land and started "moving on" as a result of this act. Missions established on the former Indian lands were abandoned or moved, and in some cases the missionaries accompanied the tribes to their new destinations.

In 1808, Baltimore was elevated to the status of an archdiocese by Pope Pius VII. As a result, Bishop Carroll gained archiepiscopal rank while being relieved of the press of duties in certain key Catholic cities. Four suffragan dioceses (dioceses serving as part of the archdiocese of Baltimore) were established. These dioceses were subject to Archbishop Carroll, but were administered locally by their own bishops. New York City became a diocese under the care of Bishop Richard Luke Concanen, a Dominican, who never arrived in America to take up his episcopal duties. Father Anthony Kohlmann, a Jesuit, served as New York's administrator until 1815.

Philadelphia was established with Bishop Michael Egan, a noted and respected Franciscan, as the episcopal authority. Boston was erected as a diocese and was administered by Jean-Louis Cheverus. (When Bishop Cheverus returned to France, in 1823, Americans protested. A petition was sent by Americans of all faiths to King Louis XVIII of France, asking that the saintly bishop be allowed to remain in New England. Daniel Webster was one of the noted signers of the petition that stated: "We hold him to be a blessing and a treasure in our social community which we cannot part with." Louis XVIII was adamant, however, and Bishop Cheverus continued his labors in his homeland and received the red hat of the cardinalate.) Bardstown, Kentucky, was the fourth diocese erected, and the famed missionary Benedict Flaget was consecrated the bishop of this see.

Archbishop Carroll's parallel pastorate, the Indian missions of America, continued outside of his actual jurisdiction and prospered within the new United States borders, despite the continued decimation or relocation of the various Native American nations. In 1778, the famed Iroquois League, or Six Nations, had been broken by deliberate military campaigns. This model of unity could not save the Iroquois League lands from the Americans who were hungry for untamed acres. The Fort Stanwix meeting in 1784 resulted in the transfer of Iroquois lands in western New York, Ohio, and Pennsylvania to the United States, and other members of the League faced similar losses.

Soon after, the Indians living in Texas, New Mexico, and parts of the Washington Territory were decimated by epidemics of smallpox and measles, the result of contact with the white settlers. Such epidemics became a vital element of American control in time, as the native populations had no protection against the white man's diseases. What the laws and wars could not gain, the illnesses provided.

In 1782, the Delaware Indians had been ruthlessly slain by federal troops at Gnadenhutten, Ohio, as part of the organized efforts to assume Indian lands. Such military actions conducted by United States forces were triggered by sudden quarrels, misunderstandings, or by the violation of existing treaties, but they were predicated upon an American desire to see the Indians banished from their ancient homelands. The year 1809, following the establishment of Baltimore as an archdiocese, witnessed the loss of two-and-a-half million acres of tribal land, taken from the Ohio and Indiana Native Americans by the Treaty of Fort Wayne.

Father Gabriel Richard, however, was laboring among the Ottawa and others at L'arbre Croche (now Harbor Springs), in Michigan. There Chief Blackbird, who had been educated at the Sulpician mission at Oka, guided his people devoutly. The mission endured until 1827, when a resident diocesan priest was appointed and a school opened as well. In Detroit, Spring Hill Academy for Native Americans was opened in 1809. Even though this academy was short-lived, it set the standard for educational pro-

grams to follow for the Native Americans. Within a decade Jesuit Joseph Sévère Dumoulin was among the Chippewa at Pembina, South Dakota, and a religious congregation of Native Americans, the Sisters of the Propagation of the Faith, was assisting in two missions and schools.

The Catholic mission apostolate also was entering into other wilderness areas or restoring once abandoned sites. By 1800, missions for the Pueblo Indians were operating in Sia, Isleta, Laguna, Picures, San Felipe, San Juan, Dandia, Poynaque, Santa Clara, Santo Domingo, Toros, and Zuñi, New Mexico, and were well sustained. Missions were serving the Pueblos as well in Acoma, Cochíti, Galistos, Jemez, Nambé, Pecos, San Felipe, San Ildefonso, Santa Ana, and Tesuque. By 1811, because of the decline in the Native American population, only five priests were in the Pueblo area. In time, the Franciscans were replaced, mainly by secular priests attached to the newly erected dioceses of those regions.

In Maine, the Abenaki had their resident missionary, and another priest, Father James René Romagné, was in the region visiting the Penobscots and Passamaquoddies in 1804.

In California, the missions had faced the onslaught of droughts and storms, changes of administration in Mexico, and the deaths of beloved pastors. Mission Santa Inés was founded in 1804 to serve another area, and the vast network of churches, schools, and residences was administered by the faithful Franciscans.

In Illinois, the Sulpician missionaries Gabriel Richard and Michael Levadoux labored among the Illinois Indians at the venerable Cahokia mission, having arrived there in 1792. Father Rivet was with the Wea (Miami), Kaskaskia, and Piankashaw.

Father Richard left the Kaskaskia mission in Illinois in 1794 and was assigned to Sault Ste. Marie in Michigan. He also served Mackinaw, Green Bay, and L'arbre Croche. Energetic and gifted with an understanding of the Native Americans, Father Richard was assigned to Detroit in 1798, where Father Levadoux was in residence. Franciscan missionaries arrived at Burt Lake and L'arbre Croche to aid in the apostolate, and the Sisters of Notre Dame de Namur entered the Michigan missions around this time. Such women religious endured many hardships in order to serve the growing number of schools, and they lived with the Native American tribes while conducting educational programs.

In Missouri, the Jesuits arrived at St. Geneviève in 1804, turning their attention to the vast mission territory of the present state. While St. Louis became an important link for Americans on their treks westward in time, the area was an early haven for many Native American tribes as well. The Jesuits strengthened their commitment in 1811 to Missouri when they opened their mission and educational programs at Florissant. These Jesuits sought ways in which to console the exiled tribes and ease their transitions in the new lands.

The War of 1812 with England took a terrible toll on the nation's capital, but it also proved disastrous for the English. British troops were slaughtered at the Battle of New Orleans, an engagement fought in vain several days after the treaty ending the war was signed in Ghent. Tecumseh, the great Shawnee chief who had recognized the American ambitions and had urged his nation to unite in defense of their sacred lands, was slain by United States troops at the Battle of the Thames in Canada.

The American Catholic Church, by this time an established and visible national entity, was involved in two profound apostolates in this period, and faced challenges that demanded both courage and zeal. These apostolates dated to the earliest eras of exploration on the continent, and both continue to the present day. The newly erected dioceses served the established regions of America, which had been cleared of the Native Americans, and new parishes were being formed in these regions to minister to the men and women who migrated to the United States from Europe. At the same time, ministries were established in newly claimed territories, and missions and parishes were nurtured in lands still free of the white American occupation. The apostolates in these missions and parishes brought yet another generation of dedicated priests and religious into the field, some leaving the routines of "civilized" life to take up their vocations in the wild lands of the continent.

Archbishop John Carroll died in 1815, mourned by people of all faiths, who formally extended their condolences to America's Catholic community. St. Elizabeth Seton was still active, inspiring her fellow Americans with her zeal and commitment as a religious foundress.

As the First Seminole War (1817-1818) raged in the southeastern part of the United States, Florida, the site of the first Catholic parish in the present United States, was ceded to American control in 1819. "Old Hickory," Andrew Jackson, the hero of the Battle of New Orleans in the War of 1812, was gaining popularity as a determined "Indian Fighter" during this period. Jackson had directed the slaughter of eight hundred Creek Indians at Horseshoe Bend, Alabama, on March 27, 1814, and relished the fame that it had brought him. His views on the Native

American nations had a harsh impact on the Indian peoples and on the Catholic missionaries in the coming decades.

Later, when Jackson served as president, the Creek Chief Speckled Snake would sum up the "Indian Fighter's" philosophy, saying: "Brothers, I have listened to a great many talks from our Great Father (President Jackson). But they always begin and end in this: 'Get a little further, you are too close to me.'"

The Native Americans were discovering that the changes coming in the United States were centering more and more upon their tribal homelands. The policy of moving the tribes West was the only consistent element in the volatile eras of America's political and social evolutions. President James Monroe occupied the White House in 1817, bringing about what was called the "Era of Good Feeling." At the time, Stephen Austin was leading more than three hundred families into the sprawling territory that would become Texas, and almost one thousand more families followed close behind, putting down roots and establishing settlements among the original Native Americans.

In 1820, the Osage Chief Sans Nerf went to St. Louis, Missouri, to ask the Catholic authorities there for missionaries to come

Chief Speckled Snake and a Creek beaded design

to his tribal lands in Kansas. Father Charles de la Croix, a Jesuit, was sent to the Osage two years later, going to a site on the Neosho River. He was followed by the Jesuits Charles Van Quickenborne, John Schoenmaker, and Christian Hoecken. These missionaries would serve the Osage, Kickapoo, and Potawátomi. To aid in this apostolate, Bishop Dubourg, in charge of this area, went to Washington, D.C., to ask for funds to start four missions among the Osage. The Secretary of War, John C. Calhoun, astounded but moved by the bishop's eloquent pleas, authorized an annual subsidy of $800 per year for the programs that would aid the tribes. In North and South Dakota, then a territory, Jesuit Joseph Sévère Dumoulin was laboring among the tribes, having been assigned there by the bishop of Quebec, still the administrator of the missions. Father George Belcourt was in the southern area of the Dakotas.

The policy of acquiring Native American lands did not abate during this era of "Good Feeling." By 1820, there were an estimated one hundred twenty thousand Indians residing on lands east of the Mississippi River. Within twenty-four years, the number would be recorded as thirty thousand. The Kickapoos were forcibly removed from their home territories in Illinois. The Creeks had lost their tribal lands six years before, and between 1814 and 1824, the Indians in Alabama and Florida had seventy-five percent of their lands taken away. One third of the Indian holdings in Tennessee were confiscated, and one fifth of Indian lands in Georgia and Mississippi. The Sauk and Fox Indians were also sent into exile.

Despite this flagrant cruelty, many of the Indians remained staunchly committed to the faith, recognizing the sincerity of their missionaries, the Blackrobes. The Ottawa chiefs in the Upper Great Lakes region were asking for missionaries at this time, and Chief Simon Pokagon, of the Potawátomi, asked for baptism. Bishop Frederic Résé of Detroit personally baptized Chief Pokagon, bringing the tribe into the faith.

When the Erie Canal opened in 1825, people began to hasten their travels to the West in even greater numbers. St. Louis, in Missouri, was the last outpost of civilization before the remaining wilderness, and a diocese had just been erected there. Missionaries such as the Jesuit Sebastian Meurin had

been in the area since 1770, but Father Meurin was the only priest in Missouri for a long time, and he was over sixty years old and exhausted by his daily rounds to the Native Americans and to the white settlers. Under the guidance of St. Louis's first bishop, Joseph Rosati, the missions were reopened and repopulated. New priests and religious were recruited and programs instituted for the Indians arriving in their lands of exile in sorrow and dire need.

Andrew Jackson followed John Quincy Adams into the White House in 1829, beginning his term in a period of disquiet. Americans had come to the realization that "all of Europe was coming across the ocean." Conditions on the East Coast were congested and chaotic as more and more immigrants crowded into the cities and seaports, and the unceasing tide of men and women threatened public services and safety. These conditions added weight to Jackson's campaign promise to make the eastern part of the country a true paradise free of all Indians. Jackson had been elected on his proposal to relocate every tribe west of the Mississippi River — a sentiment obviously shared by the voters.

Chief Black Hawk, who would begin a war during Jackson's term of office, understood what was at stake. He described the Americans at the time, saying: "The white men do not scalp the heads; but they do worse — they poison the heart."

The United States Bureau of Indian Affairs had been made part of the War Department a short time before, and military units in various locations were used to carry out the policies of Jackson's Indian Removal Act of 1830. This legislation called for the enforced march of all Native Americans out of the lands east of the Mississippi River. The Cherokees won a Supreme Court decision against the act, but President Johnson ignored the court and proceeded with the removal. When the tribal lands were taken, Catholic missionaries tried to rebuild on new allocation sites, sharing in the trials. The Five Civilized Tribes — the Cherokee, Chickasaw, Choctaw, Creek, and Seminole — lost their lands as well, but they adapted to the white styles and built new, modern enclaves in exile.

There was another breed of man in the wilderness of America in this era, the true heir of the spirit of "moving on." These rugged individuals made their way into lush valleys, followed steams and rivers, and crossed the snowy crests of towering mountains. Because they cherished the great stone spires of the wilderness, such hardy souls were called "mountain men." They were distinctly American, but they scorned the "civilization" and the progress of the settlements and cities, and they abhorred the American greed for land. The mountain men could be good friends to the Indian tribes, some being adopted into the cultures, or they could be terrible scourges, given to outrageous ferocity and cruel acts.

Jim Bridger, for example, left civilization in 1822, at the age of eighteen, seeking solitude and the natural splendors of America's wild lands. He roamed at will, trapping, hunting, and exploring the western part of the continent and proving his skills as a solitary nomad of the mountain peaks. Bridger, called "Old Gabe" by his trail companions, earned a reputation for being a dangerous enemy to Indians and whites when aroused by what he believed to be an injustice. In 1825, he followed the Bear River all the way to the Great Salt Lake, which he mistakenly identified as the Pacific Ocean at first sight. Old Gabe mapped the Oregon Trail, the vital pathway for future settlers,

Bishop Frederick Baraga
and an Ojibwa design pouch

and he made note of other overland routes. His trail companions, however, spoke of him often as a remarkable individual who displayed a unique interest around the campfires shared in the night. There Bridger liked to hear companions recite his favorite author, William Shakespeare.

In the civilized regions scorned by Old Gabe and the other mountain men, the Catholic Church was prosperous and vital. In the year 1830, some three hundred eighteen thousand Americans converted to Catholicism, an astounding number that roused Protestant enemies and renewed traditional intolerance. Several organizations arose to combat the Church on all levels and to "protect" the United States from the evils of "Popery." One such association was called the "Native Americans." The "Native Americans" were not Indians but white Anglo-Saxon Protestants who hated Catholics in general and the Irish in particular. Riots targeting the Catholics and Irish took place, and in 1834 an unruly mob, spurred to a rage by vicious tales about Catholic nuns, set fire to an Ursuline convent. This arson cooled the ardor of the bigots and brought about a new appraisal of Catholics and their contributions to the nation.

While the cities and towns raged with religious controversies, missionaries continued their labors. Father Stephen Theodore Badin, the first Catholic priest ordained in the original States of the Union, had been with Father Charles Nerinckx in Kentucky since 1801. In 1830, Father Badin was in the Ohio missions, having served with his brother, Father Vincent Badin, and with Father Gabriel Richard in Michigan during the previous two years. One of Badin's companions in the missions to the Potawátomi in Indiana was Theodore James Ryhen, who would become Brother Francis Xavier, the founder of the Xaverian Broth-

ers. This Belgian congregation was erected to serve the American missions in several areas in the United States.

The "Apostle to the Chippewas," the Redemptorist Father Frederick Irenaeus Baraga was in northern Michigan, at the Ottawa mission of L'arbre Croche. A nobleman from modern Slovenia, Father Baraga had been trained in the religious apostolate by St. Clement Mary Hofbauer and had arrived in America in 1831. Serving alone in Upper Michigan for decades, he taught farming to the local Indian tribes while caring for their spiritual needs. In 1853, Father Baraga became a bishop and vicar apostolic of the northern peninsula of Michigan and eventually made Marquette his see. His first

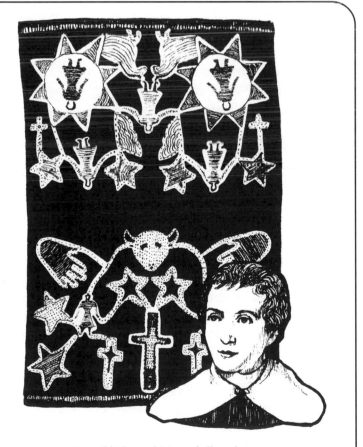

Venerable Samuel Mazzuchelli and a
Winnebago loincloth design

THE STORY OF THE CATHOLIC INDIAN MISSIONS

pastorals were issued in English and in the language of his beloved Indians. Bishop Baraga served the Native Americans on Beaver and Washington islands and on the Manistique River in Michigan. He also had missions at Grand Rapids and Muskegon, laboring among the Chippewa at La Pointe, Grande Portage, Fond du Lac, L'Anne, and Bad River. The bishop operated nine Indian schools and continued his rounds of mission visits throughout his life.

Another great Indian missionary of the era was the Dominican Venerable Samuel Mazzuchelli. Born in Milan, Italy, in 1806, he had entered the Order of Preachers and had volunteered for the American missions. He was ordained in Cincinnati, Ohio, in 1830, and went to Upper Michigan, where he served the Ojibwa, Menóminee, Ottawa, and Winnebago. His main mission was at Mackinaw. The Venerable Father Mazzuchelli traveled throughout Michigan and Wisconsin, and in 1883 served as the chaplain of the first legislative body of Wisconsin. Founding educational institutions, he wrote prayer books, liturgical guides, and calendars in the Native American languages. The Venerable Father Mazzuchelli started the Sinsinawa Dominican Sisters in 1848, and labored unceasingly among the tribes of the region until his death in 1864. Pope John Paul II declared him venerable in 1993.

Trappers and traders brought word of the missionary efforts of dedicated priests in the wilds to the Catholics residing in the heavily populated cities of America. These cities had their own models of the faith as well. The "Apostle of Philadelphia," Father Felix Barbelin, arrived in that city only four years after the burning of the Ursuline convent, and he would be followed by one of America's holiest bishops, St. John

Nepomucene Neumann. St. John Neumann, who served as the bishop of Philadelphia, walked twenty-five miles on one occasion just to confirm one small boy.

In the Potawátomi mission at Sugar Creek, Kansas, as in Florissant, Missouri, an elderly French nun entranced both the Indians and the whites as she went about her religious and missionary duties. She did not speak English. She could not carry on conversations with the Potawátomi people in their language nor provide them with an elegant dictionary. The Indians understood her without a need for words. The Potawátomi called her "the Woman Who Always Prays." They were inspired by her presence, and the white settlers of Missouri looked upon her as a "pioneer" and enshrined her in the state records. To Catholics the world over, she is St. Rose Philippine Duchesne, the American foundress of the Society of the Sacred Heart and the emissary of St. Sophie Barat to the New World. Sugar Creek Mission, graced by the presence of this saint, had been started originally in Council Bluffs by the Jesuits Pierre Jean De Smet and Felix Verreydt and was then called St. Joseph's. In 1841, the mission was relocated.

Father Christian Hoecken from the Netherlands was becoming active in the missions at the same time. A Jesuit companion of the famed Father De Smet, he had a brother, Adrian, also serving as a missionary. Father Hoecken was called "Father Kickapoo" by the Native Americans because of his fluency in the language of that tribe. In 1838, Father Hoecken founded a Potawátomi mission on the Osage River and then went to Sugar Creek, where he compiled a Potawátomi dictionary and grammar. He had given the Kickapoo a dictionary as well. In 1847, he accompanied the Potawátomi to Kaw Valley in Kansas, where he began the important work of meeting the exiled tribes who arrived in Kansas after forced marches. Father Hoecken also served the Miami, Peoria, Piankashaw, and Sauk.

Among the missionaries in the Northwest was Mother Marie Tranchepain, who labored among the Native Americans in the Rocky Mountains. Mother Marie arrived from France in 1727 with ten Sisters and founded Ursuline convents in New Orleans, Boston, Galveston, and in Montana.

Another missionary, Father Albert Lacombe, was known as the "Man-of-the-Good-Heart." The Native Americans in Buffalo, New York, Dubuque, Iowa, and St. Paul, Minnesota, as well as Montana, the Dakotas, and Canada, all knew him. Father Lacombe even hunted buffalo with the tribes in the far north. During a Cree attack on a Blackfoot encampment, Father Lacombe was accidentally wounded in the head by a stray bullet. The Blackfeet shouted: "You have wounded your Blackrobe!" The horrified Cree halted the battle and both sides looked after the "Man-of-the-Good-Heart." Father Lacombe retired to Calgary, Canada.

In the Alaskan territories, Bishop Michael Portier was trying to revive earlier gains and to recruit priests to serve the farflung outposts of the faith. He was the vicar apostolic of the immense territory after 1826, working to unite the missions and to improve the status of the chapels already in operation.

In Arizona, far to the south, the Carmelite Bishop Martínez de Ocejo toured the missions in 1814, confirming and encouraging the converts to the faith. By 1828, however, the Spanish missionaries were expelled from the region by the Mexican government, still in possession of the area, and the network of chapels and schools closed. Once again, the harsh political realities of

St. Rose Philippine Duchesne

the New World had intruded upon the apostolate of faith.

In Arkansas, where the Vincentians had been supported in their missionary efforts since 1818 by the devout Chief Sarrasin, Father John Odin was laboring among the tribes. Bishop Dubourg of New Orleans arrived in 1820 to visit the Osage and to tour the missions. The Vincentians sent more missionaries into the area in 1824 in order to rejuvenate the region, and they labored for six years there. In 1830, Chief Sarrasin was buried with Catholic honors at St. Joseph's in Pine Bluff.

In California, far removed from the American ambitions and policies concerning the Native Americans, Franciscan Andrés Quintana was slain at Santa Cruz in 1812. Five years later, Mission San Rafael Arcángel opened, followed by Mission San Francisco de Solano, which was erected in 1823. In 1833, the Mexican authorities

81

ousted the Franciscans and other missionaries and secularized all of the California missions, declaring the Catholic Native Americans homeless.

In the Midwest, which was beginning to feel the impact of the first white settlers engaged in "moving on," the Visitation Nuns started their educational apostolate in 1833 at Kaskaskia, Illinois. Father Stephen Badin revived St. Joseph's Mission, started by the Jesuit Claude Allouez, in 1832. In that same year, Jesuit Charles Van Quickenborne's apostolate with the Fox at Keokuk, Iowa, began. Venerable Samuel Mazzuchelli opened St. Raphael's in Dubuque a year later.

The Native Americans of the Great Lakes took matters into their own hands concerning local missions. In 1823, the Ottawas, led by Chief Simon Pokagon, petitioned the United States Congress to reopen the Catholic missions in their lands, and by 1825, Michigan saw a revival of the Catholic Indian apostolate. Father Joseph Badin served the Lake tribes, and Father Peter Dejean was among the Ojibwa. The Harbor Springs Ottawa mission flourished, and the Sault Ste. Marie mission was revived.

In Minnesota, Father Francis Pierz labored among the Ojibwa at Crow Wing. In Missouri, Jesuits Charles de la Croix and Charles Van Quickenborne were with the Osage and at St. Louis. A series of Osage missions was opened in 1824 in this region. In North Dakota, the initial survey conducted by Jesuits Joseph Provencher and George Anthony Belcourt started a revival soon after. Father Joseph Dumoulin went to Fort Douglas and then to Pembina. Father

Belcourt, fluent in Algonquin, served at Lake Traverse and then among the Turtle Mountain Chippewas. In 1821, he opened St. Joseph's Mission at Walhalla, as Benedictine Jerome Hunt served at Fort Totten.

In 1836, Americans heard the grim news from San Antonio and resolved to "Remember the Alamo," having no knowledge of the original Spanish mission status of that now revered shrine. The West was becoming important to the people of the United States as they began to broaden their horizons. The immensity of the continent, the splendors, riches, and beauty were all emerging in the American consciousness. More and more families began the long trek to the Pacific Ocean, many perishing on the way or discovering a site on the trail that promised the fulfillment of dreams and stopping to begin again on the new lands available.

President Martin Van Buren was in the White House, and far to the West, Father Charles Van Quickenborne died at Portage de Sioux, Missouri. For almost two decades he had served as a missionary to the Sauk, Osage, Kickapoo, Potawátomi, and others in Illinois, Indiana, and Missouri. Father Van Quickenborne was one of the pioneering Jesuits of these states, welcoming tribes in exile and trying to defend them against white aggressions. He had also founded the Jesuit provincial house in Florissant, Missouri, in 1823. Like other missionaries, Father Van Quickenborne was horrified by the devastation inflicted upon the Native Americans. These missionaries labored unceasingly to restore the health and well-being of the Indians, bracing themselves for future assaults.

Archbishop Blanchet and a Salish woven design

CHAPTER 6

The Banner Unfurled

In 1838, two Canadian missionaries headed toward the great Oregon Territory on a journey that influenced the American Indian ministry for all time. Bishop Francis Norbert Blanchet led the expedition to Fort Vancouver as vicar-general of the entire Oregon Territory, at that time under Canadian episcopal jurisdiction. He later became the archbishop of Portland, Oregon, leading Catholics in a thriving American metropolis. His companion was Father Modeste Demers, who would also be raised to the episcopacy in the region. The two set out on May 3, 1838, reaching the Rocky Mountains in the fall. Bishop Blanchet celebrated Mass at Big Bend on October 14, before moving on to the western coastal area of America. His work was just beginning, and in the years to come he was aided by his brother, Au-

gustine Magliore Blanchet, called the "Apostle of Washington," and by the missionary giant Father De Smet.

Bishop Blanchet visited the Indians at Cowlitz, founding a mission there and a second outpost on Whidbey Island in Puget Sound. Realizing that he knew nothing of the native languages of the area, he invented a device called a "Catholic Ladder" to overcome translation difficulties. The "Catholic Ladder" consisted of a flat board on which forty marks were etched to represent the forty centuries of human life before Christ's birth. There were thirty-three other marks for the years of Christ's life on earth and a cross to represent redemption. When other missionaries began to use the "Catholic Ladder" they added pictograms and illustrations.

As Bishop Francis Norbert Blanchet was opening the Oregon Territory to the mission apostolate, other regions were experiencing renewals or beginnings as well. This was a true era of expansion for the Catholic Indian apostolate on the continent. As much of the land was still in Canadian jurisdiction, religious men and women en-

83

THE STORY OF THE CATHOLIC INDIAN MISSIONS

tered the wilderness in response to their bishop's visions and displayed heroic devotion to their assigned tribes.

Alaska, for example, was being served by the Oblates of Mary Immaculate, who entered the area from their Canadian bases. Far to the south, in Yellowstone, the French Jesuit Pierre Jean De Smet celebrated Mass in 1840 and preached to the Flathead and Pend d'Oreille Indians. Father De Smet also attended the annual "Rendezvous" (the gatherings of the mountain men and the fur traders) on the Green River in Wyoming that same year. In 1841, Father De Smet, with Jesuit Nicholas Point, founded Sacred Heart Mission in Idaho for the Coeur d'Alene, and Jesuit Father Pierre Joseph Joset arrived later to serve in that outpost of the faith. In 1843, Father Point founded another mission chapel on the St. Joe River. This mission was later renamed Cataldo and moved to the Coeur d'Alene River. Missionaries in the area of Illinois honored the Miami Chief Richardville, and when he died in 1841, his passing was mourned. Father De Smet and Jesuit Felix Verreydt labored among the Potawátomi at Council Bluffs, Iowa, and Father Joseph Crétin was with the Winnebago of Iowa, building St. Patrick's at Prairie du Chien.

In Kansas, the Kickapoo mission near Leavenworth was operating. Jesuit Christian Hoecken was serving the Kickapoos, Wea (Miami), Piankashaw, and Potawátomi with Jesuit John Schoenmaker. Father Hoecken also aided exiled tribes coming into the territory, and Jesuit Paul Ponziglione labored in the southwestern part of the region; he served the tribes of the area for four decades.

The ruthless removal policies of the United States continued to exact a toll on the Native Americans and on the Catholic missions as more tribes were uprooted from

their homelands and forced into the wilderness. As the white Americans increased their treks westward, such tribes were uprooted again and sent beyond the horizon. Whenever possible, the Catholic missionaries went with their Native American flocks or sent them to waiting priests in the newly designated regions.

One such tragedy took place in 1837, when the young Father Benjamin Marie Petit arrived at the mission at Sugar Creek with his exhausted flock of Potawátomi Indians. The Potawátomi had been on an enforced march across several states to newly designated lands. Father Petit, ordained only sixteen months before, accompanied the tribe, despite official discouragement. The death toll of this march was terrible, as the young and the old could not keep up the pace set by the military.

Shocked and horrified by the atrocities being committed by American troops, Father Petit delivered the tribe to Father Hoecken and then returned to his original mission assignment in the East. Father Petit had caught a fever at the Illinois River and did not recover; he died on February 10, 1839, at age twenty-six, begging Almighty God to grant his beloved Potawátomi some measure of peace in their exile.

Sister Lucille Matheson, a Religious of the Sacred Heart, inspired by St. Rose Philippine Duchesne, was equally devoted to the Potawátomi. In 1847, she moved her school from Sugar Creek to St. Mary's, and to the Valley of the Kansas, following the tribe on another forced relocation. Sister Lucille packed up everything and went with the Potawátomi, serving them for twenty-one years. When she was in her late seventies, she was recalled to the motherhouse of the Sacred Heart to rest. The Potawátomi were outraged that their own "holy woman" had been taken from them. Sister Lucille returned to the tribe and stayed with them until her death in 1876.

On the eastern coast of Maine, Americans did not demand the removal of the faithful Abenakis. In 1848, the tribal mission at Old Town (Panawaniske) was served by Jesuit John Bapst. He suffered an outrageous assault by Protestants in 1854 because of his labors among the Abenakis and the local Catholics. In 1848, Jesuit Eugene Vetromile arrived at Old Town, and he served there until 1880, composing a much-valued Abenaki history and dictionary.

Other tribes did not fare as well. The Sioux, for example, were being pushed into North Dakota, Montana, Wyoming, Nebraska, Montana, and Canada. In 1837, the Sioux lost all of their lands east of the Mississippi River. During the following winter, a smallpox epidemic swept across the upper Missouri River, traced to a passing steamer. Some thirty thousand Native Americans died in this tragedy, a great many being the uprooted Sioux.

In order to care for the displaced tribes arriving in the district and still obligated to the local Indians, Father T. J. Van den Broeck opened St. Francis Mission on the Wolf River at Lake Powhegan, Michigan. The

Potawátomi embroidered design

Redemptorist Simon Sanderl was also laboring in the region, and in 1847, Father F. J. Bonduel built an Indian school at St. Francis Mission. The Franciscan Otho Skolla served the Menóminee missions in Michigan also.

In Minnesota, Jesuit Lucien Galtier was near modern St. Paul by 1840, and Jesuit Augustine Ravoux was with the Santee Dakota. A chapel was erected by Father Galtier at St. Paul in 1844, on the site of the future metropolis. Jesuit Father Pierz served at St. Paul's for a time and then labored among the Chippewa in nearby areas. In 1851, Bishop Joseph Crétin began revitalizing the entire mission territory.

Americans watched an ongoing struggle for Texas during this era and then mourned President William Henry Harrison, who died in office just one month after his 1841 inauguration. John Tyler followed Harrison into the White House. The war with Mexico raged from 1846 to 1848 and ended with the treaty of Guadalupe-Hidalgo, in which the Mexicans ceded California, Nevada, Utah, a portion of Wyoming, part of Colorado, and vast sections of Arizona and New Mexico to the United States, recognizing as well the prior annexation of Texas. Thousands of Native Americans residing in these lands now belonged to the U.S.

During the war with Mexico, many of the United States troops entering the battle zones were composed of Catholic soldiers. These Catholics were punished by their commanding officers for not attending Protestant services during their terms of enlistment. Some were even flogged for this "offense." Word soon reached Washington, however, and two Catholic priests were recruited as chaplains. Jesuits John McElroy and Antonio Rey were sent to assure Catholic religious liberty for the troops in Mexico, starting a tradition in the U.S. Army.

On May 6, 1844, while the Catholic missionaries were following their own trails of faith in the disputed wilds, American Catholics faced yet another tragedy that was deemed by many to be inexplicable and indefensible. Protestants, whipped into a frenzy by sermons, rumors, and slanderous assaults against Catholics, rioted in Kensington, a suburb of Philadelphia, Pennsylvania. There zealots burned down two Catholic churches, killed thirteen, and wounded others. Reaction to the events was swift on both sides.

In New York, Bishop John Hughes had no intention of sitting idly by to witness the same sort of atrocities in his diocese. He stationed armed guards in front of every parish church, convent, and school, and he publicly announced that if New Yorkers intended to emulate their Pennsylvania co-religionists, a blood bath would result. The mayor and the city council of New York pleaded with the bishop to restrain his people, but he warned everyone to be extremely cautious in dealing with New York Catholics, and to make sure that such Catholics "are not provoked." There were no riots or assaults in the city. Abraham Lincoln responded as well, offering a resolution to the Whig Party on June 12, 1844. The resolu-

tion stated that "the guarantee of the rights of conscience as found in our Constitution, is most sacred and inviolable, and one that belongs no less to the Catholic, than to the Protestant. . . ."

The word "gold" also echoed across the land from the valleys of California, starting a rush of men, sometimes accompanied by their families, to the western coast of the United States. The Native American tribes in the regions were stunned and then horrified by the avalanche of miners, squatters, and opportunists in their midst. Tent cities arose and clapboard towns dotted the landscape, and the once placid scene was devastated by gouges in the earth, ribald saloons, and palaces of pleasure. The Mariposa War was the result of the invasion of the goldfields. The Mariposa and Yuma fought the miners, as did the Miwok and Yakut.

To the north, Indian missions were opened in Yakima and Olympia. In Oklahoma, missions served the Osage, Choctaw, Miami, and Potawátomi. A new mission for the Kalispel Indians opened in Washington's wilderness, and the Jesuits in the Upper Columbia region started outposts for the Pend d'Oreille and Colville. Father Antonio Ravalli was with the Flatheads, Coeur d'Alene, and Blackfeet. He labored among these Native Americans for over forty years, demonstrating tireless devotion. Fathers John Schoenmaker and John Bax were serving the Osage, and missions for the Potawátomi, Mandan, and Miami were opened in North Dakota. The Winnebago had a new mission in Nebraska, and Jesuits Schoenmaker and Bax would expand their efforts in Oklahoma as well to serve the Kiowa and other tribes.

The chronological development of the missions provide dates and geographical specifics but do not demonstrate in full the

*Chief Four Bears of the Missouri
River Mandan and a Mundan hide*

dimensions of dedication, service, and sacrifices involved. The Catholic missionaries not only braved the natural elements but bore the brunt of American policies toward the Indians, policies that tore at the hearts of the tribal people and the priests among them. Despair and fear became vital elements of Native American life in this period, and the priests and religious going among them could only console and counsel. No promises of relief or happier horizons could be given, and there was no explanation for the unjust federal views. The missionaries of this era, and those who followed, would face a relentless policy instituted by their own government against their chosen flocks. More inhumane legislation would follow, and more missionaries would rise to the challenge of the period.

Bishop Augustine Magliore had taken up residence in his see of Walla Walla, Washington, by this time; it became Nesqually eventually, the forerunner of Seattle. A tragedy was about to unfold in this region: an Indian-white confrontation that almost brought a halt to all of the missions on the northern Pacific and thrust into the spotlight a dedicated and determined young priest who would be a decisive leader in the ongoing Catholic Indian mission apostolate. His name was Jean Baptiste Abraham Brouillet. He had accompanied Bishop Augustine Blanchet and had been appointed vicar-general of the Walla Walla (Nesqually) diocese and assigned to the Cayuse mission in the area.

Dr. Marcus Whitman, his wife, Narcissa, and other aides were already among the Cayuse in a Protestant mission on the tribal lands. A medical doctor and devout in his faith, Dr. Whitman also believed that the Oregon Territory, the area including the modern states of Washington and Oregon, was in need of settlement by sturdy, hardworking Americans. He encouraged white families to come into the region, a position that alienated the Cayuse in his mission. Dr. Whitman was not aware of the deep rancor in the hearts of the Cayuse, as he did not understand that they believed he was killing their children. The whites coming into the region brought measles and smallpox, diseases that claimed the lives of the vulnerable Cayuse, especially the young and old. Unable to bear their grief and having no reasonable explanation for the ongoing deaths, the Cayuse focused their anger on Whitman and his mission staff.

In November, 1847, the tribe sent word to the unsuspecting Bishop Augustine Blanchet that a priest was needed to start a Catholic mission in their lands. Father Brouillet was assigned the task of surveying the available sites on the Umatilla River and to organize a base camp there. He arrived among the Cayuse on November 27 and heard the complaints and the grief expressed by the tribe. Father Brouillet did not realize the extent of the their anger until November 30. He went to a Cayuse camp near the Whitman mission in order to baptize infants on that day and intended to introduce himself to his Protestant counterparts. There he discovered that Dr. and Mrs. Whitman and their mission assistants, listed in the records as nine or ten people, had been slain by the Cayuse and left unburied.

Fearing for his own life because of the tension and horror around him, Father Brouillet spent a night in solitary prayer. The next morning, with the help of a surviving mission aide, he buried the grisly remains and said a prayer over the common grave. The Cayuse did not interfere, but he could sense that their rage and lust for vengeance had not been assuaged, and he knew that another victim would be claimed as well. A Protestant missionary, one Henry Spalding, was due to enter the village soon, and he would be killed. Father Brouillet went out on the road leading to the Cayuse encampment and found Spalding, warning him about the dreadful massacre and the danger of an ambush. Spalding fled the region and days later wrote to Father Brouillet, thanking him profusely for saving his life, an act that he knew demanded courage as well as charity.

The Cayuse, hearing that Spalding had escaped their vengeance, naturally resented the priest's interference. They did not harm him, but their anger doomed his efforts in their villages. The white settlers in the area added to the problems by demonstrating their rage over the massacre immediately. When the whites organized a militia to punish the Cayuse, they sealed the mission's fate. A full-scale war resulted, and Father Brouillet closed St. Anne's Mission on the

Umatilla River on February 20, 1848. The Cayuse then burned the mission to the ground.

The missionary's return to the Cayuse after warning Spalding had demonstrated once again his courage and faith. He knew that his mission and all the other Catholic ministries in that region were in jeopardy because of the Whitman Massacre. The event took on an anti-Catholic aspect when Spalding, despite his professed gratitude for having been saved from a cruel death, claimed publicly that the local Catholics had fomented the massacre. He published such charges in the *Oregon American* and fueled anti-Catholic sentiment in the region as a result. The Blanchet brothers had to defend their ministries and rebuild good relations in many areas of society. Father Brouillet responded quickly to Spalding's charges by issuing an eloquent tract that refuted the Protestant claims. He proved the Cayuse planned the massacre even before he and Bishop Blanchet were in Walla Walla. Father Brouillet's response defused the situation, but the ghastly tragedy would haunt him when he was asked to assume a national role in defense of the Catholic Indian missions. Father Jean Baptiste Abraham Brouillet would become the first director of the Bureau of Catholic Indian Missions.

The Whitman Massacre caused a stir in America for a time, but most people were occupied by other events and news. The Oblates of Mary had also arrived in Puget Sound to begin their evangelical labors. The first American whalers had sailed into the ports of Alaska, bringing new tensions to the Indian tribes there, and in the Great Basin of the United States, cholera raged in Indian settlements.

The Gadsden Purchase of 1853 brought the remaining sections of New Mexico into the possession of the United States, along with parts of Arizona and California. Three years later the federal government acquired 174 million acres of tribal Indian lands, using fifty-two separate treaties as the means of obtaining control. All fifty-two of the treaties were violated by the whites soon after. Few Americans paid attention to such Indian land acquisitions or federal injustices, believing these actions were necessary in order to secure the nation's ultimate destiny. Americans were also distracted by the exotic spectacle of Commodore Matthew Perry sailing into Edo harbor in Japan. Edo was the ancient Japanese name for Tokyo. That mysterious land was opened to United States trade with the Kanagawa Treaty of 1854.

Zachary Taylor's sudden death in 1849 placed Millard Fillmore in the White House, signaling a bitter time for America's Catholics. Anti-Catholic demonstrations rocked towns and cities, resulting in deaths and in the destruction of Catholic homes, convents, and churches with the most vicious anti-Catholic organization of the time sponsoring this havoc and terror. This organization was the American Party, popularly called the Know-Nothing Party, because the members met in secret and consequently claimed ignorance about the intent and purposes of their leaders. The Know-Nothing Party preached that "Americans must rule America." This automatically excluded Catholics because of their spiritual allegiance to a foreign pope.

The most vicious attack on a Catholic priest took place on June 5, 1854, in Ellsworth, Maine. Father John Bapst, the pioneering Jesuit missionary from Switzerland who had labored in the region for decades among the white Catholics and the Abenaki at Old Town, was singled out by the Protestants because of his popularity and his membership in the Society of Jesus, the most feared order in the Church. An angry mob assaulted him on his rounds, tarred and feathered him, and ran him out of town on a rail. Many of the mob called for his death, but saner heads prevailed. Father Bapst recovered and returned to his ministry, a bit shaken but resolved.

The Protestants were alarmed because there were approximately 1,600,000 Catholics in America, despite the penal period and the ongoing assaults. Catholics, in turn, feared the Know-Nothing Party and President Millard Fillmore, who was the chosen candidate of that intolerant group. Across the land, Catholics watched political events and the progress of the Church in recently acquired territories and worked to support the missions and parishes in far-flung regions.

Millard Fillmore lost his bid for a second term of office, and Franklin Pierce served in the White House, followed by James Buchanan who was inaugurated as president in 1857, as tensions rose in the northwestern part of the nation. The Coeur d'Alene (Spokan) War erupted, waged by the Coeur d'Alene, Spokan, Palouse, Yakima, and Northern Paiute. These tribes could not stand by and watch their lands trampled in the rush of white settlements. In 1859, the cry of "gold" echoed from Pike's Peak in Colorado, and the mad rush started again in that state and in surrounding areas.

The ill-fated St. Anne's Mission on the Umatilla River, the scene of the Whitman Massacre, was reopened by Father Eugene Casimir Chirouse, an Oblate missionary. Father Chirouse was also extending his activities, serving the Tulalip, Puget Sound, Swinomish, Lummi, and Muckleshoot. He labored there in the northwest for over three decades, expanding into the Frasier River Valley as well.

Mother Joseph Pariseau was also in Washington. The superior of the Sisters of Charity of Providence, Mother Joseph of the Sacred Heart, and four Sisters responded to Bishop Augustine Blanchet's plea and arrived in Fort Vancouver on December 8, 1856. It took Mother Joseph only a year to convert a storage building into a convent that served as the base for a school, an orphanage, hospital, bakery, and laundry. St. Joseph's Hospital opened on June 7, 1858. Mother Joseph traveled throughout the region, even going into mining camps to beg funds to maintain her ministry to the Native Americans, the young, the poor, and the sick. She represents the state of Washington in the National Statuary Hall in Washington, D.C.

Americans, however, concentrated their attentions on the slavery debates and on the activities of John Brown at Harper's Ferry. The Civil War would start in 1861, just after Abraham Lincoln entered the White House. The Catholic Church responded to the conflict in varying ways, as did the Indian nations still residing within the areas of the battles. Pope Gregory XVI had already spoken about the evils of the slave trade, issuing a proclamation against Catholic participation in such a vile practice. In the Civil War, however, Catholics were torn by their loyalty to the opposing sides, a factor that dominated commitment and actions.

Archbishop John Hughes of New York was a staunch supporter of the Union and a friend of William Seward, Lincoln's Secretary of State. Archbishop Hughes traveled to Rome, France, and Ireland seeking aid for the northern crusade. In 1863, he also helped to quell the draft riots that erupted in New York City.

Bishop Patrick Lynch of Charleston, South Carolina — where the Civil War started on April 12, 1861, when Confederate forces fired upon Fort Sumter in that city's harbor — was loyal to the Confederacy. His own southern leaders sent him to Rome in 1864 to make the Holy See aware of the multifaceted aspects of the Confederate cause. The Catholics, however, who earned the respect and gratitude of both sides were the nursing Sisters of America.

The Daughters of St. Vincent de Paul, the Sisters of the Holy Cross, and eighteen other Catholic congregations of women religious went onto the battle sites to nurse the wounded of both the Union and Confederate forces. The Sisters labored in the filth and gore of hospitals, field clinics, and the battlefields without political discrimination. Their unceasing charity won the admiration of all the combatants.

During the Civil War, the Homestead Act of 1862 opened more Indian lands to settlers. In that same year, two hundred thousand Indians in the northwest died of smallpox brought into their camps by whites. In 1863, the Navajo endured their "Long Walk," a three-hundred-mile trek across New Mexico to Fort Sumner, where they had to construct the fort buildings and adobes. They suffered severe hardships and many died. A treaty signed in 1868 allowed the Navajo

Arapaho Chief Yellow Calf's war bonnet

survivors a 3.5-million-acre reservation on their original homelands. The "Long Walk" and the time spent in custody killed a quarter of the Navajo population.

In 1864, the Chivington Massacre took the lives of Cheyenne men, women, and children, who were attacked while sleeping beside their campfires. This horror stunned Americans and focused attention on Colorado and on the actions of Colonel John M. Chivington, a former minister in charge of the "Colorado Militia." On December 28, 1864, the colonel led his troops against an encampment of Cheyenne and Arapaho along Sand Creek. The soldiers were under the command of officers at Fort Lyon, and the Cheyenne were led by Chief Black Kettle. Chivington spurred on his seven hundred men with the shout: "Kill them all, big and small, nits make lice." The Native Americans were killed and then mutilated. Of the dead, nearly one hundred were women and children. A congressional committee investigating the incident a year later recommended no action against Chivington and his men. The general belief was that such events would take place until the Native Americans were civilized or gone.

While these terrible tragedies were visited upon the Indian nations of the United States, the federal government instituted a reversal of a former judicial policy. Earlier, there had even been calls for an end to the Indian Removal Act. In 1864, all Indians were declared legally competent witnesses in court proceedings, even when they were testifying against whites.

The Civil War was a time of tension for the Indians, despite the legal status changes. The Five Civilized Tribes (Cherokee, Chickasaw, Choctaw, Creek, and Seminole), for example, had been moved to Oklahoma, between 1830 and 1842. There the tribes built plantations, schools, newspapers, libraries, and other resplendent institutions. In the Civil War, the Five Civilized Tribes supported the Confederacy. As a result, at the end of the war the United States government relocated more than fifty tribes, so-called "uncivilized," into the Five Civilized Tribes' lands. In the West, Union soldiers deliberately penetrated into Apache Pass and the surrounding areas, sparking an Apache rebellion and tragic deaths.

All of these activities, particularly the continued relocation of tribes, had a tremendous impact on the Catholic Indian apostolate. The missionaries no longer answered to their own religious superior or regional bishops alone. Now there were government agents, commissions, and directors who set the pace for the tribal lands under their control. Such secular individuals did not have the good of the Native Americans as their sole priorities at times, and most did not value Catholic missions in their regions. The Church watched and prepared for difficult times.

In 1865, Abraham Lincoln's assassination brought Andrew Johnson to the White House. Americans were tired of war, politics, persecution of the Indians, and anti-Catholic demonstrations. Three years later, the United States Commission on Indian Affairs confirmed that Indian wars were luxuries that the nation could ill afford. The commission report stated that such ongoing campaigns cost Americans some one million dollars for each Indian slain.

The United States had a unique history, and Americans were beginning to gaze at the past, with its virtues and evils, and to seek new horizons that would honor the splendors of the continent and the richness of the sacrifices made by earlier generations. The nation was in an era of reconstruction, but individual men and women were seeking personal renewal as well. The Catholic missions came into focus as a result, as Americans took a hard look at the treatment of the Indians by the white founders of the United States.

The South Plains War, started by the Cheyenne, Sioux, Arapaho, Kiowa, and Comanche in 1868, demonstrated the ongoing destruction of the Indian lands clearly enough. These Native Americans rose up to protest because they had nothing left to lose to the American settlers. The last boundaries of the Southwest had been set in 1848, and the Americans intended to possess the land from sea to sea. The Franciscans and Jesuits had pioneered the missions of Spain and France when America opened to the Europeans, aided by the Dominicans and others. They came to a wilderness, inhabited by a people strange to them, and they wandered into campsites that were steeped in ancient traditions far removed from the trappings of civilization in the Old World. When the United States was forged in battle, the mission activities of the Church were forced to undergo strategic changes and to assume new dimensions in the face of English domination and the ever-expanding population bases of the young nation.

The missions conducted in the early eras of American exploration and colonization fell victim to the advancing trappings of "civilization" all across the continent. Even the great Spanish missions of California faced challenges brought about by local governments. The Mexican authorities secularized these missions and then ceded California to the United States, opening the way for increased secular interference and eventual domination. Other missions, especially those founded in the East, had closed because of the forced migrations of the Indian tribes residing in lands coveted by the Europeans. As a result, Catholic missionaries continued to move away from the Atlantic coastal region into the Midwest and then beyond.

Frontier bishops were obligated to organize the usual diocesan programs while they sought out the Indian nations of these regions and brought priests to serve the last remaining Indian strongholds. The vari-

ous land acts passed by the American Congress continually impacted the Indians and the missions as political events in Washington, sometimes sordid, took their toll.

The Kansas-Nebraska Act of 1854, for example, opened the door to white settle-

Father Pierre Jean De Smet and a Blackfoot stand-up bonnet

ments, and the ongoing view of the Indian lifestyles as aboriginal spurred attempts at "civilizing" the Native Americans in order to make them eligible to enter the new society being fashioned on the continent. The United States embraced the frozen north as well, and there the pioneering missionaries traveled by dogsled or skis to reach their outposts of the faith. Settlers were always close behind, even in Alaska, and towns changed the landscapes and the ways in which the missionaries fulfilled their obligations. The Church in America, always under the Congregation de Propaganda Fide (Congregation of the Propagation of the Faith) in Rome as a missionary territory, was moving rapidly toward a new status. In a matter of decades the burgeoning Catholic populations and the established dioceses would demand recognition.

In the Northwest, however, the missions continued to flourish, without too much interference, bringing frontier priests of uncommon sense and valor to the forefront of the apostolate. One such missionary, a Jesuit priest, made his way in the wilderness areas of Montana, Wyoming, Idaho, and the snow-capped Rocky Mountains. In time he became famous throughout America, but he had little use for celebrity status. Pierre Jean De Smet had come from Belgium, but he was also a tested veteran in the missions of the northwestern part of the nation. He had arrived in America in 1821 and entered the Jesuits in Maryland. Ordained in the Society of Jesus, De Smet went to Council Bluffs, Iowa, for the Potawátomi Indians in 1838. He started his mission labors with a spectacular effort that placed him squarely on his path toward national recognition. The Sioux Indians who resided near the mission at Council Bluffs had long been an enemy of the Potawátomi. Father De Smet

went to these Sioux to explain his mission and to ask them to leave his flock in peace. The Sioux agreed, and this act of daring and faith not only won the respect and admiration of the Sioux, but led to peace in the region and to a singular title bestowed on him in the missions. By Catholics and Protestants alike, he was called "the truest and greatest friend the Indians ever had."

In 1840, Father De Smet responded to a call for a "Blackrobe" and journeyed to the Rocky Mountains to begin work among the Flathead and the Pend d'Oreille nations. He also visited the Crow, Gros Ventres, and other regional tribes, a journey that took him more than forty-eight hundred miles. He was able to walk among all these Indian camps because word of his honor and devotion went ahead of him in the wilderness. In 1841, Father De Smet founded St. Mary's on the Bitter Root River, and the sheer size of the local Indian population set him on yet another quest. He sailed to Europe soon after and recruited priest workers and funds as well as six Sisters of Notre Dame de Namur. They came to the northwestern wilderness missions to care for the burgeoning faithful of the area. Returning to America with his new missionaries, Father De Smet went by canoe to Fort Vancouver after seeing them settled in their new apostolates. There he met Bishop Francis Blanchet, and set about organizing the mission territory of Oregon with that determined prelate.

The meeting with Bishop Francis Blanchet, soon to become the archbishop of Oregon City (which was renamed the archdiocese of Portland in 1928), set into motion vital and enduring mission imperatives for the nation. The two missionaries liked each other and respected their separate veteran experiences in the apostolate. Father De Smet, who was in many ways the embodi-

Chief Sitting Bull and a Sioux feather display

land, nor did he want to trade or carry on the usual white man's business ventures. He served the Indian missions because Christ had called him to such a ministry, but he stayed dedicated and enduring because he respected the tribes and their aspirations. He also had no desire to see the Native Americans assume the manner and poses of Europe or "civilized" Americans. This understanding led to Father De Smet's unceasing efforts as a spokesman for the Native American cause in white circles.

He was a leading orator at the 1851 council of ten thousand Indians at Horse Creek Valley near Fort Laramie, Wyoming, and his words calmed the assembled tribes, leading to a peaceful solution to the problem caused by the growing white populations in California and Oregon. The United States government had requested the presence of Father De Smet at this council. He also accompanied General Harney on his rounds in Utah, Oregon, and Washington, speaking on behalf of the Native Americans in each encounter with the tribes of the region. Father De Smet warned the

ment of the American Indian mission ministry, inspired Bishop Blanchet and his brother, Bishop Augustine Magliore Blanchet. These men rose up after Father De Smet's death to protect the Indian missions and to help found an organization that would become another bastion of dedication for the ministry.

Father De Smet did not covet Indian

United States authorities that a rebellion among the tribes in the Sioux territory was imminent. When the rebellion took place in 1862, he received delegations and heard views before setting out on what has been termed "the most important mission of his career." A so-called "peace commission" was instituted to start negotiations about the uprisings, and Father De Smet was asked to

THE STORY OF THE CATHOLIC INDIAN MISSIONS

accompany the representatives of the federal government. He accepted the assignment and set out with the delegation but then parted company with them. This priest was not some backwoods preacher who could be persuaded by bureaucratic double-talk. For his own reasons and because of his intelligent assessments of his companions, he decided to penetrate into the Sioux homeland without the "peace commission."

Crossing the Badlands, he reached the main camp of five thousand Sioux warriors and entered unarmed and unafraid. The Sioux recognized him instantly and honored his request to see Sitting Bull, their leader. Sitting Bull welcomed Father De Smet and heard the account of the government's intentions and the priest's analysis of the situation. As a result of the talks between Father De Smet and Sitting Bull, a peace treaty was signed on July 2, 1868. Sitting Bull would honor the treaty, but white incursions and assaults on sacred Sioux lands led him to yet another confrontation at a site called Little Bighorn, less than a decade later.

It is estimated that by the time Father De Smet died in St. Louis, Missouri, on May 23, 1873, he had traveled 260,929 miles in his ministry to the Indian peoples of America. His death was a grievous loss to the Church at a time when all of the Catholic missions were imperiled by political expediencies and a revival of intolerance. Nevertheless, Father De Smet's example served to enlighten and encourage all those who would pick up the banner of the Catholic missionaries over the centuries in America. Father De Smet used actual banners, made in Europe and Canada, to add color and religious symbolism to his ceremonies. One of those banners would remain as a distinct memento of his dedication and sacrifice and would encourage new generations.

Catholic leaders following in his footsteps fought for the Catholic missions of the Church with his example before them, but they would not face natural disasters or hostile tribes. The foes of the missions in coming eras would be bureaucrats, political patrons, and the leaders of anti-Catholic sentiments in the land. Such enemies of the Catholic mission apostolate underestimated the vitality and stamina of the defenders of the Church, and they misread the profound legacy bequeathed to all Catholic Indian ministries by Father De Smet. The Native Americans, as well as the white populations, would remember him and use his life as a standard for the missionaries of the future.

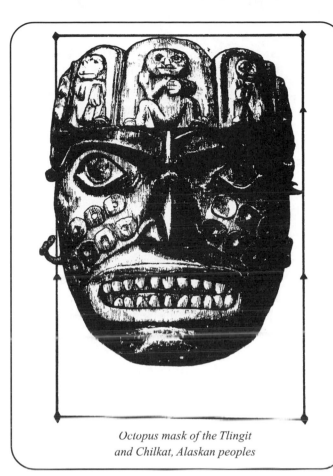

*Octopus mask of the Tlingit
and Chilkat, Alaskan peoples*

CHAPTER 7

New Mission Arenas

and the expansion of Catholic missions, the American Catholic Church experienced two pivotal events: the convocation of Vatican I and the implementation of President Ulysses S. Grant's Peace Policy.

The administration of Andrew Johnson, following the assassination of Abraham Lincoln, had come to an end. Johnson's impeachment by Congress, and the difficulties of restoring a nation ravaged by a civil war, had caused considerable pain for Americans. The land was at peace, but there were military governors in some southern regions, and debates raged over the Reconstruction Acts.

The American Catholic bishops sailed to Rome in 1869, responding to an invitation from Pope Pius IX to attend Vatican Council I, which was convened in Rome on December 8 of that year. The Holy Father opened the sessions of the council and then presided over discussions concerning doctrinal and administrative concerns. The council continued in Rome until October 20, 1870.

Vatican Council I was a rather stunning demonstration of the universality of the Church in that era, bringing prelates to the

In 1867, the territory of Alaska was purchased by the United States from Russia for $7,200,000, and "the Land of the Midnight Sun" became an American possession. Called "Seward's Folly" and "Seward's Icebox," the purchase was the result of the efforts of Secretary of State William H. Seward. The Alaskan purchase encompassed 590,804 square miles and included the islands on the coast, the Aleutian chain, and a narrow strip between the Pacific Ocean and British territory. In 1860, missionaries were at Fort McPherson with the Kutchin and Mackenzie Delta Eskimos. The Oblate Jean Seguin was at Fort Yukon. As Alaska opened to the missionaries, the priests had to adapt to travel by dogsled and snowshoes in order to serve the various tribes.

Two years after the Alaska Purchase

Eternal City from around the globe. The bishops of America made the long voyage to Rome, where they met with their counterparts on every continent. Some Americans distinguished themselves during the proceedings, adding profound concepts to conciliar pronouncements. Others voiced their opposition to proposals with gusto. These American bishops represented thriving young dioceses in the United States and the vast mission holdings as well.

In America, removed from the sacred Roman deliberations, Catholics were assessing the character of President Ulysses S. Grant's new administration. He had been inaugurated in 1869 as the hero of the Civil War, a man capable of decisive leadership. Many Americans hoped that he would heal the land and start a new generation of hope. This administration, however, was scarred by scandals and tawdry dealings that were reported in the growing daily newspapers across the nation. Grant was not deemed to be corrupt personally, but he appointed political cronies and old-time patrons to high office, thus allowing their scandalous escapades to cloud his administration permanently. A scandal concerning the cornering of gold brought Jay Gould and James Fisk into the national spotlight. The Whiskey Ring and the Crédit Mobilier affairs added new problems for Grant as well. The Union Pacific Railroad was involved in the Crédit Mobilier scandal, which had far-reaching tentacles of greed that reached even into the halls of Congress.

The most telling scandal, however, concerned the Commission of Indian Affairs in Washington, D.C. Grant had appointed Brigadier General Ely Parker, a Seneca Indian, as head of the Commission, or Bureau, of Indian Affairs, a task that the general performed ably until 1871. The scandal actu-

ally involved the Secretary of War, William A. Belknap, who was impeached in 1876 by Congress for accepting bribes in exchange for control of Indian agencies. Belknap resigned before he could be tried, but the taint of his impeachment imperiled Grant's last years in the White House.

The selling of Indian agencies climaxed years of abuse and graft in Grant's administration. Men who desired to develop or plunder Indian holdings could find ways of gaining control over such lands for their personal benefit. Investigations led to voter anger, of course, aided by two events taking place. John Muir, the beloved naturalist who was responsible for establishing Yosemite and Sequoia National Parks and the famed Sierra Club, was walking from Wisconsin to the Gulf of Mexico. On his journey through America, Muir spoke to men and women about the beauty of the land and the unspoiled splendors once cherished by the Native American tribes, who had resided as guardians of the wilderness.

At the same time, the "Iron Horse," the transcontinental railway linking the continent, was very much in the news. On May 10, 1869, at Promontory Point, Utah, the Central Pacific and Union Pacific railroads met. The "golden spike" was driven into the line by California's governor, Leland Stanford, and the continent was joined from the Atlantic to the Pacific. These rail lines crossed Indian tribal lands, confiscated by federal agencies to provide a pathway for the symbol of the nation's greatness.

Aware of the rumors surrounding his administration's Indian affairs management and alert to the growing anger of the American voters, even before the Belknap scandal filled the newspaper headlines, President Grant started a series of defensive tactics that proved disastrous in time. In 1869, Grant announced a "Peace Policy," a program for Indian affairs that he hoped would deflect the criticism being leveled at him concerning the Native Americans. The Peace Policy was implemented in the following year, serving as a spur to Catholic mission efforts, consternating Grant and his officials, and bringing into existence the Bureau of Catholic Indian Missions.

The president set about reforming the activities and attitudes of those officials responsible for the Indians by designating the various religious denominations of the nation as guardians. He announced: "Indian agencies being civil offices, I determined to give all the agencies to such religious denominations as had hitherto established missionaries among the Indians and perhaps to some denominations who would undertake the work on the same terms — that is, as missionary work."

The distribution was proclaimed as one based on longevity of missions in particular areas. Only those who had initiated or nurtured Indian missions were thus qualified, and only those willing to assume and continue that apostolate could apply. According to this policy, the American Catholic Church was entitled to thirty-eight Indian agencies, representing more than one hundred six thousand Native Americans being served in the missions at that time.

There were seventy-two agencies in existence when Grant inaugurated his Peace Policy. The Catholics had founded thirty-eight of these, being the only denomination fully engaged in such a ministry at the time and caring for more than eighty thousand professed Catholic Native Americans. The Church received only eight agencies: the Colville and Tulalip in Washington; the Umatilla and Grand Ronde in Oregon; the Flathead in Montana; Standing Rock and Devil's Lake in the Dakotas, and the Papago mission in Arizona. Initially the Church received seven — the last one was ceded later. Catholic missionaries lost nine of their eleven Sioux missions in the process, and as a result of this distribution, Catholic priests were forbidden to enter thirty of their former missions. Some who tried were threatened with arrest. Others had to watch the harsh methods employed on various reservations to force the Indians to attend the religious services of the Protestant denominations in charge.

At the same time, Grant established a Board of Indian Commissioners to oversee and advise the Bureau of Indian Affairs. This board was composed of Protestants only. Not a single Catholic was asked to serve in this capacity. The president had hoped that his Peace Policy would provide his tarnished administration with a veneer of concern and compassion. He also hoped that such a distribution of authority would clearly shift future responsibility for abuse or scandal to the religious personnel involved. The denominations would choose their own agents and set their policies.

Catholic bishops and missionaries viewed the Peace Policy as a threat to their ministries from the start. The distribution made many Americans assess President Grant's religious priorities and level of his proclaimed tolerance for the Catholic Church. In 1875, after the Peace Policy was dismantled, Grant persuaded the congressman from Maine, James G. Blaine, to aid him in his quest to make public, nonsectarian schools the only educational opportunities for the nation's youth. In 1876, Congressman Blaine introduced a constitutional amendment that would "make free public schools mandatory." The proposed amendment would also enforce taxation of property held by religious organizations and provide an absolute prohibition on the use of public money for church-affiliated schools. The amendment passed the House but was narrowly defeated in the Senate.

In 1870, Catholic groups all across the country voiced their dismay when the Indian agencies were given to Protestant groups. The plight of the various missions and Indians came to public attention when a smallpox epidemic took a terrible toll of the Blackfoot, Blood, and Piegan tribes. In the following year, General Philip Sheridan issued an order that forbade Indians from leaving their designated reservations without permission, on pain of death. As Sheridan announced the new restrictions, white hunters began the wholesale slaughter of the buffalo herds on the American plains.

In the western part of the continent, the response to Grant's unjust treatment of Catholics and their missions was not only immediate but also enduring. Archbishop Francis Norbert Blanchet was serving by then as the head of Oregon City (Portland) and was called the "Apostle of Oregon." Archbishop Blanchet had organized the Oregon missions with Father De Smet and Bishop Modeste Demers, and he was not about to surrender that ministry without a protest. When Grant's Peace Policy was announced, Archbishop Blanchet and his brother, Bishop Augustine Magliore Blanchet of Washington, began waging a campaign to limit interference in their local missions and to blunt the effects of such an unjust federal program.

These prelates wrote letters to President Grant and to administration officials, asking for redress and justice. As they received no encouraging responses, they wrote to all the bishops of the United States in November, 1871, requesting a united front against the Peace Policy. Their fellow bishops did not demonstrate much enthusiasm for the cause either and did not enroll as valiant defenders of the Indian missions. Their reluctance was rooted in several aspects of Catholic life at the time. To begin with, these bishops were administering dioceses in settled parts of America, portions of the nation cleared of Indian tribes early on. The ruthless relocation policies of the United States government had eliminated the Indian presence in such regions. The bishops were concerned more with immigrant needs, the ongoing anti-Catholic organizations, and the day-to-day administrative obligations of their sees. The Peace Policy involved lands quite distant and people no longer visible.

Archbishop Blanchet was not one to be discouraged by a lack of enthusiasm or concern on the part of others. The Indian missions in the western part of the nation had unique histories and an honor roll of Catholic tribes and missionaries who had braved hardships to nurture the faith. He was not about to see their heroic efforts squandered or lost because of inactivity or the lack of caring.

Beginning his campaign in earnest, Archbishop Blanchet sought a powerful ally, one who understood the true threat of anti-Catholic efforts in the land. He addressed, therefore, his concerns to Archbishop James Roosevelt Bayley of Baltimore. This was an inspired move, as Archbishop Bayley was not only the episcopal leader of the primal see of the United States, but he brought a rather unique perspective to the situation, being personally acquainted with the tensions that characterized Protestant-Catholic relations in that era of American history.

James Roosevelt Bayley was a nephew of St. Elizabeth Seton. Raised in the Angli-

Father Jean Baptiste Abraham Brouillet

The priest, now the vicar-general of the diocese of Nesqually, Washington, was a veteran in this sort of public-relations apostolate, and his arrival in Washington, D.C., in November, 1872, set in motion determined efforts that would result in a permanent guardianship of Catholic Indian missions.

Father Brouillet was soon working with Archbishop Bayley in alerting American bishops about the varied dimensions of interference imminent in Grant's Peace Policy. Events taking place at the time added a certain impetus to the archbishop's message and involved Modoc and Sioux Indians. First, Kintpuash (or Captain Jack, as he was called by the whites) had led the Modoc Indians in a recent rebellion in Oregon, resulting in his execution by hanging. The Modoc lived in the California-Oregon border in a region taken over by white livestock ranchers. After a series of meetings and confrontations with federal agents and troops, Kintpuash led his people into the lava beds of northern California, where sixty Modoc warriors stood off a thousand U.S. troops for more than five months. When Kintpuash and his fellow Modocs were executed, their heads were sent to Washington, D.C., for scientific study. Then, one year later, in 1874, gold was discovered in the Black Hills of South Dakota, a region sacred to the Sioux and previously protected by treaty.

can faith, he had been ordained and assigned as a minister in a parish in New York. He resigned that ministry in 1841 and traveled to Rome, where he became interested in the Catholic faith and was given the grace of conversion. Studying in Paris and New York, he was ordained a Catholic priest on March 2, 1844. Archbishop Bayley was made the ordinary of Baltimore in May, 1876, after a distinguished career as an academic leader and as bishop of Newark, New Jersey.

Archbishop Bayley responded to the concerns sent to him and encouraged Archbishop Blanchet in his campaign to protect the Catholic missions. Receiving this assistance, Archbishop Blanchet asked his brother to send Father Jean Baptiste Abraham Brouillet to Washington, D.C., to serve as a liaison to Grant's administration.

President Grant and his agents could alter and dismantle missions in existence in the United States, but they could not stop Catholics from establishing new sites and expanding their efforts. In Oklahoma, Benedictine Father Isidore Robot was about to assume the duties of a vicar apostolic for the Indian missions, aided by a fellow Benedictine, Ignatius Jean. The famed Abbey of the Sacred Heart resulted from this early mission activity.

In Montana, the missions were reaching the level of a vicariate, and in North Dakota the Benedictine Bishop Martin Marty was about to assume the leadership of a vicar apostolic of evangelical efforts. Father George Anthony Belcourt was with the Turtle Mountain Chippewa in North Dakota. The Benedictines were with the Chippewa at White Earth and Red Lake in Minnesota. In 1876, they were asked by Chief Sitting Bull to set up a series of Native American schools on Sioux lands. The famed Benedictine abbeys of the Sacred Heart in Oklahoma and Blue Cloud in South Dakota (opened in 1950) evolved from these early mission commitments. The vicariate of northern Minnesota was about to open as well, and the missions in the Northwest continued to flourish.

These missions and the new generation of men and women who served them endured, despite the efforts of the United States government. Working quietly, away from the arenas of politics and newly imposed social programs, the Catholics carried on their ministries. Word of their ongoing efforts moved the hearts of the faithful in the nation, slowly turning the tide against indifference and bringing about a response to the campaigns of the Blanchet brothers.

By January of 1873, because of this growing awareness, Archbishop Bayley and Father Brouillet had won the support of many bishops in the efforts to protect the Indian mission apostolate. The archbishop also argued successfully that these missions no longer functioned in an isolated wilderness, threatened only by natural disasters or hostile tribes. That period of American life had ended. The federal, territorial, or state governments now loomed as the great entities to be met with consolidated efforts. The Church needed a capable agency to handle the intricate, often tangled legislation and regulations issued by these local and national government units. Grant's detested Peace Policy would end in 1874, but the policies and biases inherent in that program continued and had to be met with ceaseless vigilance. The archbishop's arguments won the day, and on January 2, 1874, he issued a letter concerning that matter:

The Catholic bishops of the United States who have Indian missions within the limits of their diocese feel they have suffered great injustice at the hands of the Government in connection with those missions, chiefly an account of false and partisan information sent to the department having charge of these matters.

Not being able to come to Washington themselves to correct these misrepresentations and to oppose the plans of selfish and interested persons who are constantly at work there, they have earnestly requested me to select and appoint someone living in Washington with whom they could communicate freely and with confidence and whom they would enable to place the true state of things before the department.

In accordance with their views and at their request, I have appointed General Charles S. Ewing of Washington to act as their commissioner for these purposes. General Ewing has already done a great deal in behalf of the Indian Catholic Missions, and is in every way fitted to discharge the duties which will be required of him.

As the Indian Missionary Bishops have not the means to pay the necessary expenses of the Commission, some members of the Catholic Union in New York and elsewhere have generously offered to contribute an annual sum for the purpose and I most heartily recommend the Commissioner and the good work in which he is engaged to their favor and support.

The first commissioner of the emerging Bureau of Catholic Indian Missions, appointed actually on March 17, 1873, in an exploratory effort, was General Charles S. Ewing. A veteran of Washington, D.C.'s, political arena, General Ewing was qualified for the post, having the advantage of belonging to a remarkable family of converts to Catholicism, being the fifth son of the famous Thomas Ewing. A well-educated lawyer, General Ewing was also a veteran of the Civil War who was highly decorated and held the rank of brigadier general at the close of the conflict. He was a brother-in-law of General William Tecumseh Sherman and prominent in Washington society. Pope Pius IX would create General Ewing a Knight of the Order of St. Gregory before Ewing's death in June, 1883, at the age of forty-three.

The demands of his office led General Ewing to consult with Father Brouillet and to depend upon his experiences in dealing with proper government agencies. The Catholic women of Washington, D.C., added their own formidable social skills to General Ewing's mission as well. They began to rally behind him and formed the Catholic Indian Missionary Association. This group lobbied endlessly for the missions at events and gatherings and raised over $48,000 before disbanding in 1887 as participants' husbands were transferred to new assignments or retired.

On January 2, 1874, Archbishop Bayley formally announced the establishment of the Bureau of Catholic Indian Missions. This bureau was mandated as a true companion to the Catholic Native Americans, formed to aid the missionaries of the land. At the same time, the bureau was directed to: obtain funds for mission education programs; to repel any intolerant or unjust treatment of the Indians and their missionaries; to maintain the rights of Catholic Indians to have religious instruction; to obtain titles to all properties used for churches or schools on Indian reservations; and to provide financial aid, public relations, and whenever possible, religious personnel for the maintenance and security of the missions.

These generalized mandates of duties and obligations were based on an analysis of past difficulties and government policies that endangered the Catholic mission apostolate through the decades. All these duties were immersed in legal, legislative, or bureaucratic arenas, but they were founded in truly deep and personal commitments to the Native Americans. Each director would face changing policies and regulations, but at the same time, the director and bureau personnel would witness emerging trends among the missionaries and the Native Americans themselves.

Father Brouillet was designated as the director of the Bureau of Catholic Indian Missions, and Father Felix Baratti was appointed treasurer. General Ewing retained his position as commissioner. On June 13, 1879, the Sacred Congregation of the Propagation of the Faith issued a letter for the bureau, and Giovanni Cardinal Simeoni, the prefect of the congregation, also announced an appeal to all the dioceses of the United States, asking for their support and for their assistance in this vital mission apostolate.

This response from Rome and the obvious institutionalizing of anti-Catholic sentiment in federal programs added new imperatives to the bureau's mandates. Many former stable missions were in spiritual disarray because the priests had been excluded forcibly by rival religious denominations. Such policies outlasted Grant's Peace Policy, continuing until 1882. Two years later, Americans heard a remarkable tribute to Catholic missionaries on the floor of the United States Senate. There Senator George Vest would solemnly declare:

> Nowhere in the United States have such satisfying results been obtained as in the Jesuit missions. I defy anyone to find me a single tribe of Indians — in the plains-blanket Indians — that approximate in civilization to the Flatheads, who have been under the control of the Jesuits for fifty years. I say that out of the eleven tribes that I saw — and I say this as a Protestant — where they put Protestant missionaries, they had not made a single solitary advance towards civilization — not one; yet among the Flatheads, where there were two Jesuit missions, you find farms, you find civilization, you find Christianity. . . .

While Senator Vest's tribute to the Jesuit missions reflects the bias of the era concerning the Indian lifestyles and equates "civilization" with established European social advances as well as Christianity, his words illumined many Americans and repudiated the efforts started during Grant's administration to disengage the Catholics from the Indian mission apostolates.

In the decree issued by the American bishops at the Third Plenary Council of Baltimore, convened on November 9, 1884, and conducted until December 7 of that year, the Bureau of Catholic Indian Missions was cited and supported. The bureau was a visible agency in the land, and the bishops formed a committee to establish procedural rules and regulations and to designate episcopal membership. The original episcopal participants in the bureau were the archbishops of Baltimore and San Francisco and the bishops of Portland, Helena, and Sioux Falls. The archbishops of Santa Fe and Philadelphia became part of the bureau's operational administration within a decade.

In 1894, the bureau was chartered by an act of the General Assembly of Maryland, with the incorporator listed as the archbishops of Baltimore, Philadelphia, and New York. In 1899, Archbishop Patrick Riordan of San Francisco offered the following resolution that was unanimously accepted by the American bishops involved in Indian affairs: "That we have entire confidence in the Bureau of Catholic Indian Missions; that we use the Bureau for all Indian business, and through the Bureau transact all such business with the Government, and that the bishops should conduct all correspondence on Indian affairs with Government officials through the Bureau."

Kiowa Chief Santanta and a tribal tepee design

CHAPTER 8

The Maturing Apostolate

Kiowa, and Cheyenne were conducting a campaign called the Red River War, led by Quanah Parker and Santanta.

In North Dakota, Major Forbes of Fort Totten was welcoming the Sisters of Charity, the Grey Nuns of Montreal, into the area of his command. Such missions needed a new line of defense, and the Bureau of Catholic Indian Missions was mandated to perform this leadership.

Father Brouillet was a veteran in the Washington, D.C., political arenas, but his experience in the missions provided him with a prudent, realistic approach to those involved in evangelization. A native of Canada, he was born in the village of St. Jean-Baptiste de Rouville on December 11, 1813, and raised on a farm. In this devout, pastoral setting he received the grace of a priestly vocation and entered the minor seminary of St. Hyacinthe at the age of thirteen. There he demonstrated so many intellectual gifts during his seminary training that he was assigned to serve as a member of the faculty. He taught grammar from 1833 to 1834 and literature from 1835 to 1836. He was ordained to the priesthood on August 27, 1837, in Montreal.

Father Brouillet was appointed to the

Father Jean Baptiste Abraham Brouillet assumed the leadership of the Bureau of Catholic Indian Missions in an era that called for flexibility and a certain political astuteness in protecting and advancing various Catholic causes. America was bent on a course predicated by a certain optimism. Most citizens of the country believed that the United States was destined by Almighty God to bring the Gospel to distant shores, where democracy would bloom as well, alongside "civilization."

There were changes taking place as well in the Great Plains areas of the nation, as barbed wire had been recently invented. Fences fashioned out of this deadly metal sprang up on the plains, closing open range areas and providing protection for the farmers and their lands. Miners and adventurers were in the Sioux's sacred Black Hills of South Dakota, where gold had been discovered. Other Indian nations were fighting against intrusions as well. The Comanche,

College of Chambly soon after ordination and taught there until September, 1842. He then became the pastor of St. Georges d'Henryville and labored there until assigned to l'Acadie in 1846. It was in l'Acadie that Father Brouillet met Bishop Augustine Magliore Blanchet, the newly consecrated prelate destined for Walla Walla, Washington. In time, the diocese would be located at Nesqually, serving as the foundation of the present archdiocese of Seattle.

Bishop Blanchet was in Canada to recruit young priests for his diocesan missions, and he addressed gatherings in the area. Father Brouillet attended one of these sessions and responded with considerable enthusiasm to Bishop Blanchet's invitation to the missionary life on the American frontier. In turn, the bishop recognized the intellectual capacities of the young priest and his eagerness to accompany him to Washington. The two petitioned Bishop John Charles Prince, Father Brouillet's ordinary, and the young man received permission to join the "Apostle of Washington" on his arduous journey. Less than a week later, Father Brouillet was appointed vicar-general for the Walla Walla diocese.

On March 23, 1847, the bishop, Father Brouillet, and two other volunteers for the missions started their trek West. They did not cross Canada but went south to the United States, which offered stage lines, railroads, and boats as transportation to St. Louis, Missouri. They arrived in St. Louis on April 15 and were joined by Oblate missionaries who had been assigned to Bishop Blanchet's territory. A wagon train setting out on the famed Oregon Trail provided safety in numbers all the way to Fort Hall on the Snake River. There Father Brouillet was left behind to prepare provision wagons while Bishop Blanchet and the three

others went on to Walla Walla. He joined the missionaries there on September 5.

The diocese was part of the Oregon Territory, which included areas of Washington, along with Oregon and related wilderness regions. Father Brouillet began his ministry by being involved in the terrible Whitman Massacre and by witnessing the unleashing of anti-Catholic sentiments. Legislation had been introduced to expel Catholic missionaries from the region as a result, and military campaigns had been conducted in retaliation. The Cayuse burned Father Brouillet's first chapel on the Umatilla River, and he traveled to St. Peter's in The Dalles region to work with Bishop Blanchet.

In the following summer, word of the gold strike in California reached Bishop Blanchet, who recognized an opportunity to raise funds for the missions. He sent Father Brouillet to the mining camps around the California strike areas in December, 1848, with this mission in mind. Father Brouillet also established a chapel on Vallejo Street in San Francisco and celebrated Mass there on June 17, 1849, becoming the first pastor of the city. He recruited priests and the Sisters of Notre Dame de Namur for the establishment of Catholic schools at the same time. Ordered back to Oregon, Father Brouillet left San Francisco one year after his arrival. He visited the city one more time to raise funds, but then assumed the duties of his position in the diocese.

In 1850, Bishop Blanchet was transferred to the newly erected diocese of Nesqually, headquartered in Vancouver. Father Brouillet served as vicar-general there also, administering the diocese when the bishop went on fund-raising trips. One of his most pressing obligations was the task of obtaining clear titles to the lands of the Catholic missions in the territory. This process demanded two journeys to Washington, D.C. In 1859, he went to the nation's capital, where he managed to obtain a legal title to the Cowlitz mission and began proceedings to secure other Catholic lands.

During his 1862 visit, Father Brouillet visited government agencies associated with the Indian missions and the far western dioceses. He pleaded with these agencies for demonstration of religious toleration in such enterprises and even wrote to President Lincoln, requesting that government agencies act to promote religious identities on such missions. This request was a foreshadowing of President Grant's Peace Policy of 1869, but it was received with little enthusiasm in Lincoln's administration.

William Dole, the Commissioner of Indian Affairs at the time, received a copy of the request and declared it unreasonable. Father Brouillet had asked that Indian reservations served by Catholic missionaries "be placed under the religious care of the Catholic missions." Dole and his agents did not intend to relinquish powers to religious denominations, believing that the policies in effect were generous and sensitive to the needs of the faiths involved.

Father Brouillet stayed in Washington caring for diocesan matters for the Blanchets from 1864 until 1867. He was able to settle the claim issue for St. Joseph's Mission in the Oregon Territory before returning to Nesqually. In November, 1872, as the furor over Grant's Peace Policy was raging, Father Brouillet was sent to Washington again. Aiding Archbishop Bayley and General Ewing, he put his experiences to good use and proved himself capable in dealing with government agencies and his Protestant counterparts. There was considerable disagreement between Bishop Blanchet and General Ewing about Father Brouillet's in-volvement in the bureau's affairs, as the bishop did not want to lose the valuable abilities of his vicar-general. In December, 1874, however, Bishop Blanchet gave his permission, and the priest was free to assume leadership in the Catholic Indian affairs.

The following year, the American Catholic Church reached a milestone, as the first cardinal in the United States was named by Rome. Archbishop John McCloskey of New York received the red hat, a symbol that the American Church was coming of age. Father Brouillet understood the new vitality in the Church and worked to make the Native American apostolate part of the national Catholic agenda. He raised funds, encouraged the Ladies of the Catholic Indian Missionary Association, and started a collection in Catholic schools. Father Jean F. Malo was also sent to the dioceses on the East Coast to raise consciousness about the Indian missions and their truly dire needs with a series of sermons and lectures.

The prefect apostolic of the Indian territory of Oklahoma was established in 1876, the same year that Chiefs Sitting Bull and Crazy Horse made good on their vow to repay the whites for desecration of their sacred lands and decades of abuse. Sitting Bull had declared openly: "I am a red man. If the Great Spirit had desired me to be a white man, he would have made me so in the first place. . . ."

The war had started with raids in 1875, but then the Sioux allied themselves with the equally irate Cheyenne and Arapaho and left destruction in their wake. On June 25, 1876, General George Armstrong Custer was on the move against the tribes. The Sioux especially viewed Custer as a ruthless enemy, and as a slaughterer of defenseless women and children, and they watched as the general divided his forces and went to the Little Bighorn in Montana. That site became a historical landmark honoring "Custer's Last Stand." There he faced three thousand Indian warriors bent on avenging the treacherous deeds of the whites of America.

Grant's troubled administration came to an end soon after Custer's death, as Rutherford B. Hayes became the president of the United States and the Catholic mission activity continued in the wilderness. In Alaska, the Oblate Jean Seguin started evangelizing the Native Americans at Fort Yukon in 1862, and by 1867 Oblate Joseph Mandart was laboring in the panhandle district. Three years later, Oblate Emil Petitot took up mission work at Father Seguin's mission. In 1872, Oblates Bishop Isidore Clut and Father Auguste Lecorre were touring Sitka, Kodiak, and Unalaska. The arrival of Bishop Charles John Seghers in Alaska spurred the mission activity pioneered by the Oblates of Mary Immaculate.

Arizona's missions were being guided by Bishop John Baptist Salpointe by 1868. The Sisters of St. Joseph and the Sisters of Loreto were serving the Native Americans as well. In 1868, Colorado, which had pre-

An example of Tlingit artistry

Bishop Martin Marty and a Sioux shirt
from the Rosebud Reservation

viously been under the jurisdiction of New Mexico, became part of a new vicariate apostolic guided by Bishop Joseph Machebeuf.

Idaho's missions came under the jurisdiction of Bishop Louis Lootens in 1868. Jesuit Joseph Cataldo had just started his half-century apostolate among the Nez Percé and Slickapoo, and another Jesuit, Father Gozzoli, was laboring as a medical missionary to the tribes. In 1876, Archbishop Francis Blanchet administered Idaho. Bishop Alphonse Glorieux became the vicar apostolic of the region in 1884.

In Maine, the Abenaki maintained their devout loyalty to the faith. The Sisters of Mercy arrived among the Abenaki in 1870. Chief Stockvesin Swassin provided them with a four-room wigwam for their convent. By 1879, the Pleasant Point School was open, and a mission was established at Dana's Point.

In Michigan, Bishop Baraga's diocese was transferred to Marquette in 1865. In 1878, Bishop Benedict Flaget was at a rally for ten thousand Native Americans at St. Mary's (Sault Ste. Marie), and he toured Detroit's missions and Catholic facilities in Monroe. In 1875, Minnesota was declared a vicariate apostolic in part, and the Jesuits were laboring in the Mankato mission. The

Benedictines opened the Crookston mission three years later, and the remaining portions of Minnesota were declared part of the vicariate apostolic in 1879.

In Mississippi, a group of Dutch Carmelites had entered the mission in 1883. Two years earlier, Bishop Francis Janssens had founded a Choctaw community at Philadelphia. The Carmelite Bartholomew Bekker was at Tucket, and the Carmelite Augustine Breek served the Choctaw.

St. Stephen's Mission for the Arapaho was founded on the Wind River Reservation in Missouri in 1884. The Jesuits were in Montana, at St. Paul's Mission, in 1863. The Flathead missions were also revived there soon after, and in 1867, St. Michael's was founded for the Spokan. The Yakima and Nez Percé were served by St. Joseph's Mission in 1872. The great Ursuline foundation in Montana aided the missions and provided systematic records of activities. One such record, at St. Peter's, lists 2,732 baptisms as of 1879. Montana was already a vicariate apostolic, having been so designated in 1877. In 1884, the diocese of Helena was established. One year later, Father Frederick Eberschweiler opened St. Paul's. In 1886, St. Xavier's was founded for the Crow, followed by St. Mary's for the Okanagon. By 1890, nine missions and stations were operating with nine Indian schools, conducted by the Ursulines and the Sisters of Providence.

In North Dakota, Benedictine Claude Ebner was at Fort Totten in 1877, and in that same year Standing Rock Mission was served by other Benedictines as Bishop Martin Marty, O.S.B., was reviving the Catholic Indian apostolate. He made his headquarters in Yankton. A unique congregation of Sioux Sisters were also in the area. Founded by Father Francis Craft, these Sisters served at Standing Rock and Fort Berthold.

In Oklahoma, Bishop Isidore Robot, O.S.B., was serving the missions in 1876 as prefect apostolic. One year later, the Benedictines founded Sacred Heart Mission for the Potawátomi. The Sisters of Mercy opened schools for the Choctaw and white children at Krebs in 1887 also.

In South Dakota, Bishop Martin Marty served the Sioux at Fort Yates in 1876. The Benedictines opened a school two years later on Standing Rock Reservation. Bishop Marty was vicar apostolic and worked to bring qualified religious into the territory. The Presentation Sisters aided the missions, and the Jesuits were laboring at Holy Rosary Mission on Pine Ridge Reservation and at St. Francis Mission on Rosebud Reservation. The diocese of Sioux Falls was erected in 1889.

In Washington, the Oblates recorded 3,811 baptisms on Puget Sound in 1868. Missions were being served in Clark, Skomonia, and Lewis counties, and Father Adrian Croquet was at Grand Ronde. The Franciscan Sisters were at St. George Mission school in 1888, and one year later all of Washington mourned the death of Father Jean-Baptiste Bolduc, called the "Apostle of Puget Sound." In Wyoming, the Jesuits assumed the missions to the Shoshone and Arapaho in 1884. The Sisters of Charity were also in the missions, and Jesuits John Jutz and Paul Mary Ponziglione served at St. Stephen's.

The tragedy of the Native Americans was being played out relentlessly elsewhere. Chief Crazy Horse was killed while in U.S. custody, and the Nez Percé odyssey caught the attention of Americans. Chief Joseph (*Hin-mah-too-yah-lat-kekht*, "Thunder Soaring to Loftier Realms") had watched the lands in Oregon being opened to white settlements and had moved to a reservation with his people. Being forced to live on yet another smaller reservation when gold was discovered in the region, the Nez Percé vowed to return to their own lands in Wallowa Valley in Oregon. Chief Joseph led fifteen hundred Nez Percé there but realized they would have

Chief Joseph and a Nez Percé design

to return to Idaho. In June, 1877, they set out on the journey, and some young warriors attacked local settlers. Chief Joseph, seeing a cavalry unit approaching, flew a white flag in hopes of conducting a peace conference. The cavalry charged at White River Creek despite the truce sign, and suffered thirty-four dead with no Nez Percé losses.

Realizing that their only hope for safety and freedom was now Canada, the Nez Percé traveled seventeen hundred miles in four months, all the while fighting a rear guard action against General Oliver Howard, who stayed in pursuit. A battle at Clearwater River allowed Chief Joseph to lead the old and young into Montana, where they were joined by the warriors. In Montana, the Nez Percé were attacked at Big Hole, and suffered many casualties. Another battle on September 13 exhausted the warriors, but they pushed on. On September 30, the Nez Percé rested at Snake Creek on the southern side of the Bear Paw Mountains, only forty miles from Canada. There Colonel Nelson A. Miles attacked with troops, and a ferocious battle erupted with a standoff lasting five days. Some two hundred Nez Percé escaped and found refuge in Canada, but Chief Joseph and four hundred more were unable to flee. Chief Joseph surrendered on October 5, and Colonel Miles agreed to take them back to Idaho.

General William Tecumseh Sherman, however, demanded that the survivors be imprisoned in Fort Leavenworth, Kansas, for a time. The Nez Percé were then moved to various sites, settling finally at Colville Reservation in Washington. Both Colonel Miles and General Howard interceded for them on several occasions, and Chief Joseph appeared before a gathering of government, political, and diplomatic officials, but to no avail. He died in 1904 on the Colville Reservation. His words at surrender were recorded and published, chilling the hearts of Americans who had remained oblivious to the plight of the Indians: "I am tired of fighting. Our chiefs are killed. . . . The old men are all killed. . . . It is cold and we have no blankets. The little children are freezing to death. . . . Hear me, my chiefs, I am tired; my heart is sick and sad. From where the sun now stands, I will fight no more forever."

The horrors of such Indian policies impelled the Catholic missionaries to redouble their efforts to awaken their fellow Americans to the ongoing plight of the Native Americans. Some progress was being made concerning the legal status of the remaining Native American tribes. The Bannock War in Idaho and Oregon, involving the Bannock, Northern Paiute, and Cayuse, led the United States Congress to establish legislation guaranteeing recognition of Indian tribal governments and police forces as legal entities on tribal lands. The tribal governments were assaulted again within a decade, but at this time, they were providing stability and comfort in places of exile.

A remarkable Sister of Charity, Blandina Segale, was becoming well known and honored for serving both Indians and whites in this era. Laboring in the communities of Colorado and New Mexico, Sister Blandina was determined and dedicated; moreover, according to one story, she was protected by a young man who did not tolerate any opposition to her labors. Sister Blandina's patron and protector was none other than William Bonney, known to Americans as Billy the Kid.

He took Sister Blandina's remonstrance to heart after she cared for one of his companions, and, in turn, shielded her and her Sisters in the rough frontier outposts.

The Sisters of Charity, under Sister Blandina's leadership, founded a school in Colorado, hospitals and schools in Albuquerque, New Mexico, aided the local Native Americans, and built a hospital in Santa Fe. Sister Blandina's fame spread rapidly after an Apache raid on one of her outposts. Seeing the Apaches approach the settlement, she went on foot to meet them, armed only with a crucifix and her reputation for honesty, caring, and compassion. She spoke truthfully about a white man who had wantonly slain an Apache, declaring the man had fled the area. The Apaches honored her honesty and left to search for him elsewhere.

While the Sisters of Charity were laboring on the frontier, Father Jean Baptiste Abraham Brouillet was facing a different sort of enemy in the Catholic press. He understood that the Bureau of Catholic Indian Missions would not survive in the political world or even in the ranks of the American Catholics if he did not obtain an official endorsement from Rome. The bureau was clearly under attack by James McMaster, the editor of the *Freeman's Journal and Catholic Register* in New York. This editor had launched a campaign to have the bureau disbanded, claiming the agency had no purpose. McMaster was a convert to Catholicism who targeted various groups and agencies in his editorials. He also accused the Protestants of the era of ruining the nation by their own assaults on Catholics. During the Civil War, McMaster had printed such ferocious comments about President Abraham Lincoln that he was arrested and briefly imprisoned from 1861 to 1862.

McMaster's assault, however, prompted action in the Bureau of Catholic Indian Missions. Father Brouillet undertook a campaign to gain Vatican approval, visiting Rome to plead his cause. The formal

Vatican endorsement, announced in June, 1879, accompanied by the exhortation of Giovanni Cardinal Simeoni, prefect of the Congregation of the Propagation of the Faith, assured the survival of the bureau. The American Church, still a mission territory, was functioning under Cardinal Simeoni's jurisdiction, which added weight to the announcement and urgings.

Father Brouillet was still concerned with the damage done to Catholic Indian missions by the Peace Policy, but he was able to secure only one additional agency for the Church. He realized then that a new approach had to be taken in order to safeguard the great mission legacy and, as a result, started a series of programs to strengthen the Catholic missions in operation. Education thus became a valuable aspect of the apostolate, coinciding with the generally accepted viewpoints of the time. The United States government was still intent on "civilizing" the Native Americans by teaching them how to farm and keep house with time-honored European methods. In order to carry out this "civilizing" effort, the government contracted with religious groups to educate Indian children in agricultural and domestic arts. Father Brouillet was the first religious leader to enter into such contracts. By 1873, three Catholic boarding schools were established in the northwest region to conduct the mandated "civilizing" efforts.

Chief Geronimo and an Apache ceremonial crown

A decade later, the Church was operating eighteen "contract" schools, all with financial aid from the government.

On July 2, 1881, President James A. Garfield was shot by a deranged political office seeker and lingered some weeks before dying of the wound and subsequent infections. Chester A. Arthur entered the White House in time to face the "Last Indian War" in America, as Geronimo started his campaigns, which lasted until 1886. This Apache warrior was originally named *Goyanthlay*, "One Who Yawns." In 1858, a Mexican military unit murdered his family, and he attacked the local Mexicans with such ferocity that they bestowed the name Geronimo on him, Spanish for Jerome. The actual significance of this new name has been lost, but Geronimo was no longer "One Who Yawns." He became the scourge of the United States-Mexican border region after joining forces with the Chiricahua Apaches, led by the great Chief Cochise.

Cochise and his father-in-law, Mangas Coloradas, had granted the Americans the use of an area called Apache Pass in Arizona's Chiricahua Mountains. In 1861, Cochise was charged by the white settlers coming into the area with the crimes of cattle stealing and the kidnapping of a white child. As Cochise was not guilty of such crimes, he went to the station at Apache Pass to discuss the charges, taking his brother and two nephews as companions. The Americans tried to arrest them all, violating the truce arranged for the meeting, but Cochise escaped. He took three American civilians as hostages and in a rage killed them. In turn, the army hanged his brother and nephews. The Cochise War that resulted brought about the death of a hundred fifty Americans. Mangas Coloradas was wounded, captured, and hanged. Cochise continued to fight until 1872, closing Apache Pass and American trade in the region.

When Cochise made peace, Geronimo fought on, stirring up problems until 1886. After his surrender to the Americans, he was held locally and then sent to Florida and eventually to Fort Sill, Oklahoma. Americans loved seeing great chiefs such as Sitting Bull on display, and they applauded them when they performed at various exhibitions. Geronimo was so popular that he was one of the dignitaries in the inauguration parade of President Theodore Roosevelt.

Father Brouillet and the Bureau of Catholic Indian Missions watched these Indian wars with concern and with a certain horrified awareness of the inevitable outcome. Such campaigns and the atrocities conducted on both sides reinforced the stereotype of the Native Americans as savages in need of European education, discipline, and training. The bureau contracted schools in order to keep a truly Catholic presence among the Indians, and these schools were mandated to operate as part of the mission legacy of the faith, bringing the same spirit to each new generation while fulfilling the roles assigned to them by the prevailing political and social views. Father Pierre Jean De Smet had been known as a true friend of the American tribes. Father Brouillet wanted to maintain the same level of honor, mutual respect, and cooperation that the famed Jesuit missionary had accorded the Native Americans in his own time, despite the ongoing concepts of "civilizing" the Indians.

He was particularly concerned about one of the schools contracted in the ongoing federal programs, where the bureau had guaranteed a certain quality of education and care. This guarantee was being called into question at the Boys' Industrial School in the Devil's Lake Agency in the Dakota Territory. Conditions there had deteriorated over the previous months because of personnel problems involving the superintendent and a faculty member, who were reported to have displayed intemperate behavior that jeopardized the entire program. Father Brouillet went to the school, planning to remain there for three months in order to address the faculty situation and to institute the necessary personnel changes.

While he was at the Devil's Lake Agency, he also agreed to go to Fargo for a special meeting. A severe blizzard struck the region, causing a delay in Father Brouillet's intended journey to Fargo. Unable to wait any longer, he set out in the blizzard and was eventually forced to seek haven in an abandoned cabin while the storm raged on.

Mangas Coloradas and a
Chiricahua Apache design on a hide

The snow and the temperature, which dropped lower than forty degrees below zero, claimed several lives in the region, and Father Brouillet was confined to the cabin for a week, enduring considerable hardship, including snow blindness. He lost the sight of his left eye and had severe damage to his right also. The experience drained his physical reserves, and Father Brouillet was unable to serve as director of the bureau until the summer of 1883. The following winter months sapped the last of his physical strength, and he suffered complications that led to his death on February 5, 1884.

Father Brouillet was a missionary priest called upon to assume the leadership of a new and vital Catholic apostolate; a ministry that demanded updated awareness and vital commitments in the changing political scene of America. He witnessed tragedies and losses among the Native Americans and labored to forge an agency that challenged prevailing government policies and blunted their disastrous consequences for the Indian peoples. In the coming decades, the white populations and the Indi-

THE STORY OF THE CATHOLIC INDIAN MISSIONS

ans themselves would reassess the concepts about the "civilizing" efforts of Father Brouillet's era, but no one would question his determined defense of the faith and the Bureau of Catholic Indian Missions' mandated apostolate. A contemporary called Father Brouillet "a most lovable character, full of the milk of human kindness . . . the nearest approach to a saint of any man I have known."

Father Joseph Stephan, "the fighting priest"

CHAPTER 9

New Federal Assaults

A few months after Father Jean Baptiste Abraham Brouillet died, some four thousand devout pilgrims attended a service at a shrine in Auriesville, New York, commemorating the Jesuit martyrs of the region. The memorial ceremony was conducted on August 15, 1884, by the Jesuit priest Joseph Loyzance, and it was held on ten acres of land deemed the actual site of the martyrdoms. Father Loyzance had purchased the land after determining its historical value and had erected the shrine in order to revive Catholic awareness of the missionary heritage of America. The Catholics of the nation had already forgotten their own history in the raw wilderness of the continent. Few Catholics had heard of the sacrifices of the early missionaries, and the Native Americans were no longer a presence in American cities and towns, especially in the East.

A particular Native American was honored in the services as well, a woman who contradicted all of the stereotypes about In-dians being touted across the land at the time. Her name was Kateri Tekakwitha, affectionately called the Lily of the Mohawks, and she had graced new trails of the spirit in an untamed world. Kateri was born at Gandaouague, the Mohawk fortress at Ossernenon, present-day Auriesville, New York, in 1656. The Jesuit martyrs commemorated by Father Loyzance had pioneered the faith embraced by Kateri and had offered her a haven in the Church. The Society of Jesus was still laboring among the Native Americans, some just having founded St. Stephen's Mission in Wyoming and then St. Francis and Holy Rosary missions in South Dakota.

The Third Plenary Council, also held in Baltimore in 1884, not only supported the Bureau of Catholic Indian Missions and the missionaries honored at Auriesville but also provided American Catholics with the famed Baltimore Catechism. There were approximately seven million Catholics in the country at the time, served by seventy-one bishops and almost seven thousand priests. The main imperative of the Church's role within the United States was that of parochial education, and throughout the land the faithful were opening new schools. These Catholics joined their fellow Americans in welcoming the Statue of Liberty, a gift from France that arrived in New York in October and was erected in New York harbor as a shining symbol of the nation's hopes and aspirations.

At the Bureau of Catholic Indian Missions, Father Joseph Stephan, called "the fighting priest," assumed the directorship left vacant by Father Brouillet's passing and began his seventeen-year term of dedicated service. Father Stephan was a European, born in Gissigheim, Baden, Germany, on November 22, 1822. He studied at local academies and then entered military service, becoming an officer under Prince Chlodwig K. Victor von Hohenlode. Distinguishing himself, he was sent to Karlsruhe Polytechnic Institute and to the University of Freiburg to further his education in military engineering.

While at the University of Freiburg, however, he was struck blind by an unknown medical cause, suffering a loss of sight that lasted two years. Praying for the restoration of his sight, Joseph promised to become a priest if cured of the mysterious illness. In 1845, with his sight restored as strangely and suddenly as it had disappeared, he studied Scholastic philosophy at Freiburg with the intention of completing seminary classes and being ordained. His parents, however, had emigrated to the United States, and in 1847 he received word that his father was dying in that far-off land. He set sail immediately and reached his father's deathbed in time.

Following the funeral, Joseph applied to the diocese of Cincinnati for holy orders and was admitted to the seminary. He was ordained by the newly elevated Archbishop John Baptist Purcell on March 19, 1850. Father Stephan was then assigned to local parishes and orphanages, even as his con-

cern for the Native American missions grew steadily. In 1856, he was sent to northern Indiana, where there was a need for German-speaking priests. Two years later, Father Stephan founded a German Catholic community on three thousand to four thousand acres of land near modern Rensselaer, in Jasper County. Fort Wayne had just been erected as a diocese, and he won considerable admiration from the new bishop for his parish and mission foundations and for bringing back lapsed Catholics.

In 1863, however, Father Stephan, still a military man at heart, became a Union Army chaplain in the Civil War. He was commissioned as an officer on May 18 and joined the Indiana 47th Regiment. During campaigns, he distinguished himself and displayed his engineering skills to such an extent that the army offered him a permanent commission within its ranks. He declined this honor, and at the end of the war started his ministry in the Native American missions.

Hearing that the agent at the Standing Rock Sioux mission in the Dakotas was going to be replaced, Father Stephan contacted General Charles S. Ewing, whom he had met while in the military. On October 16, 1878, he became the official agent of that mission, working with the Benedictines, who were involved in the school. His military discipline, however, prompted him to set standards of efficiency that were not embraced enthusiastically by his co-workers. Father Stephan also viewed the enlisted personnel at the local military garrison to be a disruptive element. The situation deteriorated to the point that on March 31, 1881, he tendered his resignation. He remained at Standing Rock until the end of the year and then founded other ministries in the Dakota Territory. Bishop Martin Marty enlisted his aid and named him vicar-general and consultor as well. It was Bishop Marty, among others, who recommended Father Stephan to replace Father Brouillet at the Bureau of Catholic Indian Missions. He was confirmed by the Third Plenary Council of Baltimore on December 20, 1884.

The Peace Policy instituted by President Grant was no longer a paramount factor in Indian affairs, but the drive to "Americanize" the Native Americans was a thriving impetus for federal and state projects. Such a policy embraced programs that belittled Native American traditions and history and introduced European values and modern concepts about work and commitment. Chester A. Arthur was in the White House, and Father Stephan maintained relatively cordial relations with Arthur's administration and worked to adapt the bureau's programs to the prevailing political imperatives because it was the only avenue at the time.

He also recognized the value of the "contract schools" financed by the government in areas not served by nonsectarian public educational institutions. The Catholic missionaries conducted such mission schools in truly isolated regions, and these qualified for government subsidies. Father Stephan was convinced that the so-called nonsectarian schools, touted by government agencies, were Protestant-dominated, so he set about increasing the number of Catholic schools under "contract" to serve as a buffer for the faith. When he assumed the directorship of the bureau, the government was paying $54,000 to support eighteen Catholic Indian schools. By 1900, Father Stephan had thirty-eight such schools operating with $394,533 in federal funds.

The Protestants were horrified to see tax money being used to nurture "Popery" in the nation and mounted a campaign to put an end to the "contract schools." The Indian Rights Association, a group composed mainly of sympathetic white Protestants in political circles, led the opposition to the success of the Bureau of Catholic Indian Missions. The battle lines were joined, positions stated, and events set in motion without concern for the realities of the Indian schools at the time. No thought was given to the actual ramifications of such programs, in fact, because the prevailing sentiments blinded all those involved.

Some Indian schools provided truly happy and spiritually fulfilling experiences for the children enrolled, and some Native American youths viewed such programs as opportunities for advancement in the new order in America. Too often, however, the end results of such schools proved disastrous for the students and their tribes. Trained to function as "Americans," with European standards of civilization imposed even upon their manners and dress, such Indian children were set adrift in a terrifying limbo between the white man's domain and their tribal realities. Indian elders referred to such educated children as "the lost ones" in some regions, defining the fact that their acquired education served as an alienating factor that separated the students from their ancient traditions and the tribal values passed down over generations. Indian youths had to undergo rigorous warrior rites upon returning to various reservations in order to prove that their spirits were not contaminated permanently by their contact with the whites.

The Catholics and Protestants involved in such educational programs at the time genuinely cared about the Native Americans, striving to bring them into the social arenas of the country. They were guided, however, by the prevailing concepts and attitudes of their own era; views of the Indians as individuals needing change and improvement. The beauty of the Native American's ancient ways, particularly the honor and innate dignities of tribal traditions, did not register with the whites of that historical period. White children could not succeed without education, everyone knew, so the Indians needed the same advantages, perhaps even more so.

Americans of the last century also failed to grasp the simple fact that the majority of Indians had no ready access to the white world, educated or not. They resided in remote sites that were constantly coveted by white settlers, and they had no legal protection against the devastation of their lands and lifestyles. An even more bizarre dichotomy of thought was evident in the celebrity status of defeated Indian chiefs. Sitting Bull and Geronimo had been hunted down and taken prisoner because they fought against the white man's desire to take their lands and decimate their tribes. Once defeated, however, the chiefs were invited to address political and social gatherings or to appear in the popular "Wild West" shows. These views ran parallel, thereby confusing issues and values.

In 1885, Grover Cleveland became president of the United States, the same year in which the last great buffalo herd was exterminated by white hunters. Approximately sixty million buffalo, or bison, had roamed freely over the American landscape when the Europeans arrived. These animals were revered by the Native American tribes and served as a mainstay of the Indian lifestyle and sustenance. No part of the great beast was wasted, normally, when slain by the Indians, and some tribes recited litanies of thanksgiving and apologies for the deaths. When the buffalo disappeared, the lifestyle of the tribes was disrupted and endangered. An even crueler impact upon the Indians was

to follow: the Dawes General Allotment Act of 1887.

In 1886, Archbishop James Gibbons became the second cardinal of Baltimore, attesting to the growing maturity of the American Church. In Alaska, the saintly Bishop Charles Seghers was killed on the trail by a deranged lay companion, and his death signaled changes in the Alaskan missions. Two Jesuits, Fathers Paschal Tosi and Louis Aloysius Robaut, had served as Bishop Seghers's companions for a time. When the bishop was slain, Father Tosi met with his superior, the famous Father Joseph Cataldo, a veteran of missions among the tribes. It was decided that the Jesuits would assume the Alaskan missions, a move later supported by Pope Leo XIII. Father Tosi had a personal audience with the pope in 1892 and gave him a colorful description of Alaska and its people. The Jesuits went to Alaska in 1886, serving the Yup'ik, Inupiat, Aleut, Athapaskan, and other Native Americans. The Sisters of St. Anne, who also served the Choctaw in Krebs, Oklahoma, entered Alaska and began Catholic school programs.

New Mexico was once again serving as a vital mission area. In 1899, Archbishop Peter Bourgade asked the Franciscan Sisters of Lafayette to open schools at Jemez, Peña Blanca, San Fidel, Cuba, and Gallup. In 1890, Blessed Katharine Drexel's* Sisters had opened St. Catherine's Indian School. The Sisters of Loreto were in the schools at Taos and Mora, having opened them four decades earlier.

In South Dakota, the Jesuits were with the Sioux at Rosebud and Pine Ridge reservations, and the Franciscan and Presentation

---

*Blessed Katharine Drexel is scheduled to be canonized by Pope John Paul II on October 1, 2000, and will be referred to as St. Katharine Drexel from this point on.

Sisters were teaching in the local schools. The Benedictine Sisters conducted a school at Mount Angel Mission in Oregon. The Jesuits were also in Wyoming at the Shoshone Arapaho Reservation on the Wind River. Far to the south, Father Adrien Rouquette turned his back on his growing fame as a preacher in order to become a chaplain of the Choctaw remaining in Bayou La Combe, Louisiana. St. Anne's Mission on the Umatilla River in Father Brouillet's Cayuse mission was rebuilt and called St. Andrew's.

In 1887, the United States Navy signed a contract to open a new base in the Pacific, on the Hawaiian Island of Oahu. That base was at a site called Pearl Harbor. In Iowa, another anti-Catholic organization was formed in that same year by Henry F. Bowers and by six others. This group would prove more virulent than previous assaults on the Church. The American Protective Association, as it was called, was dedicated to the taxation of Catholic properties, to the end of naturalization of immigrants, mostly Catholic at the time, and to the outlawing of Latin in religious services. By 1896, one million Americans joined the American Protective Association, vowing never to hire or vote for a Catholic.

The year 1887, however, was noted by the Native Americans and the Catholic mission apostolate for yet another event, the passage of the Dawes General Allotment Act, also called the Dawes Severalty Act or, simply, the Dawes Act. A Creek Indian sage commented that Egypt had locusts, Asia cholera, and England, the Black Plague. He added that the American Indians, however, were inflicted with "the worst scourge," the Dawes Commission.

Senator Henry L. Dawes of Massachusetts, originally considered a friend of the Native Americans, pushed through an act that provided the distribution of reservation land among the individual tribe members. The intended goal was to create solid farmers among the tribes, families that could be assimilated easily into western culture. Reservation lands were distributed to the Indians in lots of eighty to one hundred sixty acres. Actually, these Native Americans were reduced to the status of tenant farmers, as the lots were to be held in trust by the federal government for twenty-five years.

The devastation of the tribes, the loss of entire homelands, and the wholesale deterioration of Native American enclaves were not intended, obviously, but such were the results of the Dawes Act. The legislation also provided for the disposal of "surplus" reservation holdings of those acres not bestowed upon the Indians, thus freeing these lands for sale to the migrating whites. When the Dawes Act was signed into law on February 8, 1887, the Native Americans held 138 million acres of land. By 1932, because of this act, two thirds of that land ended up in the hands of whites. The former reservations, reduced and broken, became disease-ridden sites, subject to poverty and despair.

The Sioux of the Dakotas were among the first Native Americans targeted by the Dawes Act. Rosebud Reservation was carved up, followed by other Indian holdings. The Catholic missions in these reservations faced great hardships and devastation as a result. Father Stephan and the Bureau of Catholic Indian Missions labored with other Catholic leaders to maintain the mission apostolate in the resulting chaos but faced terrible enemies.

The Dawes Act may have been enacted as a reform measure, but it resulted in wholesale ruination for the Native Americans. The Indians were swindled out of their allotted acres in some instances, as fast-talking whites moved in with money and promises, and the nomadic tribes were unable to adjust to the agricultural existence thrust upon them. All were bereft of their cultural traditions and spiritual cores. Father Stephan responded whenever possible, fearing future problems as well. These materialized in 1889, when Benjamin Harrison was elected president of the United States by the Electoral College in that year and set about opening new lands for settlement. The Oklahoma Territory was declared available to whites and an unbelievable 1.9 million acres of land were claimed in a single day. A Shawnee commented: "The whole white race is a starving beast, and what that beast dines on is land."

In Catholic circles, the American Church celebrated the long-awaited opening of the Catholic University of America, sanctioned by Pope Leo XIII in his apostolic letter *Magni nobis Quadii* and empowered "to provide instruction in every department of learning to the end that the clergy and laity alike might have an opportunity to satisfy fully their laudable desire for knowledge." In New York, an Italian nun arrived with a small group of Missionary Sisters of the Sacred Heart to begin work among the Italian immigrants. Her name was Frances Xavier Cabrini, and she would become the "Patroness of Emigrants" and a canonized saint of the Church.

President Harrison, forming his administration, appointed a Baptist minister, Thomas Jefferson Morgan, as the Commissioner of Indian Affairs, and a Methodist minister, Daniel Dorchester, as the superintendent for Indian schools. Both men were advocates of public education, and both set about eliminating the Catholic "contract schools." Father Stephan pleaded in vain and went to Congress directly to secure funds for three more such institutions. As a result, Commissioner Morgan severed all ties with the Bureau of Catholic Indian Missions, a state of affairs that continued throughout Harrison's term of office.

In 1890, Congress announced that America's "frontier" was closed. The continental settlement was successful, and the Indian population was recorded at two hundred fifty thousand nationwide. This shockingly low number assured white Americans that the Indians had been subdued, removed from view for all time. Chief Red Crow of the Blood nation, died in the faith, and Sitting Bull was slain brutally on the Grand River Reservation of South Dakota, where he was living quietly with his people. The local Indian agent, Major James McLaughlin, reportedly despised Sitting Bull and feared the chief's power. When rumors about the Ghost Dance circulated

Arapaho Ghost Dance shirt

*Miniconjou Chief Big Foot and a
tribal saddle decoration*

years later, and a granite marker was erected there.

The Ghost Dance rumors that had prompted Sitting Bull's arrest and death alarmed many whites in the region, combining dread about another Indian uprising but involving mysterious elements as well. The United States government had forbidden the Ghost Dance among the Plains Indians, but it was conducted in secret. Sitting Bull had been rumored to have led such a ceremony at Standing Rock, fueling apprehension among the whites. The first Ghost Dance cult started in 1869 but died out among the tribes before it caused alarm in white communities. The second, more enduring celebration of the cult's religious aspirations began during the solar eclipse in January, 1889. Wovoka, a Paiute prophet, had a vision during the eclipse and began preaching about spiritual powers that could be attained in the rituals. The Ghost Dance would supposedly allow the Native Americans to ride free again, immune to the horrors visited upon them by the whites. During the Ghost Dance rituals, participants wore deerskin shirts covered with mystical symbols.

When Sitting Bull was killed, the Miniconjou Chief Big Foot, a Ghost Dance participant, fled to the south with over a hundred warriors and two hundred fifty women and children. A cavalry unit, led by Colonel James Forsythe, caught up with them and persuaded Big Foot to take his people to Pine Ridge Reservation. The chief was dying of pneumonia and anxious to see his women and children out of harm's way. At the reservation, the Indians were taken to a site on Wounded Knee Creek. When they camped for the night, the U.S. cavalry broke out a keg of whiskey to celebrate the American victory.

The next morning, armed with rifles,

through the area, McLaughlin issued orders for Sitting Bull's arrest. He was dragged from his bed as a result and killed in the ensuing melee. Sitting Bull never signed a treaty with the United States and believed all white men were liars. The exception to this, of course, was Father Pierre Jean De Smet, the Jesuit missionary, who had been received with utmost warmth by the great Sioux leader. Sitting Bull's celebrity status with Buffalo Bill's Wild West Show only five years before did not save him from being slain. Originally buried near the site of his murder, the remains of Sitting Bull were transferred to Mobridge, South Dakota, ten machine guns, and small cannons, the United States soldiers began to disarm the Indian warriors. A scuffle broke out, and the cavalry began to fire point-blank on the captives. When the women and children fled from the horror, the soldiers followed, stalking the fugitives and killing them at random, in some instances miles away from the original camp. The slaughter ended with about three hundred Indians as victims, mostly women and children. Some of the soldiers in the massacre reportedly received the Congressional Medal of Honor "for their gallantry." Wounded Knee would remain a symbol for the Sioux over the coming decades. It was a place of reverence even before the massacre, as the heart of Chief Crazy Horse had been buried somewhere in the area after his slaying while in U.S. captivity.

In 1893, Grover Cleveland became president of the nation, and the dispute between the Bureau of Catholic Indian Missions and federal agencies dissolved temporarily as Harrison's appointments were dismissed. At the World's Columbian Exposition held in Chicago, approximately twenty-five million Americans were thrilled by the exhilarating new ride called the Ferris wheel. "Little Egypt," a dancer with unusually provocative hips for the time, was another sensation. The stellar attraction, however, was the "Death Cabin." Visitors flocked to a small house reported to be the original cabin in which Chief Sitting Bull had been slain. The building had been relocated to Chicago for the exhibition. While Americans visited the attractions at the Columbian Exposition, Queen Liliuokalani, the rightful ruler of the Hawaiian Islands, was overthrown by American businessmen in Honolulu.

The Catholic Church in America was distinguished by yet another event in 1893

as well, as the Vatican apostolic delegation was opened in Washington, D.C., on January 24, despite Protestant objections. This was the first diplomatic office of the Vatican ever tolerated in the United States. Archbishop Francis Satolli, who had served on the faculty of the Catholic University of America, was the first apostolic delegate to this nation. Two years later he received the red hat of the cardinalate from Cardinal Gibbons in Baltimore, in a ceremony promoted by Rome.

Welcoming the delegate, Father Stephan and his staff braced for yet another round of assaults by the advocates of the public, or "nonsectarian," school systems. The Bureau of Catholic Indian Missions worked to fend off new attacks by inculcating an awareness of the need for religious and spiritual values in all areas of education, especially in educational programs for the Native Americans. Father Stephan believed that the Protestant values incorporated into public schools would not survive the coming social changes and would fail to train upright moral generations. He feared that the Catholic mission schools would be targeted, and he was correct in his assessment of the era and its social imperatives.

Hoke Smith, the Secretary of the Interior in the administration of Grover Cleveland, proposed putting an end to the Catholic "contract schools." He did not want to halt the system abruptly, however, and offered a method of gradually reducing federal funds for the Church related schools, believing that to be a fair method of closing down the entire system. Smith's proposal became part of the Indian Appropriations Act of 1896, lowering federal subsidies for Catholic "contract schools" by ten percent each year until such subsidies were ended in 1900.

Desperate to find support within the Catholic community, Father Stephan turned to a remarkable woman, St. Katharine Marie Drexel. One of the wealthiest women in America at the time, the second daughter of Francis M. Drexel, she had been raised by a devout stepmother, Emma Bouvier. When her father and stepmother died, Katharine and her sister received an inheritance amounting to a thousand dollars a day for each one of them. St. Katharine had urged the founding of the Bureau of Catholic Indian Missions and had discussed the need for such an agency during an audience with Pope Leo XIII. The Holy Father told her to commit herself personally to the missions, and she set about funding schools in the Dakotas, Wyoming, Montana, California, Oregon, and New Mexico. In 1891, she professed her vows as the first member of the Sisters of the Blessed Sacrament for Indians and Colored People. Within a year the congregation had twenty-one members and was assuming an important role in Church mission affairs. St. Frances Xavier Cabrini was one of St. Katharine's close advisers in her apostolate.

Funding Indian missions and schools, St. Katharine Drexel also established Xavier University in New Orleans, the first United States Catholic institution of higher education for blacks. With St. Katharine's generous aid and the annual collection taken up in Catholic parishes across the country, Father Stephan's schools survived. Some bishops aided the cause by visiting the larger city parishes to explain the pressing needs. Father Stephan, exhausted by the ongoing political skirmishes over the Catholic Indian missions, retired unofficially to Cornwall Heights, the motherhouse of the Sisters of the Blessed Sacrament, in order to regain his strength. He

St. Katharine Drexel

then went to Europe in 1900, hoping that his health would improve.

In that same year, the Native American Indians were centered in Santa Fe and Gallup, New Mexico; Tucson, Arizona; Santa Rosa, California; Rapid City, South Dakota; and Great Falls and Billings, Montana. In Alaska, the Jesuits were serving the mission apostolate. Holy Cross Mission was opened for the Ingalik Eskimos, and Nulato was in the Koyukum area. The Ursuline Nuns were at St. Michael's and at Valley. In Juneau, the Sisters of St. Anne were at Holy Cross, and Nelson Island Mission had been opened. Six more Jesuits entered the area in 1890, and in 1901, the Sisters of Providence started educational programs. In 1905, there were more than six missions in Alaska, and

125

the Christian Brothers had joined the educational systems.

In Arizona, the Franciscans were operating missions for the Navajo and Pueblo at Cochíti, Santo Domingo, San Felipe, and Jemez. St. John's at Gila Crossing had started in 1899, offering education to the Papago, Pima, and Maricopa. St. Katharine Drexel's Congregation would open St. Michael's Mission in 1902.

In California, Father Luciano Osuna had established St. Turibius Mission near modern Kelseyville, and St. Mary's had been opened near Ukiah. The missionaries had founded an outpost for the Southern Ute in Colorado in 1900, continuing the apostolate there.

In Montana, the Okanagon Indians had St. Mary's, and there were nine Indian schools in the region, served by the Ursulines and Sisters of Providence. In 1900, missions were serving the Northern Cheyenne, Assiniboin, Crow, Gros Ventre, and Piegan Blackfeet. St. Labré Mission was serving the Northern Cheyenne, and the Ursulines were at the mission, along with Jesuits A. van der Velden and Peter Prando. St. Paul's had been opened by Father Frederick Eberschweiler, and St. Xavier's Mission was founded for the Crow.

In Fort Berthold, North Dakota, a remarkable group of Sioux Indian Sisters served their own people as religious. Father Francis Craft had established this unique congregation at Standing Rock Reservation and had applied to Rome for approval. The congregation was never formally approved, but the Sioux religious served faithfully for many years. There was a mission for the Sioux as well on the Cheyenne River. Missions recorded here in 1905 included Our Lady of Sorrows at Devil's Lake, St. Elizabeth at Standing Rock, St. James at Standing Rock, and St. Bede, St. Benedict, St. Edward, and St. Aloysius.

In Idaho, Father Joseph Cataldo, the Jesuit pioneer, was laboring at St. Joseph's Mission in Slickapoo. He served the Nez Percé, Sahaptin, Lapwai, and Spokan, and was an apostle to the Kalispel, becoming fluent in their language. Father Cataldo was a missionary for over half a century and was considered a wise veteran of the apostolate, revered by other Jesuits in the field. He and his fellow missionaries continued to expand their efforts, despite the obstacle put in their way by government policies. There were 140 Catholic Indian missions in operation by the turn of the century, with 175 chapels, 60 schools, and 50,000 Catholic Native Americans. Federal subsidies would not keep these missions operating because of the new changes, and American Catholics would have to assume that responsibility in time and would have to become aware of the ongoing ministry.

In Oklahoma, Bishop Theophile Meerschaert, vicar apostolic of the territory, had established a chain of mission schools, starting in 1891. When the Oklahoma diocese was erected in 1905, Indian schools were operating at Anadarko, Antlers, Ardmore, Chickasha, Gray Horse, Muskogee, Pawhuska, Purcell, Quapaw, Tulsa, and Vinita.

In 1905, the Jesuits in Oregon were operating a mission on the Umatilla Reservation, with a school staffed by the Franciscan Sisters and the Christian Brothers. The diocese of Sioux Falls, South Dakota, erected in 1889, aided the mission apostolate in that area. The Benedictines were serving the Sioux on the Cheyenne River, and missions reported in the state in 1905 included: Immaculate Conception at Crow Creek, St. Matthew's in Veblen County, Corpus Christi on the Cheyenne River, St. Francis on Rosebud, and Holy Rosary on Pine Ridge. In 1908, St. Paul's was opened.

In Washington, the Franciscan Sisters were at St. George Mission School. In 1900, the Jesuits opened the Colville and St. Francis Regis missions. Jesuit John Jutz was serving at St. Stephen's, Mississippi, joined by the Sisters of Charity.

In 1901, as Theodore Roosevelt was inaugurated president, Father Stephan recovered energy enough to resume his work in Washington, though he died quite suddenly on September 11 of that year. His body was taken to a cemetery at Cornwall Heights, Pennsylvania, where he was laid to rest in St. Katharine Drexel's haven. The Catholic missionaries in the nation were stunned to hear the news of his sudden death. Father Stephan had explored every avenue possible to keep the Native American missions and schools operating. He had introduced fund-raising innovations and had sent veteran missionaries into the nation's parishes to make the people aware of the need. Father Stephan had secured the funding necessary for such activities before he died, but that task and the daily tensions and stresses of dealing with government bureaucracies had claimed his last physical reserves. All across the mission territories, prayers were recited for his repose and for the coming of another bureau director equal to the crises facing the faithful. Almighty God would send *Wambli Wakiata*, "the Watching Eagle."

Arapaho feather bustle for rituals

CHAPTER 10

The Turning Point

The frontiers of America may have been "closed" by the United States Congress in 1890, but vast stretches of continental wilderness remained. At the turn of the century, Catholic missionaries to the Native Americans continued their labors in the regions still unclaimed by the whites. In the process, these missionaries earned unique nicknames from the tribes that they served — generally predicated upon characteristics, physical build, rank, or particular gifts of personality.

Father Bellarmine Lafortune, for example, who conducted missions at Teller, Sinuk, Mary's Igloo, Wales, Pilgrim Springs, and Little Diomede in Alaska, was called the "Little Father." The Inupiat Inuit stated the obvious when they referred to him in this fashion. Father Lafortune was remarkably short of stature. Bishop Martin Marty, the Benedictine pioneer, was called the "Black-robe Lean Chief" by the Sioux, denoting both his physical appearance and his episcopal rank. The great Jesuit Father Joseph Cataldo carried the name "Dried Salmon" in the Rocky Mountains, where he established twelve additional Indian boarding schools and Gonzaga College for Native Americans and whites in the region. He was pale, weathered, and gaunt.

A priest named William Henry Ketcham became *Wambli Wakiata*, "the Watching Eagle," among the Sioux. He earned this title after many years of missionary service and by his championing of the Native Americans in the volatile arena of Washington, D.C., politics. Father Ketcham came to this daunting apostolate with two special capabilities. He was a veteran missionary, which ensured his understanding of the day-to-day struggles in far-flung outposts. He was also a convert to Catholicism, raised in the Protestant traditions and thus well aware of the tensions involved in the interdenominational relationships of the times.

William Henry Ketcham was born in Summer, Iowa, on June 1, 1868, the son of a Puritan family. His father, Alonzo, was a direct descendant of John and Priscilla Alden of Plymouth Colony in the beginning of the Massachusetts settlements. Alonzo Ketcham was also a veteran of the Civil War. Marrying a Michigan woman, Josephine Shanafelt, he moved his family to Iowa. After William was born, the family relocated yet another time to Wills Point, Texas. William was educated in private schools in the area and raised in a wholesome family-style life. Learning about the Catholic faith while maturing in Texas, he received the grace of conversion and stated his spiritual desires to his family without hesitation. Perhaps he realized that this intended conversion would not bring about the usual Protestant response from his parents. Instead, they encouraged him to grow spiritually and to attend the Catholic college of his choice. William elected to enter St. Charles College in Grand Coteau, Louisiana, a Jesuit institution. He took instructions while studying in the college and was baptized on April 4, 1885. His parents and sister, Ella, eventually followed him into the Church.

William earned his bachelor's degree in 1888 and in that same year entered St. Mary's Seminary of the West in Norwood, Ohio, to study for the priesthood. However, he became ill during his studies at St. Mary's and was forced to withdraw in order to recuperate at his parents' home. They had taken up a new residence in Oklahoma City, Oklahoma, where William remained for a year before returning to his seminary training. Recovered, he entered Sacred Heart Monastery in the Indian territory, preferring to remain close to his family. Two Native American schools were operating near the monastery, St. Benedict's Industrial School for Boys and St. Mary's Academy for Girls. William was actively involved in projects in both institutions as a result of seminary commitments and was familiar with the customs and traditions of the Indian children enrolled in the programs. He felt at home with the Indians and was accepted by them.

This introduction to the Native Americans had an effect on William and led to his application to Bishop Theophile Meerschaert as a possible seminarian. Bishop Meerschaert, the vicar apostolic to the Indian territory, was a Belgian who had studied at the American College, Louvain. A dedicated missionary and administrator, the bishop later became the head of the newly erected diocese of Oklahoma and main-

William Ketcham, first priest to be ordained in Oklahoma Territory

130

tained missions for the Potawátomi, Choctaw, and Osage at Pawhuska, Purcell, Anadarko, Chickasha, Antlers, Gray Horse, Quapaw, Ardmore, Muskogee, and Vinita. Bishop Meerschaert welcomed William to Guthrie, Oklahoma, the episcopal residence at the time, and there he instructed him and conferred upon him holy orders. William was thus the first person to be ordained in the vicariate of the Indian territory of Oklahoma. The ceremony was held on March 13, 1892, and marked a turning point for the entire apostolate.

Following his ordination, Father Ketcham was assigned to Muskogee, a mission that was designed to serve the Creek nation. The mission, however, extended over the entire northeastern part of the modern state of Oklahoma. Within its borders were members of the Choctaw, Delaware, Modoc, Ottawa, Peoria, Quapaw, Seneca, Shawnee, and Wyandotte nations. Finding the area in the grip of an economic depression and rife with agricultural failures, Father Ketcham set about establishing a genuine Catholic presence that would have an impact on the severe conditions. Aware of her generosity and concerns, he contacted St. Katharine Drexel and asked for financial aid for the region. She responded as generously as ever, and he was able to finish the half-completed church in Muskogee and to open Nazareth Institute for Boys and Nazareth Academy for Girls. By 1894, more than a hundred Indian students were being educated in these institutions.

The Protestant Creeks, horrified that a descendant of the original Plymouth Colony was teaching "Popery" with such success, moved to dismantle Ketcham's ministry. In 1893, the Creek council formally charged the missionary with violating a tribal law that forbade opening a school without tribal permission. Father Ketcham responded to the charge by showing that he had received such permission from the local chief, a leader named Perryman. Thwarted legally, the Protestant Creeks then conducted an illegal search of the convent of the Sisters of St. Joseph, who formed part of the faculty of Father Ketcham's educational programs. These intruders did not find the evidence they sought, whatever that was, but they bullied the Sisters and threatened arrest and other disasters during their search of the convent. The Sisters did not flee from their ministry, and Father Ketcham dismissed the threats that he received personally. The campaign withered, and the mission thrived. Father Ketcham received similar threats and insults from the Native American Protestants in Eufaula, where he erected another church. Bishop Meerschaert arrived there to dedicate the new building in 1892, ignoring the implied threats.

By 1895, Father Ketcham had constructed a church in Vinita, another in Wagner, and one at Quapaw. With additional funds donated by St. Katharine Drexel, he constructed a church in the Native American settlement in Tulsa as well. These accomplishments, and the unending concerns that he demonstrated, brought Father Ketcham recognition as a true pioneer. Accordingly, he was transferred in 1897 to the southern region of the mission territory to develop the same sort of organization there. His new headquarters was at Antlers, where he served the Choctaw nation. Arriving in the area with no funds, and no immediate prospects, he appealed again to St. Katharine Drexel and soon had a residence built and then a school, St. Agnes, which was designed with a chapel.

Father Ketcham also set about learning Choctaw, becoming fluent in the tribe's native tongue. His ministry at Antlers, how-ever, was short-lived, as Archbishop John Ryan of Philadelphia summoned him to Washington, D.C., to assist the ailing Father Stephan at the Bureau of Catholic Indian Missions. Bishop Meerschaert protested this assignment, citing the needs of the Indian territory and the commitment made to the Oklahoma region by Father Ketcham. The episcopal advisers of the bureau pressed the needs of the national apostolate in return and demonstrated the advantages of having such a capable missionary serving the Catholic Indian missions on a national stage. By August, 1900, Father Ketcham was in control of the bureau. Father Stephan's return was brief, in 1901, and the bureau's directors named Father Ketcham as his successor.

When Father Ketcham began his na-tionwide ministry to the Native Americans, he faced a desperate situation brought about by the discontinuation of federal funding for Catholic Indian schools. The subsidies ended officially, and "contract schools" were only memories. Many in the secular and religious communities recommended the closing of these schools or the surrender of them to state or federal authorities. Father Ketcham would not consider such courses of action, coming from a Protestant background that gave him a profound awareness of the doc-trinal advantages of each stage of education in the young. He also understood that the Native Americans needed continuing dem-onstrations of the Church's commitment to their welfare.

Father Ketcham redoubled the efforts of the Bureau of Catholic Indian Missions and revived the lecture circuit once again so that more and more American Catholics would have a personal awareness of the needs and aspirations of the Native Ameri-can schools. He raised $140,000 in 1900,

and in the following year established the Society for the Preservation of the Faith Among Indian Children, an association that had national appeal. The annual member-ship fee for the society was twenty-five cents. Members received the prayers of the Native American children and a subscrip-tion to *The Indian Sentinel*, a news bulletin concerning the bureau's apostolate. Father Ketcham wrote for the mission publication, stating: "The life or death of the Catholic Indian schools is the issue at this hour, and view it as we may in all its vast responsibili-ties, the time and opportunity for action are now upon us, and delay in any event is most hazardous."

If the message appears dire, even omi-nous, it reflected the realities of the Ameri-can Catholic efforts to maintain an educa-tional program for the Indians who were forgotten in their exiles. The society raised over $21,000 the first year and almost $26,000 in the second year, but these amounts still left the bureau with ever in-creasing debts. St. Katharine Drexel once again saved the situation, providing over $100,000 per year to the Catholic Indian schools. A Snake rebellion in Oklahoma and a Creek demonstration against the Dawes General Allotment Act made more Ameri-cans aware of the plight of the reservations and Indian enclaves.

Another Catholic religious was also inspiring Americans and alerting them to the needs of the Indian mission apostolate. Her name was Mother Bernardine Wachter, a German-born Benedictine from the famed Maria Rickenbach Abbey. In 1876, Mother Bernardine volunteered for the missions in Missouri. She taught at Maryville and then at Fort Yates in the Dakota Territory until 1882, when she was asked by Abbot Adelhelm Odermatt, the Benedictine pioneer, to establish a Benedictine community in the West. With three professed nuns and recruits who arrived from Europe, Mother Bernardine went to Oregon. At Gervais, the Benedictines lived in an abandoned saloon until they could erect their convent and school. In 1887, Mother Bernardine was formally elected the superior, and she began erecting residential schools for the Native Americans in Grand Ronde, Oregon, and in British Columbia, as well as schools for local white children. Mother Bernardine founded Queen of Angels Monastery at Mount Angel, Oregon. She died on June 3, 1901.

From Rome a papal message saluted these missionaries and their efforts. In 1895, Pope Leo XIII wrote *Longinqua oceani,* "The Far Regions Beyond the Ocean." This remarkable document evoked memories of centuries past, when Europeans had gazed upon a wild continent and had committed themselves to exploration and settlements. The America addressed by Pope Leo XIII, however, was a land filled with industries and communities consisting of towns and cities linked by modern vehicles of transportation.

The Holy Father praised American democratic processes but provided insights, as well, concerning the effects of such a government. Pope Leo XIII begged American Catholics to support educational and evangelical efforts and to provide families with the sacred doctrines that would help them prosper and defend their hard-won freedoms. This message addressed a Church that was maturing and prospering after several centuries in the New World, and it signaled that American Catholics were ready to take their place among the Churches of the world.

To aid in the continuing apostolate outlined in the document and in the mandates of the American Church, Father Ketcham was involved in applying to the federal government's Bureau of Indian Affairs for permission to use tribal revenues for educational purposes, but he was sharply rebuffed by that agency. He then set about openly attacking the Browning Ruling of 1896, a regulation still in effect at the time. The Browning Ruling declared that since the Native Americans were mere wards of the United States, they were not entitled to decide where or how their children would be educated. Only the federal agencies were deemed capable of making such a determination under the Browning Ruling. Father Ketcham, seeing the manner in which the desires of the Catholic Native Americans were being thwarted by such a policy, contacted the involved agencies with no success.

He then managed to speak to the Secretary of the Interior, Ethan Allen Hitchcock, and to President William McKinley, providing them both with detailed information about the injustices involved. Father Ketcham won their support, and the Commissioner of Indian Affairs, W. A. Jones, was ordered to rescind the ruling as of October, 1901. Jones stalled but was forced to put an end to the Browning Ruling on January 18, 1902.

The year before, however, the commissioner had decided to discontinue the policy of providing food and clothing to all Native American children attending denominational or religiously oriented schools. This move alienated the Protestants as well as the Catholics and provided Father Ketcham with powerful allies in a campaign of protest. He labeled the decision as a "decided injustice," an act that not only violated existing treaties but openly deprived Native American children of necessities. An intense campaign of lobbying moved Congress to respond. The rations discontinued by Commissioner Jones were restored by the Indian Appropriations Act. Father Ketcham was also able to force the government agencies to allow Catholic Indian children in federal schools to receive catechetical instructions and to receive Catholic sacraments. This put an end to the policies of harassment conducted by some reservation agents against local Catholic missionaries.

This particular political battle was conducted during a time of national turmoil. On September 6, 1901, President William McKinley was shot by an anarchist named Leon Czolgosz at the Pan-American Exposition in Buffalo, New York. The assassin shot at McKinley from only two feet away. The resulting wounds were treated immediately but became infected, and the president died on September 14. Theodore Roosevelt succeeded McKinley and became the twenty-sixth president of the United States.

In 1904, the Marquette League was founded by Father H. G. Ganss of Lancaster, Pennsylvania. Members of the councils of St. Vincent de Paul Society joined as well to aid the Catholic Indian missions. During its first years, the Marquette League established chapels at Holy Rosary and St. Francis missions in South Dakota and aided the Moqui Indians of northern Arizona and the Winnebago of Nebraska. The league also erected two chapels on Fort Berthold Reservation in North Dakota.

Soon after the assassination of President McKinley, the entire Eskimo population of Southampton Island, in Hudson Bay, died of typhus, a disease brought into their settlements by outsiders. Also, in 1902, the Oklahoma reservation lands served by Bishop Meerschaert, Father Ketcham, and other dedicated priests and religious were opened by federal authorities for leasing. Gas and oil reserves had been discovered in the area, and American companies set about bidding for the rights of exploration and development.

Father Ketcham and the Bureau of Catholic Indian Missions continued the day-to-day fund-raising and defense campaigns in the midst of the political and social unrest caused by the assassination of President McKinley and the unending assaults on Native American lands. They hoped that somehow Catholics would achieve recognition and status in the Indian apostolate. The changes desired did take place because of an extraordinary Catholic layman who entered the political scene and set into motion new attitudes and understandings.

His name was Charles Joseph Bonaparte, the grand-nephew of Emperor Napoleon of France. Charles was the grandson of King Jerome of Westphalia, who had been placed on the throne by his brother, Napoleon, when the Bonapartes wielded power in Europe. Born in Baltimore, Maryland, in 1851, Charles belonged to a branch of the Napoleon family that had recognized the end of their ambitions in Europe and had taken up a new life in America. The Bonapartes of Baltimore were wealthy, educated, socially prominent, and devoutly Catholic.

Charles was a graduate of Harvard University and a trained lawyer. A close friend of Theodore Roosevelt, he was an authority on Church-state affairs and a defender of the faith. President Roosevelt appointed him to the Board of Indian Commissioners, where he was rather warmly welcomed by the Protestant members. His presence on that board and his ongoing explanations of Catholic intentions and aspirations brought a certain sanity to the continual Catholic-Protestant debates. Charles's wealth, family ties, and political allies added to his prestige, opening doors to events and groups normally closed to Catholics in the nation's capital.

In 1905, as a dedicated enthusiast of Roosevelt's naval policies, Charles became the Secretary of the Navy. In 1906, he was appointed and confirmed as the Attorney General of the United States and served with distinction. He was also founder and president of the National Municipal League, a reform organization that was highly respected by Americans. A recipient of the Catholic Laetare Medal, Charles Joseph Bonaparte died at his Maryland estate, Belle Vista, on June 28, 1921.

His presence on the Board of Indian Commissioners not only altered policies during his immediate term of service but also allowed other prominent Catholics to participate in decisions involving Indian missions. James Cardinal Gibbons of Baltimore would also serve on the board, and in his person the Protestants found an erudite, informed, and charming Catholic prelate among them. Bishop James Healy of Portland, Maine, also held rank as a consultor for the Indian affairs agencies.

Another element in the political struggle undertaken by Father Ketcham and the Bureau of Catholic Indian Missions came to light slowly and brought about a genuine turning point for the mission apostolate. This was the innate sense of fair play demonstrated by President Roosevelt. As Father Ketcham noted: "One thing is beyond question, President Roosevelt, in his official as well as private acts, has risen above un-Christian racial and partisan prejudices, and has manifested a determination to mete out equal justice to all men."

Americans did not grasp the significance of the Catholic political breakthrough concerning the Indian missions. Other events caught their fancy and earned newspaper headlines. Among such events was the Wright brothers' historic accomplishment of December 17, 1903, when they flew their biplane eight hundred fifty-two feet for fifty-nine seconds. In that same year America received the Panama Canal Zone in the Hay-Bunau-Varilla Treaty. In 1904, the most popular fast food in America was the recently introduced hot dog. The St. Louis Exposition opened to record crowds, and Francis Cardinal Satolli, the former apostolic delegate to the United States, attended as the personal representative of Pope St. Pius X.

In the Oglala Sioux lands, the holy man Black Elk converted to Catholicism. This great Sioux sage had survived the terrible era of the Wounded Knee Massacre as a member of the Ghost Dance celebration. His only surviving child, Lucy Looks Twice, and other Oglala Sioux knew Black Elk as the wilderness ascetic and philosopher, but they also remembered him as "Nicholas," the devout Catholic catechist. He prepared his people for baptism, led prayer services, and did missionary work on other reservations, remaining faithful until his death. Books recording Black Elk's religious and ecological reflections have long been popular in America, but few detail his spiritual journey as a Catholic convert and catechist.

In 1904, Father Ketcham attempted again to have tribal funds used to support the schools on Indian lands. President Roosevelt intervened and decided that such funds could be used for sectarian educational programs if the local tribes approved of such action. The federal Indian department therefore issued contracts for eight Catholic schools, a move that alarmed the Protestants. They went to President Roosevelt to demand that he reverse the policy, but he refused. The Protestants began a campaign to force the annulment of such contracts, and Father Ketcham testified before a Senate subcommittee investigating the affair on February 3, 1905.

Oglala Sioux Chief Red Cloud and his horse decoration

When legislative action proved futile, the Protestants turned to the Indian Rights Association for legal redress. The association instituted a suit against the Secretary of the Interior in *Quick Bear* v. *Leupp* and watched as the case moved through the various processes, finally reaching the Supreme Court. In February, 1908, the justices determined that tribal funds could be used for Catholic schools on reservations.

In 1905, the Franciscans opened an Indian mission in Bayfield, Wisconsin, and the Sisters of the Divine Providence were teaching in missions for the Quapaw in Oklahoma. Bishop Meerschaert became the first bishop of the diocese of Oklahoma City, Oklahoma, and the Catholic Church Extension Society was established. In the following year, the federal government confiscated fifty thousand acres of Indian land, including Blue Lake, New Mexico, a site sacred to the Taos Pueblos. Used as a national park, this site was returned to the Native Americans in 1970.

Another missionary was also active at the time, and the Indians called her the "Chief Lady Blackrobe." She was Mother Mary Amadeus Dunne, an Ursuline superior who began her labors at St. Labré Mission in Montana. Mother Mary Amadeus also founded missions among the Inuits and Aleuts in Alaska. Born in Ohio in 1846, Mother Amadeus was the first elected superior of the American Province of the Ursulines and a remarkable pioneer in the Catholic missions. Another religious congregation, the Oblate Sisters of the Blessed Sacrament — composed of Native American women — was started in 1908 at St. Paul's Mission in South Dakota.

The year 1908 was a momentous one for Catholics of America, as Pope St. Pius X issued *Sapienti consilio*. This papal document placed the American Church on an equal footing with the other ancient Churches of the world. The United States Catholics were no longer under the jurisdiction of the Congregation of the Propagation of the Faith but were of equal rank with European and other Churches. The Americans were no longer part of a mission territory but a recognized Church. The burgeoning Catholic population, the leadership of the various bishops, and the unswerving fidelity of the United States Catholics had prompted this move by the Holy See. The American Church had come of age and would need new bureaucracies and agencies to fulfill its role in the nation.

The next year, President William A. Taft entered the White House. In Montana, the Oglala Sioux mourned the passing of *Mahpiua Luta*, Chief Red Cloud. This warrior had defeated the United States cavalry in a dispute over the Bozeman Trail and at Fort Laramie had extracted a treaty to protect Sioux lands. The treaty proved false, however, and Red Cloud stated: "They made us many promises, more than I am able to remember. They did not keep any of these promises, except one. They promised to take our land, and they took it."

In 1910, a mission school was opened at Harbor Springs (originally L'arbre Croche), Michigan, directed by Franciscan missionaries and staffed by the local Sisters of St. Joseph. Catholic missions to the Native Americans were thriving. The church operated fifty-five Indian boarding schools and eight day schools on the various reservations. There were one hundred thirty-seven actual Catholic Indian missions, supported by approximately ten million Catholic Americans nationwide.

Protestant extremists were alarmed by these continued endeavors and sought legal ways in which to dampen the Catholic ardor. A campaign was started by some of these Protestants to make the wearing of religious garb, the clear insignia of "Popery," illegal in any school operated with federal subsidies. In January, 1912, the Commissioner of Indian Affairs, Robert Valentine, issued a circular throughout the nation to institute the Protestant demands. Religious habits were forbidden, and the various orders and congregations conducting Indian schools had to remove all religious-symbol displays from public classrooms.

A furor developed instantly as a result, and Father Ketcham arranged a meeting with President Taft to discuss the issue. The president ordered that Valentine's circular be withdrawn until a sensible, orderly open hearing could be conducted. The Catholics and Protestants were given equal opportunity to present their arguments during the sessions held in April, 1912. The Secretary of the Interior, Walter Fisher, made the final decision, based on the evidence provided. He declared that in the future, all such religious employees of federally sponsored schools would be required to put aside their traditional attire. Fisher, however, added a "grandfather clause" to this decision. All religious presently in the service of such schools were exempt, unaffected by the ruling. The hearings provided another blessing to the Bureau of Catholic Indian Missions as well. Father Ketcham had conducted himself so intelligently and with such tact that he was appointed by President Taft to the Board of Indian Commissioners.

Father Ketcham was in the public eye as well as an authority on Native Americans. Everyone in Washington, D.C. — from the common man on the street to those in power — was talking about members of the Cherokee, Chickasaw, Choctaw, and Creek nations who had appeared before the United States Congress to protest the Dawes General Allotment Act, still in existence and still wreaking havoc.

Chief Trucha and an Apache basket

CHAPTER 11

The 'Great War'

a newly minted coin, the Indian head nickel. The Native American depicted on this nickel was described by government authorities as a composite of the profiles of the chiefs of the Cheyenne, Seneca, and Sioux nations. On the reverse of the coin was an engraved buffalo, or bison, happily honored after being slaughtered to the brink of extinction.

When Woodrow Wilson entered the Oval Office as president of the United States, the Bureau of Catholic Indian Missions was involved in a comprehensive health campaign on Native American reservations. Tuberculosis and trachoma (which is caused by chlamydia and causes blindness and other health problems) were prevalent in these enclaves, and other diseases were taking a deadly toll especially among the young and elderly. As a member of the federal Board of Indian Commissioners, Father Ketcham had increased powers as he visited the various missions and reservations. As a result, his requests and suggestions were given prompt responses from the various authorities in the regions affected by the Native American health crisis.

As he toured the missions, Father

The truly modern era for America and the Catholic Church of the United States opened with the inauguration of President Woodrow Wilson in 1913. As the largest single religious denomination in the land, the Catholic Church provided a vast multicultural awareness and a rather comprehensive agenda of education and service to all Americans. But the world was entering into a troubled and tragic era, and the coming problems would have a significant impact on the rich European heritage of Catholic immigrants, who watched events and pondered their ramifications.

Americans discovered that they were subject to a new "income tax," and they used

Ketcham received word of the reopening of an apostolic relic from the past. The Arizona mission, called San Xavier del Bac, was once again serving the Pima and Papago. Over the decades, San Xavier del Bac had been abandoned and forlorn and stood hauntingly empty as a "solitary monument in the wilderness." Now it was restored and serving the surrounding Native American communities.

Father Ketcham heralded the reopening of this venerable mission as he continued the health programs on the reservations. He received generous and professional assistance from federal and state officials, especially in Oklahoma, a state with a vast Indian population. Governor Williams, a Dr. Duke of the State Health Commission, and the medical personnel of the Oklahoma Tuberculosis Association instituted a drive to assist the Native Americans. Health programs were initiated, and a sanitarium was opened near Fort Sill. A second sanitarium was operating at Tolihima.

Father Ketcham, still fluent in the Choctaw language, spent a good portion of every year in Oklahoma. He was collaborating with a group of scholars to provide the Choctaws with a catechism and a series of pamphlets instructing them in hygiene and preventive health measures. Such efforts had to be ongoing, as the medical crises on the reservations had to be addressed repeatedly. The shadow of a global war loomed even over the Native American tribal lands at the time, alarming many in the mission apostolate. Father Ketcham addressed such concerns when he announced: "I believe Indian missions work to be the work of God, and I am not looking forward to any possible interruptions as this would savor a feeling of distrust."

The mission apostolate had survived many eras of conflict, and European wars had imperiled the Church's efforts in decades past, he assured everyone. The Catholics of America were no longer singled out as victims of such wars on their home grounds. The missions would survive no matter what the nation faced in the months to come.

Then on June 28, 1914, an event took place that would change the world forever. Archduke Francis Ferdinand, the heir to the throne of the Austro-Hungarian empire, and his wife were assassinated while on a visit to Sarajevo in what is now Bosnia-Herzegovina. Within a month the European continent was spiraling toward a disastrous confrontation. Americans celebrated the completion of the Panama Canal and then read the horrifying news of the sinking of the *Lusitania* on May 7, 1915. The tragic sinking took the lives of 1,198 passengers, including citizens of the United States.

Almost two years later, on April 2, 1917, President Woodrow Wilson asked the United States Congress to declare war against the Central Powers: Germany, Austria, Hungary, Turkey, and Bulgaria. This would be a conflict to make the world "safe for democracy," and Americans entered the fray as the ally of Great Britain, France, Italy, and, until 1917, Russia.

The declaration of war and the subsequent mobilization of American troops would put 4,791,172 citizens of the United States on active duty. A recorded seventeen thousand Native Americans entered military service during World War I. They served valiantly and brought distinction to their ranks, earning praise from military officers who had campaigned against them in the past. General John J. Pershing, the general of the armies during World War I, used Apache scouts and others, descendants of the very Native Americans that he had fought as a member of the United States Army only three decades earlier. The Indian soldiers served in all units of the military during the war with honor. It must be remembered that the Native Americans were not citizens of the United States at the time, and could have avoided such military service. About thirty percent of all adult Indian males put on the uniform of America and fought in the war.

The American Catholic Church was also involved in the war efforts starting in 1917. Catholic officials aided the mobilization crisis and then served in numerous capacities on the various fronts. James Cardinal Gibbons of Baltimore was asked by President Wilson to head the newly formed League of National Unity, an organization designed to spearhead a rigorous response from Americans to mobilization and the conversions of industries to wartime efforts. The League of National Unity stressed sacrifice, industrial might, and moral resolve as key elements for ultimate victory over the enemy in Europe. In an interview Cardinal Gibbons stated quite firmly the demands of the time, announcing: "In the present emergency it behooves every American citizen to do his duty, and to uphold the hands of the President. . . . The primary duty of a citizen is loyalty to country. . . . It is exhibited by an absolute and unreserved obedience to his country's call. . . ."

That interview and his tireless administration of the League of National Unity brought Cardinal Gibbons into the national spotlight. Theodore Roosevelt summed up America's response to the cardinal by saying that this prelate was "the most respected and venerated, and useful citizen of our country."

In another area of the war effort, the American Church was provided with a military ordinariate, a unique diocese for military personnel and their families. The Holy See appointed Bishop Patrick J. Hayes, auxiliary bishop of New York, as the bishop ordinary for the United States military forces on November 24, 1917.

There were twenty-five chaplains on duty at the time, and within eighteen months some 1,026 Catholic priests had entered military service. The military ordinariate was divided into five vicariates to serve their needs in the United States, the Pacific, and Europe. One of the most celebrated of the Catholic chaplains was Father Patrick Duffy of the "Fighting 69th." Father Duffy earned the Distinguished Service Cross, the Croix de Guerre of France, and membership in the French Legion of Honor.

The American bishops also organized the National War Council in 1917 to coordinate the Catholic responses to the country's crisis. Pope Benedict XV had promoted the development of such an association, and the apostolic delegate in that era, Archbishop Giovanni Bonzano, made the Holy Father's sentiments known. In 1919, the National War Council would become the National Catholic Welfare Council, the parent organization of today's United States Catholic Conference-National Conference of Catholic Bishops.

While these various levels of organization and conversion to the war efforts were taking place, Father Ketcham was asked by the Commissioner of Indian Affairs, Cato Sells, to aid in the care of the Native Americans in military service. Commissioner Sells knew of the Knights of Columbus, founded in 1882, and asked if the Knights would assume the task of assisting the Indians in uniform. The Knights of Columbus responded with generosity, and they instituted a program of free recreational and aid centers for the Native American and white servicemen in the United States and overseas. Over 250

Shoshone hide shield

ing on the tribal lands during the war, however, faced a series of events that further eroded their security. The dreaded Dawes General Allotment Act was discontinued, prompting a period of turmoil because Indian lands were no longer federally protected. Corrupt officials and swindlers descended upon the tribes and robbed some of them of the acres remaining in their possession.

The Papago (Tohono O'odham) Reservation was established in Arizona, the last such Native American enclave erected in the United States. For the first time in fifteen years, the birth rate of the Indians exceeded the death rate, as the Native American nations began an era of recovery and regrowth. Congress also ended federal subsidies to religious groups involved in Indian educational programs. As in the early periods of the continental wilderness, the missions and schools conducted by Catholics would have to survive on their own resources and vigor.

The armistice that ended World War I was signed on November 11, 1918. The war had claimed the lives of 320,710 Americans

such centers were opened in Europe and 360 sites in the U.S., with 2,000 secretaries being involved in this charitable service, as well as 27,000 Knights of Columbus volunteers.

The American government was awed by the response of the Indians to the war effort and made efforts to offer them considerable benefits and opportunities while in service. The Native Americans remain-

and introduced the Indians to the white man's world, both in the states and across the sea. One year after the war ended, Congress gave United States citizenship to all of the honorably discharged Indian veterans. Universal citizenship came only in 1924.

Father Ketcham was made a domestic prelate on April 15, 1919, given the rank of monsignor by Pope Benedict XV. He put on his monsignorial attire for the first time on the Rosebud Reservation in South Dakota while attending the Sioux Catholic Congress held in July, 1919. This congress and other developing programs signaled the vitality of the Native Americans and their readiness to participate in the ongoing religious, educational, and social programs being discussed at the time. The Indians would participate but would not accept wholesale the various ideas being presented. The ways of their fathers taught them to be wary and cautious in each new venture concerning whites.

The Catholic Church in America was receiving thirty thousand converts annually, and the Indian missions were thriving. In Alaska, the Pilgrim Springs Indian mission and school were opened, and the Ursuline Sisters were teaching and providing care. In the Southwest, Mission San Carlos opened for Apaches, followed by another on Fort Apache Reservation, in Arizona. Both of these missions represented new advances among the Apaches, who were not noted for welcoming whites into their lands. In 1761, a Franciscan missionary had opened San Lorenzo on the Río San José, in Apache territory, but the Comanches destroyed the site eight days later. Few lasting missions had been erected since that time.

In Washington, D.C., the Shrine of the Immaculate Conception was started. This basilica, the largest church in the Western Hemisphere and the eighth largest in the world, was inspired by a papal suggestion. Pope Pius IX wrote to the American bishops in 1847 concerning devotion to the Patroness of the United States and an appropriate structure announcing that role. Cardinal Gibbons laid the cornerstone of the basilica on September 23, 1920.

Monsignor Ketcham was spending his time on the Choctaw mission in Mississippi, where he continued to work on devotional and medical tracts in the language of the tribe. In October, 1921, he was preparing a report in Choctaw and English concerning the ongoing debate over government schools in the area. He complained of fatigue while working on the report, and on November 9 collapsed while working on the school grounds. Unable to breathe and choking, he was revived by a staff member and put to bed to await the local doctor.

The medical practitioner diagnosed Monsignor Ketcham's condition as acute indigestion and prescribed medication to give him relief. He felt better within a few days and resumed his work schedule, celebrating Mass on November 13. The following morning, November 14, 1921, Monsignor William Henry Ketcham died of a massive heart attack.

Only fifty-three years old when he suffered his fatal attack, Monsignor Ketcham's death stunned Church and government authorities involved in Native American services. The Board of Indian Commissioners stated that their loss was irreparable, while praising the monsignor's interdenominational cooperation and sensitivity. A funeral Mass was conducted at his home parish in Oklahoma on November 18, and his remains were interred there. A Solemn Requiem Mass was celebrated in Washington, D.C., on November 22, attended by prominent officials of all walks of life. Another Mass was celebrated on the same day at St. Basil's in Los Angeles.

Monsignor Ketcham's successor in the Bureau of Catholic Indian Missions, Father William McDermott Hughes, provided the tribute at the Los Angeles Mass declaring that *Wambli Wakiata*, "the Watching Eagle," had proven himself "the truest and most powerful friend of the Indians of his generation." In this tribute, Father Hughes was echoing the beautiful summation of Monsignor Ketcham by the Sioux nation.

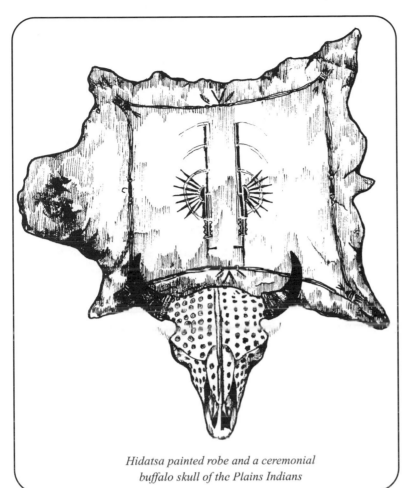

Hidatsa painted robe and a ceremonial buffalo skull of the Plains Indians

A Heart for the Indians

ern California tribes and a profound appreciation for Indian traditions. He attended public schools and then St. Mary's College in Oakland, graduating in 1900.

Receiving the grace of a vocation, William studied at St. Thomas College in Washington, D.C., and then at St. Joseph's Seminary in Dunwoodie, New York. He was ordained a priest by Bishop Thomas Conaty on August 5, 1905, the first native of Sacramento to enter the priesthood. Father Hughes's first assignment was St. Agnes Parish in Los Angeles. He remained there until 1907, when he was sent to Pasadena for a year. Father Hughes was then assigned to mission work among the Native Americans. In 1908, he went to Mexico to study Spanish and to learn about Mexican native cultures. Upon his return to California he was assigned to St. Mary's, in San Jacinto, where he labored among the Murietta, Perris, and Temecula, and visited the Soboba, Cahuilla, and Los Coyotes reservations on a two-hundred-mile circuit.

In 1921, Warren G. Harding became the president of the United States, opening the nation to yet another scandalous administration. The Catholic Church in America was still growing, with fourteen archdioceses, a hundred dioceses, and two vicariates serving the faithful. Within the Catholic Church structure, the Bureau of Catholic Indian Missions was being directed by Father William McDermott Hughes, who had replaced Monsignor Ketcham.

Father Hughes was from Sacramento, California, born there on January 9, 1880, the son of an Irish immigrant named Owen, and Catherine Ellen McDermott. As a young lad, William hunted and fished with the Native Americans of nearby reservation lands, developing a rapport with the north-

145

During this ministry, Father Hughes began to witness the suffering endured by the Native Americans and the relentless measures carried out in the name of "civilizing" the Indians. Later he would declare: "Is it any wonder they are a sad and demoralized race? Is it any wonder that they suspect the white man, and almost distrust the padre himself, because he is white?"

Father Hughes welcomed the opportunity of hearing about ancient traditions and spent hours with tribal elders, trying to learn the legends and concepts that had endured over the centuries. He raised a beautiful chapel on the Soboba Reservation, based on Native American art forms. His labors, of course, brought him some attention, and eventually an interview with Father Ketcham. The director of the Bureau of Catholic Indian Missions had been looking for a dedicated missionary who understood the Native Americans and labored with zeal and enthusiasm. Father Hughes was exactly the man he sought. As Father Ketcham ex-

plained to the young priest: "You are an American, a westerner, an idealist not wanting on the political side; you could get along with our public men, and I think with our churchmen. You have had experience on the missions and know a good deal of the Indians, and you have a heart for the Indians."

Father Hughes did not want to leave his diocese but agreed to work for six months each year. Travel expenses would be assumed by the bureau, and as an assistant director, he would earn $1,500 over and above the $1,000-to-$2,000 stipend as a lecturer. Father Hughes was responsible for the support of his aged father and in need of such money. He agreed but discovered that Bishop Conaty was not willing to part with his services in the diocese at first. When a replacement priest was found, Father Hughes was able to go to Washington.

The new lecturer for the bureau had enthusiasm and innovative ideas for raising funds. Father Hughes wanted to use stereopticon slides (the accepted visual aids of the era) in his lectures, depicting missions and Native Americans. He contacted the officials of the Southern Pacific Railroad to ask for their sponsorship of such programs. Father Hughes had hoped to receive free transportation and slides in exchange for various advertisements during his lecture tours. The Southern Pacific authorities declined these advertisements and the request for the free railway passage, but they did provide beautiful slides. Father Hughes used them on his November, 1910, lecture circuit with considerable success. In time, his lectures were expanded to western dioceses as well, and he proved himself so valuable that the board of directors appointed Father Hughes the assistant director of the Bureau of Catholic Indian Missions on April 17, 1912.

Father William Hughes

The lectures and the constant travel took a toll, however, and in 1915, Father Hughes resigned from the bureau, citing a need to return to the pastoral ministry and to have contact with Native Americans on a close, personal basis. He returned to California and was assigned to a small parish in Coalinga, where he was able to combine his pastoral labors with research and writing. Father Hughes assembled his collection of Indian myths and also put together a course of doctrinal sermons. He experienced some regrets about leaving his post in Washington in letters to Father Ketcham, but he remained in the parish until the start of World War I.

Then he was commissioned as a chaplain on November 27, 1917, and assigned to the army's 87th Division at Camp Pike, Arkansas. He served with the 87th Division when it was sent to the battle sites in France and then with the 1st Division, which was occupying a defeated Germany. Father Hughes left active military service in June, 1919, but maintained a reserve status in the army. In 1931, the Military Chaplains Association, in a tribute to his status and leadership, elected him president of the organization. In 1932, he was promoted to the rank of lieutenant colonel in the Chaplain Corps Reserves.

Returning once again to California, Father Hughes was appointed pastor of a new parish, St. Basil's, in Los Angeles. With the aid of an enthusiastic and truly generous parishioner, he completed a wood-framed church that was dedicated on November 21, 1920. Father Hughes remained there, however, for only a year. The untimely death of Monsignor Ketcham brought Father Hughes to the Bureau of Catholic Indian Missions as the new director.

President Warren G. Harding was in the White House, presiding over his brief administration, and the Teapot Dome Scandal was about to break into the headlines of newspapers across America. There were now more than eighteen million Catholics in the land, and Catholic prelates had leadership roles in national affairs. Protestant responses varied according to region and issues, but the ongoing debate about public school funding continued. In Oregon, there began a debate on a legal and legislative statute that threatened the entire Indian mission apostolate.

The Oregon School Law of 1922 was an overt display of Protestant sentiment on the issue and is still regarded by many scholars as the most serious challenge ever mounted against Catholics in an American state. Called the Oregon Compulsory Education Act, this legislation was promoted through the initiative political process. The first such legislation was supported by the Masonic Lodge of Oregon and the Ku Klux Klan, and they gathered enough signatures throughout the state to have the issue placed on the Oregon ballot in November, 1922. The Oregon Compulsory Education Act passed by a wide margin, and anti-Catholic groups joined the Masons in bringing voters of like mind to the polls. The act became law as a result, and every child in Oregon between the ages of eight and sixteen had to be enrolled in a public school by September 1, 1926.

The voters of Oregon had clearly demonstrated their views, but few of them, including their leaders, grasped the constitutional and judicial ramifications of that legislation. Other groups in the land did understand what had happened and reacted quickly. All of these groups viewed the legislation as a dire threat aimed "at the roots of American toleration." Protestant, Jewish, and secular organizations recognized that such a law targeted Catholics within Oregon but paved the way to systematic persecution of other denominations, or even other political aspirations, in the future.

The Church in Oregon established the Catholic Civil Rights Association immediately, and an appeal was sent to the National Catholic Welfare Conference for financial and legal assistance. By December, 1923, a grant of $100,000 was received from the Administrative Council of the NCWC, and a case was introduced in the courts on behalf of the Sisters of the Holy Names of Jesus and Mary, a teaching congregation disenfranchised by the law. An injunction against the law was granted by a panel of federal judges on March 31, 1924. The appeal of the state of Oregon led to the involvement of the Supreme Court of the United States, and Protestant and Jewish groups as well as the American Civil Liberties Union supported the Catholics of Oregon during the proceedings. On June 1, 1925, the high court nullified the Oregon Compulsory Education Act, and many in the nation were relieved to see this assault on the Church and cultural pluralism thwarted.

The Bureau of Catholic Indian Missions had watched the case closely, as it would have an impact on the Native American schools in the region. Father Hughes was made a monsignor by Pope Pius XI, and he accepted the new rank and readied himself and his co-workers for the newest assault, led by a man named John Collier. Collier was a social worker who had spent some time with the Pueblo Indians and felt obliged to speak out as a defender of the Native Americans. A dispute over Pueblo land rights brought Collier to the attention of many, and he began to make known his views and ideals.

Founding the American Indian Defense Association, Collier attacked the Catholic missions as persecuting the Indians on religious grounds. This charge was based on the current policies of government officials and missionaries to "civilize" the Indians by rejecting the ancient rituals of the tribes. Collier's arguments were based on his views that the Native Americans were remnants of a "Red Atlantis," a form of ancient treasures, somehow outside of human time and worthy of being protected at all costs.

The Secretary of the Interior, Hubert Work, created the Advisory Council on Indian Affairs in response to Collier and his supporters. Monsignor Hughes was made a member of that select council of one hundred leaders in Indian concerns. He defended the missionaries and the Commissioner of Indian Affairs, Charles Burke, and he took part in the debates. When the term "sovereign nations" became part of Collier's arguments, Monsignor Hughes demanded to know if Christian members of the tribes were being protected. Such members did not want to take part in revived ancient rites because of their beliefs and were being punished as a result. Discussions conducted in Washington, D.C., offices and chambers were totally irrelevant to the stark realities of reservation life in that era. The diseases and despair that were rampant during Ketcham's term as director of the bureau still took their deadly toll. Monsignor Hughes hoped the new administration of President Calvin Coolidge would remedy such situations.

Warren Harding died suddenly in San Francisco on August 2, 1923, after returning from a vacation in Alaska. Calvin Coolidge was sworn in as president and formed his own cabinet. He started his efforts concerning Indian affairs by directing that an independent group begin a thorough assessment of policies and programs.

The universal bestowal of citizenship on all Native Americans in 1924 was the result of the heroic efforts of the thousands of Indians in World War I and demonstrated changing ideas concerning them. Americans still regarded these Native Americans as exotic creatures isolated from the day-to-day life of the nation. Catholics, African Americans, and Jews were also considered alien to the American culture, and demonstrations continued to protest their presence. In 1925, the Ku Klux Klan paraded down Pennsylvania Avenue in Washington, D.C., some thirty five thousand to forty thousand strong.

A year later, in Chicago, the Catholic Church celebrated an International Eucharistic Congress, and the sheer spectacle of it stirred interest. Over a million Catholics were on hand, some arriving from the East Coast on special trains that honored past Catholic heroes. The ceremonies of the Congress were lavish and inspirational and included 57 archbishops and 251 bishops as well as 12 cardinals of the Church. A Mass was celebrated in Soldier Field on the shores of Lake Michigan, accompanied by a choir of sixty-two thousand Catholic schoolchildren.

Also in 1926, the Meriam Report, "The Problem of Indian Administration," requested by President Calvin Coolidge, was released to the American public and received considerable attention. This report assailed allotments, an opinion long held by everyone concerned with Indian affairs, and generally criticized the federal government's handling of Native American needs and concerns. The Meriam Report, however, did not call for an end to the policies but offered some systems and safeguards for improving the overall activities.

Americans heard about the report and conditions on the reservations, but other events distracted them. Herbert Hoover was elected president, defeating the Catholic candidate Alfred E. Smith, and Charles Curtis, a Kansa Indian, was inaugurated as his vice president. On October 29, 1929, the stock market crashed, and by November of that year the Great Depression gripped America. Stocks valued at approximately thirty billion dollars became worthless, and fifteen million Americans were to face unemployment as a result.

The 1930 United States Census reported a Native American population of 332,397, a remarkable display of a renaissance on Indian lands, despite diseases, poverty, and government mismanagement. In that same year, Congress accused the Bureau of Indian Affairs of actually kidnapping Navajo children in order to enroll them in schools in the region. The "Dust Bowl," the vast stretches of arid lands, appeared in Kansas, Nebraska, Texas, Oklahoma, and New Mexico, affecting the reservations in these states. The Great Depression continued, and in 1932, Americans were provided with a stunning image of coast-to-coast suffering and desperation.

Franklin D. Roosevelt became president in 1933 and began a new approach to stem the ravages of the Great Depression. One of his most famous supporters, John Collier, received the appointment he had been seeking. He became the Commissioner of Indian Affairs and promised one and all an "Indian New Deal." Collier began to implement his views on the Native Americans and worked toward proposing a legislative package, the Indian Reorganization Act, or the Wheeler Howard Act. In its final form, the act was passed in 1934 by Congress and reestablished most tribal govern-

149

ment rights, funded the study of Indian culture, reversed allotted lands, and returned other areas to the Native Americans.

Monsignor Ketcham supported Collier's efforts, despite his misgivings about certain aspects. The Catholic missions were not endangered, although problems arose as Native Americans became embroiled in the processes of receiving federal recognition and funding. Distinctions about "blood" status also proved troublesome. While all these bureaucratic activities were taking place, the Bureau of Catholic Indian Missions procured $44,750 in emergency relief funds for the mission schools suffering from the Great Depression.

Monsignor Hughes had worked diligently for the Catholic Indian apostolate, but his fervor and resources had been drained. He resigned from the bureau on June 30, 1935, and returned to California to work with Dr. John Harrington of the Bureau of Ethnology on his Indian myths and costume collection. Less than a year later, in February, 1936, he was appointed as the pastor of St. Catherine's on Catalina Island. The following December he assumed the pastorate of St. Catherine's Parish in Laguna Beach. He labored there in contentment until contracting pneumonia during the winter months of 1938-1939. Complications developed in the spring, and Monsignor William Hughes died on May 6, 1939.

A Mass was celebrated at St. Vibiana's for the repose of Monsignor Hughes's soul on May 9. Over one hundred fifty members of the clergy attended, and messages of condolences came from government officials and missionaries. Monsignor Hughes had clearly demonstrated his "Heart for the Indians" in maintaining seventy Catholic schools on eighty-one Native American reservations and in his day-to-day administration and by conducting the ongoing defense of the Catholic Indian apostolate in the hallowed halls of the United States government.

Father John B. Tennelly

CHAPTER 13

The Looming Darkness

seminaries, earning his Bachelor of Arts in 1910, and Master of Arts degree in 1911. He was ordained to the priesthood in Baltimore, Maryland, on June, 17, 1913.

A year later, Father Tennelly entered the Sulpicians, the pioneering congregation that had responded to the call of America's first bishop, John Carroll, and had started the nation's first seminary. The Sulpicians served the entire American Catholic Church with devout and scholarly concerns, and they welcomed the young priest. He demonstrated intellectual brilliance, academic thoroughness, and dedication, and he would prove himself to be a winning and popular teacher to the new generations of Americans.

Father Tennelly began his religious commitment as an instructor at St. Austin's College in Washington, D.C., and then, in 1915, at St. Mary's University in Baltimore. He earned his Doctorate in Sacred Theology at the Angelicum in Rome in 1917, and became a professor of Sacred Scriptures and Dogmatic Theology at the Sulpician seminary in Washington, D.C., in 1920, serving for a time as rector as well.

In 1925, Father Tennelly was asked to assume the post of Secretary-Treasurer of the Commission for the Catholic Missions

America was still in the grip of the Great Depression in 1935 when Father John B. Tennelly, a Sulpician scholar, was asked by Dennis Cardinal Dougherty and the board of directors of the Bureau of Catholic Indian Missions to become the successor to Monsignor Hughes. The United States was not only poverty stricken but demoralized by the suffering and want. The Native Americans were caught in the debates and activities caused by Collier's "Indian New Deal," and the nation as a whole looked toward Europe, where a barbaric system was rising and threatening world peace.

John Benjamin Tennelly was originally from Colorado, born to Robert and Madeleine Tennelly on June 8, 1890, in Denver. The family moved soon after to Lebanon, Kentucky, where the young man decided very early on to study for the priesthood. He entered St. Gregory's Seminary in Cincinnati, Ohio, at the age of twelve and then attended various other colleges and

Among the Colored People and the Indians, a role that he was able to fulfill along with his professional duties. This commission had been established by the Third Plenary Council of Baltimore and was mandated to take up annual mission collections throughout the parishes of the United States. This was Father Tennelly's first experience with the Native American Catholic missions, and he approached his duties with a precise and scholarly dedication. Monsignor Hughes also conferred with him on bureau matters and was aided by Father Tennelly's historical and philosophical awareness. The two men were totally different in their approaches to current events and problems, but Monsignor Hughes found Father Tennelly's overviews of such concerns to be correct and worthwhile. Monsignor Hughes recommended the Sulpician as his successor.

Upon assuming his duties following Monsignor Hughes's retirement, Father Tennelly contacted the Commissioner of Indian Affairs, John Collier, and stated that he would endeavor to cooperate with him to the best of his ability. He also stressed his interest in maintaining the present "cordial relationship" between the Bureau of Catholic Indian Missions and the government agencies. In 1937, proof of this "cordial relationship" was demonstrated in the fact that the federal subsidies for Catholic Indian schools had increased by $74,100, even as President Roosevelt had reduced all congressional allotments.

At the Bureau of Indian Affairs, Commissioner John Collier was facing struggles of his own, with or without Father Tennelly's cooperation. Critics within other agencies and many outside of Washington voiced their opposition to his reforms and focused on his view of the Native Americans. Such critics condemned Collier for sponsoring a resurgence of paganism and atheism, and some equated his programs with the newest peril facing the world, Communism. Collier could repel such outside attacks, but he was vulnerable within the Native American community, and he was alarmed by what he faced there.

Most of the Oklahoma tribes, many landless, took a dim view of the "Indian New Deal," and they were not reticent in voicing their opinions. These Native Americans had been offered other programs in the past, all announced as solutions or forms of salvation. Some also questioned Collier's views of them as "noble savages" who somehow remained outside of time and history, standing only as relics of forgotten mystical eras of the past. Some seventy-seven Native American tribes apparently refused to endorse the work, education, and training programs offered to them by the Indian Reorganization Act, thus absenting themselves from this new social experiment. That meant that Collier was working with only forty percent of the Indians, thus reducing his program in status and in effectiveness. Many tribes did participate and did benefit from their experiences and opportunities. He needed total cooperation, however, to add credence to the "Indian New Deal," and he faced shortages, cutbacks, and slashed appropriations if the dread clouds of war embraced America as they had other continents of the world.

Father Tennelly did not allow the Bureau of Catholic Indian Missions to become involved in any of the debates concerning Collier and his views, demonstrating a remarkable single-mindedness about the Catholic Indian apostolate amid trends and political intrigue. He preserved all that had been hard-won over the centuries and watched the spreading areas of combat abroad. Even in the Vatican, change was evident in that tense era. Eugenio Cardinal Pacelli became Pope Pius XII in 1939.

In that same year, new avenues opened for evangelization of the Native Americans. Bishop Aloysius Muench of Fargo, North Dakota, instituted this new form of Indian ministry. In time he would become a cardinal of the Church, and in Fargo he was demonstrating his concerns and leadership. Bishop Muench called together a group of missionaries involved in the Indian apostolate — men of experience who understood the need for mutual action, unified programs, support, and inspiration. These veteran missionaries, under the leadership of Bishop Muench, started a new apostolate, a new expression of devotion and unity, called the Tekakwitha Conference. Kateri's canonization cause had been opened in Rome sometime before, and Americans were beginning to hear about the Lily of the Mohawks, as she was known. The Benedictines also joined the Tekakwitha Conference, which evolved through the decades to become a significant factor in the Native American ministry.

In the following year, 1940, there were twenty-one million Catholics in the United States, all sharing to some degree in the recovering economy and relatively free of intolerant assaults from their fellow citizens. It was difficult to start a petty, vindictive campaign against a particular group at the time because of the horrendous spectacle of hatred and cruelty being played out in Asia, Europe, and Africa. The nation was turning to a wartime industrial footing as the Europeans facing the Nazi menace needed supplies. The German-Soviet invasion of Poland on September 1, 1939, resulted in declarations of war by Great Britain and France, prompting Congress to pass a Lend Lease Act on March 11, 1941. President Roosevelt was thus able to transfer munitions and other military equipment to Great Britain even amid calls for neutrality in some American circles.

December 7, 1941, ended all such calls for neutrality in the United States. Pearl Harbor, on the Hawaiian Island of Oahu, was attacked by Japanese planes, which resulted in some eighteen United States ships being sunk or severely damaged, with 2,380 Americans killed in the raids. America was at war and preparing to conduct campaigns on two different fronts, and an estimated sixteen million men and women would serve in the nation's armed forces during World War II. Catholics would make up twenty-five to thirty-five percent of the military personnel in the conflict.

When the war started, Brigadier General (Bishop) William K. Arnold was Chief of Army Chaplains, and 3,270 more priests would serve as "Padres" as well. Some were awarded the Congressional Medal of Honor for their bravery, among which sixty-seven Catholics received the nation's highest military honor.

The Native Americans, having been given United States citizenship in the past, were eligible for the "draft," the compulsory entrance into the armed forces under the Selective Service Act of 1940. By the end of World War II, twenty-five thousand American Indians were on active duty. This figure includes one thousand American Indian women. One such Native American, Clarence Tinker, an Osage, became a brigadier general in the United States Army Air Corps before being killed in combat in 1942. Almost four hundred Osage Indians were in uniform.

Father Tennelly, who was entering into

negotiations with federal agencies to fund twenty-two Native American schools, did not believe that the war would seriously cripple the Indian missions. He refused as well to institute programs for the displaced Native Americans, knowing the war would

A Navajo rug and a ritual sand figure symbol

not last forever. The most prudent response, as far as he was concerned, was to keep the mission schools intact and stable. When the Native Americans returned home, he said, missionaries laboring on eighty reservations would be there to greet them. Francis Cardinal Spellman, as the Catholic Military Vicar of the United States, did spearhead relief services and programs oversees and stateside.

The year 1942 started calamitously, but the Battle of Midway in June brought about the reversal of Japanese naval fortunes. Americans did not know it at the time, but another military front had opened as well, called the Manhattan Project. On the battlefields of war, the Native Americans were serving with distinction and writing new front-line history for the American armed forces.

The Native American code talkers were involved in battlefield communication on all fronts. The most famous was a contingent of Navajo Indians, all U.S. Marines, whose 540 members included between 375 and 420 trained to be code talkers and by 1945 had taken part in every battle in the Pacific Theater of Operations from Guadalcanal to Okinawa. These Navajo code talkers and their counterparts elsewhere served as radiomen. The official communication experts between units and command posts, their messages remained secure because no enemy intelligence measures could be used to decipher the "codes" being used. Actually, the Navajo operators spoke in their own language, incorporating as well several hundred words that identified military objectives, personnel, equipment, or logistical maneuvers. There was no elaborate codebook, no searching for words during transmissions. The Navajos made contact, chatted freely in their own tongue, and kept communications clear. The Chippewa, Comanche, Fox, Hopi, Lakota Sioux, Oneida, and Sauk Native Americans conducted similar radio services in Europe and in the Pacific.

In 1943, despite the ongoing ravages of war, Pope Pius XII declared Kateri Tekakwitha venerable and a Servant of God. Her cause had been forwarded, having been in process in 1938, as noted in *The Positio of the Sacred Congregation of Rites on the Introduction of the Cause for Beatification and Canonization and on the Virtues of the Servant of God Katherine Tekakwitha, the Lily of the Mohawks*. This document stated: "The Servant of God Katherine Tekakwitha, was a North American Indian, a genuine redskin, the first of that great and sorely tried human family to be presented to the Sacred Congregation of Rites as a candidate for the honors of the altar."

Calling Kateri Tekakwitha a "genuine redskin" seems a little odd in light of today's terminology, but it has to be remembered that this was a popular appellation for the Native Americans in times past. Denoting the fact that Kateri was a "genuine redskin" adds a note of wonder and delight as well. Europeans have retained their fascination with the Indians and their view of America's Wild West over the years.

The war progressed, and on June 6, 1944, the Allies landed on the European mainland, in D-Day, which clearly signaled a new phase of the combat. In Denver, Colorado, a group of Indians met to form the National Congress of American Indians. The organization also signaled a change within the Native American community in its perceptions of white policies and in the responses deemed appropriate or necessary.

President Franklin D. Roosevelt died on April 12, 1945, and Harry S. Truman entered the White House as Commander in Chief. He authorized the use of the terrible weapons that resulted from the Manhattan Project, and on August 6, an atom bomb demolished the Japanese city of Hiroshima. The city of Nagasaki was hit by a second bomb three days later, and the Japanese surrendered. As Europe's battles had ceased earlier, the world was at peace. More than 405,000 Americans had given their lives in that conflict. Worldwide the death toll was staggering, particularly as the Holocaust had cost so many innocent civilian lives, including women and children.

The victorious men and women of the American armed services returned home to rebuild their lives and the nation. World War II had served to make such men and women alert to the cruelty and evil rampant in an unguarded world. They had fought and won combative campaigns. Now they had won the peace.

*An Ojibwa tabernacle from L'arbre Croche
(now Harbor Springs), Michigan*

CHAPTER 14

The 'Indian Business'

tions, in industrial, defense, and military structures, and in the nation's resolve in the growing aggression. A Western ally in World War II, the Union of Soviet Socialist Republics (officially dissolved in 1991) was now opposing America and other European nations as it occupied countries and expanded its empire. In the era following surrender of the Axis forces, America was embroiled in what was known as the "Cold War." New imperatives resulting from this Cold War

The end of World War II signaled a new era in Indian affairs in the United States. As early as 1944, members of Congress were demanding an end to Collier's "Indian New Deal," believing that legislation was necessary to provide coherent policies concerning Native American lands and lifestyles. Actually, across the nation more and more officials were speaking of the day when the United States government would be "out of the Indian business" entirely.

There were several reasons for the adoption of this new approach. The war had demonstrated changes in international rela-

prompted Americans to clear up old problems and to streamline policies in order to be prepared for the growing Communist threats. The Native Americans were categorized as "old problems" by many in government, and the policies in their efforts needed to be clarified and modernized.

The Indian Claims Commission, put into effect by Congress in 1946, was the initial effort on the part of the government to overhaul old policies and to implement the newer slogans about Indian self-determination. At the root of this effort were the older concepts concerning the assimilation of the tribes into the American mainstream. The Indians had taken part in the war and in the home-front efforts. They had been introduced to the new inventions, the urban splendors, and the highways of the land. It was unthinkable that after having shared in such fruits they would want to return to their reservation ways.

Assimilation, self-determination for American Indians, and housecleaning in government agencies thus prompted the new approaches, and the Indian Claims Commission was the first tangible effort in the campaign. The commission was mandated to settle old treaty disputes, to resolve land claims, and to regulate matters concerning such lands and issues. The Indian Claims Commission heard pending cases and distributed vast amounts of money in awards. Records indicate that these awards included $14,789,000 to the Cherokee nation, $10,242,000 to the Crow, $3,650,000 to the Snake-Paiute, and $3,000,000 to the Nez Percé. The awards were all monetary, and no actual lands were returned to the tribes as a result.

The Catholic missions were affected by this effort, but the entire school system of the Church came into the national spotlight in the following year, 1947. A Supreme Court decision on a case, *Everson* v. *Board of Education*, brought about a resounding Protestant response. The court ruled that the state of New Jersey could use tax funds to bus Catholic children to Catholic schools. Within a year, the "Protestants and Other Americans for Separation of Church and State," including Paul Blanchard, were issuing warnings about a Catholic takeover of America. President Truman attempted to open diplomatic relations with the Vatican in 1947, going so far as to appoint an ambassador to the Holy See. The furor resulting from the school issue dashed Truman's hopes for such a diplomatic beginning, and no such ambassador was delegated to Rome.

In 1948, Arizona was forced to give Native Americans voting rights, and Americans of all faiths were being entranced by the sermons of Bishop Fulton J. Sheen. The best selling book was Thomas Merton's *The Seven Storey Mountain*. Merton, a Trappist at Gethsemani Abbey in Kentucky, was hailed by one and all as "the American Augustine" and caused a renaissance of spiritual pursuits in the United States.

The Cold War continued to drain the exuberance of the era, as nations across the world sought to maintain a certain military readiness in the face of Communist aggression. The Korean War, starting in 1950, brought home the dangers of the political confrontations taking place around the world. Once again the American military mobilized for devastating battles.

In that same year, in northeastern South Dakota, a Yankton Sioux elder named Blue Cloud followed in the footsteps of Sitting Bull. Blue Cloud owned a rounded hill overlooking the Mission River. As Sitting Bull had done in 1876, Blue Cloud invited the Benedictines to open a school there. The first Benedictines to accept the invitation lived on a small farm and then built an abbey that today bears the Yankton elder's name. Blue Cloud Abbey serves as well as the American Indian Culture Research Center for the area.

Blue Cloud recognized the changes taking place in the world and sought a way to broaden the horizons of the young Yanktons. Other Native Americans were discovering changes and challenges as well. Indian lands were being bombarded with posters and various signs designed to lure them into the white world. Industries seeking workers were part of the campaign, but the underlying policy came from the federal Indian agencies.

Dillon S. Meyer, President Truman's new Commissioner of Indian Affairs, viewed reservations as American "concentration camps" and worked in earnest to put an end to such enclaves. Concerted efforts were thus made to pursue the younger Indians with promises of a good life in the white cities and in the mainstream of society. Meyer's views were supported by the Special Presidential Commission on the Organization of the Executive Branch of Government, which issued the Hoover Report. The relocation of all Indians and the end of federal support for the tribes became the new watchword of this era.

At the Bureau of Catholic Indian Missions, Father Tennelly watched the agencies and officials dismantle Collier's work and begin their own solutions to the "Indian business," but he did not respond publicly. He believed that the Catholic mission schools were the only answer to the problems and refused to embroil the bureau in any response that might endanger these schools.

Father Tennelly believed that Native Americans needed the education provided by the schools if they intended to compete in the white man's world. He also wanted to keep these schools secure for those Indians who decided to return to the reservations. The United States government was free of the financial burdens of the war and could afford the subsidies for such institutions. In 1948, the Catholic Indian day and boarding schools received $91,637 in federal funds. In 1949, the amount allocated was $231,650, and in 1952, the schools received $289,495.

It was prudent therefore, to continue mission work away from the arenas of combat. Another aspect of Blanchard's attack on Catholics alarmed Father Tennelly and other Catholics because it heralded the rise of a new facet of assault. Blanchard and his supporters declared that the Catholics of America were unfit to be part of the great national experiment because the Church taught that there was a source of truth beyond the values of the majority, the scientists, and the secular humanists. Catholic Indian missions and schools fostered such doctrines and were therefore vulnerable to assault by modern idealists.

The Vatican responded as well to the introduction of such changes. Pope Pius XII issued *Evangelii Praecones*, an encyclical concerned with developing a true mission-mindedness among American Catholics. Recognizing the forces arrayed against the Church, the Holy Father called for a balancing counter mentality to protect Catholic interests.

The disastrous legislation passed by the Congress in August, 1953, alerted Father Tennelly to the dangers inherent in the new policies and solidified his resolve to keep a low profile in order to protect school funding. Congress passed House Concurrent Resolution 108 and Public Law 280 in order to institutionalize the policies of the termination of reservations and assimilation of the Native Americans. These legislative enactments were designed to make Indians subject to the same laws, rights, and responsibilities as other citizens of the United States. Their status as wards of the government was to end, and all tribes considered reasonably immersed in modern culture were to be freed from federal supervision, controls, and disabilities or limitations that might impede their journey toward cultural equality with whites. In California, Minnesota, Nebraska, Oregon, and Wisconsin, for example, the states were to receive jurisdiction over criminal and civil matters instead of federal agencies.

The administrations of Truman and his successor, Dwight D. Eisenhower, who entered the Oval Office in 1953, also instituted other policies along the same lines. Some one hundred nine Indian groups were formally recognized by the federal government and received benefits in land-status debates and increased health services. The unrecognized tribes were placed in an administrative limbo, while Native Americans left the reservations in search of economic survival. Between 1952 and 1972, more than a hundred thousand Indians were relocated. Moving into urban areas, these Native Americans began to organize into groups that put aside tribal imperatives and provided the beginnings of tribal survival techniques.

The successor to Meyer in the Bureau of Indian Affairs, Glenn Emmons, was a supporter of the policies and worked with Senator Clinton Anderson of New Mexico to dismantle the status and privileges that were in effect. Emmons pushed for greater assimilation and tried to end the tax exemptions and the privileged status of Indian lands.

Ellis Island, the gateway to America for millions of Americans since 1892, was closed in 1954. In the same

Crow tobacco plan design on a parfleche

year, the Native Americans residing in Maine received the right to vote in elections. One year later, America was involved in the Vietnam War, entering an era of unrest and violence that would unleash new policies and outlooks in the nation.

If Father Tennelly clung to a unified, unwavering position concerning the Catholic Indian missions, he did so because of the upheavals and changes coming to America. Events and personalities intruded upon everyday routines, and new tensions and strident demands were being made throughout the social and political arenas. The pluralism of the past, along with the give-and-take and the positioning of opposing views, was being lost in a new flurry of media coverage and staged demonstrations. Father Tennelly knew that dedication and adherence to the truth of the faith were the only keys to the survival for the Catholic Indian apostolate. He did not appear capable of modernizing approaches or techniques in some instances because he saw the dangers in the new mania of abandoning the past among American leaders. In this he was not alone. Many government, religious, and social institutions in the United States found themselves adrift in new philosophies, new standards, and new expectations.

On October 28,

1958, Giovanni Battista Cardinal Roncalli was elected pope, taking the name John XXIII. His pontificate opened the entire Church to new processes that altered the lives of Catholics everywhere. Vatican Council II, which was opened by Pope John XXIII on October 11, 1962, and continued, with varied interim periods, until September 14, 1965, had a tremendous impact on all aspects of Catholic life, including the mission apostolates.

In the election year of 1960 there were 42,000,000 Catholics in the United States, served by 10 cardinals, 37 archbishops, 306 bishops, 59,892 priests, and 126,517 women religious. John F. Kennedy was elected president of the United States, demonstrating a remarkable reversal of past prejudices that focused on Catholics in general and on the Irish in particular. The era called "Camelot" took hold in Washington society as a result.

The Native Americans recognized the political changes taking place and positioned themselves to press their concerns on the new administration. The appointment of Philleo Nash as the Commissioner of Indian Affairs under President Kennedy aided their cause and promoted their new approaches to the problems facing them. Nash was an anthropologist, a former member of the Task Force on Indian Affairs, and an expert in the studies of Indian religious revivalism. Nash dedicated himself to enlarging government appropriations for educational and resource development and to strengthen tribal operations. He visited reservations and took part in ceremonies and regional and national meetings.

The Native Americans had discovered the value of gatherings and public relations. Many groups were active and visible, including the National Congress of American Indians, which dates to 1944. New organiza-tions were started as well, such as the National Indian Youth Council, formed in Gallup, New Mexico, in 1961, and the American Indian Movement, founded in Minneapolis.

The American Indian Chicago Conference in 1961 pulled together many urban Indian groups and focused on a declaration of Indian purposes. At the same time, another aspect of American preoccupation with Indians lent new interest and popularity to the cause. Groups throughout the United States, and particularly in the Midwest, began to sponsor powwows and other activities that demonstrated Native American cultural traditions. Such events, staged in parks, public centers, and on private estates, allowed whites to wear Indian-style attire and to participate in Indian celebrations. A publication called *American Indian Hobbyist* appeared in 1954, vividly demonstrating the popularity of such activities. The Society of American Indian Traditions assumed the editorship of the publication in 1960, renaming it the *American Indian Tradition*. Other groups and other publications followed.

Vatican Council II, the Cuban Missile Crisis, and John Glenn's space orbiting in *Friendship 7* caught the attention of Americans as well. The nation was plunged into shock and mourning on November 22, 1963, when John F. Kennedy was assassinated. Lyndon Baines Johnson became the president of the United States, and a new era of American politics began. Assassinations of public figures continued, and American streets became scenes of antiwar demonstrations as the Vietnam saga took an even greater toll of military and civilian personnel.

Throughout all of this turmoil, the Native Americans focused on their own purposes and strengthened their positions. The situation was made more dramatic in 1968, when Congress passed Title II of the Indian Civil Rights Act. This particular legislation concerned Indian and non-Indian individuals who lived under tribal jurisdiction. Such individuals were deemed protected by the Bill of Rights, whether they were tribal members or not. This act was comprehensive and was somewhat remiss in certain areas because it was recognized as an intrusion into tribal affairs.

Father Tennelly at the Bureau of Catholic Indian Missions was faced with incredible changes on the social and political stages of the nation. He maintained his steady guardianship of the Catholic Indian schools, keeping them secure and financially supported. The changes taking place among Catholic missionaries, however, troubled Father Tennelly, who could not embrace the growing Indian Rights Movement. He watched with genuine astonishment the Thanksgiving Day demonstrations by Indians on the *Mayflower* replica at Plymouth, Massachusetts, the march called "the Trail of Broken Treaties," the Indian occupation of Alcatraz, and the confrontation at Wounded Knee on the Pine Ridge Reservation in South Dakota.

At the 1974 Tekakwitha Conference, Father Tennelly, now in his eighty-fourth year, was stunned to hear Catholic missionaries assail past efforts in the Catholic Indian apostolate as "impersonal." The year before, 1973, had heralded this new approach. At this gathering many Catholic missionaries had demonstrated their full support of the Native American goals. Father Tennelly did not debate the opinions expressed, but he would not endorse the new approaches and would not fund them.

By 1975, Tennelly was ready to resign the directorship of the bureau. He requested that Cardinal Krol and the board of directors find a successor, although he continued working until July 5, 1976, when Monsignor Paul A. Lenz was named to the post. Father Tennelly retired to St. Charles Villa and then St. Martin Home. He died on October 18, 1981, Mission Sunday, and was buried in the Sulpician seminary at Catonsville. At the funeral, he was praised for his dedication and service. Father Robert Paul Mohan, giving the eulogy, stated:

> The greater part of Father Tennelly's apostolate was served in an older tradition, yet he accepted change with grace, if not enthusiasm. Yesterday's world was perhaps in many ways a simpler world, and his style was primarily adapted to that world. But even the critics of our own time have been known in a later vision of earlier years, to see fidelity and firmness where once they tended to severity and intransigence.

Blessed Kateri Tekakwitha

CHAPTER 15

The Lily of the Mohawks

ity and survival. Monsignor Lenz, unknown to Washington, D.C., and to the Native American community, came to his new responsibilities with a wide range of missionary and administrative experiences. He would need all these skills and acquired abilities in order to revive the bureau and to renew the liaison role of the organization in trying times.

Paul A. Lenz was from Gallitzin, Pennsylvania, named after the dynamic missionary Prince Demetrius Augustine Gallitzin, the "Apostle of the Alleghenies." Paul was the second of six sons, born on December 15, 1925, to Raymond and Aimee Lenz, and was raised in a devout, close-knit family. He was educated in local schools in Gallitzin and in Altoona and then earned a Bachelor of Arts degree at St. Vincent's College in Latrobe, Pennsylvania, in 1946.

Receiving the grace of a vocation and wanting to be near his family after the death of his father, he entered St. Vincent's Seminary and was ordained to the priesthood on April 2, 1949. His first assignments were in local parishes of the diocese, and in 1953 he became curator of the diocesan Prince Gallitzin Chapel at Loretto, a shrine commemorating the life and labors of the "Prince

When Monsignor Paul A. Lenz became the sixth director of the Bureau of Catholic Indian Missions on July 5, 1976, he faced many difficulties within the parameters of the organization and factors in the Native American responses to recent events. The Catholic Indian apostolate was at a crossroads in the nation, and the missions were enduring critical pressures from social and political forces that threatened their stabil-

163

of Pastors." There he labored to coordinate historical materials and to make Prince Demetrius Gallitzin known in the area. Father Lenz also served as the diocesan director of the Society for the Propagation of the Faith.

From 1956 until 1962 he had the additional duties of serving as head of the theology department at Mount Aloysius College, and from 1962 until 1970 taught theology at St. Francis College, Loretto. He was elevated to the rank of domestic prelate, monsignor, on December 16, 1960. At the time he was as an assistant editor of the diocesan newspaper and pastor and administrator of St. Michael's Parish, Loretto.

In 1970, the monsignor's life changed abruptly when he was asked to go to Paraguay by Bishop Jerome Pechillo. Responding to the invitation with enthusiasm and receiving permission from the bishop of Altoona-Johnstown, Monsignor Lenz went to the prelature of Coronel Oviedo, a remote jungle region some one hundred forty miles from Paraguay's capital, Asunción. There, in a primitive jungle wilderness, he learned Spanish and the dialect of the local Guarani Indians and worked in the mission offices.

The Guaranis were being abused tragically by the Paraguayan authorities, and Monsignor Lenz added his protests to those voiced by other Catholic officials. As a result, he and his fellow missionaries were arrested and imprisoned by the authorities, who threatened them with punishments, even death; luckily, their American citizenship saved them from such dire consequences and secured their release in time. The harsh treatment did not silence the Church, however, and did not dampen the priests' commitment. Monsignor Lenz and the other missionaries continued their labors, despite ongoing threats. He was not destined to remain among the Guaranis, however, as another apostolate awaited in his own country.

In 1974, he was recalled to the Altoona-Johnstown diocese to become the pastor of St. John the Evangelist Parish in Bellefonte, and the following year brought yet another, even more drastic change to his life. Monsignor Lenz received a call from John Cardinal Krol, informing him that he was being considered for the office of director of the Bureau of Catholic Indian Missions. When Monsignor Lenz expressed some hesitation, Cardinal Krol assured him that if the "Church calls . . . you should respond." Monsignor Lenz took Father Tennelly's office at the bureau as a result of that call. In accepting the directorship, he was assuming a myriad of difficulties — problems that would demand innovative measures and sustained responses to evolving situations.

The events that had taken place during Father Tennelly's last years as director had not distracted him from his steadfast guardianship of the Catholic Indian missions and schools. He had held firm to his principles in the face of such events, but the Native American communities and the Catholic Indian apostolate had endured impacts on many levels. Such happenings altered views about the roles of the Native Americans and set new agendas for actions. Indians lived through such events and decided upon courses of response that would complicate federal and social programs while establishing new precedents within the Indian communities.

In 1972, Raymond Yellow Thunder was found beaten to death in Gordon, Nebraska. The regional coroner attributed the cause of death to suicide, which meant that somehow Raymond Yellow Thunder had managed to

Monsignor Paul A. Lenz

policy change, made a public statement about the centuries of federal enactments and programs that had altered their routines in each new presidential administration. Three caravans set out across the United States in response to the new policies, converging on Washington, D.C., as a staged "Trail of Broken Treaties." The federal Bureau of Indian Affairs was occupied by members of that Indian caravan and renamed "the Native American Embassy."

In 1973, the American Indian Movement, with two hundred Oglala Sioux, took over Wounded Knee at Pine Ridge Reservation, South Dakota, and held it against U.S. government forces for seventy-one days. The American Indian Movement occupied Alcatraz Island as well in another symbolic assault on government policies. Americans watched these demonstrations, but they were focused on another grave issue: Watergate. The ensuing congressional investigation and the media coverage blunted all other concerns and led to the resignation of Richard Nixon in 1974. President Gerald Ford was in the White House, immediately after, promising an end to the turmoil.

In 1975, yet another legislative policy was introduced, the Indian Self-Determination Act. This legislation ceded oil production, timberland projects, water distribution, and even hydroelectric dams to the control of the local tribes. As a result of the publicity concerning this act, Americans discovered that Indian reservations in the United States were reported to contain half of the

assault himself and to inflict mortal injuries on his own person. This autopsy satisfied local authorities but received public scorn from many outside of the region, particularly the Native Americans. Some eleven hundred Sioux on the Pine Ridge Reservation demonstrated their concerns and ridiculed the coroner and his medical conclusions, leading to media coverage of the affair and national attention. The original autopsy was ruled out as a result and charges of murder were laid against local whites, who were later convicted and imprisoned.

While the Native Americans were coping with the tragedy of Raymond Yellow Thunder, the Indian Education Act, passed in 1972, added new complications to their lives, especially on the reservations. This legislation provided the tribes with a certain level of self-determination and control in school concerns. The Native Americans, viewing this act as just another momentary nation's uranium deposits, ten percent of the oil and gas reserves, and a third of the country's strippable coal. The water deposits, the forests, and pasturage on the reservations also came under the media spotlight. Within the tribes, as a result of the legislation and media coverage, levels of stress emerged alongside the newly granted controls. Native Americans were faced with harsh choices concerning financial security and progress versus traditional lifestyles and the safeguarding of ancient heritages.

The Bureau of Catholic Indian Missions kept watch as these political changes were reflected across the land, but Monsignor Lenz was focusing on the role of his agency in maintaining the network of Catholic Indian missions and schools that anchored the apostolate and served as ongoing symbols of the Church's historical labors. Shocked to discover that bishops in some parts of the United States were unaware of the Bureau of Catholic Indian Missions, Monsignor Lenz started a new program of communications. He personally visited dioceses, supervised the establishment of diocesan liaisons, and in 1978, began the bureau *Newsletter*, a publication that was sent initially to Church leaders, government officials, and mission affiliates. The *Newsletter* started with a distribution of seven hundred names and now reaches twenty thousand individuals with news of Indian mission affairs.

He then turned his attention to the Tekakwitha Conference, the organization that was founded in 1939 and has continued over the decades, despite adversities. Father Tennelly had refused to fund Tekakwitha Conference programs during his last years as director of the bureau, but Monsignor Lenz was determined to see this vital apostolate flourish in all of the Native American communities. In 1976, the Tekakwitha Conference reflected new outlooks and changed considerations, as Indians demanded an increased role in their own affairs. When asked to support a review of past efforts and the exploration of new courses for the future, the Bureau of Catholic Indian Missions responded generously. Monsignor Lenz arranged for a meeting of the leaders in Washington and paid their expenses. Father Gilbert Hemauer, O.F.M. Cap., became the president, assisted by Sister Genevieve Cuny and Deacon Francis Hairy Chin.

Monsignor Lenz attended the Tekakwitha Conference meeting in 1977 and introduced himself, spurring a sense of renewal within the group. Since that time, the Tekakwitha Conference has grown and expanded and has offered new insights into the political and social problems facing the Native Americans. By 1980, at Denver, Colorado, the potential of the Tekakwitha Conference was manifesting itself to the more than six hundred Native Americans present. At this tribal gathering, Mass was celebrated and then tribal ceremonies performed to honor the cultural traditions of the past. The Association of Native Religious was supported by the members of the Tekakwitha Conference, and social issues of concern to Native American communities were openly addressed.

In this modern era, the conference is directed by the Native Americans, with support of the Bureau of Catholic Indian Missions and other affiliated Church agencies. The Tekakwitha Conference is a functioning organization that is able to unite the Native Americans while promoting tribal differences and varied native spiritual traditions. As a group, the conference members can also address issues and conduct ongoing communications with the American Catholic hierarchy.

One of the singular apostolates of the Tekakwitha Conference is the promotion of the Kateri Circles, the organizations formed on reservations and in urban centers. These circles are involved in making evident Native American heritage and wisdom. The Bureau of Catholic Indian Missions supports the Kateri Circles and provides them with monthly agendas for the meetings. Monsignor Lenz recognizes the value of these active organizations. They are echoing Pope John Paul II's call to make known the richness of the Indian presence in the faith. The conferences and the circles also seek to heal the wounds inflicted upon the Native Americans in the past eras of the United States. This unusual and vital apostolate is centered in the faith and is critical, deserving support of Catholics throughout the country. The past will remain a vital element in Indian life, but the members of the Tekakwitha Conference recognize the future of grace now opening to them. The conference is also focusing on the urban centers serving the Indians estranged from their own people. (For a list of the Kateri Circles, see Appendix 3.)

While the bureau and the Tekakwitha Conference were exploring avenues of new cooperation, the political attitudes of Washington were changing again. The American Indian Review Policy Commission, reinvigorating Collier's views of the past, declared in 1977 that Native American tribes were sovereign political bodies, entities that must be protected by the federal government in order to maintain their ancient spirituality and cultures.

The following year, 1978, the American Indian Freedom of Religion Act came into being. This legislation provided recognition of traditional religious practices of the tribes and declared them protected under the First Amendment of the Constitution. Under this act, tribes were entitled to use the skins and feathers of federally protected animals in religious rites, were entitled to use peyote for ceremonial purposes, and could preserve sacred lands for religious use. Monsignor Lenz testified at federal hearings in support of the act and hired Jesuit Father Ted Zuern to serve as a liaison with Congress, monitoring all legislation concerning Native Americans and to write of ongoing enactments.

Recognizing the cultural and religious heritage of the surviving tribes of the nation did not repudiate the centuries of the Catholic Indian apostolate in America. The Bureau of Catholic Indian Missions was dedicated to preserving the cultural heritage of the tribes in many ways, while promoting the evangelizing efforts so valiantly demonstrated by the great missionaries of the past. The bureau's efforts were seconded by the National Conference of Catholic Bishops in May, 1977. (See Appendix 4.)

Kateri Tekakwitha, a shining light for the Native Americans, took her place of honor in the Universal Church three years later. In Rome, the splendor of Kateri Tekakwitha shone for the faithful everywhere. On June 22, 1980, Pope John Paul II beatified Kateri, raising her to the altars as the Lily of the Mohawks.

Kateri Tekakwitha was a convert to the Church and a mystic who lived in North America long before the United States came into existence. She was born in Ossernenon (Auriesville), New York, about 1656, the daughter of a Mohawk war chief and an Algonquin Christian woman, Kahenta. When Kateri was only four years old, an epidemic of smallpox ravaged the Mohawk settlements, killing her parents and a brother and leaving her with a scarred face and damaged eyesight. She was young and vulnerable but a high-ranking Mohawk maiden, and was cared for by an uncle and his family. Kateri grew up in a kindly environment, and she learned all the tribal traditions concerning her rank and her expected role.

She was gentle, popular, and esteemed until she began to refuse the offers of marriage made by young men of her tribe. This continued obstinacy troubled her relatives because it went contrary to the accepted role of women among the Mohawks. When Kateri approached the newly arrived missionary at Ossernenon, Jesuit Jacques de Lamberville, for baptism, her family was further alienated. Kateri became a Catholic and then began to display the intense ardor and mystical gifts that would become the hallmarks of her spiritual life.

Such alien ways enraged the Mohawks of her community, of course, and Kateri began to endure various forms of abuse. The torments from rejected suitors reached such a level that Father de Lamberville enlisted the aid of visiting Christian Indians and sent Kateri to the mission of Sault Ste. Marie near Montreal, Canada. This journey on foot took Kateri four hundred miles to the north. There she grew spiritually, confounding many who could not reconcile her profound mystical gifts to their wilderness setting. A little over a year after her baptism, Kateri received her First Communion, on Christmas Day, 1677, and this union with Christ in the sacraments added to her spiritual graces. In 1679, she took a vow of chastity and even asked to be allowed to enter religious life, a request that was declined.

Kateri Tekakwitha died at Caughnawaga, near Montreal, Quebec, New France (Canada), on April 17, 1680. As she lay in state in the mission, her face took on a clear luster. Word of her demise spread quickly among both Indians and whites with this simple phrase: "The saint is dead." She was declared venerable by Pope Pius XII and beatified by Pope John Paul II.

The Bureau of Catholic Indian Missions, the Tekakwitha Conference, and Monsignor Lenz have promoted Kateri's cause over the decades, and many Native Americans made a special pilgrimage to Rome, sponsored by the bureau, to witness the magnificent ceremonies conducted in her honor there. At the beatification rites, Pope John Paul II declared:

> This wonderful crown of new Blesseds, God's bountiful gift to his Church, is completed by the sweet, frail yet strong figure of a young woman who died when she was only twenty-four years old: Kateri Tekakwitha, the Lily of the Mohawks, the Iroquois maiden, who in seventeenth-century North America was the first to renew the marvels of sanctity of Saint Scholastica, Saint Gertrude, Saint Catherine of Siena, Saint Angela Merici, and Saint Rose of Lima, preceding, along the path of Love, her great spiritual sister, Thérèse of the Child Jesus.
>
> She spent her short life partly in what is now the state of New York and partly in Canada. She was a kind, gentle and hard-working person, spending her time working, praying and meditating. At the age of twenty she received Baptism. Even when following her tribe in the hunting seasons, she continued her devotions, before a rough cross carved by herself in the forest. When her family urged her to marry, she re-

plied very serenely and calmly that she had Jesus as her only spouse. This decision, in view of the social conditions of women in the Indian tribes at that time, exposed Kateri to the risk of living as an outcast and in poverty. It was a bold, unusual and prophetic gesture: on 25 March 1679, at the age of twenty-three, with the consent of her spiritual director, Kateri took a vow of perpetual virginity, as far as we know the first time that this was done among the North American Indians.

The last months of her life were an ever clearer manifestation of her solid faith, straightforward humility, calm resignation and radiant joy, even in the midst of terrible sufferings. Her last words, simple and sublime, whispered at the moment of death, sum up, like a noble hymn, a life of purest charity: "Jesus, I love you. . . ."

Full of deeply felt joy we thank God who continues to bestow bountifully the gift of holiness on the Church, and we bow reverently to venerate the new Blesseds, whose spiritual portrait we have sketched briefly. Let us listen docilely to the message they address to us by the power of their witness. Really, by means of faith their hearts opened generously to the Word of God and they became Christ's dwelling, and, rooted and based in charity, they reached a particular depth of knowledge and understanding of the mysterious divine plan of salvation, and knew the love of Christ that surpasses all knowledge (cf. Eph 3:17-19). On this day of glory they remind us that we are all invited and bound to pursue the holiness and perfection of our own state (cf. *Lumen Gentium*, 42), and that the Church, which lives in time, is missionary by her very nature and must follow the same path followed by Christ, that is, the way of poverty, obedience, service and self-sacrifice until death (cf. *Ad Gentes*, 15).

O Blesseds, whom the pilgrim Church glorifies and exalts today, give us the strength to imitate your limpid faith, when we find ourselves in moments of darkness; your serene hope, when we are disheartened by difficulties; your ardent love of God, when we are tempted to idolize creatures; your delicate love of brothers, when we would like to shut ourselves up in our selfish individualism!

O Blesseds, bless your countries those of your origin, and those given to you by God, like the "Promised Land" to Abraham, and which you loved, evangelized and sanctified!

O Blesseds, bless the whole Church, a pilgrim that is awaiting her lasting Country!

O Blesseds, bless the world, which is hungry and thirsty for holiness!

Blessed Joseph of Ancheta, Blessed Mary of the Incarnation, Blessed Peter de Betancur, Blessed François de Montmorency Laval, Blessed Kateri Tekakwitha, pray for us!

In a special audience for the Native Americans attending the beatification, the Holy Father stated:

169

Dear brothers and sisters in Christ,

It is a joy for me to meet today with all of you, representatives of the North American Indians of Canada and the United States. I greet you in the name of Christ. . . . When you return home, please tell your families and friends that the Pope loves them, and that he invokes upon them joy and strength in the Holy Spirit. You have made this long journey to Rome to participate in a special moment in the history of your people. You have come to rejoice in the beatification of Kateri Tekakwitha. It is time to pause and give thanks to God for the unique culture and rich human tradition which you have inherited, and for the greatest gift anyone can receive, the gift of faith. Indeed, Blessed Kateri stands before us as a symbol of the best of the heritage that is yours as North American Indians. But today is also a day of great happiness for the Church throughout the world. All of us are inspired by the example of this young woman of faith who died three centuries ago this year. We are all edified by her complete trust in the providence of God, and we are encouraged by her joyful fidelity to the Gospel of our Lord Jesus Christ. In a true sense, the whole Church, together with you, says, "Glory be to him whose power, working in us, can do infinitely more than we can imagine; glory be to him from generation to generation in the Church and in Jesus Christ forever and ever" (Eph. 3:20-21). The Church has declared to the world that Kateri Tekakwitha is blessed, that she lived a life on earth of exemplary holiness and is now a member in heaven of the Communion of Saints who continually intercede with the merciful Father on our behalf.

Her beatification should remind us that we are called to a life of holiness, for in Baptism, God has chosen each one us "to be holy and spotless and to live through love in his presence" (Eph. 1:4). Holiness of life — union with Christ through prayer and works of charity — is not something reserved to a select few among the members of the Church. It is the vocation of everyone.

My brothers and sisters, may you be inspired by the life of Kateri. Look to her for an example of fidelity; see in her a model of purity and love; turn to her in prayer assistance. May God bless you as He blessed her. May God bless all the North American Indians of Canada and the United States.

Blessed Kateri Tekakwitha is a unique figure in the Catholic Indian missions of America, and she stands as an enigma and a wondrous chosen soul from the nation's past. No stereotypes can be applied to this mystic, who confounded her contemporaries and unites her own people, believers and non-believers, even today. The Tekakwitha Conference promotes her spirit, her dedication, and her cause among the Native Americans. Blessed Kateri's authentic Catholicity also appeals to Americans of all races, and groups and individuals across the land are joined in praying for her eventual canonization.

The Native Americans across the country are involved as well in offering prayers and good works for that intention. The

Blessed Kateri Tekakwitha League at the Martyrs Shrine in Auriesville, New York, serves as a powerful resource for the ongoing program. (The shrine is also known as the Auriesville Shrine and the National Shrine of the North American Martyrs.) Jesuit John J. Paret is the American vice-postulator for the cause of Blessed Kateri, and he serves that cause at Auriesville. There he publishes a newsletter, the *Lily of the Mohawks*, to keep the faithful aware of activities and devotions relating to the ongoing efforts. Father Paret also conducts novenas and promotes the cause of Kateri through letter writing campaigns and the marketing of devotional books and articles. The Auriesville apostolate encourages the Native Americans in seeking the spiritual horizons evident in the life of the Lily of the Mohawks.

Following the celebrations honoring Blessed Kateri in June, 1980, Monsignor Lenz and the Bureau of Catholic Indian Missions turned again to the massive task of providing for the Catholic Indian schools in the various dioceses. Federal funding for these schools had steadily dwindled and then ceased at the beginning of Monsignor Lenz's term as director. By 1983, in fact, the four Catholic secondary schools and the forty-three primary schools were threatened financially. To aid the situation, Monsignor Lenz founded the Association of Catholic Indian Schools in June of that year and supplemented school incomes through direct mail campaigns, personal appeals, and wills of request. The campaigns secured the future of all but one school.

Funding such massive mission and education programs made it necessary for the Bureau of Catholic Indian Missions to find not only new avenues of support but to openly defend the traditional collection methods designed in the past. Monsignor Lenz was able to finance the bureau's new efforts to educate and integrate Native Americans into the various structures of the Church. Honoring Monsignor Lenz's initiative and leadership in this endeavor, Rome conferred the rank of papal chamberlain upon him (the highest monsignorial rank) on December 10, 1982.

One of the first efforts undertaken was the support of the Sioux Spiritual Center at Plainview, South Dakota. This retreat house and educational institution provides leadership programs for Native Americans in liturgical apostolates and educates candidates for the permanent diaconate. The Sioux Spiritual Center was in need of textbooks designed especially for the Native American diaconate candidates. Jesuits Patrick McCorkell, John Hatcher, and Tibor Horvath designed a series of such texts, and the bureau funded the printing and distribution of the books throughout the country. A fund for Indian seminarians was also established. The Sioux Spiritual Center has trained a large number of Native American deacons, who serve the missions among their own tribes.

Another goal adopted by Monsignor Lenz and the Bureau of Catholic Indian Missions was the introduction of Native Americans to the episcopacy in the American Church. On February 24, 1986, Pope John Paul II appointed Father Donald E. Pelotte, S.S.S., an Abenaki Indian, as the coadjutor bishop of Gallup, New Mexico. A former provincial of the Congregation of the Blessed Sacrament, Bishop Pelotte is a distinguished author and scholar. In 1990, he became bishop of the Gallup diocese, and on September 4, 1999, Bishop Pelotte ordained his twin brother, Dana, to the priesthood in Waterville, Maine.

On July 26, 1988, the second Native American priest, a Capuchin Franciscan, Charles J. Chaput, was ordained as the bishop of Rapid City, South Dakota. In April, 1997, Bishop Chaput was installed as the archbishop of Denver, Colorado. He is a member of the Prairie Band Potawátomi Tribe and is a well-known retreat master and theologian.

In 1984, Catholics witnessed another event in Washington, D.C., when Archbishop (later Cardinal) Pio Laghi, the apostolic delegate to the United States, became the apostolic nuncio or pro-nuncio and presented his full credentials to the United States government. Full diplomatic relations were at long last established between the Vatican and the United States of America. The Vatican was very much evident in the United States three years later, when Pope John Paul II visited Miami, Columbia (South Carolina), New Orleans, San Antonio, Phoenix, Los Angeles, Monterey, San Francisco, and Detroit. At each stop, the Holy Father addressed Americans intimately and lovingly.

In Phoenix, Arizona, the pope met with more than ten thousand Native Americans at the Veteran's Memorial Coliseum. Some two hundred tribes were represented at the gathering in which the Indians greeted the Holy Father face to face. Emmett White, a Pima medicine man from the Gila River Reservation, opened the ceremonies with a ceremonial fire and eagle feather ritual. Bishop Donald Pelotte officially greeted Pope John Paul II, and then Mrs. Alfretta M. Antone, vice president of the Salt River Pima-Maricopa Indian Community, spoke

Taos Pueblo elk-hide robe, Ute style

on behalf of Catholic Native Americans. Mrs. Antone recounted the missionary efforts over the centuries and the fact that thousands of Indians had chosen the Catholic way of walking with Christ.

The Native Americans at the papal audience asked for cultural empowerment and the realization that the Indian traditions could be translated into Catholic liturgical observances. The Holy Father responded to their requests by declaring: "The cultural oppression, the injustice, the disruption of your life and your traditional societies must be acknowledged." He added that the Church is enriched by the presence of Native Americans, and he urged the Indians of the nation to seek their spiritual and moral goals and to trust in their own future. It was noted that the Catholic Native Americans have taken steps to conduct an evangelical apostolate within their own ranks. Witnessing the tragic past and the legacy of disruptions and forced relocation, these American Indians have not retreated from the faith. Rather, they are now exploring new avenues of participation in the Church and new evangelical apostolates. Pope John Paul II recognized the potential of such renewal, and he urged the Native Americans to seek their spiritual horizons and to hone their traditional and cultural skills. The missions operating on the modern reservations, the urban Native American centers, and the diocesan Indian ministry offices encourage this awareness and this powerful resolve.

The federal government was working at the same time to secure the treasures of the Native Americans. In 1989, President George Bush signed a measure mandating the Smithsonian Institute to erect and furnish an Indian museum on the National Mall. In the following year, the Native American Graves Protection and Repatriation Act was passed with President Bush's support. The act declared that all five thousand federally funded museums had to return sacred and cultural objects, including human remains, to individual owners or tribes that could demonstrate prior claims. All trafficking in Indian remains or artifacts assumed the status of federal crimes with severe penalties.

The Native American Graves Protection and Repatriation Act was a great step forward in the government's treatment of Indians and it was deemed a certain atonement for past crimes. Over the decades, the heads of Native Americans were sent to Washington, D.C., for forensic studies, thus marking the Indians as alien beings warranting scientific analysis. The graves of ancestors were despoiled by federal units or by avid speculators and collectors. Such practices were not only at an end, but beloved ancestors were being restored to their tribes.

In May, 1999, for example, the skeletal remains of 1,912 people exhumed more than sixty years earlier were returned to Pecos National Historical Park. Members of the Pueblo nation and delegates from other tribes walked for three days from Jemez to the park, escorting their ancestors to their restored resting places. Other repatriations of Native American remains are planned, as some seven hundred museums have submitted inventories of skeletons and sacred artifacts. The Smithsonian Institute alone has repatriated more than 3,225 skeletons since 1990.

Efforts to establish rules and procedures to restore all of the Native American remains and artifacts and to halt looting or development of sacred sites are being made. The various sciences involved in anthropological, archaeological, and forensic studies are also training students to be aware of the status of the Native Americans and to remain sensitive to legal and human rights.

Also in 1990, the Federation of Catholic Indian Leaders and the Native American Native Religious organization were formed. In the following year, the United States Census reported 1,959,234 Native Americans in the nation, a demonstration of the resurgence of the Indians and the revitalization of their tribal communities. Some of these tribes gathered in Albuquerque, New Mexico, in 1991, to demand a new level of spiritual determination and to protest against the development of oil fields, mines, gas companies' roads, and telescopic foundations that Indians believe threaten the ecological balance of their lands and intrude upon sacred sites. The National Congress of American Indians and the Native American Rights Fund supported the conclusion of the Albuquerque gathering.

In 1992, a group of Native Americans went to Rome to ask the Vatican to force the United States to guarantee greater freedom of religious practices. This pilgrimage to Rome was perhaps prompted by the message given to all native peoples by Pope John

Paul II. When the Holy Father met with Inuits and Metis in the frozen lands of the far north in September, 1987, his words had profound meaning for the Indians when he declared:

> For untold generations, you the native peoples have lived in a relationship of trust with the Creator, seeing the beauty and the richness of the land as coming from his bountiful hand as deserving wise use and conservation. Today you are working to preserve your traditions and consolidate your rights as Aboriginal peoples. . . . As native peoples you are faced with a supreme test: that of promoting the religious, cultural and social values that uphold your human dignity and ensure your future well-being. Your sense of sharing, your understanding of human community rooted in the family, the . . . relationships between your elders and your young people, your spiritual view of creation, which calls for responsible care and protection of the environment — all of these traditional aspects of your ways of life need to be preserved and cherished.
>
> This concern with your native life in no way excludes your openness to the wider community. It is a time of reconciliation, for new relationships of mutual respect and collaboration in reaching a truly just solution to unresolved issues. . . . The pioneering efforts of the missionaries — to whom once again the Church expresses her profound and lasting gratitude — have given rise among you to living communities of faith and Christian life. The challenge is to become more active in the life of the Church . . . [to] become more effective witnesses of God's kingdom of love, justice, peace, forgiveness and human solidarity.

Father Pierre Jean De Smet's banner

CHAPTER 16

The New Apostolate

Mission San Xavier del Bac has weathered decades of storms and droughts, invasions and rebellions, and the splendors of the liturgical seasons that filled the Arizona desert with hymns of praise. This great bastion of the faith still serves the Native Americans of the region, surrounded by newer enclaves of the Church raised up by later generations. An architectural marvel and a cherished treasure of the southwestern region of the United States, San Xavier del Bac symbolizes the Catholic Indian apostolate in a unique fashion. The historical significance of the mission, its noted isolation over the centuries, and its endurance as a haven of the faith mark San Xavier del Bac as a striking symbol of the Catholic Indian apostolate in the new millennium.

In this age, the roles of governments, social and religious institutions, and individual citizens have been altered by modern technology and the new priorities. Moreover, the physical wilderness of the American continent has vanished over the centuries, as towns and cities formed by immigrants and new lands claimed for growing populations moved in. There is a new wilderness in the nation, however, having little to do with geological splendors or untrammeled regions. The barren landscape evident in America, and mirrored in other areas of the modern world, has to do with the spirit. The new millennium opened in America in a certain wilderness of the heart and mind, where the old certainties and the courageous adherence to the truths of faith are challenged daily by secular demands and doubts about the values that govern the human society.

In order to survive in the modern eras, not as a relic of older times but as a vital force for evangelization and authentic faith, the Catholic Indian apostolate has undergone dramatic changes and reformations. The traditional aspects of the apostolate remain firmly in place, but the Bureau of Catholic Indian Missions and other groups across the

175

country are demonstrating a maturing awareness of the challenges and opportunities of the new millennium.

The Catholic missions established so long ago have served the Native Americans since the earliest eras of this apostolate. Many of these original havens of the faith, such as San Xavier del Bac, stand as sentinels of commitment and devotion from times long past. Others have been erected to meet more modern needs, adapted to new approaches and to the leadership of the Native Americans themselves.

The Oblates and the Benedictines, for example, have broadened their horizons of service beyond the traditional parish approach. In Sisseton, South Dakota, the Oblates of Mary Immaculate have established a variety of ministries for the Sisseton-Whapeton Sioux. Originally the Oblates conducted the Tekakwitha Children's Home for orphaned and underprivileged Native American boys and girls. With the introduction of foster care programs, the home was adapted to other pressing needs, such as adolescent drug and alcohol treatment. The Oblates then added a thrift store and food pantry and a program to promote the sale of Native American art. Parish and religious education programs continue, side by side with centers providing meals for the hungry. At White Earth Reservation, the Oblates serve the Ojibwa and Chippewa Native Americans of Minnesota with similar approaches. This mission provides ongoing parish activities, religious education, youth programs, and various aid projects to local families.

The Benedictines at Blue Cloud Abbey in Marvin, South Dakota, reside in a monastic setting begun in 1950. The abbey bears the name of an elder of the Yankton tribe who provided the land. Blue Cloud was designed as a home for the Benedictine missionaries serving the Native Americans in the Dakotas. The Benedictines arrived in the area in the 1870s and labored on four reservations. Blue Cloud serves modern Native Americans as a retreat center, parish ministry program, and as a summer camp.

The era of dedicated missionaries thus lives on in America. The modern priests and religious no longer face hostile tribes or murderous English colonial governments, but the day-to-day apostolate commitments take their own toll. The Native Americans of Montana and Alaska, for example, recently mourned the loss of one such dedicated evangelizer. Father Bernard Francis "Barney" McMeel, a Jesuit missionary and pastor, died in 1994 after decades of commitment and service. A licensed bush pilot and ham operator, Father Barney was born in Great Falls, Montana, and was ordained to the Society of Jesus in Spokane. He was assigned to the arduous Alaska missions in 1955. There he traveled on the vast mission circuits by dogsled and then by plane. Father Barney also served as a chaplain to the members of the United States armed forces on duty at the defense outpost called the DEW (Distant Early Warning) Line. For five years he was the Alaska Jesuit superior, directing the far-flung mission apostolate in the forty-ninth state. Father Barney was made pastor of St. Paul's Parish (Indian Mission) in Hays, Montana, in 1979. He remained part of that Native American community until his death on January 6, 1994. A memorial now stands in front of St. Paul's Mission Church to honor his life of service.

In June, 1999, the Native Americans of New Mexico suffered the loss of another modern apostle when Father Bernard Loughrey died in his sleep at Isleta Pueblo. Beloved in the area, Father Loughrey had come to New Mexico from Philadelphia, Pennsylvania. Ordained in Philadelphia, he had volunteered for the Native American missions and was assigned to Isleta Mission. There he renovated St. Augustine Church, maintained the parish, and welcomed visitors and dignitaries to the historic site. Eleven priests, including Father Loughrey's brother Tom, also a priest, concelebrated the funeral Mass. Monsignor Lenz then expressed the sympathy of the Native Americans and the Bureau of Catholic Indian Missions.

Monsignor Lenz and the bureau maintain support and contact with missionaries such as Father Barney and Father Loughrey. The missions operating today serve the modern Indian reservations or large Native American populations within certain dioceses. Such a network of missions includes the original foundations of past historical periods and newer missions to serve modern evangelical imperatives.

The Catholic dioceses in the state of Montana, for example, have not surrendered their historical mission apostolates, despite the ongoing changes and pressures of the modern world. St. Labré, St. Ignatius, St. Mary's at Rocky Boy, and St. Anne's are serving the Native American agencies and communities, alongside numerous other missions and ministries. In the Dakotas, once a wild terrain, the missions operating today mirror decades of Native American history at Wounded Knee, Fort Totten, Belcourt, Fort Yates, Rosebud, and elsewhere.

In the far north region of Alaska, the missions serve almost every parish outside of the city of Anchorage because such communities are the historical abodes of that state's Indian populations. The missions of Fairbanks serve Nome, Bush Village, Newtok, Hooper Bay, and other locales, and missions are thriving in Juneau, St. John's Prince of Wales Island, and the Northern Indian Mission Territory.

The dioceses of California maintain the famed missions of *El Camino Real* ("The Highway"), the trail of faith blazed by Blessed Junípero Serra and his Franciscan companions. There are also mission parishes on the Cauhilla, Soboba, and other reservations. In Arizona, the San Carlos Apaches, the Tohono O'odham Reservation Indians, and other Native Americans are served by a network of missions that stand proudly beside San Xavier del Bac. The famed missions of New Mexico, part of the American Southwest territory, dating to the earliest eras of the Catholic Indian apostolate, receive diocesan support and the dedicated efforts of mission priests and religious.

The state of Minnesota, along with the Great Lakes regions of America, has a long and complex history of evangelization. The missions there, as in Oklahoma, Utah, and the states east of the Mississippi River, are supported by dioceses and the Offices of Indian Ministry in the various locales.

Such Offices of Indian Ministry offer unique opportunities for furthering the Catholic Indian apostolate. In Michigan, for instance, the combined resources of the archdiocese of Detroit and the diocese of Grand Rapids provide the Native Americans of the state with a variety of programs and gatherings. The *Native American News*, published in conjunction with the combined efforts, communicates announcements about activities and promotes the cause of Blessed Kateri Tekakwitha.

The Michigan Tekakwitha Conference was held in 1999 at Lake Huron, focusing on the needs and aspirations of the local tribes. Other activities included a *She she behn-Kweh kush weh win*, a traditional Duck

Nootka painted panel

Race, with a picnic sponsored by the Grand River Bands of Ottawa Indians. In Port Huron, the Blue Water Indian Celebration was held in August, and an Autumn Moon Festival evoked the spirits of the past when it was conducted at the CYO camp at Sanilac Township.

Such programs provide solidarity, traditional ceremonies, and companionship for the Native Americans. The Michigan combined resources offer Native American Masses and gatherings announced with this admonition: "Please bring memories!" The ministry also includes "God's Kitchen Mobile Food Pantry," and traditional home blessings upon request by the Morningstar Kateri and Detroit Tekakwitha Circles.

As in the past, the Franciscans, famed for the missions of Florida, the Southwest, and California, remain at their posts with unsung devotion. The Jesuits, pioneers in the early apostolate from coast to coast, have not forsaken the sacrifices of their martyrs and have maintained their original ministries and taken on apostolates demanded by the times.

The Bureau of Catholic Indian Missions has long served the Native Americans as the guardian and defender of the varied schools opened across the nation by missionaries. The battles against religious intolerance and federal bureaucratic interference were heightened in some eras by the ongoing and prevailing views of political leaders in power. Maintaining schools for relocated tribes proved impossible in some instances, while in others the missionaries and religious educators were able to load the schools onto wagons and set out to the place of exile with their students.

Funding the schools has always been part of the mandated duties of the bureau, sometimes with help from missionaries such as St. Katharine Drexel and at other times through innovative measures. Native American schools are now involved in massive fund-raising campaigns themselves, using modern communication techniques. Native American websites for schools, tribal cultures, declarations of purpose, and general history are readily available today.

The Native American urban centers are another adjunct to the modern apostolate. These centers, located in cities and towns all across the country, provide services for the Indians living in modern settings, cut off from the traditions and ceremonies of their reservations. The various tribal centers serve much the same purpose in America's cities and towns. The Tekakwitha Conference and other Catholic organizations receive support and members from the urban areas alongside the traditional Native American homelands.

The Bureau of Catholic Indian Missions maintains the same level of service for the Indian missions, ministries, and schools today as in the past. The bureau is mandated to assist these educational institutions financially, but added concerns and familiarity with the local regions and tribes prompts Monsignor Lenz to visit the apostolic centers as often as possible and to labor in the political and social arenas for their advancement.

Part of this educational apostolate involves cooperation with people of other faiths. At such sessions, the bureau can explain the purpose of the Native American schools, seek unified programs or efforts for their continuance, and blunt any lingering bias toward the Church and the Native Americans. The bureau also keeps an up-to-date analysis of legislative actions, federal or statewide, on matters pertaining to Indian affairs. Such analyses are included in the monthly newsletter sent out to Native Americans and interested groups.

The banner of faith unfurled by Father Pierre Jean De Smet and other dedicated missionaries and martyrs is not lost to time. Father De Smet and his missionary counterparts across the nation bequeathed the Church and the Native Americans a heritage of honor, devotion, and vigor. It appears that this "greatest friend" of the American Indians left another cherished gift as well, one recently uncovered.

Monsignor Paul Lenz and the staff members of the Bureau of Catholic Indian Missions were alerted recently to the presence of this gift. Mark Thiel, an assistant archivist at Marquette University in Milwaukee, Wisconsin, who aids Monsignor Lenz in projects, called the bureau to discuss an inquiry concerning a gilded Blessed Sacrament banner supposedly carried by Father De Smet on his mission rounds. Mark, who serves as a valued resource person for the bureau, relayed the story of the banner as well, prompting an immediate search.

In 1840, according to available records, Father De Smet, who distributed holy cards, prayers, and pious illustrations throughout his mission territories, stopped at a Lakota village in Wyoming and gave the banner to a tribal leader. This banner was treasured and passed from father to son in the Native American family, eventually coming into the possession of a Dakota Sioux woman, Marie McLaughlin, the wife of a former agent on Standing Rock Reservation. In 1910, Mrs. McLaughlin displayed the beautiful banner at the Catholic Sioux Congress. The work, featuring a communion chalice, colorful flowers designed in cross stitch and glass beads, bordered by a metallic fringe, was presented to Monsignor William Ketcham, the bureau director at the time. He put it away carefully, and the banner disappeared from view.

Not having seen the banner, Monsignor Lenz and his assistants began a diligent search. It was located in the bureau building attic by assistant treasurer Miss Patricia O'Rourke. The De Smet banner has since been cleaned and placed in a protective covering to preserve it for all time. That symbol of faith represents the bureau and the entire panorama of the Indian mission apostolate.

The men and women in the mission fields and in the bureau have learned Father De Smet's other secrets in dealing with the American Indians and their lifestyles as well. He went among them as a Christ-bearer, asking only that they consider the truth of his words and his beliefs. Father De Smet, in turn, honored the Native Americans for their unique strengths and their wisdom.

Pope John Paul II communicated the same sense of respect and honor when he urged the Indian peoples to seek their spiritual horizons and to enrich the Church with their presence. The Holy Father demonstrated that message in quite dramatic terms during the last days of October, 1999. In the Vatican City State, the Holy Father welcomed leaders of the world's faiths to a meeting concerning religious persecutions and the abuse of fellow human beings in the name of faith. Christians, Hindus, Jews, Muslims, Buddhists, and members of other religious groups gathered to discuss intolerance, "holy wars," and wholesale crimes inflicted supposedly in God's cause during the past centuries. On the last day of the gathering, the religious leaders called for an end to such travesties, declaring them unproductive and injurious. The leaders then took part in a unique ceremony that expressed their unity of purpose.

Pope John Paul II, seated with other participants, watched as colorful circles of lamas and religious formed undulating circles, representing patterns of prayers and religious joy. Then a single figure appeared in the center of these circles, acknowledging the sincerity and the resolve of all. There, before the pope and people of all faiths, a lone Native American, in ceremonial regalia, lifted up his eyes and began the ancient Indian ritual of saluting the four corners of the world. One American Indian stood in the heart of the ceremony, invited by the Holy Father to send good will to all people and to enrich the believers of all faiths in every land with the heritage of the Native Americans and with the wisdom born of suffering, endurance, and loyalty to the memories of their ancient forebears.

Mississippi shell with crested woodpeckers,
the guardians of the four corners of the earth

Sioux Chief Short Bull and his traditional shirt

Indian Missions to 1908

served by French missionaries and linked in this apostolate with Arkansas, Louisiana, Mississippi, and Missouri. (See the other states for additional details.)

1519 — Alonso Álvarez de Piñeda expedition at Mobile Bay.

1540 — French priests with Hernando de Soto in area.

1560 — Dominicans conduct a mission at Santa Cruz de Nanipacna in present-day Wilcox County.

1682 — Territory claimed for France by René-Robert Cavelier, Sieur de La Salle.

1699 — Pierre Le Moyne, Sieur d'Iberville, begins colony with Father Anastase Douay.

1700 — Father Antoine Davion labors among the Tunicas with Father Dougé.

1702 — Fort Louis de Mobile founded by La Salle at 27 Mile Bluff.

1704 — Father Anastase Douay at the D'Iberville colony at Mobile. Seminarist Fathers Jean François de Saint-Cosmé, François de Montigny, and Dougé labor on Mississippi River. Father Alexis de Guyenne with Creeks. Father de la Vente at Fort Louis at Mobile. Church built at Mobile.

In the year 1908, the Catholics of the United States received word, in Pope St. Pius X's declaration *Sapienti consilio,* that the Congregation of the Propagation of the Faith would no longer be in charge of the American dioceses as mission territories. For centuries the United States had functioned as a mission region. Each of these areas comprising the modern states of America was visited in some capacity by missionaries, and most have unique histories concerning the Native American apostolate. The following account is a chronological summary of the Catholic Indian missions across the nation during the missionary era.

Alabama

The area comprising this state was once part of the vast Louisiana missions

1709 — Chapels erected for Apalachee near Mobile.

1711 — Fort Louis moved to Mobile.

1721 — Carmelite Charles of St. Alexis among the Apalachee, north of Mobile. Capuchin Franciscans serving in region.

1724 — Jesuit Michel Baudoin with Chickasaw and Choctaw. Missions established at Fort Toulouse, Fort Tombeché, and Chickasaway.

1726 — Jesuit Mathurin le Petit serving Choctaw.

1736 — Capuchin Franciscan Jean Francis with Chapitoula, Natchitoches, and Natchez. Additional Jesuits enter regional missions.

1763 — British authorities close Catholic Indian missions.

Alaska

1779 — Franciscans Juan Rioba and Matías de Santa Catarina y Noriega celebrate Mass on Lower Bucareli Bay on May 13 in area to become Alaska.

1826 — Bishop Michael Portier named vicar apostolic of territory.

1844 — Oblates of Canadian province begin mission explorations in Alaska.

1859 — Our Lady of Good Hope founded in Arctic Circle. Oblate Father Grolier visits Fort Norman and Good Hope.

1860 — Missionaries at Fort McPherson with Kutchin and Mackenzie Delta Eskimos.

1862 — Oblate Jean Seguin at Fort Yukon.

1865 — Oblate Emil Petitot tours region on Anderson River.

1867 — Oblate Joseph Mandart in panhandle area.

1870 — Oblate Emil Petitot at Fort Yukon.

1872 — Bishop Isidore Clut and Oblate Auguste Lecorre to Fort Yukon and Kotlik.

1873 — Father Auguste Lecorre to St. Michael's on Yukon River.

1874 — Bishop Charles Seghers in Alaska, touring Sitka, Kodiak, and Unalaska.

1877 — Bishop Seghers promotes Nulato mission activities with Father Joseph Mandart.

1879 — Father John Althoff becomes first resident missionary at Wrangel mission.

1885 — Archbishop Seghers erects Sitka mission with Father William Heynen as pastor and visits Juneau.

1886 — Archbishop Seghers murdered by demented guide on the trail.

1887 — Jesuits enter Alaska missions. Holy Cross Mission (Koserefsky) for Ingalik and Eskimo mission at Akulark, St. Mary's, founded. Nulato mission serves Koyukum. Ursulines at St. Michael's for Inuits and at Valdez. Sisters of St. Anne in Juneau.

1888 — Sisters of St. Anne at Holy Cross Mission after Juneau foundation.

1889 — Nelson Island mission opened.

1890 — Six more Jesuits enter regional missions.

1894 — Alaska made prefecture apostolic under Jesuit Paschal Tosi. St. Joseph's Mission at Akulark opened with Sisters of St. Anne teaching in school.

1901 — Sisters of Providence enter regional missions. Jesuit Francis Barnum provides Eskimo grammar and dictionary.

1904 — Jesuit Joseph Crimont becomes prefect apostolic of area.

1905 — Christian Brothers at Holy Cross School. Ursulines extend mission apostolate in area. Six missions reported flourishing.

Arizona

1539 — Franciscan Marcos de Niza explores area that became the state of Arizona.

1540 — Franciscans Juan de Padilla and Marcos de Niza with Francisco Vásquez de Coronado expedition through Arizona territories.

1581 — Franciscans Augustín Rodríguez and companions slain at Tignex.

1582 — Antonio Espejo expedition in region. Franciscan Father Bernardino Beltrán tours Indian Pueblos.

1598 — Franciscans scout region for missions.

1617 — Franciscans operating eleven missions.

1621 — Franciscan Alonso de Benavides heads missions.

1629 — Franciscans labor among Moqui and Hopi Indians. Chapel erected at Awátovi (San Bernardino) by Franciscan Francisco de Porra. Chapels also erected at Shongópovi (San Bartolomé) and at Oraibi (San Francisco). Mission stations founded at Walpi, Awátovi, and Mishóngnovi.

1632 — Franciscan Martín de Arvide slain at mission at Zipias.

1633 — Franciscan Francisco de Porra slain at Awátovi.

1680 — Pueblo Revolt claims lives of Franciscans José de Espeleta, Augustín de Santa María, José de Figueroa, José de Trujillo, and others.

1687 — Jesuit Eusebius Kino in area, founds Nuestra Señora de los Dolores for Papago Indians at Cosari on San Miguel River and baptizes the Pima Chief Coxi. Missions established between 1687 and 1720 include: San José, Tumacacuri; Santa Gertrudis, Tubac; Santa Ana, Arivaca; and San Cayetano, Calabasas.

1695 — Southern Pima Revolt.

1699 — Father Kino establishes original San Xavier del Bac for Sobaipura Indians near Tucson and San José at Tumacacuri, north of Nogales. Erects Santa María de Suamca on the Mexican border. Father Kino also visits Gila at Casa Grande.

1700 — Father Juan Garaycoccha at Awátovi mission and with the Pueblos.

1726 — Hopi missions opened.

1732 — Father Kino founds San Miguel de Guevavi near Nogales. Jesuits Felipe Segesser and Juan B. Grashoffer revive San Xavier del Bac and San Miguel.

1736 — Jesuit Fathers Keller and Sedelmayer to Pima and Papago missions.

1745 — Franciscans begin Hopi missions.

1767 — Jesuits expelled from Arizona missions. Franciscans assume ten apostolates.

1768 — Franciscan Francisco Garcés at San Xavier del Bac.

1781 — Yuma Revolt takes lives of Franciscan Francisco Tomás Hermenegildo Garcés and three companions.

1783 — Cornerstone laid for new San Xavier del Bac Mission; completed in 1797.

1814 — Carmelite Bishop Martínez de Ocejo visits mission territory.

1828 — Spanish missionaries expelled by Mexican authorities.

1863 — Jesuits return to San Xavier del Bac briefly and serve at Tucson.

1864 — School opened at San Xavier del Bac.

1866 — Sisters of St. Joseph at Papago mission.

1868 — Bishop John Baptist Salpointe assumes jurisdiction of Arizona.

1869 — Sisters of Loreto in Arizona missions.

1897 — Bishop Peter Bourgade of Tucson expands missions.

THE STORY OF THE CATHOLIC INDIAN MISSIONS

1898 — Franciscans serve Navajos and Pueblos at Cochíti, Santo Domingo, San Felipe, and Jemez. Father Bernard Haile with the Navajos.

1899 — St. John's at Gila Crossing opened by Franciscans with schools for Papago, Pima, and Maricopa.

1902 — St. Michael's Mission for Navajo opened with support of St. Katharine Drexel.

Arkansas

1541 — Priests with Hernando de Soto expedition visit Quapaw Indians in the area comprising modern Arkansas.

1673 — Jesuit Jacques Marquette in region with Louis Joliet.

1682 — René-Robert Cavelier, Sieur de La Salle, visits five Quapaw villages. Recollect Franciscan Zenobius Membré plants cross in Arkansas territory.

1700 — Jesuit Jacques Gravier celebrates Mass in Arkansas. Father Nicholas Foucault laboring in missions for Quapaw.

1726 — Fort Toulouse mission opened for Choctaw and prospers until 1763.

1727 — Jesuit Paul du Poisson labors among Arkansas tribes but is slain two years later.

1750 — Jesuit Louis Carette serves area missions for eight years.

1764 — Jesuit Sebastian Meurin serves local tribes.

1792 — Father Pierre Gibault serves in area missions.

1795 — Father Paul de St. Pierre visits local tribes.

1805 — Bishop John Carroll appointed administrator apostolic of Arkansas missions.

1818 — Sarrasin, local chief, supports Vincentian missions. Vincentian John M. Odin labors in region.

1820 — Bishop Louis Dubourg of New Orleans visits Osages in the area.

1824 — Vincentians work to revive missions for six years. Bishop Joseph Rosati assumes Arkansas missions.

1830 — Chief Sarrasin dies and is buried with Catholic honors at St. Joseph's Mission in Pine Bluff.

1891 — Arkansas territory becomes a vicariate apostolic.

(Arkansas was part of the vast Louisiana missions. See Louisiana for additional accounts.)

California

1535 — Franciscan Martín de la Coruña with Hernán Cortés expedition at Santa Cruz Bay.

1542 — Priests accompany Juan Rodríguez Cabrillo expedition to Upper California.

1602 — Carmelite Anthony of the Ascension celebrates first recorded Mass in California at San Diego.

1642 — Jesuit Hyacinth Cortés explores the region.

1683 — Jesuit Eusebius Kino and companions explore area.

1687 — Eusebius Kino in Baja region.

1697 — Jesuit Juan María Salvatierra lands in San Diego, San Dionisio Bay. Mission Nuestra Señora de Loreto founded by Jesuits Victorian Arnes and John Joseph Diez. The Pious Fund for the California Missions started. Jesuit Wenceslaus Link explores region.

1699 — San Francisco Xavier Mission opened by Jesuits.

1705 — Mission San Juan de Ligné and Mission Santa Rosalia de Malegé founded.

1708 — Mission San José de Comundú founded.

1718 — Mission Purísima Concepción de Cadegomó erected.

1720 — Nuestra Señora de Guadalupe Mission established. Jesuit Fathers Bravo and Ugarte in regional missions, founding Nuestra Señora del Pilar in La Paz.

1721 — Mission Santiago de las Coras opened.

1728 — San Ignacio Mission opened.

1730 — Mission San José del Cabo established.

1733 — Mission Santa Rosa (Todos los Santos) founded.

1734 — Jesuits Carranco and Tamaral slain in La Paz revolt. Missions Santiago, San José, Santa Rosa, and Nuestra Señora del Pilar plundered and burned.

1737 — San Luis Gonzaga Mission established.

1752 — Santa Gertrudis Mission founded.

1759 — Mission San Francisco de Borja opened.

1766 — Mission Santa María de los Ángeles in operation.

1767 — Only fourteen missions opened by Jesuits remain due to illnesses among Indians, wars, and tribal relocations.

1768 — Jesuits exiled from California by King Carlos III of Spain.

1769 — Blessed Junípero Serra leads Franciscans into California, establishing Mission San Diego.

1770 — Mission San Carlos Borromeo de Monterey, called Carmelo, opened.

1771 — Mission San Gabriel erected. Mission San Antonio de Padua also established.

1772 — Mission San Luis Obispo de Tolosa opened.

1775 — Franciscan Luis Jayme slain in San Diego while defending the Blessed Sacrament.

1776 — Missions San Juan Capistrano and San Francisco de Asís erected.

1781 — Pueblo de Nuestra Señora de los Ángeles founded by Franciscans of San Gabriel Mission. Franciscans Francisco Tomás Hermenegildo Garcés, Juan Antonio Barrenechea, Juan Marcello Díaz, and José Matías Moreno slain.

1782 — Mission San Buenaventura founded.

1784 — Blessed Junípero Serra dies.

1786 — Santa Barbara Mission erected.

1787 — La Purísima Concepción Mission founded.

1791 — Missions Nuestra Señora de la Soledad and Santa Cruz established.

1797 — Missions San Miguel Arcángel, San Juan Bautista, San Fernando Rey de España, and San José opened.

1798 — Mission San Luis Rey de Francia in operation with adjunct Mission San Antonio de Pala.

1804 — Mission Santa Inés founded.

1812 — Franciscan Andrés Quintana killed at Santa Cruz.

1817 — San Rafael Arcángel Mission opened.

1823 — Mission San Francisco de Solano erected.

1833 — California missions secularized by Mexican government.

1850 — Bishop Joseph Alemany assumes Monterey diocese, then San Francisco.

1870 — Father Luciano Osuna establishes St. Turibius Mission near modern Kelseyville.

1889 — St. Mary's Mission opened near Ukiah.

Colorado

1540 — Franciscan priests with Francisco Vásquez de Coronado expedition in area of what is now Colorado.

1682 — Region claimed for France by René-Robert Cavelier, Sieur de La Salle.

1700 — Colorado in jurisdiction of vicariate apostolic at Leavenworth, Kansas, under Spanish. Unidentified missions serve the region briefly.

1762 — Region becomes an actual Spanish territory.

1776 — Franciscan Silvestre Vélez de Escalante on local expedition in area.

1800 — France regains territory of modern Colorado.

1803 — Colorado becomes United States land.

1860 — Colorado under vicar apostolic of New Mexico.

1868 — Colorado and Utah become part of new vicar apostolic directed by Bishop Joseph Machebeuf.

1900 — Southern Ute mission opened.

Connecticut

No Indian missions of any permanence are recorded in the area of present-day Connecticut. The major Indian tribes in Connecticut were the Mohawk, Mohican, Nipmuc, Pequot, Podunk, Sequin, and the Wappinger Confederacy. These Indians may have been served by missionaries in the early eras, but no mission efforts were recorded. The first recorded Catholic Mass in the state was probably celebrated by Abbé Claude Robin, a French chaplain during the Revolutionary War. Jesuit Gabriel Druillettes served as the envoy of the governor of New France (Canada); he was in the state in 1651 and may have celebrated Mass during his stay.

Delaware

1674 — Father Jean Pierron visits the area of the present state of Delaware for the bishop of Quebec but founds no missions.

1750 — The Jesuits establish the Apoquiminck mission in New Castle County, Delaware.

1772 — First permanent parish established at Coffee Run.

Florida

1513 — Juan Ponce de León expedition discovers the area that will become the state of Florida.

1516 — Florida visited by Mirvelo expedition.

1517 — Francisco Hernández de Córdova tours Florida.

1519 — Alonso Álvarez de Piñeda tours Florida.

1520 — Lucas Vásquez de Ayllón visits Florida.

1521 — Priests with second Ponce de León exploration company celebrate Masses.

1524 — Florida visited by Estevan Gómez expedition.

1527 — Pánfilo de Narváez and company tour Florida.

1528 — Franciscans, including Bishop Suárez and companions, slain with Narváez expedition.

1538 — Hernando de Soto expedition in Florida.

1539 — Twelve missionaries land at Tampa Bay with De Soto expedition. Franciscans slain.

1549 — Dominican Luis Cáncer de Barbastro and companions slain near Tampa Bay.

1559 — Expedition of Tristan de Luna in region.

1564 — Colony of St. Caroline flourishes briefly.

1565 — City of St. Augustine founded by Pedro Menéndez de Avilés, an explorer who had four secular priests in his company.

Nombre de Dios established as a mission. Father Francisco López de Mendoza Grajales begins parish. Calusa and Timucua missions opened.

1566 — Jesuits open missions at Charlotte Harbor and Miami. One Jesuit is slain near mouth of St. John's River. Jesuits Juan Rogel and Brother Francisco de Villareal in missions.

1568 — Jesuits open Calusa mission and take young Indians to Havana, Cuba, for education. Jesuit Juan Bautista Segura among the Calusa, Miami (Tekesta), and Tocobaga. Jesuit Alonso de Reynosa serves the Timucua, Yamasee, and northern tribes. Jesuit Antonio Sedeño labors among the Yamasee.

1572 — St. Francis Borgia, general of the Society of Jesus, withdraws Jesuits from Florida missions.

1573 — Franciscans open missions near St. Augustine.

1577 — Franciscan Alonso de Reynosa opens Timucua mission at St. Augustine.

1586 — British, under Sir Francis Drake, attack St. Augustine.

1592 — Franciscans serve Timucua and Yamasee.

1593 — Franciscans Juan de Silva, Francisco de Pareja, and ten companions enter Timucua missions. Priests serve Yamasee also and begin site on Little Talbot Island, north of St. Augustine.

1597 — Yamasee Revolt destroys tribal missions and takes lives of five priests in area.

1598 — Franciscan Francisco Pareja prepares first Indian language book in United States history.

1602 — Mission for Timucua started at St. John's River with three other outposts.

1606 — Bishop Juan de las Cabezas Altamirano, O.P., confirms fifteen hundred on mission tour.

1607 — Franciscans at Palatka and Gainesville, also at juncture of Santa Fe and Suwannee River and at Tallahassee.

1609 — Florida chiefs baptized.

1612 — Florida becomes mission province, and more Franciscans arrive.

1620 — Chapel of Nombre de Dios dedicated to Blessed Virgin as Nuestra Señora de la Leche y Buen Parto (Our Nursing Mother of the Happy Delivery), oldest Marian shrine in the United States.

1633 — Apalachee mission opened in west.

1655 — Franciscans operating thirty-eight missions in Florida and Georgia.

1657 — Apalachee War closes western missions.

1665 — British attack St. Augustine.

1674 — Apalachee missions reopened. Bishop Gabriel Díaz Vara Calderón confirms 13,152 Indians on tour of thirty-six missions.

1684 — Havana diocese promulgates regulations to protect Native Americans.

1702 — Timucua Mission Santa Fe destroyed by Creeks.

1704 — Northern mission destroyed by English and Indian troops led by Governor James Moore of South Carolina. Franciscans Juan de Parga, Dominic Criodo, Tiburcio de Osorio, Augustín Ponce de León, and Marcos Delgado, along with two Native Americans, Anthony Enixa and Amador Cuipa, slain cruelly.

1720 — Six Florida missions reopened.

1726 — Christian Apalachee missions restored.

1735 — Bishop Francisco Martínez de la Tejadu Díaz de Velasco takes up residence in St. Augustine.

1740 — Governor James Oglethorpe of Georgia destroys St. Augustine.

1743 — Jesuits José María Monaco and José Xavier de Alana reopen other missions for Ais and Jobe Indians.

1763 — Florida missions closed when area became English domain.

1800s — Seminole Wars break out in region (1817-1818, 1835-1842, and 1855-1858).

Georgia

1526 — Priests with colony of Lucas Vásquez de Ayllón in area comprising the state of Georgia.

1540 — Priests with Hernando de Soto perform baptisms at Macon.

1566 — Jesuits start Mission Santa Catalina de Guale on St. Catherine's Island near Savannah.

1567 — Pedro Martínez, Jesuit protomartyr, slain on Cumberland Island with two companions.

1569 — Jesuit missions reopened on St. Catherine's Island and at Port Royal. St. Catherine's served by Jesuits Juan de la Carrera and Juan Rogel. Jesuit Antonio Sedeño visits Yamasee.

1572 — Jesuits withdrawn from Georgia region.

1592 — Franciscans enter missions.

1595 — Five Franciscans assigned to Guale Indians. Some fifteen hundred converts recorded.

1597 — Guale Revolt takes lives of Franciscans Pedro de Corpa, Blas de Rodríguez, Miguel de Anón, Francisco de Beráscola, and Brother Antonio de Badajoz in coastal missions.

1606 — Dominican Bishop Juan de las Cabezas Altamirano tours area.

1655 — Franciscans operating nine Indian missions.

1676 — St. Catherine's mission attacked and destroyed.

1680 — Georgia missions closed by English troops.

1702 — Guale missions reopened but attacked by English in the Juanillo Revolt.

1742 — Spanish missions ended.

Idaho

1812 — Christian Iroquois, led by Old Ignace, enter the future Idaho area with fur trappers.

1831 — Flathead and Nez Percé send delegation to St. Louis to ask for missionaries.

1840 — Jesuit Pierre Jean De Smet celebrates Mass near western end of Yellowstone, preaches to Flathead and Pend d'Oreille tribes.

1841 — Jesuits Nicholas Point and De Smet establish Sacred Heart Mission for Coeur d'Alene in northern area, followed by Father Pierre Joseph Joset.

1843 — Father Point establishes church on St. Joe River near St. Marie's. This mission was moved to Coeur d'Alene River and later called Cataldo Mission.

1845 — Salish Indians reported maintaining Catholic faith despite lack of missionary contact.

1850 — Jesuit Antonio Ravalli with Coeur d'Alenes.

1867 — Jesuit Joseph Cataldo begins fifty years of missions among the Nez Percé and Slickapoo.

1868 — Idaho becomes vicariate apostolic under Bishop Louis Lootens.

1876 — Archbishop Francis Norbert Blanchet named administrator of Idaho. Jesuit Father Gozzoli serves as medical missionary to area.

1884 — Bishop Alphonse Glorieux made vicar apostolic of Idaho.

1900 — Sacred Heart mission for Coeur d'Alene prospering.

Illinois

1673 — Jesuit Jacques Marquette among Peoria Indians in region.

1674 — Father Marquette establishes Kaskaskia mission of the Immaculate Conception near Utica and erects chapel near modern Chicago. A Jesuit is slain at Seneca.

1677 — Jesuit Claude Allouez revives Kaskaskia mission, aided by visits from Recollect Franciscans Louis Hennepin, Zenobius Membré, and Gabriel de la Ribourde.

1680 — Kaskaskia mission and Indians moved south to escape Iroquois incursions. Father Ribourde slain by Kickapoo Indians. Father Claude Allouez and Jesuit coworker Jacques Gravier compile Native American dictionaries.

1682 — Father Jacques Gravier at Peoria and Starved Rock.

1684 — Father Allouez opens mission for Peoria and serves Kaskaskia and Rockford.

1685 — Father Gravier compiles Peoria dictionary.

1689 — Father Gravier at new Kaskaskia mission on the eastern bank of the Mississippi River. Father Allouez at Peoria. Seminary Priests of the Foreign Missions of Quebec, New France (Canada), found Cahokia mission, part of the Louisiana missions, dedicated to the Holy Family and called Tamaroa.

1692 — Father Gravier labors among the Wea (Miami) near present-day Chicago. Jesuit Sebastian Rale serves missions in region.

1693 — Father Gravier becomes mission superior.

1699 — Seminarist Father Jean François de Saint-Cosmé at Chicago.

1702 — Jesuits found Piankashaw mission near Vincennes.

1705 — Father Gravier wounded in attack, dies in 1708.

1711 — Father Jean Baptiste Chardon among Illinois Indians.

1728 — Jesuit Ignatius Guignas captured and adopted by Kickapoos and Mascoutens.

1730 — Secular Father Gaston slain at Cahokia mission.

1763 — Jesuits banished from Illinois.

1768 — Father Pierre Gibault serves as vicar general of the Illinois Territory at Kaskaskia.

1792 — Sulpicians Gabriel Richard and Michael Levadoux among the Illinois at Cahokia.

1795 — Father Rivet serves the Wea (Miami), Kaskaskia, and Piankashaw in area.

1804 — Fort Dearborn established.

1820 — Vincentians enter Kaskaskia mission.

1821 — Father Richard serves at Fort Dearborn (Chicago).

1822 — Father Stephen Badin at Fort Dearborn.

1833 — Visitation Nuns at Kaskaskia in education apostolate.

1841 — Miami Chief Richardville, devout Catholic patron, buried with Church honors.

Indiana

1675 — Jesuit Jacques Marquette explores region of modern-day Indiana.

1679 — Recollect Franciscans Louis Hennepin and Gabriel de la Ribourde visit the local tribes and begin mapping territory.

189

1685 — Mission St. Joseph founded near South Bend.

1686 — Jesuits receive land at present South Bend for missions.

1687 — Jesuit Claude Allouez founds St. Joseph's Mission near Indiana border.

1689 — Father Allouez dies, replaced by Jesuit Claude Areneau.

1706 — Jesuit Jacques Gravier in area missions.

1711 — Jesuit Peter F. X. Chardon on St. Joseph River.

1719 — Jesuits open Fort Miami (Fort Wayne) mission.

1732 — Fort Vincennes opened and St. Francis Xavier Church founded. Jesuit Stephen Doutreleau at mission.

1756 — Jesuit Pierre du Jounay with Miami Indians in Lafayette.

1832 — Father Stephen Badin revives St. Joseph's Mission.

1834 — Bishop Simon Gabriel Bruté at Vincennes.

1838 — Schools operating in Lowell, La Porte, Michigan City, and Mishawaka. Holy Cross priests and Sisters in missions.

Iowa

1673 — Jesuit Jacques Marquette visits Peoria village in Montrose.

1679 — Recollect Franciscans Louis Hennepin and Gabriel de la Ribourde labor among tribes.

1832 — Jesuit Charles Van Quickenborne with Fox Indians at Keokuk.

1835 — Dominican Venerable Samuel Mazzuchelli opens St. Raphael's at Dubuque.

1838 — Jesuits Pierre Jean De Smet and Felix Verreydt labor among Potawátomi at Council Bluffs. St. Joseph's Mission opened, moved in 1841.

1839 — Father Joseph Crétin among Winnebago, builds St. Patrick's at Prairie du Chien. Bishop Pierre Jean Mathias Loras in Davenport.

Kansas

1535 — Expedition of Álvar Núñez Cabeza de Vaca in region.

1541 — Francisco Vásquez de Coronado in territory with expedition.

1542 — Franciscan Juan de Padilla slain while laboring among the Wichita (Quiveria) Native Americans, becoming America's protomartyr.

1673 — Jesuit Jacques Marquette maps area.

1719 — Du Tissenet expedition erects a cross in the Padoucas region.

1745 — Franciscans begin work among the Potawátomi and Osage.

1820 — Sans Nerf, Osage chief, journeys to St. Louis to ask for missionaries.

1832 — Jesuit Charles de la Croix on Neosho River with Osage. Bishop Louis Dubourg of Louisiana gains federal funds for Osage missions.

1836 — Jesuit Charles Van Quickenborne establishes Kickapoo mission near Leavenworth, abandoned in 1847. Jesuit Christian Hoecken serves Kickapoo, Wea (Miami), Piankashaw, and Potawátomi with Jesuit John Schoenmaker.

1837 — Father Benjamin Petit delivers exiled Potawátomi Indians to Father Hoecken.

1839 — Father Hoecken establishes Potawátomi mission at Sugar Creek.

1840 — St. Rose Philippine Duchesne at Sugar Creek to found Sacred Heart convent and school.

1842 — Jesuits open boys' school.

1847 — Jesuits John Schoenmaker and John Bax labor among the Osage at St. Paul's. Sisters of Loretto open academy for

Potawátomi girls. Miami mission started.

1848 — Father Hoecken aids exiled tribes at St. Mary's. Jesuit Paul Ponziglione labors in southwestern area of Kansas, devoting forty years to this mission.

1851 — Jesuit Bishop Jean-Baptiste Miège becomes vicar apostolic of territory.

Kentucky

There are no records available to indicate Indian missions were established in the region of modern Kentucky. The Mound Builders were the original inhabitants of the territory. The Catawba, Cherokee, Chickasaw, Delaware, Shawnee, Wyandotte, and other Native Americans were in the region when Thomas Walker entered Kentucky in 1750, followed by Daniel Boone. Settlements started in 1774. Missionary agents such as Fathers Stephen Badin and Charles Nerinckx labored in Kentucky among the white communities and many Indians.

Louisiana

The Louisiana missions in the French colonial period included the area comprising the present states of Missouri, Arkansas, Louisiana, Mississippi, and Alabama. Also part of the Louisiana missions were the Tamaroa mission at Cahokia, Illinois, and the Caddo settlements of Texas. The actual Louisiana missions are listed below. See other states for related evangelization efforts.

1526 — Álvar Núñez Cabeza de Vaca expedition in Louisiana.

1682 — Recollect Franciscans Anastase Douay, Maxime LeClerq, Paul du Ru, and Zenobius Membré in area with the expedition led by René-Robert Cavelier, Sieur de La Salle.

1698 — Seminarists François de Montigny, Antoine Davion, and Thaumer de la Source enter Louisiana missions.

1699 — Seminarist Jean François de Saint-Cosmé in area. Father Douay offers Mass in vicinity of New Orleans. Father de Montigny serves Taensa Indians, in modern Alexandria. Father Davion labors among the Tunicas. Father de Saint-Cosmé works among Natchez Indians.

1700 — Jesuit Paul du Ru builds chapel for Bayougoula Indians.

1706 — Father de Saint-Cosmé slain.

1708 — Mission for Tunica Indians abandoned. Father Jacques Gravier slain.

1716 — Caddo missions and outposts for the Ais and Adai tribes established by Franciscans.

1717 — Franciscan Venerable Antonio de Margil de Jesús establishes Mission San Juan Bautista in north central Louisiana. Franciscans found Missions San Francisco, La Purísima Concepción, San José, Dolores, and San Miguel de Cuellar in Louisiana regions.

1722 — Jesuits enter missions. Father Mathurin le Petit goes to the Choctaw. Father Paul du Poisson serves the Arkansas; Father Stephen Doutreleau serves on the Wabash. Fathers Tartarin and Le Boulinger labor at Kaskaskia. Father J. C. Guymonneau serves a Michigamea mission. Father Jean Souel serves the Yazoos. Father Michel Baudoin works with the Chickasaw.

1727 — Ursulines open school for Native American girls.

1728 — Father Michel Baudoin among Choctaws.

1729 — Natchez War claims lives of Fathers Paul du Poisson and Jean Souel.

1730 — Jesuit Stephen Doutreleau assaulted by local tribes. Jesuit Antoine Senat martyred.

1760 — Sulpician François Picquet serves region for three years.

1764 — St. Louis de Apalachees

founded at Pineville. Father Nicholas le Febvre ends Choctaw labors.

1769 — Father Michael Baudossin serves Choctaws, beginning eighteen-year mission.

1800 — Capuchin Luis de Quintanilla erects chapel at Fort Miro in Monroe. Our Lady of the Pillar founded at Nuestra Señora del Pilar.

1859 — Father Adrien Rouquette to Choctaw Indians at Bayou La Combe.

(See other state lists for complete mission designation.)

Maine

1541 — Diego Maldonado expedition visits territory that comprises modern Maine.

1603 — Father Nicholas Aubry accompanies Pierre du Guast, Sieur de Monts, expedition at Sainte-Croix (now De Monts Island), erecting a chapel at the mouth of the Passamaquoddy.

1604 — Samuel de Champlain explores region.

1605 — Secular priests serve as chaplains at Sainte-Croix.

1610 — Jesuit Jesse Fleché baptizes Micmac Chief Memberton and tribe.

1611 — Jesuits Pierre Biard and Enemond Massé at Kennebec.

1613 — Father Biard founds Saint-Sauveur for Abenaki on Mount Desert Island. Jesuits attempt permanent settlement at Kennebec River. Jesuits Quentin de la Saussaye and Lalamant follow Biard to missions. English attack missions. Jesuit Brother Gilbert du Thet slain.

1619 — Recollect Franciscans enter missions, serve until 1630.

1630 — Capuchin Franciscans assume Maine missions, while Jesuits expand their own efforts. A Capuchin mission operating on the Penobscot River at Fort Pentaquet (Castine).

1636 — Jesuit Gabriel Druillettes begins work among the Abenaki at Kennebec.

1639 — Our Lady of Hope, Capuchin mission for Penobscot, operating.

1646 — Father Druillettes founds Assumption Mission for Abenaki.

1656 — Capuchins conduct chain of missions in Maine, suffering losses but resume rebuilding.

1657 — Franciscan Laurent Molin at Pentagoet.

1665 — Father de Crespy captured by English.

1667 — Father Jean Morain labors among the Penobscot and Passamaquoddy tribes.

1668 — Jesuit Jacques Bigot restores Norridgewock Abenaki mission chapel with his brother, Father Vincent. Jesuits in the missions include Joseph de la Chasse, Julian Binnéteau, Joseph Aubéry, Alexis d'Eschambault, Sebastian Rale, Sebastian Lauvergat, and Philip Rageot. Jesuit Louis Thury begin labors at Old Town (Panawaniske), Sainte Anne, and serves at Castine, laboring in area until his death in 1699.

1689 — Abenaki mission, St. Francis de Sales, opened by Jesuits Jacques Bigot, Vincent Bigot, and Joseph Aubéry.

1693 — Jesuits receive Maine missions.

1694 — Father Jacques Bigot to Penobscot at Saint-Sauveur. Father Sebastian Rale to Norridgewock Abenaki mission.

1701 — Father Joseph Aubéry labors among the Malisit Indians at Meductic.

1703 — Jesuits assume Old Town and Kennebec mission expansions.

1718 — Jesuit Étienne Lanverjet in mission expansions, laboring until 1731.

1724 — Father Sebastian Rale slain at Norridgewock.

1728 — Norridgewock reopened by Jesuit Jacques de Sirisme (Sirrene).

1731 — Jesuit missions close in some parts of region. Jesuits de Sirisme and Lanverjet leave region.

1746 — Jesuit Claude Coquart composes Abenaki grammar.

1754 — Jesuit Jean-Baptiste Brosse to Abenaki, composes Abenaki and Micmac dictionaries.

1757 — Jesuit Father Claude Virot labors in area.

1776 — French chaplains assigned by French navy to the Abenakis.

1785 — Sulpician François Ciquard labors at Old Town.

1794 — Father Ciquard labors at Etchimin for Malisit.

1797 — Father Jean-Louis Cheverus at Pleasant Point.

1802 — Penobscot Chief Orono buried with honors.

1804 — Father James René Romagné serves Penobscots and Passamaquoddies for two decades.

1825 — Dominican Bishop Edward Fenwick on mission tour, assisted by Dominicans Ffrench and Demillier.

1848 — Jesuit John Bapst at Old Town.

1855 — Jesuit Eugene Vetromile at Old Town until 1880, composes Abenaki dictionary and history.

1870 — Sisters of Mercy at Abenaki mission, receiving four-room wigwam from Chief Stockvesin Swassin.

1879 — Pleasant Point school opens. Missions started at Dana's Point.

Maryland

1634 — Jesuits Andrew White and John Altham arrive in the colony of Lord Calvert, with Brother Thomas Gervase. They are sheltered by Yaocomoco Indians, and Father White celebrates the first Mass in Maryland on St. Clement's Island on the Lower Potomac River. Establishes St. Mary's.

1635 — Father White labors among the Piscataway. Other Jesuits, including Father Rigby, serve tribes on the Patuxent River.

1637 — Jesuits Philip Fisher (Thomas Copley) and John Knoller take up mission labors.

1639 — Kittamaquindi mission opened by Father White for Piscataway with stations, including Mattapony on the Patuxent, the Anacostan in modern Washington, D.C., and the Potopaco at Port Tobacco.

1640 — Father White baptizes the "Emperor of the Piscataway," Chitomachon, on July 5, with Governor Calvert in attendance at the ceremony.

1642 — Father White baptizes another Piscataway chief at Nacochtank. Secular priests Gilmett and Territt enter Maryland missions.

1643 — Jesuit Gabriel Druillettes founds missions in region.

1645 — Fathers Phillip Fisher and Andrew White taken by British to London in chains.

1648 — Father Fisher returns to area and labors four years until his death.

1653 — Jesuit Father Lawrence Storkey replaces Father White.

1673 — Father Masseus Massey leads six Franciscans into missions in area.

1706 — Jesuit Thomas Mansell founds St. Xavier Mission in Cecil County.

Massachusetts

1611 — Jesuit Pierre Biard enters region comprising modern Massachusetts to labor among local tribes.

1643 — Jesuit Gabriel Druillettes founds missions in territory.

1647 — Catholic priests declared criminals in Massachusetts and denied entry.

1650 — Father Druillettes arrives in colony as representative of the governor of New France (Canada) and is cordially received during negotiations on a treaty.

Michigan

1622 — Recollect Franciscan Guillaume Poullain in Sault Ste. Marie region.

1624 — Recollect Franciscan Jacques de la Tayer in Sault Ste. Marie region.

1641 — Jesuits St. Isaac Jogues and Charles Raymbault visit Sault Ste. Marie area, planting a cross on the banks of St. Mary's River and naming the rapids in region of modern Michigan. Jesuit Claude Pijart at Nipissing and Georgian Bay with Jesuit Charles Raymbault.

1644 — Jesuit Leonard Gareau with Jesuits Joseph Poncet and Adrian Daran. Missions Saint-Esprit, Saint-Charles, and Saint-Pierre in operation.

1660 — Jesuit René Menard at Keweenaw Bay with Ojibwa. He is slain one year later in Wisconsin. Jesuit Jacques Marquette establishes Sault Ste. Marie Mission, and St. Michael's opens in territory. Jesuit Claude Dablon establishes St. Ignace Mission on Mackinaw and labors at Sault Ste. Marie.

1665 — Jesuit Claude Allouez at Saint-Esprit in Chegoimegon (Bayfield).

1668 — Jesuits, including Fathers Louis André, Henri Nouvel, and Pierre Bailloquet, serving missions.

1670 — St. Ignatius Mission moved north. St. Joseph's Mission opened in Detroit for Ottawa by Jesuit François Dollier. Jesuit Gabriel Druillettes in area.

1675 — Jesuit Henri Nouvel labors at Thunder Bay and Saginaw.

1677 — Father Marquette buried at St. Ignace Mission.

1686 — Jesuit Jacques Gravier in Michilimackinac.

1687 — St. Francis Xavier Mission burned in French-Iroquois War. Jesuit Jean Enjahan escapes fire and rebuilds mission in the following year.

1689 — Father Claude Allouez dies near Niles.

1691 — Jesuit Sebastian Rale compiles life and customs of Ottawas at St. Ignace Mission, serves Illinois around Great Lakes.

1701 — Recollect Franciscans open St. Anne-de-Detroit chapel at Fort Ponchatrain (Detroit).

1706 — Recollect Franciscan Nicholas Constantine Delhalle slain at Detroit.

1721 — Jesuits Charlevoix and Jean Baptiste Chardon at St. Francis Xavier Mission.

1747 — Jesuit Armand de la Richardie in Detroit with Hurons.

1781 — Father Jean François Hubert (future bishop of Quebec) with Hurons at Detroit.

1794 — Father Gabriel Richard at Sault Ste. Marie, Green Bay, and L'arbre Croche (Harbor Springs). Franciscans at Burt Lake and L'arbre Croche. Sisters of Notre Dame de Namur in missions.

1798 — Father Richard appointed to Detroit to aid Father Levadoux.

1823 — Missions restored in area when Ottawa Indians appeal to the United States Congress for aid. Chief Simon Pokagan spearheads restoration.

1825 — Father Joseph Badin serves Lake tribes.

1827 — Jesuit Father Peter Dejean among Ojibwa at Mackinaw.

1829 — Ottawa missions reopened at L'arbre Croche.

1830 — Father Irenaeus Frederick Baraga begins mission to Ottawa, is stationed at L'arbre Croche (now Harbor Springs). Father Stephen Badin with Potawátomi Indians. Venerable Samuel Mazzuchelli opens school for Menóminee in Green Bay.

1833 — Father Baraga goes to Grand Rapids, replaced by Redemptorist Simon Sanderl.

1834 — Sault Ste. Marie Mission revived.

1835 — Father Baraga at La Pointe, Keweenaw Bay. Father Andrew Viszoczky, a Hungarian, was in Grand Rapids.

1836 — Father Jean B. Prouix at Manitoulin Island.

1838 — Father Francis Pierz founds Grande Portage and Michipicoton.

1840 — Father Ignatius Mrak labors with Father Pierz at L'arbre Croche.

1843 — Father Baraga founds L'Anse mission.

1844 — Father T. J. van den Broeck opens St. Francis Mission at Lake Powhegan on Wolf River.

1845 — School opened at Pokagon by Sisters of the Holy Cross.

1847 — Father F. J. Bonduel builds school at St. Francis Mission.

1848 — Jesuits, operating missions at Garden River, found Pigeon River mission.

1852 — Franciscan Otho Skolla labors in Menóminee missions.

1853 or 1857 — Bishop Frederick Baraga consecrated as vicar apostolic of territory.

1866 — Bishop Baraga transfers see to Marquette.

1869 — Bishop Ignatius Mrak assumes diocese of Marquette.

Menóminee thunderbird design

1878 — Bishop Benedict Flaget at St. Mary's for rally of ten thousand Indians, then visits Detroit and Monroe.

Minnesota

1655 — Jesuits (led by French explorers Médard Chouart des Groseilliers and Pierre Esprit Radisson) labor among Dakota Sioux near present Hastings.

1680 — Recollect Franciscan Louis Hennepin discovers Falls of St. Anthony, rescued from Sioux by Daniel Greysolon, Sieur Du Lhut.

1683 — Jesuit Joseph Marest among the Sioux. Jesuits serving in several areas.

1721 — Jesuit Michel Guignas celebrates Mass at Fort Beauharnois near Frontenac.

1727 — Jesuits Nicholas de Gonnor and Michel Guignas start St. Michael Archangel chapel for Sioux at Fort Beauharnois. Lake Pepin mission founded. Expedition of René Boucher in territory.

1732 — Jesuits at Fort St. Charles on Northwest Angle Inlet, Lake of the Woods. Jesuits Charles Messaiger and Jean-Pierre Aulneau labor in region.

1736 — Jesuit Aulneau slain with twenty companions.

1737 — Jesuit Christian Hoecken serving Minnesota missions.

1830 — Father Francis Pierz labors among the Ojibwas at Crow Wing.

1839 — Father Joseph Crétin starts labors in area. Jesuit Pierre Jean De Smet in region.

1840 — Father Lucien Galtier at St. Paul.

1841 — Father Augustine Ravoux with Santee Dakota Indians near St. Paul.

1844 — Father Galtier builds St. Paul chapel. Father Pierz labors among the Dakotas.

1851 — Bishop Joseph Crétin revives St. Paul area missions. Father Pierz begins Chippewa missions.

1869 — Jesuit Joseph Marest at Sioux ceremonies in Minnesota.

1875 — Minnesota declared a vicariate apostolic in part. Jesuits laboring in Mankato missions.

1878 — Benedictines open Crookston, White Earth, and Red Lake missions.

1879 — Remaining parts of Minnesota become attached to a vicariate apostolic.

1894 — Benedictine Bishop Martin Marty at St. Cloud.

Mississippi

1540 — Missionary priests accompany Hernando de Soto expedition into territory.

1682 — Recollect Franciscans Zenobius Membré and Anastase Douay labor among the Taensa and Natchez near Fort Adams while on expedition with René-Robert Cavelier, Sieur de La Salle.

1699 — Foreign Mission Seminary of Quebec establishes Natchez mission. Seminarist Jean François de Saint-Cosmé begins work among Taensa. Father Antoine Davion at Fort Adams, with the Tunica and Yazoo, Father François de Montigny and Father Thaumer de la Source among the Natchez.

1700 — Father Jacques Gravier serves Tunica Indians.

1702 — Father Nicholas Foucault slain at Koroa.

1706 — Father Jean François de Saint-Cosmé slain. Father Anthony Davion accompanies the Tunica to Red River.

1720 — Carmelite John Matthew serves Biloxi mission.

1721 — Missions partly abandoned. Father Juif remains with Yazoo. Jesuit Jean Rouel visits Yazoo.

1726 — Jesuit Mathurin le Petit labors among Choctaw in northern area.

1729 — Natchez War claims lives of Jesuits Paul du Poisson at Fort Rosalie and Jean Souel in Yazoo area.

1730 — Jesuit Antoine Senat burned at stake with French officers at Chickasaw mission.

1765 — Jesuit Sebastian Meurin serves Illinois and Mississippi tribes.

1768 — Recollect Franciscan Luke Collet dies in mission.

1772 — Capuchin Franciscans from New Orleans enter mission territory.

1787 — Fathers McKenna, White, and Savage serve at Natchez.

1822 — Mississippi becomes part of vicariate apostolic.

1825 — Mississippi becomes separate vicariate apostolic.

1881 — Bishop Francis Janssens founds Choctaw community at Philadelphia.

1883 — Dutch Carmelites serve Choctaw missions. Carmelite Bartholomew Bekker at Tucker.

1899 — Dutch Carmelite Augustine Breek labors among Choctaw.

(See Louisiana for more details about this mission.)

Missouri

1542 — Priests accompany Hernando de Soto expedition in area.

1659 — Jesuits at St. Geneviève on western bank of Mississippi River.

1673 — Jesuit Jacques Marquette with Louis Joliet in region.

1700 — Jesuit Gabriel Marest founds mission near St. Louis.

1734 — St. Geneviève Mission operating, attended by priests from Cahokia, who also serve Old Mines area.

1760 — Recollect Franciscan Luke Collet and Jesuit Sebastian Meurin at St. Geneviève and St. Louis.

1762 — Indian mission started at St. Charles.

1766 — Father Sebastian Meurin serves in Cahokia.

1767 — Carondolet mission opened.

1768 — Father Pierre Gibault serving tribes in area.

1804 — Father James Maxwell working at St. Geneviève.

1811 — Jesuits establish Indian mission school at Florissant.

1818 — Bishop Louis Dubourg arrives in St. Louis with Vincentians Joseph Rosati and Felix de Andreis. St. Rose Philippine Duchesne at St. Charles, then Florissant.

1822 — Father Charles de la Croix among the Osage.

1823 — Jesuit Charles Van Quickenborne at St. Louis.

1824 — Jesuits begin labors in new Osage missions.

1827 — Father Van Quickenborne on Neosho River.

1840 — Bishop Joseph Rosati revives Indian apostolate, invites Jesuits to missions.

1847 — Jesuit John Schoenmaker opens Osage mission, erects church in area.

1851 — Jesuit Paul Mary Ponziglione serves the Osage, Quapaw, Ottawa, Chippewa, Sauk, Fox, Kansa, and Ponca tribes.

1884 — St. Stephen's Mission for Arapaho opened on Wind River Reservation.

(See Louisiana for more details about this complex mission territory.)

Montana

1743 — Jesuit Claude Coquart in area with expedition of Pierre and François Verendrye.

1816 — Caughnawaga Iroquois visit Flatheads and Nez Percé, and spread word of the faith.

1821 — Flatheads and Nez Percé go to St. Louis, Missouri, seeking missionaries.

1835 — Flathead representatives renew pleas for missionaries in St. Louis, repeated in 1837 and 1839.

1840 — Jesuit Pierre Jean De Smet among the Flatheads at Three Forks and Great Falls, also visits Potawatomi and Pend d'Oreille tribes.

1841 — Father De Smet opens St. Mary's Mission on Bitter Root River near Stevensville; also opens Sacred Heart for the Coeur d'Alene. Jesuits Gregorio Mengarini and Nicholas Point enter missions in territory.

1844 — Kalispel mission of St. Ignatius established and St. Francis Xavier opened. Father De Smet with Flatheads.

1845 — Jesuit Antonio Ravalli at St. Mary's Mission. Jesuit missions started: Assumption for Lower Kalispel Indians, Holy Heart of Mary for the Kutenais, St. Francis Borgia for the Pend d'Oreilles and Upper Kalispels, St. Francis Regis for the Crees, St. Peter for the Lakes, St. Paul for the Colvilles, and St. Joseph for the Okanagons.

1846 — Jesuit Nicholas Point at St. Peter's with Blackfeet.

1850 — Father De Smet at Great Point (Fort Benton).

1851 — Flatheads enter St. Ignatius

197

Assiniboin war shirt

mission. Montana becomes part of vicariate apostolic of Idaho.

1857 — St. Peter's mission operating for Blackfeet.

1863 — Jesuits revitalize St. Paul's.

1866 — Mission for Flatheads revived.

1867 — St. Michael's established for the Spokan.

1868 — Helena region supports missions for Blackfeet, Flatheads, and Cheyennes.

1872 — St. Joseph's mission serves the Yakima and Nez Percé in area.

1877 — Montana becomes a vicariate apostolic.

1879 — St. Peter's Ursuline mission records show 2,732 baptisms in territory.

1884 — Diocese of Helena established. St. Labré Mission opened for Northern Cheyenne by Father Joseph Eyler.

Ursulines at mission, assisted by Jesuits A. van der Velden and Peter Prando.

1885 — St. Paul's Mission established by Father Frederick Eberschweiler for Gros Ventre and Assiniboin tribes. Holy Family mission serving Blackfeet.

1886 — St. Xavier's Mission opened for the Crow.

1887 — St. Mary's Mission founded for the Okanagon.

1890 — Nine missions and stations operating, with nine Indian schools, assisted by Sisters of Providence and Ursulines.

1900 — Missions founded for Northern Cheyenne, Assiniboin, Crow, Gros Ventre, and Piegan Blackfoot tribes.

Nebraska

1541 — Franciscan Juan de Padilla, the protomartyr of the United States, at Platte

River with Francisco Vásquez de Coronado expedition.

1662 — Father Nicholas de Freitas with expedition of the Count of Penelosa, Don Diego, in region.

1673 — Jesuit Jacques Marquette visits Nebraska Indians.

1682 — Nebraska placed under jurisdiction of the bishop of Quebec.

1720 — Franciscan Juan Mingües slain near Columbus while on Pedro de Villasur expedition.

1739 —Mallet expedition in region.

1837 — St. Joseph's Mission opened for the Potawátomi by Jesuits Pierre Jean De Smet, Felix Verreydt, and Andrew Mazella at Council Bluffs.

1838 – Father De Smet with the Otoe tribe on Platte River. Jesuits serve local tribes near Omaha.

1848 — Local Jesuits serve Ponca Indians on Niobrara River.

1851 — Jesuit Bishop Jean-Baptiste Miège becomes vicar apostolic of Rocky Mountain missions.

1856 — Father Jeremiah Trecy starts colony in northeastern part of state, called St. Patrick's.

1857 — Vicariate apostolic of Nebraska started.

1859 — Trappist James Miles O'Gorman serves as vicar apostolic.

Nevada

1774 — Franciscans enter region of modern Nevada on the way to California missions.

1775 — Franciscan Francisco Garcés in Nevada with Juan Bautista de Anza expedition.

1776 — Franciscans Atanasio Domínguez and Silvestre Vélez de Escalante in area.

(No missions were opened in the region comprising the state of Nevada on a permanent basis until the establishment of white settlements, although Spanish missionaries did record visits to the region.)

New Hampshire

1691 — First Mass in the modern state of New Hampshire celebrated at Durham by Jesuits with a French military expedition during King William's War.

(No permanent missions were recorded in this region, as a law passed in 1647 decreed death for any Catholic priests found in the territory.)

New Jersey

1672 — Jesuit priests explore present Woodridge.

1762 — Mass is celebrated by a missionary at Macopin.

(No Indian missions of a permanent nature are recorded in this state as the law of 1698 forbade any such activity. The missionaries to New Jersey, exemplified by Father Farmer [Ferdinand Steinmeyer], the Jesuit "Apostle of New Jersey," served the scattered white Catholic communities.)

New Mexico

1539 — Franciscan Marcos de Niza enters the area, planting a cross forty miles south of today's Gallup and claiming the region as "the new kingdom of St. Francis." He also visits the Zuñi at Hawikuh.

1542 — Francisco Vásquez de Coronado expedition reaches area.

1563 — Francisco de Ibarra enters region and names it "New Mexico."

1581 — Antonio Espejo expedition reaches New Mexico, accompanied by Franciscans Augustín Rodríguez, Juan Santa María López, and Francisco López. All are slain. Father Bernardino Beltrán begins work in territory.

1595 — Don Juan de Oñate expedition sets out for the region that became modern Santa Fe.

1598 — Franciscan Alonso Martínez leads nine Franciscans into area. They settle at San Juan de los Caballeros, thirty miles north of Santa Fe. San Gabriel settled nearby (moved to what is now Santa Fe, about 1602). A chapel is erected at Chamita. Franciscan Andrés Corchado labors among the Zuñi at Hawikuh.

1599 — Franciscans led by Juan de Escalona enter area.

1608 — Franciscan Alonso Peinada and eight companions in missions.

1612 — Franciscans arrive under leadership of Martín de Arvide, open eleven missions.

1617 — Eleven mission churches in operation.

1620 — San Gerónimo de Taos founded for Taos Pueblos by Franciscans.

1621 — Franciscan Alonso de Benavides leads twenty-seven Franciscans into area missions. Franciscan Gerónimo Zarate Salméron translates Jemez devotional work.

1626 — Franciscans report forty-three churches and twenty-seven missions operating in region.

1628 — Franciscan Father de Arvide labors among Jemez in mountains for four years.

1629 — Permanent mission established at Hawikuh. Franciscan Father de Benavides founds Santa Clara de Capo. Apache Chief Sanaba converted.

1630 — Franciscans in Socorro, Senecu, Sevilleta, Sandia, and Isleta, serving Piros, Picos, Liguas, Keres, Tompiros, Tanos, Pecos, Taos, Tehuas, Toas, and Zuñis.

1631 — Franciscan Pedro de Miranda slain in Taos mission.

1632 — Franciscan Father de Arvide slain on trip to Sonora. Franciscan Francisco Letrado also slain. Report indicates ninety pueblos in twenty-five missions served by fifty Franciscans.

c. 1670 — Franciscan Pedro de Ávila y Ayala slain at Hawikuh.

1675 — Franciscan Alonso Gil de Ávila slain in area.

1678 — Franciscan Francisco de Ayeta predicts Pueblo Revolt after tour of missions.

1680 — Pueblo Revolt closes missions. Christian Indians flee to El Paso, Texas.

1692 — Franciscan missions reopened under Father Francisco Vargas.

1693 — Franciscan Father Tarfan establishes Santa Cruz de la Cañada.

1696 — Indian revolt claims lives of five Franciscans.

1732 — Jesuits Felipe Segesser and Juan B. Grashoffer establish local missions.

1733 — Apache mission founded at Jicarillas.

1742 — Jesuit John Menchero begins work among Moquis and Navajos.

1768 — Franciscans arrive in large number to restore missions.

1780 — Isleta missions decimated by smallpox.

1800 — Reported missions in territory include: Asunción (Sia), San Augustín (Isleta), San José (Laguna), San Lorenzo (Picures), San Felipe, San Juan, Dandia (Asunción or Dolores), Guadalupe (Poynaque), Santa Clara, Santo Domingo, Toras (San Gerónimo), and Guadalupe (Zuñi). Visiting stations reported include: Acoma, Cochíti, Galistos, Jemez, Nambé, Pecos, San Felipe, San Ildefonso, Santa Ana, and Tesuque.

1811 — Only five Franciscan missionaries remain in area.

1850 — Bishop John Baptiste Lamy named vicar apostolic of New Mexico. Sisters of Loreto open schools at Mora and Taos.

1894 — St. Katharine Drexel opens St. Catherine's school for Pueblos.

1899 — Archbishop Peter Bourgade invites Franciscan Sisters of Lafayette to open mission schools at Jemez, Peña Blanca, San Fidel, Cuba, and Gallup.

1900 — Schools operating at Santa Fe and Jemez.

New York

1524 — Long Island listed on Spanish maps as *Isleta de los Apóstoles,* so named by Estevan Gómez and Francisco Gordillo.

1614 — Recollect Franciscans tour region, enter Oswego territory.

1626 — Recollect Franciscan Joseph de la Roche Daillon founds Niagara Indian mission.

1642 — Jesuit Sts. Isaac Jogues and René Goupil mutilated at Auriesville (Osscrnenon). St. René slain.

1644 — Jesuit Francisco Giuseppe Bressani tortured at Auriesville but released. St. Isaac Jogues tours region.

1646 — Sts. Isaac Jogues and Jean Lalande martyred at Auriesville.

1651 — Jesuit Joseph Poncet captured and tortured at Auriesville but released.

1654 — Jesuit Simon Le Moyne visits Mohawks. Jesuits Pierre-Joseph Chaumont, René Menard, and Claude Dablon at Indian Hill, Fort Ste. Marie de Gannentaha. Father Dablon opens St. John the Baptist Mission at Syracuse. Father Le Moyne finds salt deposits at Indian Hill, near Manlius.

1656 — Missions started for Cayuga, Oneida, and Seneca tribes. Jesuits at St. Michael's on visits.

1658 — Indian uprisings destroy missions started two years before.

1663 — Seneca chief baptized by missionaries.

1667 — Garaconthié, Onondaga chief, sponsors restoration of Indian missions in region. Jesuit Jean Pierron with Iroquois.

1668 — Jesuit Jacques Fremin in Huron Christian village of St. Michael's at Gandougarae, near modern East Bloomfield. Also serves Seneca in area. Jesuits Pierre Millet (called "the Looker-up-to-Heaven") and Étienne de Carheil at St. John Baptist Mission. Father de Carheil serves Cayuga at St. Joseph's Mission near Great Gully Brook. Immaculate Conception Mission founded at Totiakton, Lima, New York. Father Pierron replaces Father Fremin at Tinnontoguen for Mohawks.

1669 — Jesuit Julian Garnier composes Seneca dictionary at Immaculate Conception Mission at Gandacheragou. René-Robert Cavelier, Sieur de La Salle, expedition and two Sulpicians arrive at Niagara River.

1670 — Jesuit Pierre Raffeix at St. James Mission for Seneca. La Prairie mission opened for Iroquois.

1671 — Jesuit Jean Pierron at St. James (Gannagaro) at Boughton Hill for Senecas.

1678 — Recollect Franciscan Louis Hennepin celebrates Mass within limits of present-day Buffalo.

1679 — Jesuit Vaillant de Gueslis with Mohawks.

1683 — New York Governor Thomas Dongan brings Jesuits Thomas Harvey, Henry Harrison, and Charles Gage to missions.

1684 — Jesuit missionaries, including

Jacques de Lamberville, Jean Pierron, Jacques Bruyas, and Jacques Fremin, in Mohawk missions.

1689 — Jesuit Pierre Millet taken prisoner by Iroquois, remains a captive for five years.

1700 — Anti-Catholic laws passed in New York, threatening missions.

1702 — Jesuits Jacques de Lamberville, Julian Garnier, and Vaillant de Gueslis serve at Onondaga and Seneca settlements.

1709 — Jesuits forced to give up New York missions.

1748 — Sulpician François Picquet at Presentation Mission (Oswegatchié) on St. Lawrence near Ogdensburg, serving Iroquois.

1756 — Jesuits operating St. Regis Mission at Aquasane.

1760 — Presentation Mission abandoned.

1791 — St. Regis flourishing with liturgy using the Mohawk language in part.

North Carolina

1526 — Lucas Vásquez de Ayllón in area.

1540 — Priests accompany Hernando de Soto expedition into region.

(See South Carolina and Florida missions for additional information about this area. No permanent Indian mission records for North Carolina are available.)

North Dakota

1742 — Pierre and François Verendrye expedition accompanied by Jesuits Jean-Pierre Aulneau and Claude Coquart to local tribes.

1818 — Jesuit Joseph Sévère Dumoulin sent to Fort Douglas, St. Boniface, by bishop of Quebec. Jesuits Joseph Pro-

vencher and George Anthony Belcourt also in missions. Father Dumoulin stationed at Fort Douglas and then at Pembina. Father Belcourt, fluent in Algonquin, serves at Lake Traverse and then with Turtle Mountain Chippewas; also compiles dictionary.

1821 — Father Belcourt opens St. Joseph's Mission at Walhalla. Benedictine Jerome Hunt at Fort Totten.

1840 — Jesuit Pierre Jean De Smet among Mandan and Gros Ventre tribes. Jesuit Christian Hoecken serves local missions.

1847 — Devil's Rock mission and school opened by Benedictines. The Grey Nuns of Montreal, the Sisters of Charity, arrive to conduct school programs.

1865 — Jesuit Jean Baptiste Marie Genin founds Fort Totten at St. Michael's.

1874 — Grey Nuns at Fort Totten school.

1877 — Benedictine Claude Ebner at Fort Totten. Standing Rock mission opened by Benedictines, with school. Benedictine Bishop Martin Marty serving missions.

1879 — Bishop Marty heads Dakota vicariate apostolic, headquartered in Yankton. Sioux Sisters labor at Sacred Heart in Elbowoods.

1882 — Benedictine Jerome Hunt at Fort Totten.

1884 — Mercy Sisters teach Chippewa at Belcourt until 1907.

1887 — Father Francis Craft and Sioux Sisters serve at Standing Rock and Fort Berthold.

1893 — Benedictines found St. Gall's at Devil's Lake, moved to Richardton in 1899.

1905 — Missions recorded in area include: Our Lady of Sorrows, Devil's Lake; St. Elizabeth, Standing Rock; St. James,

202

Standing Rock, St. Benedict, St. Aloysius, St. Edward, and St. Bede.

Ohio

1749 — Jesuits accompany Pierre-Joseph Céloron de Blainville into territory. Jesuit Joseph Bonnecamps celebrates Mass on Little Miami River. Jesuit Father Potier in missions.

1751 — Jesuit Armand de la Richardie founds Huron mission near Sandusky, bringing Indians from Lake Erie region.

1795 — Father Edmund Burke (future bishop of Halifax) labors among Maumee at Fort Meigs, near Toledo (Maumee) for two years.

1818 — Dominican Edward Fenwick builds St. Joseph's Church, becomes bishop of Cincinnati.

Oklahoma

1540 — Priests accompany Hernando de Soto expedition into Oklahoma territory.

1541 — Franciscan Juan de Padilla in region with Francisco Vásquez de Coronado expedition.

1630 — Franciscans labor among Oklahoma tribes, led by Father Juan de Sales.

1820 — Jesuit missionaries tour region.

1824 — Jesuit Charles Van Quickenborne visits local tribes.

1830 — Father Van Quickenborne in northeastern region seeking Osage.

1846 — Mission St. Francis opened by Fathers John Schoenmaker and John Bax. St. Mary's of the Quapaw opened, with Sisters of the Divine Providence coming to the school soon after.

1850 — Oklahoma designated as an Indian territory.

1876 — Prefecture apostolic established in Oklahoma with Benedictine Isidore Robot as prefect.

1877 — Benedictines establish Sacred Heart Mission for Potawátomi.

1887 — Sisters of Mercy open school for Choctaw and whites at Krebs.

1891 — Bishop Theophile Meerschaert named vicar apostolic of Oklahoma and the Indian Territory. He opens chain of mission schools. Anadarko, St. Patrick's, for Kiowa opened by St. Katharine Drexel.

1900 — Cherokee schools established at Vinita, Tulsa, and Muskogee.

1903 — Dutch Carmelites labor at Antlers.

1905 — Oklahoma diocese established. Indian schools in operation include institutions at Purcell, Anadarko, Chickasha, Antlers, Pawhuska, Gray Horse, Quapaw, Ardmore, Muskogee, Tulsa, and Vinita.

Oregon

1602 — Sebastian Vizcaíno explores northern Oregon coast with priest chaplains.

1774 — Franciscans accompany Juan Perez on his expedition into area.

1775 — Spanish explorer Bruno Heceta, accompanied by Franciscans, claims area for Spain.

1838 — Father Francis Norbert Blanchet and Father Modeste Demers arrive in Oregon. Headquartered at Vancouver, they open missions at Cowlitz and in the surrounding Oregon area for the local tribes, using the "Catholic Ladder," *Sa-cha-lee-stick,* for catechetical instructions. Log church erected at St. Paul's in Willamette Valley.

1840 — Jesuit Pierre Jean De Smet begins work among Flatheads in area. Church founded on Whidbey Island on Puget Sound. Oblates enter Oregon missions.

1843 — Oregon becomes vicariate apostolic, headed by Bishop Francis Norbert

Cayuse Chief Umapine

bishop of Vancouver. Bishop Augustine Blanchet in Walla Walla, present state of Washington. Pendleton site of new St. Andrew's Mission.

1860 — Father Adrian Croquet at Grand Ronde and Siletz reservations.

1901 — Benedictine Mother Bernardine Wachter dies after laboring in area missions.

1905 — Jesuits open mission on the Umatilla Reservation, staffed by Sisters of St. Francis and Christian Brothers.

Pennsylvania

1643 — Jesuit St. Isaac Jogues labors in Susquehanna area, followed in the 1670s by other Jesuits, Recollect Franciscans, and Sulpicians.

1687 — Jesuit Henry Harrison in missions until 1700.

1720 — Jesuits Joseph Greaton and Richard Molyneux visit local tribes.

1744 — Father Molyneux attends Indian council at Lancaster.

1749 — Jesuit Joseph Bonnecamps with Pierre-Joseph Céloron de Blainville expedition in region.

1754 — Chapel erected at Fort Duquesne, called "The Assumption of the Blessed Virgin of the Beautiful River [the Ohio River]." The Recollect Franciscan Denys Baron begins his work there, with Franciscans Gabriel Amheuser and Luke Collet.

1755 — Jesuit Claude François Virot labors among the Delawares, Shawnees, and Mingos at Sawcunk on the Delaware River.

1891 — St. Katharine Drexel founds Sisters of the Blessed Sacrament.

Rhode Island

No Indian missions are recorded in this state. Catholics fared well in Rhode Island,

Blanchet. Fathers Langlais and Jean-Baptiste Bolduc at Walla Walla.

1844 — Father De Smet founds St. Francis Xavier Mission near St. Paul. Sisters of Notre Dame de Namur enter educational missions. Jesuit Antonio Ravalli at St. Paul's, Champoeg.

1846 — Archbishop Blanchet at Oregon City.

1847 — Whitman Massacre by Cayuse Indians threatens all missions on the Northwest Coast. Father Demers made

but the Native Americans lost their homelands in the region at an early date.

South Carolina

1521 — Priests, including Dominicans
Antonio de Cervantes and Antonio Montesino, accompany Lucas Vásquez de Ayllón
into region.

1523 — Father Sebastian Montero labors at Guatari mission near Anderson
County.

1525 — Dominicans visit Indians in
area.

1526 — Ayllón establishes Winyah
Bay colony, north of Charleston, called San
Miguel de Guandape. Ayllón dies of ship
fever. Dominicans Cervantes and Montesino
labor among local tribes.

1569 — Jesuits Juan de la Carrera and
Juan Rogel at Port Royal, south of Charleston, called Orista (Edesto). Mission abandoned.

1573 — Franciscans start missions in
southeastern section.

1697 — Religious liberty denied to all
Catholics.

South Dakota

1665 — Jesuits Claude Allouez and
Jacques Marquette visit Sioux Indians in
mission explorations.

1674 — Jesuit Gabriel Druillettes labors among Sioux.

1742 — Priests accompany Pierre and
François Verendrye expedition. Jesuits Jean-
Pierre Aulneau and Claude Coquart leave
plaque on the Missouri River near Pierre,
discovered in 1913.

1822 — Jesuit George Belcourt visits
local tribes.

1839 — Jesuits Pierre Jean De Smet
and Christian Hoecken visit Yankton Sioux
on the Vermillion River, serving as well the

Teton and others. Father De Smet labored
among the Potawátomi at Fort Vermillion.

1841 — Father Augustine Ravoux
serves Dakota Sioux in Brown County.

1842 — Fathers De Smet, Christian
Hoecken, and Adrian Hoecken visit local
tribes. Father Ravoux labors at Fort Vermillion and Prairie du Chien, composes Sioux
devotional books.

1858 — Father De Smet baptizes
Yankton Dakota Chief Padanniapapi and his
wife, Mazaitzashanawi.

1876 — Benedictine Bishop Martin
Marty at Fort Yates, works among Sioux.

1878 — Benedictines open school at
Fort Yates on Standing Rock Reservation.

1879 — Dakota Territory established
as a vicariate apostolic. Benedictine Bishop
Marty assumes jurisdiction.

1880 — Presentation Sisters enter
Dakota missions.

1886 — Jesuits serve at St. Francis
Mission on Rosebud Reservation.

1888 — Jesuits labor at Holy Rosary
Mission on Pine Ridge Reservation. Sioux
Sisters in Dakota missions.

1889 — Sioux Falls diocese established.

1892 — Benedictines serving on
Cheyenne River in Sioux mission.

1905 — Missions reported in area in-
clude: Immaculate Conception, Crow Creek;
St. Matthew, Veblen County; Corpus Christi,
Cheyenne River; St. Francis, Rosebud; Holy
Rosary, Pine Ridge.

1908 — Oblate Sisters of the Blessed
Sacrament open St. Paul's.

Tennessee

1541 — Hernando de Soto expedition,
accompanied by Fathers Juan de Gallegos
and Louis de Soto, plants cross on the banks
of the Mississippi River.

1673 — Jesuit Jacques Marquette welcomed by Chickasaw in the area.

1682 — Recollect Franciscans Zenobius Membré and Anastase Douay on René-Robert Cavelier, Sieur de La Salle, expedition to Memphis.

(No permanent Indian missions were founded in Tennessee.)

Texas

1541 — Priests accompany Francisco Vásquez de Coronado expedition into the territory. Hernando de Soto explores region.

1544 — Franciscan Andrés de Olmos visits Pakawá and other Indians in Texas and takes them south to Tamaulipas, Mexico, establishing a secure mission there.

1553 — Dominicans Diego de la Cruz, Hernando Méndez, Juan Ferrer, and Brother Juan de Mina slain in area.

1659 — Franciscan Mission Nuestra Señora de Guadalupe established, serves local tribes.

1675 — Father Juan Larios celebrates High Mass in territory with expedition led by him and Fernando del Bosque.

1682 — Corpus Christi de Isleta Mission founded near El Paso by Franciscans for Jumanos.

1685 — Expedition led by René-Robert Cavelier, Sieur de La Salle, arrives in region, accompanied by Franciscans Zenobius Membré, Maxime LeClerq, and Anastase Douay, with two Sulpician priests named Chefdeville and Cavelier. Fort St. Louis, Bahía, founded. All missionaries slain.

1689 — Franciscan Damian Massenet leads companions into region with expedition of Alonso de León, meets Payaya Indians.

1690 — Father Massenet returns to Texas with Franciscans Miguel Fontcubierto, Francisco Casañas, Antonio Borday, and Antonio Pereira. Welcomed by Asinais Indians and founds San Francisco de las Tejas in eastern area. This mission abandoned in 1693 when epidemic kills seven thousand Indians.

1691 — Father Massenet serves Pakawá Indians. Franciscans Francisco Hidalgo, Nicolás Recío, Miguel Estelles, Pedro Fortuny, Pedro García, Ildefonso Monge, José Saldona, Antonio Miranda, and Juan de Garayuschea enter missions on the Red River, Neches, and Guadalupe.

1700 — Additional Franciscans enter Texas.

1703 — Mission San Francisco de Solano established on Rio Grande River. This mission was later moved and renamed.

1716 — Venerable Antonio Margil de Jesús leads nine Franciscans into region. Establishes six missions and Nuestra Señora del Pilar de los Adayes near Natchitoches. La Purísima Concepción opened for Caddo, Sanipao, and other tribes.

1718 — Mission San Francisco de Solano moved to San Antonio and renamed San Antonio de Valero, the Alamo.

1720 — Venerable Antonio Margil founds San José y San Miguel de Aguayo Mission.

1721 — Franciscan Brother José Pita slain at Carnezeria.

1722 — Venerable Antonio Margil named guardian of the missions. Espíritu Santo founded near Fort St. Louis and La Bahía, later transferred to Goliad.

1731 — La Purísima Concepción, San Juan Capistrano, and San Francisco de la Espada founded in San Antonio. La Purísima, originally a Caddo mission in eastern Texas, founded on the San Marcos River.

1734 — San Saba Mission and San Luis de Amarillos founded for Apaches and Comanches by Father Aponte y Lis.

1748 — Franciscan Francisco Año de los Dolores establishes San Francisco Xavier at Horcasitas for the Tónkawa on the San Gabriel River.

1749 — La Bahía opened at Goliad for Karánkawas.

1752 — Father José Ganzabal slain.

1754 — Rosario Mission established near San Juan.

1757 — San Saba attacked; Franciscans Alonso Terreros and José Santiesteban slain.

1760 — Texas missions record fifteen thousand Christian converts.

1761 — San Lorenzo Mission in operation but destroyed by Comanches.

1772 — Mission San Francisco Xavier de Naxera erected.

1791 — Refugio Mission opened on the Mission River.

1793 — Last mission founded at Goff Bayou, Nuestra Señora del Refugio. Mexican government secularizes missions soon after.

Utah

1776 — Franciscans Silvestre Vélez de Escalante and Atanasio Domínguez reach Salt Lake.

1841 — Jesuit Pierre Jean De Smet guest of Brigham Young near Council Bluffs.

1858 — Father De Smet serves as chaplain for General Harney on an expedition to Utah.

1859 — Franciscan Bonaventure Keller offers Mass at Camp Floyd near Lehi.

1861 — Utah and Colorado formed as vicariate apostolic. Bishop Joseph P. Machebeuf assumes leadership.

1866 — Father Edward Kelly offers Mass in Salt Lake City in the Mormon Assembly Hall.

1886 — Utah vicariate apostolic established.

(No permanent mission for Native Americans resulted from any of these events.)

Vermont

1609 — Samuel de Champlain visits region and provides name of state.

1666 — Sulpician Dollier de Casson celebrates Mass at Fort Ste. Anne on Isle La Motte.

1668 — Blessed François de Montmorency Laval, first bishop of Canada, visits region. Jesuit Jacques Fremin labors among Mohawks, founds mission.

1710 — Jesuits among Native Americans near Lake Champlain. Swanton and Ferrisburg missions opened.

1749 — Jesuits labor among local tribes.

Virginia

1526 — Dominican Antonio Montesino celebrates Mass at settlement of Lucas Vásquez de Ayllón. Dominican Antonio de Cervantes and Brother Pedro de Estrado present at Guandape mission, named St. Michael's.

1561 — Dominicans explore coastal areas for mission sites.

1570 — Jesuit Juan Bautista Segura leads seven companions to mission sites of Ajacan near future Jamestown with Jesuit Luis de Guiros and Brothers Solís, Méndez, Linares, Redondo, Gabriel, and Gómez. All are slain in 1571 at Ajacan on the Rappahannock River.

1571 — Jesuit Father Rogel returns to Rappahannock River missions. Jesuits slain in area.

1634 — Jesuit John Altham serves tribes in area.

1642 — Catholic priests outlawed in Virginia.

1687 — Jesuits Edmonds and Raymond arrested by English.

1689 — Capuchin Franciscan Christopher Plunket arrested, dies on a coastal island in exile in 1697.

Washington

1774 — Priests with expeditions from Mexico.

1838 — Fathers Francis Norbert Blanchet and Modeste Demers arrive in region.

1839 — Father Demers on Puget Sound.

1840 — Cross erected on Whidbey Island.

1843 — Area made vicariate apostolic. Father Jean-Baptiste Bolduc at Puget Sound and Lower Vancouver Island.

1844 — Mission founded at Colville, called St. Paul, by Jesuit Pierre Jean De Smet, staffed by Sisters of Notre Dame de Namur.

1846 — Diocese of Walla Walla erected.

1847 — Bishop Augustine Magliore Blanchet arrives at Walla Walla with Oblates and seculars. Whitman Massacre causes conflict. Oblate Eugene Casimir Chirouse, the "Apostle of Tulalip," in region. Jesuit Adrian Hoecken at St. Paul's for Lake Indians.

1848 — Oblates Eugene Casimir Chirouse and Charles Pandosy to Yakima at St. Rose Mission.

1850 — Father Chirouse among Swinomish, Lummi, and Tulalip tribes. Diocese of Nesqually erected.

1856 — Father Chirouse serves at Priest's Point, Olympia.

1858 — Tulalip school opened for Swinomish.

1859 — Father Chirouse begins missionary work on Puget Sound.

1860 — Tulalip mission serving Snohomish, Swinomish, Lummi, and Duwamish tribes.

1866 — Jesuit Joseph Cataldo serves Spokan Indians.

1868 — Puget Sound mission records 3,811 baptisms by Oblates.

1872 — Lake Indians moved to St. Francis Regis at Ward.

1875 — Missions in Clark, Skamania, and Lewis counties. Father Adrian Croquet at Grande Ronde.

1888 — St. George Mission school conducted by Franciscan Sisters.

1889 — Father Bolduc dies, honored as the "Apostle of Puget Sound."

1900 — Jesuits laboring at Colville, St. Francis Regis missions.

West Virginia

1749 — Jesuit Joseph Bonnecamps visits region with Pierre-Joseph Céloron de Blainville expedition.

(No permanent Indian missions were recorded in this state.)

Wisconsin

1634 — Region explored and recorded by Samuel de Champlain expedition.

1636 — Jesuits labor at Green Bay with Winnebagos.

1658 — Jesuit Gabriel Druillettes at Green Bay, Oumamik.

1661 — Jesuit René Menard disappears in area, believed slain.

1665 — Jesuit Claude Allouez founds Holy Ghost Mission at La Pointe de Esprit on Madeleine Island at Chegoimegon Bay (Bayfield).

1669 — St. Francis Xavier Mission founded at De Pere (Green Bay). Jesuits

Claude Allouez and Jacques Marquette in missions.

1670 — Twenty Jesuit missionaries enter Wisconsin missions. Father Allouez at St. Michael's on the Menóminee River. Mission St. Jacques opened on the Fox River.

1671 — Father Allouez and Jesuits Louis André and Claude Dablon labor in local missions.

1673 — Father Marquette visits Miami villages. Father Louis André to Menóminee Indians.

1677 — Jesuit Charles Abanel at de Pere mission.

1698 — Seminarist Jean François de Saint-Cosmé at Sheboygan, Milwaukee, and Racine regions.

1701 — Jesuit Jean Baptiste Chardon goes to Green Bay to assist Jesuit Henri Nouvel, who labored there for forty years.

1711 — Father Chardon visits Illinois Indians, then returns to Green Bay.

1763 — Jesuits forced out of missions.

1836 — Dominican Venerable Samuel Mazzuchelli begins serving Native Americans in local missions.

1854 — Menóminee mission founded. Franciscan and Sisters of St. Joseph of Carondelet in schools. Benedictines start labors among Chippewas. Oblates open missions at Nett Lake. Missions founded at Fond du Lac, New Ulm, and other sites.

1880 — Franciscan Zephyrin Engelhardt serves the Menóminee at Kenosha and Ottawa.

1900 — St. Michael's opens at Keshima.

1905 — Franciscans found mission at Bayfield.

Wyoming

1840 — Jesuit Pierre Jean De Smet celebrates Mass at Rendezvous on Green River on July 4. Jesuits P. de Vos, Christian Hoecken, Zerbinate, Pierre Joseph Joset, and Gregorio Mengarini also in regional settlements.

1851 — Bishop Jean-Baptiste Miège named vicar apostolic of territory. Father De Smet conducts peace conference at Fort Laramie.

1884 — Jesuits assume missions for Shoshone and Arapaho. Jesuit John Jutz at St. Stephen's Mission for Northern Arapaho on Wind River Reservation. Sisters of Charity in mission by 1890.

1887 — Jesuit Paul Mary Ponziglione at St. Stephen's.

1900 — New missions for Arapaho and Shoshone founded.

Menóminee Chief Bear's Oil, from an 1831 painting

Missionaries of the Native Americans

through the Great Lakes region and beyond. He even mapped the western end of Lake Superior. Some twenty-three Indian nations benefited from his devotion in an area covering three thousand square miles. His missions were also hampered by the presence of the unfriendly Iroquois, who were being driven west by the increasing white populations in their homelands.

In 1665, Father Allouez was in Wisconsin, where he made his headquarters on Madeleine Island for over two decades. From there he labored among the Huron, Nipissing, Wyandotte, Ottawa, Potawátomi, Sauk, Outagami, Miami, Chippewa, and Illinois tribes. When fourteen Indian nations met to form an alliance at Sault Ste. Marie in 1671, Father Allouez was asked to give the main address to the assembled participants.

He served as well as the first vicar-general of the missions of the territories that would become the United States, an office conferred upon him by Blessed François de Montmorency Laval of Quebec in 1663. Father Allouez's jurisdiction was not limited to the missions, as he had authority over French traders and settlers as well. Father Allouez reportedly baptized as many as ten

Claude Allouez

Called "the founder of Catholicism in the West," this Jesuit was one of the most famous explorers and missionaries of the western United States. He was born in France in June, 1622, and as an ordained priest of the Society of Jesus was sent to Canada in 1658. From the beginning of his ministry, Father Allouez mastered the Native American languages of the tribes in his mission territory. He was a co-laborer with Jesuit Jacques Marquette, and he prepared devotional works to aid in the missions. A book was discovered containing prayers in French and in the Illinois language, with a note stating that Father Allouez provided this work to his companion, Father Marquette.

Father Allouez labored among the Native Americans for thirty years, traveling all thousand Native Americans. The renovations of Kaskaskia and other missions were due to his efforts also. No missionary of his era traveled over a wider area, and few could converse in the Native American languages with such ease. Considered by many to be the greatest Jesuit missionary of the period, Father Allouez continued his labors until his death, among the Ottawas, in 1689.

John Altham

Considered a co-founder, with Father Andrew White, of the Catholic Church in the Maryland colonies, Father Altham was a Jesuit missionary. He was born in England in 1589 and arrived in Maryland in 1634, with Father White and a Jesuit Brother, Thomas Gervase. Both priests started their missionary labors immediately among the local Native American tribes and the Catholic colonists. Father Altham fell ill in 1637, having cared for victims of yellow fever. He recovered and labored in Chesapeake Bay, near modern Annapolis, until 1640. Taken aboard ship to be returned to St. Mary's Mission near Baltimore, he died of the fever. Father White was arrested with another Jesuit in 1645, ending his role in the mission.

Louis André

One of the most gifted of the Jesuit missionaries in Native American languages, Father André was born in France in 1631. He was ordained a priest and assigned to the American missions, laboring with Father Gabriel Druillettes at Sault Ste. Marie in northern Michigan. When the Ottawa Indians fled the oncoming eastern Indian tribes, Father André accompanied them out of the region and then went to the Algonquin missions on the Great Lakes. He established his base mission at Green Bay, Wisconsin, in 1671.

There he labored for over a decade, traveling by canoe or on foot to tour the mission outposts. St. Francis Xavier served as his residence when he was not on the trail. He also served the Chicoutimi and Sept-iles (Seven Isles) Indians. Father André compiled dictionaries and catechisms for the Algonquins and Ottawas. He died in Quebec in 1714.

Anthony of the Ascension

A Discalced Carmelite missionary, Anthony of the Ascension set sail with Sebastian Vizcaíno in May, 1602, and landed in San Diego, California, celebrating Mass there on November 12, 1602. Exploring the area, the missionaries reached the Monterey peninsula, calling it Carmelo. The local Native Americans were kindly and hospitable and receptive to the faith. When Anthony and the others ended the expedition, they urged missionary activities in the California region, but did not return themselves. The Spanish merchant Vizcaíno is credited with providing several California communities with their present names. He did not return to the area either.

Martín de Arvide

Called the "Apostle of Picuris," this Franciscan missionary to New Mexico was born in Puerto de San Sebastian, Spain, probably around 1586. He entered the Franciscan Order, and in 1612, was sent with twenty-five companions to the New Mexico missions. There he established San Lorenzo Mission at Picuris and served until 1628. When word came that the local Jemez Indians had fled to the mountains to escape Navajo assaults, Father Arvide joined them and served as their missionary for four years.

In 1632, Father Arvide was asked to open a mission among the Zipias of Sonora.

He was on his way to his new station when he was slain by Zuñis. A monument honors Father Arvide at San Lorenzo.

Stephen Theodore Badin

The first Catholic priest to be ordained in the original states of the Union, Father Badin was a pioneering missionary in Kentucky, Michigan, Illinois, and Ohio. He was born in France in 1768, becoming a Sulpician. Fleeing the French Revolution, he sailed to Baltimore in 1792 and was ordained by Bishop Carroll in May, 1793. Father Badin was then assigned to Kentucky, where he rode horseback on a mission circuit covering over a hundred thousand miles.

Returning to France in 1819, Father Badin was back in America in 1828, going to Michigan and then to Kentucky. Two years later he was serving the Potawátomi in Ohio. He served as vicar-general of the diocese of Bardstown, Kentucky, and celebrated his golden anniversary of ordination in 1843 in Lexington. Three years later he was the pastor of a parish in Kankakee County, Illinois. Before his death, Father Badin donated land to Father Edward Sorin, who erected Notre Dame University on the site. Father Badin died in the residence of Archbishop Purcell in Cincinnati, Ohio, in 1853. His remains were transferred to Notre Dame University in 1904.

Pierre Bailloquet

Beloved missionary to the Ottawa, this Jesuit served the Native Americans from Acadia on the eastern coast to what is now Illinois. He was born in 1612 in France and was assigned to the Catholic Indian missions after ordination, arriving in Quebec in 1647. For over forty-five years, Father Bailloquet would travel the Native American settlements, enduring physical torments and pri-

vations. He dragged himself on his rounds even at the age of eighty in order to comfort the ill or dying among the Indians. Father Bailloquet himself became ill, and eventually he was unable to complete his rounds. He died on his Ottawa mission in June, 1692, mourned by the tribes.

Irenaeus Frederick Baraga

The "Apostle to the Chippewas," Father Baraga was a Redemptorist missionary in the northern peninsula of Michigan. He was born a noble, in a castle in a region now called Slovenia, in 1797. St. Clement Mary Hofbauer recognized Frederick's spiritual gifts and served as his spiritual director when he entered the Redemptorists, receiving ordination in 1823. He volunteered for the American missions soon after and arrived in Cincinnati, Ohio, in 1831.

Father Baraga began his mission labors with the Ottawa at L'arbre Croche (now Harbor Springs), in northern Michigan. He also served at La Pointe, Wisconsin, L'Anse, Michigan, and in the region now known as Grand Rapids. Alone in the area, he built churches and schools for the Native Americans and the white families working for the local copper mine. He made two trips to Europe, however, to collect funds and personnel for the missions.

In 1853, Father Baraga was named vicar apostolic of the northern peninsula of Michigan. Consecrated a bishop, he also presided over the erection of a new diocese, moving his see from Sault Ste. Marie to Marquette in 1865. His first pastoral letters were issued in Chippewa and in English. He also compiled a grammar for the Native Americans, and his sermons and prayer books were popular. Bishop Baraga suffered a stroke while attending the Second Plenary Council in Baltimore, and he was taken to

Marquette, where he wanted to breathe his last. He died on January 19, 1868. His canonization cause was opened in Rome.

Michel Baudoin

Called the "Apostle to the Choctaw," this Jesuit missionary was one of the few members of the Society of Jesus not expelled from the missions when the order was suppressed. He was born in Canada in 1692 and entered the Jesuits at twenty-one in France. Ordained, he was assigned to Louisiana and arrived in New Orleans in 1728. His mission apostolate there centered around the Choctaw, whom he served faithfully.

In 1749, Father Baudoin was assigned to New Orleans, where he served as the superior general of the Louisiana missions until 1763, when the Jesuits were expelled. Father Baudoin, however, was beloved by whites and Native Americans alike. He was given a pension and a retirement residence on a planter's estate. Father Baudoin accepted the offer and stayed in New Orleans until his death, about 1768.

Pierre Biard

A Jesuit missionary to the Native Americans on the eastern coast, he was from France, born in Grenoble in 1567. Father Biard was noted for his brilliance and spiritual insights. He was a professor of Scholastics, theology, and Hebrew at Lyons, when he was assigned to the Society of Jesus missions in Acadia, New France (Canada). The Calvinists opposed his journeying to America, and Father Biard and his companions had to purchase their own ship in order to secure safe passage. They arrived in Port Royal, Canada, in May, 1613.

Father Biard went to Saint-Sauveur, in Maine, where he began his labors. Within months, however, English troops arrived at the mission and took the Jesuits prisoner. They were marched to the English at Jamestown and then forced to accompany a second English expedition to complete the destruction of Saint-Sauveur. It was hoped that the presence of the Jesuits in this final raid would turn the local Indian tribes against them and all of the French — a tactic that did not succeed.

Father Biard was placed on board a ship bound for England and was then returned to France. Knowing that he could not hope to continue his missionary efforts in America, he returned to his academic career. In time, however, he became quite famous in southern France as a military chaplain and missionary. Father Biard died in Avignon in 1622.

Augustine Magliore Blanchet

Revered as the "Apostle of Washington," Augustine Blanchet, the brother of Archbishop Francis Blanchet, was born in Saint-Pierre, Rivière de Sud, Quebec, Canada, in 1797. Educated with his brother in Quebec, he was ordained to the priesthood on June 3, 1821. He labored in the Îles de la Madeleine (Magdalen Islands) and Cape Breton Island and in 1842 became a canon of the Montreal Cathedral.

In that same year, he was consecrated as the bishop of Walla Walla, which was the forerunner of the present archdiocese of Seattle. He arrived in Walla Walla on September 5, 1847, with Father Jean Baptiste Abraham Brouillet and other missionaries, including Oblates, and worked in the region called The Dalles. The Whitman Massacre, involving St. Anne's Mission on the Umatilla, caused Bishop Blanchet problems, but he continued his efforts and made his commitment public by becoming a United States citizen in 1847. He established missions, academies, schools, hospitals, and parishes throughout the diocese.

In 1850, the diocese was moved to Nesqually, and Bishop Blanchet made his residence in Fort Vancouver. He built a log cathedral as well. In 1852, he attended the First Plenary Council in Baltimore, and in 1876, with Archbishop Blanchet, spearheaded the organization of the Bureau of Catholic Indian Missions. Bishop Blanchet retired in 1879 and suffered considerably from physical ailments before his death at Fort Vancouver on February 25, 1887.

Francis Norbert Blanchet

The first archbishop of Oregon City, now Portland, he is revered as the "Apostle of Oregon," and one of the driving forces for the establishment of the Bureau of Catholic Indian Missions. He is the brother of Bishop Augustine Magliore Blanchet and was born in 1795 at Saint-Pierre, Rivière de Sud, Quebec. Ordained to the priesthood on July 18, 1819, Father Blanchet served seven arduous years in New Brunswick, among the Acadians and Micmacs.

In 1827, he was made pastor of St. Joseph de Soulanges, Montreal, and so distinguished himself by his tireless labors during the cholera epidemic of 1832 that the local Protestants gave him a testimonial. In 1837, Father Blanchet set out with Father Modeste Demers for Fort Vancouver, in the Oregon Territory, taking nine days to cross the Rocky Mountains. His territory included 375,000 square miles, and he brought priests from Canada to serve the local Catholics and the Indian tribes in residence in the region.

On July 25, he was consecrated a bishop and appointed vicar apostolic. He went to Rome to gather priests and religious Sisters, and worked with Jesuit Pierre Jean De Smet to plan a vigorous and comprehensive mission apostolate. In 1846, he became the archbishop of Oregon City and continued his labors among the Indian missions, going to South America to gather funds and mission personnel.

The Whitman Massacre of 1847 almost destroyed all the missions in the region, and the California Gold Rush added new complications. Archbishop Blanchet persevered and moved to Portland in 1862. His main concern, even amid his many archdiocesan labors, was for the Native Americans. The Bureau of Catholic Indian Missions resulted from his defense of the Catholic Indian apostolate.

In 1869, Archbishop Blanchet celebrated his golden jubilee of ordination. He labored on until 1881, when he retired to the Sisters of Providence Hospital in Portland. Archbishop Blanchet died on June 18, 1883.

John Baptist Boulet

A secular missionary to Washington's tribes, John Baptist Boulet was born in Quebec in 1834. He was educated locally and then at Saint-Hyacinthe's, going soon after to Vermont and Holyoke, Massachusetts. In his studies, John Baptist met Napoleon St. Onge, a seminarian who had volunteered to assist Bishop Augustine Magliore Blanchet at Holy Angels College in Vancouver, Washington. John Baptist joined St. Onge and was ordained for the Washington missions on July 19, 1874.

He was assigned to all the tribes in Clark, Skamania, and Lewis counties. He conducted missions throughout the vast area and also served the Northwest Coast. Father Boulet then decided to start a printing apostolate for the region and founded St. James Press. When he moved to Tulalip, he renamed the press in honor or St. Anne. Father Boulet, who printed pamphlets and magazines to aid the missions, was made a monsignor in 1911. He died at Bellingham on August 4, 1919.

St. Jean de Brébeuf

Martyred Jesuit missionary to the Huron nation, he was honored as *Echon*, "the Strong One," by that nation. He was born in Condé-sur-Vire in 1593 and raised as a rural noble. In 1617, St. Jean entered the Society of Jesus; he was ordained and sent to Canada in 1625. He labored among the Algonquins and then went to the Hurons in 1626. Taken prisoner by the English and returned to France, St. Jean was back with the Hurons by 1633, founding missions. In 1639, he opened St. Marie Mission and labored there until the Iroquois captured him ten years later. Called "the Huron among the Hurons," St. Jean and his Jesuit companions were tortured and slain on March 16, 1649, at Sault Ste. Marie near Georgian Bay. He converted seven thousand Native Americans and composed a Huron catechism and dictionary.

Francisco Giuseppe Bressani

A missionary to the Hurons, this Jesuit was born in Rome in 1612 and entered the Society of Jesus at age fourteen. Educated at Rome and at Clermont in France, he was ordained and assigned to the Quebec missions. Father Bressani was a brilliant scholar who taught in Jesuit institutes in Sezza, Tivoli, and Paris before being sent to Canada (or New France as it was known at the time).

He labored among the Algonquins at Three Rivers, Michigan, soon after his arrival in Quebec and then set out in April, 1644, to the Huron missions, accompanied by six Christian Hurons and a young French boy. The Iroquois captured the party and killed the Hurons. Father Bressani was tortured by his captors for two months and then ransomed by the Dutch at Fort Orange. The Mohawk Great Council sanctioned Father Bressani's release in order to open negotiations for future Catholic missions in their lands. He returned to France to recuperate, but was back in Quebec in 1645.

Once again he went to the Hurons, establishing a mission, which was destroyed by the Iroquois. With his health shattered, Father Bressani returned to Italy in 1650, where he wrote of his captivity. He died in Florence on September 9, 1672.

Luis Cáncer de Barbastro

Called the "Apostle of Guatemala," this Dominican was martyred near Tampa Bay, Florida, while attempting to begin missions for the local tribes. He was born in Saragossa, Spain, around 1510; he entered the Order of Preachers (Dominicans) and was ordained to the priesthood in Spain.

In 1543, Father Cáncer de Barbastro was sent to the order's Guatemalan missions, where he became known as the "Standard Bearer of the Faith." In December, 1547, he received permission and support for a mission in Florida, and on May 29 of that year went ashore at Tampa Bay with two companions and an interpreter. Father Cáncer de Barbastro returned to the ship moored nearby to get presents for the local Indians. Going ashore again, he discovered that his Dominican companions had been slain. On June 26, he tried to make contact once again with the Florida tribes and was clubbed to death.

Magín Catalá

Called the "Holy Man of Santa Clara," this Franciscan missionary spent his life in the Mexican-sponsored Indian apostolate. Born in Spain, he entered the Franciscans, being ordained to the priesthood in 1785. He volunteered for the Mexican missions and set out from Cádiz in 1786.

For six years, Father Catalá served at the Apostolic College of San Fernando in Mexico City. In 1793, he was sent to Monterey, California, and became the chaplain of an expedition sailing to Nootka Sound, Vancouver Island, Canada. Upon his return he was assigned to the mission at Santa Clara, where he labored until his death. He suffered from severe crippling arthritis but did not allow the pain to halt his efforts. Father Catalá baptized 3,067 Native Americans and performed 1,905 marriages. His endless suffering and goodness won the respect of the local Indians, who aided his work. Father Catalá died as the "Holy Man of Santa Clara" on November 22, 1830.

Joseph Cataldo

Called the "Dried Salmon" by the Native Americans, this Jesuit missionary and superior was laboring in his late eighties to evangelize local tribes. Born in Tersasini, Sicily, in 1837, he became a Jesuit at age fifteen and had to leave his native land to study for the priesthood in Rome. He was ordained at Louvain, Belgium, and then volunteered for the American missions.

Sent to Boston to study English, Father Cataldo developed tuberculosis and was assigned to Santa Clara College in California to recuperate. By 1865, he was well enough to be assigned to the missions for the Coeur d'Alene and Spokan Indians, and he started his lifelong labors among the Nez Percé. He became superior of the Rocky Mountain missions in 1877 and served in that capacity until 1893. Revered by the Native Americans, Father Cataldo under-

stood Indian culture, having been trained by Father Gregorio Mengarini, a Jesuit companion of the famed Jesuit Pierre Jean De Smet.

Father Cataldo established boarding schools on many reservations and founded Gonzaga College for Indians and whites. He died in his beloved missions in 1928.

Jean Baptiste Chardon

A gifted linguist and a trusted friend of the Native Americans in the Great Lakes region, this Jesuit missionary was born in Bordeaux, France, in 1672. By 1700, he was in the Ottawa missions, and the following year went to Green Bay, Wisconsin, to aid Jesuit Henri Nouvel, who had been at that post for over forty years.

Able to learn the Native American languages with ease, Father Chardon served the Illinois Indians on the St. Joseph River in 1711. He returned to Green Bay in 1728 and labored there for the rest of his missionary apostolate. For much of that time, Father Chardon was believed to be the only priest west of Lake Michigan. He died in Quebec in 1743.

Pierre-Joseph Chaumont

A Jesuit missionary and founder of the Congregation of the Holy Family, he was born near Châtillon-sur-Seine, France, in 1611. Some records list his family name as Calvonotti. Entering the Society of Jesus in Rome, he was ordained and sent to Canada in 1639. St. Jean de Brébeuf was his superior in the missions at Lake Huron, and when the saint was martyred, Father Chaumont helped four hundred Catholic Hurons to reach safety in Quebec.

He was then sent to New York, to the Onondaga mission founded by Jesuit Simon Le Moyne. His Jesuit companion was Claude Dablon. The mission lasted two years, and in 1657 the missionaries and some fifty colonists had to flee the area because of unrest. Father Chaumont remained with the Hurons until his death in Quebec on February 21, 1693.

Jean-Louis Cheverus

An Oratorian missionary and a cardinal of France, Jean-Louis Cheverus was born in Notre Dame de Mayenne, France, in 1768. He was educated at the Oratorian seminary of St. Magliore on December 18, 1790, just as the French Revolution was threatening the faithful in his homeland. Father Cheverus had to leave France and labored in England before coming to America.

In 1796, he arrived in Boston, where he served with Father François Matignon among French and Irish immigrants. Father Cheverus also worked among the Native Americans in Maine. In 1803, the two missionaries opened Holy Cross Church on Franklin Street in Boston. In 1808, Father Cheverus was named the first bishop of Boston by Pope Pius VII. He continued to labor in Maine throughout his episcopacy, as he had many Native American converts.

In 1823, Bishop Cheverus returned to France to become the bishop of Montauban despite the pleas of Catholic and Protestant Americans who petitioned the king of France to allow him to remain in the United States. In 1826, he became the archbishop of Bordeaux and was made a cardinal in 1836 by Pope Gregory XVI. He died on July 19, 1836, and was buried in the nave of Saint-André's Cathedral, Bordeaux.

Eugene Casimir Chirouse

Revered as the "Apostle of Tulalip," this tireless Oblate missionary was born in France in 1821. Entering the Oblates of Mary Immaculate in his homeland, he was assigned to the American missions while he was still in the seminary. He traveled across the sea, then across the region of America as he followed the Oregon Trail to Walla Walla (Nesqually), Washington. There he was ordained to the priesthood on January 2, 1848.

Father Chirouse went to St. Rose in Yakima following his ordination and in 1852 reopened the Cayuse mission on the Umatilla River, which had been involved in the Whitman Massacre. He renamed the mission St. Anne's and labored to build a solid congregation. Four years later, Father Chirouse went to Priest's Point (Olympia), on Puget Sound, where he started his mission apostolate of over three decades. At Tulalip he built a chapel, residence, and school in one log building.

Father Chirouse offered the Native Americans a full program in his missions. He instructed them, conducted liturgies, and brought them the holy sacraments, but he also fed and clothed the members of his flock and knew them as individuals. In this fashion he ministered to the Swinomish, Lummi, Muckleshoot, and Fort Madison tribes. For a time he also served as a reservation agent for the federal Bureau of Indian Affairs and was respected for his knowledge of Native American culture and needs.

Father Chirouse's death on May 28, 1892, in British Columbia, where he had retired in 1878, was mourned by everyone in the northwest region of the United States. He was trusted and respected by the Indians he had served for so long.

Louis Lambert Conrardy

A unique missionary, whose apostolate spanned continents, he was born in Liège, Belgium, in 1841. Educated locally and ordained on June 15, 1866, Father Conrardy became a missionary in India, serving in the Pondichery region from 1871 to 1874.

He then attended the American College at Louvain, Belgium, and arrived in Oregon in 1874 to begin labors among the Native Americans. By 1875, he was the resident on the Umatilla Reservation and revered by the Indians and local whites. In 1888, Father Conrardy, called a "hero" by the American Church leaders, went to Molokai, Hawaii, and administered the last sacraments to Blessed Damien de Veuster, S.S., C.C. He stayed on Molokai, serving the lepers for eight years, and then enrolled in the University of Oregon Medical School in Portland.

Earning his medical degree in 1900, he went to Shek Lung Island, near Canton, China, to begin a leper colony. He eventually won the respect of the Chinese authorities and received assistance in this apostolate. Father Conrardy died of pneumonia in Hong Kong on August 24, 1914. At his request, he was buried with two other lepers, wrapped in a mat, in the Hong Kong cemetery.

Pedro de Corpa and Companion Martyrs

These Franciscans, part of the vast Florida mission, were concentrated among the Indians in Georgia, on Cumberland and Parris islands. They arrived in 1584 and began their apostolate, only to be slain in 1597.

Father Pedro de Corpa, from Villabilla, Spain, was the first victim of a revolt started by Juanillo, the local Indian chief. Father de Corpa was clubbed to death on September 14, 1597.

Father Blas de Rodríguez, from Caceres, Spain, was slain on September 16. Father Miguel de Anón, from Badajoz, Spain, was killed at Mission Santa Catalina de Guale, St. Catherine's Island, Georgia, on September 17. The Franciscan Brother Antonio de Badajoz died with Father de Anón.

The last martyr was Father Francisco de Beráscola on the island of Asao. He had been absent during the revolt but was slain upon his return.

Joseph Crétin

A missionary bishop and friend of St. John Vianney, the Curé of Ars, he was born in 1799 at Montluel, Ain, France. Educated at the University of Paris with St. John, Joseph also attended the seminaries of Meximieux, L'Argentière, Alix, and Saint-Sulpice in Paris. He was ordained to the priesthood on December 20, 1823, and assigned to Ferney, where he founded a school for boys.

In 1838, Father Crétin responded to the plea of Bishop Pierre Jean Mathias Loras and volunteered for mission work in Dubuque, Iowa. There he served the Winnebago Indians and in 1839 was made vicar-general of the diocese. In 1850, Father Crétin was appointed the first bishop of St. Paul, Minnesota. He was consecrated on January 26, 1851, and began his ministry to a diocese that contained thirty thousand Native Americans.

He served six years in St. Paul, revitalizing the Indian missions and bringing religious orders and congregations to the region. Bishop Crétin died in St. Paul on February 22, 1857.

Charles de la Croix

A missionary to the Osage Indians of the Missouri plains, and a pioneer, he was born in Hoorbeke-St.-Corneille, Belgium, in 1792. He studied for the priesthood at Ghent and was imprisoned by Napoleonic authorities in the fortress of Wesel, where his

Gros Ventre shield

In 1828, Father de la Croix was in the Lower Louisiana parish of St. Michael's. He completed the church there in 1832. In 1833, he returned to Belgium and served as a canon of the cathedral of Ghent until his death on August 20, 1869.

Adrian Croquet

One of the most committed missionaries to the Native Americans in the northwest, he was born in Braine-l'Alleud, Belgium, in 1818. He attended Malines seminary and was ordained in 1844, returning to the Catholic University of Louvain for more study. In 1858, Father Croquet volunteered for the American missions and was trained at the American College, Louvain. He started his Indian mission apostolate at Grand Ronde Reservation in 1860.

For four decades, Father Croquet served the Indians at Grand Ronde on the Siletz Reservation and in the Willamette Valley of Oregon. The local Native Americans recognized his good heart and his profound respect for their traditions. He retired to Belgium in 1898 and died in his hometown on August 15, 1902.

Claude Dablon

The Jesuit missionary superior of New France (Canada) and a companion of the famed explorer Jesuit Jacques Marquette, he was born in Dieppe, France, about 1618. He entered the Society of Jesus at age twenty-one. Following his ordination he was assigned to the American missions. In 1655, Father Dablon served the Onondaga Indians, and in 1661, accompanied Jesuit Gabriel Druillettes on an expedition to Hudson Bay. Seven years later, he was with Father Marquette and Jesuit Claude Allouez on Lake Superior.

Father Dablon helped to establish Sault

brother died from the harsh conditions. When Napoleon I fell from power, Father de la Croix was released and followed Bishop Louis Dubourg to Louisiana after ordination to the priesthood.

In 1818, Father de la Croix was sent to Borrens, Missouri, where he labored as a missionary and supervised the building of a seminary. He then went to Florissant, near St. Louis. The Religious of the Sacred Heart aided him there in his work among the Osage and the white Catholic settlements. He prepared the way for the Jesuits in Florissant, then called St. Ferdinand's.

Ste. Marie Mission in Michigan and sent his companions on a celebrated journey down the Mississippi River. He recorded and published the journeys of Fathers Jacques Marquette and Charles Abanel's travels in Hudson Bay. Father Dablon, who was the superior of Sault Ste. Marie from 1668 until 1679, bequeathed maps, detailed accounts, and studies of his labors to the Jesuits. He died in Quebec in 1697.

Modeste Demers

Revered as the co-founder of the Oregon Church and the founder of the Church in British Columbia, he was born in Quebec, Canada, in 1809. He was educated at the Quebec seminary and ordained on February 7, 1836. Father Demers served in Quebec until 1837 when he labored among the Native Americans at Red River Mission.

One year later he set out with Bishop Francis Norbert Blanchet for Oregon, where he demonstrated his dedication and his facility with Indian languages. Within weeks he knew the local languages well enough to translate hymns and prayers for his mission flocks. He served the district of the Columbia River and then labored in the interior of British Columbia.

From 1844 until 1847, Father Demers served as a pastor in Oregon City, which became an archdiocese. He erected St. John's, the future cathedral, and was vicar-general of Oregon while Archbishop Blanchet toured Europe soliciting funds and qualified mission religious.

In 1847, Father Demers reluctantly accepted the post as the bishop of Vancouver Island and was consecrated on November 30. He also went to Europe to raise needed funds and to recruit priests. In 1852, he assumed episcopal jurisdiction in Victoria.

The Sisters of St. Anne arrived in the missions in 1858, and the Oblates of Mary Immaculate began their labors among the Native Americans of the region. In 1869, Bishop Demers attended the First Vatican Council. He was in a train accident in France and suffered a compound leg fracture. Returning to Victoria, he also suffered a stroke. He died on July 28, 1871, and was buried in the cathedral that he built in Victoria, St. Andrew's.

Pierre Jean De Smet

The famed Jesuit and peacemaker, probably the best-known mid-nineteenth-century missionary to the Native Americans west of the Mississippi River, he was born in Termonde, Belgium, in 1801. In May, 1823, he immigrated to the United States and entered the Jesuit novitiate at Whitemarsh, Maryland, completing his studies at Florissant, Missouri. He was ordained in 1827.

In 1833, Father De Smet, who suffered repeated illnesses, was sent to Belgium to recover. In 1838, he returned to St. Louis and began working with the Potawátomi near Council Bluffs, Iowa. His no-nonsense missionary style was demonstrated at this stage in his apostolate. His mission, St. Joseph's, was endangered by the nearby Sioux, who threatened attacks. Father De Smet walked into the Sioux camp, introduced himself, and asked the Sioux to leave the Potawátomi and the mission in peace. The astonished Sioux heard his pleas and agreed to refrain from any such assaults.

In 1840, Father De Smet responded to a call for a "Blackrobe" and went to the Rocky Mountains, where the Jesuits were establishing a missionary province. He was welcomed by the Flatheads and Pend d'Oreilles, and he went among the Crows, Gros Ventres, and others on a journey of

4,814 miles. In 1841, Father De Smet founded St. Mary's Mission on the Bitter Root River, thirty miles north of Missoula, Montana. Realizing the vast populations of the local tribes and their receptive acceptance of the faith, Father De Smet went to Europe to recruit six Sisters of Notre Dame de Namur and other workers as well as funds.

On his return to his mission area, he went by canoe to the residence of Bishop Francis Norbert Blanchet, at Fort Vancouver. The two men spent time planning the missions in the region. Father De Smet, who attended the "Rendezvous of the Mountain Men and Fur Trappers," came to this planning session with vast experiences. He even spent time with Brigham Young in Utah, welcomed there because of his knowledge of the district and the tribes.

The hallmarks of Father De Smet's missionary apostolate were manifold. He was a no-nonsense traveler who endured hardships without complaint. He respected the Native American traditions and values and never took sides in debates. Because he spoke only the truth, he served as a mediator in tribal conflicts, such as the Blackfoot and Flathead confrontation in 1846. Father De Smet also served as a mediator at Fort Laramie (1851), in the Mormon Wars (1858), and in other regional disputes.

Founding the Kalispel St. Ignatius Mission as part of the overall mission strategy for the territory, he accompanied the Blackfoot Indians into the Yellowstone Valley in 1846. He and the tribe then went to Fort Lewis and there the Blackfeet adopted peaceful relations with their neighbors.

He addressed the ten thousand Indians holding a council in Horse Creek Valley near Fort Laramie, urging peace. The United States military forces also asked him to intercede in events that threatened disaster.

Father De Smet's most unforgettable feat took place in 1868 as a result of the federal government's requests for his assistance. Sitting Bull and the Sioux threatened war as a result of white treachery concerning their lands, and a federal peace commission was formed to avoid such a conflict. Father De Smet joined the commission on their way to the Sioux enclave but soon left the whites and went on his own way. He walked unarmed into a camp of five thousand Sioux warriors and asked to see Sitting Bull. Warmly received, Father De Smet and the great chief talked alone over a long period. The Jesuit missionary left the Sioux camp with a pledge of peace.

Father Pierre Jean De Smet was honored by Native Americans and whites alike as "the truest friend the Indians ever had." He logged nearly 261,000 miles through the wilderness to serve the tribes. He spoke with candor and showed respect and honor in his dealings with all the Native Americans. Such views were evident in his writings and reports. Father De Smet died in St. Louis, Missouri, on May 23, 1873.

St. Katharine Marie Drexel

Called "the Million-Dollar Nun," and serving as the sponsor of untold Native American and black educational programs and missions, St. Katharine was born in Philadelphia in 1858. She was the daughter of Francis Martin Drexel, a noted Philadelphia banker. When her mother died soon after Katharine's birth, her father married Emma Bouvier, a devout Catholic. Katharine and her sister, Elizabeth, were raised in the faith.

When their parents died, they left Katharine and Elizabeth a sizable fortune. During an audience with Pope Leo XIII in 1883, Katharine asked what could be done about the Native and "Colored People" (the term used at the time). The Holy Father asked in return: "Daughter, why don't you become a missionary?"

Returning to Philadelphia, St. Katharine started the Sisters of the Blessed Sacrament for Indians and Colored People, canonically founded on February 12, 1891, and now called the Sisters of the Blessed Sacrament. She became Mother Katharine Drexel. Over the next decades, St. Katharine Drexel spent nearly twenty million dollars of her inheritance on missions and schools, including Xavier University in New Orleans. She also founded forty-nine convents and sixty-two schools.

St. Katharine died on March 3, 1955, revered by Americans for her holiness and generosity. Her cause was opened in 1964 by John Cardinal Krol. Pope John Paul II beatified Mother Katharine Drexel on November 20, 1988, and is scheduled to be canonized on October 1, 2000.

Gabriel Druillettes

A far-ranging Jesuit missionary and Canadian legate, he was born in France in 1610. Entering the Jesuits, Father Druillettes was ordained and assigned to the American missions, arriving in Canada around 1633. He served in New England and around the Great Lakes for four decades. In 1636, Father Druillettes labored among the Abenaki Indians of Maine. He was at the mission on the Kennebec River and stayed in the area until 1652. He then labored in the Canadian Indian missions and served in an official capacity for the governor of New France (Canada). The Canadian governor wanted to arrange a treaty with the Protestants of New England colonies and sent Father Druillettes to attend meetings with the leaders of the colonies. These sessions proved futile, but Father Druillettes, a recognized authority on the American Indians, was treated with kindness and respect. He was a very holy man, and miraculous events are associated with his name in many Native American mission regions.

In 1670, Father Druillettes was in Sault Ste. Marie and other Michigan missions. He had labored as well in Green Bay, Wisconsin, twelve years earlier. Exhausted by his travels, Father Druillettes returned to Quebec, where he died on April 8, 1681.

St. Rose Philippine Duchesne

The foundress of the Society of the Sacred Heart in America, called "The Woman Who Always Prays" by the Native Americans, she was born in Grenoble, France, in 1852. The daughter of a prominent lawyer, she was educated by the Visitation Nuns and entered the convent just as the French Revolution closed the religious houses of the nation. When the revolution ended, St. Rose Philippine tried to revive the Visitation Convent and asked St. Madeleine Sophie Barat to assume the house. St. Madeleine declined that offer but welcomed St. Rose Philippine into the Society of the Sacred Heart. She took her vows on December 31, 1804.

Fourteen years later, when St. Rose Philippine was forty-nine, the Society of the Sacred Heart responded to the invitation given by Bishop Dubourg of New Orleans. St. Rose Philippine was assigned to lead four companions to Louisiana. She did not speak English, but she opened the first school in St. Charles, Missouri, and then founded Indian schools, orphanages, and an American novitiate for the congregation.

She even spent time with the Potawátomi at Sugar Creek Mission in 1841; she did not speak to the tribal members in words but in recollection, prayer, and compassion.

223

She was not able to remain with the Potawátomi but was recalled to St. Charles, Missouri, the following year, where she died on November 18, 1852, at the age of eighty-three. She is honored as a pioneer in the Hall of Fame of the state of Missouri. She was canonized by Pope John Paul II on July 3, 1988.

Mary Amadeus Dunne

This Ursuline superior, called the "Teresa of the Arctic," was born in Ohio in 1846 and entered the Ursulines in Toledo, Ohio. Called Mother Mary Amadeus of the Heart of Jesus in religious life, she led five Ursuline companions to Miles City, Montana, on January 17, 1884. There she started a school called the White House and won the respect of the local Cheyenne and others at St. Labré Mission. In 1887, she opened a school for the Crow and then led the Ursulines to Alaska. Mother Mary Amadeus opened schools in St. Michael's and at Valdez. She died in Alaska in 1919. Mother Mary Amadeus was affectionately called "Chief Lady Blackrobe" by the Native Americans, who respected her no-nonsense approach to the apostolate.

Zephyrin Engelhardt

A publisher and promoter of the Native Americans, this Franciscan missionary was born in Bilshausen, Germany, in 1851. His parents migrated to Covington, Kentucky, and he was raised in his adopted land. In 1873, he entered the Franciscans in Illinois and was ordained five years later.

Father Engelhardt was sent to the Menóminee mission at Kenosha, Wisconsin, in 1880, and spent two decades serving that tribe in Kenosha and Superior. He also labored among the Ottawas at L'arbre Croche (now Harbor Springs), Michigan.

Father Engelhardt published the "Guide to Heaven," *Kachkenohamatwon Kesekoch*, translated from Ojibwa to Menóminee. In 1884, he published *Kateshim*, a catechism, and he founded the *Praying Indian, Anishina Enamiad* for the Ottawa in 1896.

Father Engelhardt also compiled histories of the Franciscan missions in Arizona and California. He died in 1934 in Santa Barbara, California, and his archives are preserved there.

Jacques Fremin

This Jesuit missionary to the Mohawks, the guardian of some ten thousand Native Americans, was born in Reims, France, in 1628. He entered the Society of Jesus in 1646 and was ordained before being sent to the American continent. Father Fremin arrived in the Onondaga mission in 1655. In 1666, he was invited to the Cayuga settlement at Lake Tiohera, near modern-day Cayuga, and remained a year.

Father Fremin then went to Isle La Motte in Vermont and to Tinnontoguen, the Mohawk capital at the time. Most of his ministry there was aimed at caring for the Christian Huron captives being held at the Mohawk settlements. In October, 1668, he went to the Seneca lands, and in August of the following year visited Onondaga with other priests.

In 1670, Father Fremin, who was fluent in the local Indian languages, took charge of La Prairie Mission near Montreal. At the time of his death, on July 2, 1691, he had served over ten thousand Native Americans in their homelands.

Pierre Gibault

The famed "Patriot Priest" who aided the American Revolutionary War, he was born in Montreal, Canada, in 1737. Educated in Quebec, he was ordained on March 19, 1768. Soon after, he was assigned to the Illinois missions as vicar-general, and after visiting Mackinaw, established his headquarters at Kaskaskia. He also labored among the Native Americans at St. Geneviève, Vincennes, and Cahokia.

For a long period, Father Gibault was the only priest in Illinois and Indiana, at a time when white settlers were teeming into the region. In 1778, Colonel George Rogers Clark captured Kaskaskia for the Americans, and Father Gibault led the whites in accepting the cause. Cahokia and Vincennes also joined the Americans under his leadership.

The Canadians had forbidden such activities, and the British authorities were enraged by Father Gibault's actions. Father Gibault was forced to leave his post and went to Spanish-held lands in the area called New Madrid, beyond the Mississippi, in modern Missouri. He died there on August 15, 1802.

Joseph Giorda

This Jesuit missionary of the Rocky Mountains, called *Mil'Kokan*, "Round Head," by the Coeur d'Alenes, was born to a noble family in Turin, Italy, in 1821. Brilliant, he entered the Society of Jesus at age twenty-two, and taught in a seminary after ordination. In 1861, he volunteered for the Indian missions and was assigned to Sacred Heart Mission for the Coeur d'Alenes. He then went to St. Peter's in eastern Montana and won the trust and respect of the Native Americans and whites in the area. Father Giorda was so popular that he became the first chaplain of the Montana Territorial Legislature at Virginia City.

When the Jesuits in the area were reassigned to California, Father Giorda, who had been appointed superior of the Rocky Mountain missions, went to California and brought back his much needed priests. When he retired in 1866, he had eight missions in operation, six of which he had started. From 1869 until 1877, he served again as Jesuit superior, dying at Sacred Heart Mission on August 4, 1882.

Jacques Gravier

This Jesuit missionary, who traveled up and down the Great Lakes for the Native Americans, was born in Moulins, France, in 1651. Joining the Society of Jesus in 1670, he was ordained and then assigned to the Canadian missions in 1685. Traveling through the Great Lakes district, Father Gravier succeeded Father Claude Allouez at Kaskaskia in Illinois in 1689. For over a decade he served the Kaskaskia and Peoria Indians and compiled a grammar of the Illinois languages.

In 1696, at Michilimackinac (Mackinaw) in Michigan, he served as superior and vicar-general. In 1700, he returned to the Illinois mission, where the Peorias rebelled six years later. Father Gravier was wounded, and the arrow embedded in his arm could not be removed. He went to Paris to have surgeons extract the arrow, which was causing infections, but they were unable to aid him. Father Gravier, still carrying the arrow in his arm, went to Louisiana in 1708. He died of an infection soon after.

François Vaillant de Gueslis

A Jesuit missionary among the Mohawks and the Native Americans in the region of Detroit, he was born in Orléans, France, in 1646. He entered the Society of Jesus in 1665 and was ordained in Quebec ten years later. Father Vaillant de Gueslis was then assigned to the Mohawk Indians, among whom he labored from 1679 to 1684.

Father Vaillant de Gueslis also served as a liaison between the Catholics in Canada and Governor Thomas Dongan of New York. Governor Dongan was able to promote the faith but was overthrown by the Protestant authorities.

Father Vaillant de Gueslis aided the Jesuit missions around Detroit, Michigan, demonstrating respect and concern for the Native Americans there. He was recalled to Canada's missions and then returned to France, where he died at Moulins on September 24, 1718.

Louis Hennepin

A Franciscan missionary and one of the famous explorers of seventeenth-century America, he was born in Belgium in 1640. Entering the Recollect Franciscans, he volunteered for the missions after his ordination and was assigned to various European houses until 1675, when he set sail for Quebec. There he learned Indian languages and began his famous records and descriptions.

He sailed down the American waterways with René-Robert Cavelier, Sieur de La Salle, in 1679, and parted with the explorer in order to proceed down the Illinois River. Father Hennepin was in the company of two Frenchmen when they reached the Mississippi River and were captured by Issati Sioux on April 12, 1680. Father Hennepin and the others traveled with the Sioux from that day on, reaching Minneapolis, Minnesota, and they were not released until the explorer Daniel Greysolon, Sieur Du Lhut, demanded their freedom.

Father Hennepin went to St. Ignace Mission and then to Quebec, where he met Blessed François de Montmorency Laval, the first bishop of Canada. After a brief rest, he retired to a monastery and then sailed for Europe for monastic enclosure. He wrote accounts of his travels and descriptions of his encounters with the local tribes. Father Hennepin died in Rome around 1701.

Christian Hoecken

The Jesuit missionary companion of Father Pierre Jean De Smet and the guardian of the Native Americans in exile, he was born in the Netherlands in 1808. Educated in Belgium, he entered the Society of Jesus in 1832. Following his ordination, Father Christian Hoecken sailed to America and labored among the Kickapoos from 1836 to 1838, in Missouri and Kansas. He was called "Father Kickapoo" because of his fluency in the tribal language. He even wrote a dictionary for the tribe.

In 1838, Father Hoecken founded a Potawátomi mission on the Osage River, remaining there for three years and then going to Sugar Creek, Kansas. There he wrote a Potawátomi dictionary and grammar. In 1847, he accompanied the tribe to Kaw Valley in Kansas. He also served the Miami, Peoria, Piankashaw, and Sauk in the region. When eastern tribes arrived in their new lands of exile, Father Hoecken was waiting with medicines, blankets, food, and words of comfort. His brother, Adrian, also served in the Jesuit missions.

In 1851, Jesuit Pierre Jean De Smet was asked to take part in a journey to attend the Great Council of Indians. Father Hoecken went with the famous Jesuit and died on the trail of cholera.

St. Isaac Jogues

Martyred French Jesuit to the Hurons and Iroquois, he was born in Orléans, France, in 1607. St. Isaac entered the Society of Jesus in 1624. In 1636, an ordained priest, St. Isaac volunteered for the missions of America. He arrived at the main Huron village, Ihonateria, in September of that year and served the Catholics there and in the Tobacco and Chippewa settlements. Three years later he built Sainte-Marie on Georgian Bay.

In 1642, the Mohawks captured St. Isaac while he was journeying to Quebec. He spent a year as a tortured slave before being released through the efforts of a Dutch trader, who arranged his voyage back to France. St. Isaac was acclaimed in the court of Anne of Austria, the regent of France, but he longed for his missions and returned to Canada in 1644. Two years later, St. Isaac was asked to undertake peace negotiations with the Mohawks. He made two separate journeys into the Mohawk territory, the first proving a successful start. On his second journey, however, Isaac faced danger. His vestments and liturgical objects that he had left in the Mohawk settlement at Ossernenon (Auriesville), New York, had alarmed the Indians. Upon entering into negotiation in vain, St. Isaac was killed by a hatchet blow in October, 1646. He was a priest of courage and devotion, a writer of classical eloquence, and a mystic. St. Isaac was canonized by Pope Pius XI in 1930.

Pierre Joseph Joset

This "Apostle to the Coeur d'Alenes" was a Jesuit missionary, born in 1810, in Bern, Switzerland. Trained in the Society of Jesus, he was ordained on September 19, 1840. He promptly volunteered for the American missions and arrived in New Orleans with Jesuit companions in 1843. In the following year he was assigned to the Rocky Mountain missions and went to Wyoming to meet Jesuit Pierre Jean De Smet at the

Young Ignace

Green River Rendezvous. Father De Smet did not arrive, so the Jesuit party went in search of St. Mary's Mission in Montana. "Young Ignace," an Iroquois who had converted to Christianity, met them and led them safely through the wilderness to their destination.

Assigned then to the Coeur d'Alenes, at Sacred Heart Mission, Father Joset moved the outpost to Cataldo in Iowa. He served as the local Jesuit superior there and maintained his Coeur d'Alene apostolate, visiting St. Paul's on the Columbia River and St. Michael's near modern Spokane, Washington. He died on June 19, 1900, with his beloved Coeur d'Alenes.

Eusebius Francisco Kino

The Jesuit missionary called the "St. Francis Xavier of Pimería," he was born in Segno, Tyrol, in 1645. He was of noble lineage, and his family name was spelled Chino or Chini, which he changed to Quino or Kino. He entered the Society of Jesus in

1665 and was ordained in 1677. (Because of his association with the Jesuit province of Upper Germany, some historians have classified him as a German under the name Kühn.) The following year he studied agriculture in Seville and served as spiritual adviser to the duchess of Aveiro. He also taught mathematics and science and in 1680 wrote a well-received book about comets.

Arriving in Mexico in 1681, after volunteering for the Spanish missions, Father Kino was sent on an expedition to California. He set out from La Paz Bay, in California, and explored the region with Matías Goñi, his Jesuit companion. In 1685, he returned to Mexico, where he was assigned to Pimería Alta, which included Sonora and the deserts of the American Southwest. He established his mission headquarters at Mission Dolores in 1687, where he baptized the Pima Chief Coxi and labored among the Papago. In 1699, among other sites, Father Kino founded San Xavier del Bac, near Tucson, and Mission San José. He continued his labors until 1698 or 1699, when he explored Baja California, founding nine missions there. Father Kino, as mentioned earlier, was the one who determined that Baja California was not an island but a peninsula. His work, *Favors From Heaven*, recounts his missionary efforts.

He is called the "Padre on Horseback," and statues of him, equestrian style, were raised in various southwestern cities. His statue also stands in the National Statuary Hall in Washington, D.C., as a representative of the state of Arizona. He died in Magdalena, Baja California, on March 15, 1711. That site is now called Magdalena de Kino. Father Kino's canonization cause was introduced in 1995.

Albert Lacombe

This Oblate missionary to the Native Americans was called the "Man-of-the-Good-Heart" and was born in Canada in 1848. One of his ancestors had been captured by the Ojibwa but rescued. He was educated locally by the Oblates and ordained, then sent to the missions. Father Lacombe traveled from Montreal to Buffalo, New York. He went as well to Dubuque, Iowa, and St. Paul, Minnesota, in his mission assignments.

Fluent in Native American languages, he compiled dictionaries and grammars for the tribes. He hunted buffalo with the Indians, explored Hudson Bay, and met with Blackfoot, Blood, Piegan, Strongwood, and Plains Cree at

Cree painted coat

Edmonton. He also gave missions to the tribes at Peace River, Little Slave, and Lesser Slave lakes. He was laboring in Montana and the Dakota Territory up until 1877.

The traditional account of Father Lacombe's involvement in a Cree attack on the Blackfeet states that during the conflict he was accidentally hit by a stray bullet that grazed his head. The Blackfeet shouted the news to the Cree: "You have wounded your Blackrobe!" The Cree, horrified, stopped the battle, and both sides tended Father Lacombe's wound. He retired to Calgary, Canada, where he died in 1890.

Bellarmine Lafortune

Called the "Little Father," this Jesuit missionary to Alaska was born in Saint-Roch-de-l'Achigan, near Montreal, Canada, in 1869. Small but energetic, he entered the Society of Jesus and was ordained on July 27, 1902. He was about to begin four decades of missionary labors among the Native Americans. In 1903, Father Lafortune landed in Nome, Alaska. The Inuit of the Seward Peninsula were the focus of his efforts, and he built a chapel in 1905.

Father Lafortune then founded missions at Teller, Sinuk, Mary's Igloo, Pilgrim Springs, Wales, and on Little Diomede Island. He became in time the main missionary for the King Islanders, visiting them in 1916. In 1922, he built a mission on the island. Father Lafortune died after suffering a stroke on October 22, 1947.

Jacques de Lamberville

This Jesuit missionary, called the "Divine Man" by the Native Americans, instructed and baptized Blessed Kateri Tekakwitha. He was born in Rouen, France, in 1641, and entered the Society of Jesus two decades later. Ordained, Father de Lamberville was sent to Canada, where he started his labors among the Iroquois. At Ossernenon, now Auriesville, New York, Father de Lamberville recognized the unique spiritual gifts of Blessed Kateri and aided her in entering the Church and in seeking the safety of a Christian Indian community.

He served the Iroquois with his brother, Jean, and was considered "one of the holiest missionaries of New France." Father de Lamberville died at Quebec in 1710.

Jean de Lamberville

The elder brother of Jesuit Jacques de Lamberville, this missionary of the Society of Jesus was born in Rouen, France, in 1633. Ordained in 1656, he arrived in Canada in 1669. There he began his missionary work among the Onondaga Iroquois of present-day New York, a labor lasting fourteen years. It was a difficult era, beset with the rivalries of France and England. Father de Lamberville mediated peace on several occasions and was assaulted by opposing tribes. His health was shattered by his harrowing experiences, and he retired to France to recover, planning to return to the missions. Father de Lamberville died in Paris in 1714.

St. Jean Lalande

This lay missionary companion of St. Isaac Jogues was born in Dieppe, Normandy, France. Volunteering as a layman for the Jesuit missions, he arrived in Canada and labored in the Three Rivers district until 1646. St. Isaac Jogues was returning to the Mohawks at Ossernenon (Auriesville), New York, to negotiate a peace and St. Jean accompanied him to the meeting. The Mohawks had decided against the peace, however, and made them prisoners. St. Isaac Jogues and St. Jean Lalande were slain on

October 18 and 19, 1646. Both missionaries were canonized in 1930.

Simon Le Moyne

A famous Jesuit missionary, friend of Chief Garaconthié of the Onondagas, Simon Le Moyne was born in 1604 at Beaudois, France. Joining the Society of Jesus in 1622, he was educated, ordained, and assigned to the Canadian missions, arriving there in 1638. Father Le Moyne was a gifted linguist, mastering Huron and Iroquois and displaying a remarkable awareness of Native American diplomatic and ceremonial observances.

In 1654, he was among the Onondagas and then the Mohawks, who martyred St. Isaac Jogues and others. Father Le Moyne went among the Mohawks time and again. On his fifth visit he was tortured and condemned to death but was saved by Chief Garaconthié. When Father Le Moyne died in 1665 at Cap de la Madeleine, near Three Rivers, Chief Garaconthié delivered the eulogy, describing the missionary's virtues and courage.

Michael Levadoux

One of the first Sulpicians to serve in the United States, and a tireless missionary to the Native Americans, Michael Levadoux was born in Clermont-Ferrand, Auvergne, France, in 1746. He entered the Sulpicians in 1769 and, after his ordination, was assigned as the director of the seminary at Limoges.

Father Levadoux, appointed vicar-general of the Illinois missions, went to that region in 1792. His labors centered around Cahokia and Kaskaskia, serving Vincennes, Indiana, as well. In 1796, he was stationed at Detroit and labored among the Indians from Sandusky, Ohio, to Mackinaw, Michigan, and Fort Wayne, Indiana.

In 1803, Father Levadoux was recalled to France, where he held many offices among the Sulpicians. He died at Le-Puy-en-Velay on January 13, 1815.

Francisco López de Mendoza Grajales

This founder of the first parish in today's United States arrived in Florida in 1565, accompanying the expedition of Pedro Menéndez de Avilés. Arriving from Havana, Cuba, he had probably been born in Spain, and was a secular priest recruited by de Avilés.

Father López de Mendoza Grajales celebrated Mass for the first time in Florida on the feast of the Nativity of the Blessed Virgin Mary. Remaining in the region, he tried to found a mission at Santa Lucia but was forced to flee from attacks by local tribes. He tried then to return by ship to Havana, but his vessel was caught in a storm and blown back on the Florida coast. There he was rescued by Spanish settlers.

By June, 1566, Father López de Mendoza Grajales was the pastor of the mission church at St. Augustine. He was joined by five more priests and continued his labors. The last documented records of his presence in Florida dates to 1569.

Venerable Antonio Margil de Jesús

A Franciscan missionary veteran and a profoundly holy man, this Servant of God was born in Spain, probably about 1657. Volunteering for the missions in June, 1683, Venerable Antonio Margil de Jesús labored in Mexico and Costa Rica and then actually walked across Guatemala, evangelizing the Maya and other tribes. He helped to found Cristo Crucificado College in Guatemala City and Nuestra Señora de Guadalupe College in Zacatecas, Mexico. Venerable Antonio Margil also administered Santa Cruz de Querétaro College.

In 1716, he led a band of three Franciscan priests and two lay brothers into the region of the present United States. He built three missions on the Rio Grande, but they were destroyed by the French in the area. By 1717, he was in Louisiana, working in Sabine Parish, where he founded Mission San José y San Miguel de Aguayo. He also erected a chapel near Nuestra Señora del Pilar. Venerable Antonio Margil walked twenty miles to the settlement at Natchitoches to instruct and baptize the local tribes.

In 1718, he was in Texas to found Missions Guadalupe, Dolores, San José, and San Miguel. He then went to San Antonio and in 1722 was made the guardian, or superior, of the Mexican missions. This demanded his return to Mexico City, where he labored until his death on August 6, 1726. He was described by contemporaries as tall and thin, walking barefoot through his mission areas. Penitential and praying throughout each night, Venerable Antonio Margil fasted every day of his life. He was declared venerable by Pope Gregory XVI in 1836.

Jacques Marquette

This famous Jesuit missionary-explorer, the companion of Louis Joliet, was born in Laon, France, in 1637. Entering the Society of Jesus in 1654, he was ordained on March 7, 1666, volunteering immediately for the American missions. He was sent to Canada to learn the Native American languages and became fluent in seven Algonquin dialects. He then went to Lake Superior, where the Indians detected his priestly qualities and called him the "Young White Father." His fame spread, and Illinois Indians invited him to visit them on the "Great River." Father Marquette had already journeyed to Sault Ste. Marie, Michigan, in 1668.

In May, 1673, Louis Joliet arrived at Father Marquette's mission, sent by Count Frontenac of Canada (Louis de Buade, comte de Palluau et de Frontenac) with permits and provisions for a lengthy expedition. The two men set out in canoes, crossing Lake Michigan to Green Bay, where they visited the tribe called the Wild Oats. They pushed on to St. Francis Xavier Mission on the Fox River, a route that forced Father Marquette, Joliet, and five French companions to carry their canoes overland. They visited the Miami, Mascouten, and Kickapoo there, and the Miami guided them to the Wisconsin River.

Arriving at an Illinois village, Father Marquette and his party were feted and treated with kindness. They entered the Mississippi River on June 17. The trip was arduous because of the heat and the mosquitoes, but they journeyed to the Arkansas River, where they heard that the Spanish controlled the area to the south. That news caused them to turn back. On the journey north, Father Marquette suffered severely, probably from amoebic dysentery. By the end of the year, the party was safely back at Lake Michigan.

During the following years, Father Marquette pioneered many Great Lakes missions, beloved by the Kaskaskia and Illinois tribes. Exhausted from his travels and his missionary circuits, Father Marquette visited these Native Americans, then fell ill not long after. He wanted to return to his mission at Mackinaw and was escorted by an Indian retinue. Slowly the party moved northward, but he could not hold off his death and stopped his journey at present-day Ludington, Michigan. While in his last ago-

231

nies, Father Marquette gave instructions about his burial.

Gazing upon his crucifix and thanking God for dying in the Society of Jesus as a missionary, he sighed: *Mater Dei, memento mei*, "Mother of God, remember me," and died calmly and gently on May 18, 1675. He was buried at Ludington, where his bones were dried and placed in a birch-bark casket. His remains were taken solemnly to St. Ignace Mission, Mackinaw, on June 8, 1677.

Pedro Martínez

This Jesuit protomartyr of America was born to a noble family in Aragon, Spain, and desired to become a religious. Given the gift of a priestly vocation, he entered the Society of Jesus and served as the rector of several Spanish colleges and then accompanied the Spanish military forces on an expedition against the Moors.

Father Martínez volunteered for the American missions and went with the expedition of Pedro Menéndez de Avilés to an area on the coastal region of Georgia called Guale by the Spaniards. The Jesuits, led by Father Martínez, established a mission on Cumberland Island, then called Tacatucuru. On October 6, 1567, these missionaries were slain. When Father Martínez volunteered for the American missions, the perils of the apostolate were well known by the Spanish. Before he embarked on his apostolate and eventual martyrdom, Father Martínez received personal blessings from Pope St. Pius V and St. Francis Borgia.

Martin Marty

A Benedictine abbot and bishop who answered the call for missionaries to the Native Americans, he was affectionately known as "Blackrobe Lean Chief" by the Indians. He was born in Schwyz, Switzer-land, in 1834. He entered a Jesuit school and then the Benedictine monastery of Maria Einsiedeln and was ordained to the priesthood on September 14, 1856.

In 1860, Father Marty arrived in St. Meinrad, Indiana, and ten years later served as the first abbot of the American abbey. The Bureau of Catholic Indian Missions asked him to send Benedictines to the Indian missions, and Father Marty undertook the apostolate personally, in 1876, going to Yankton, a site in Dakota on the Missouri River. Slowly he began his ministry, working to make the care of the Native Americans a permanent part of the Benedictine mission in the United States.

On August 5, 1879, Pope Leo XIII named Abbot Marty vicar apostolic of the Dakota Territory. He was consecrated a bishop in Indiana and resumed his ministry, tireless in his efforts. He became the bishop of Sioux Falls in 1899, and was transferred to St. Cloud, Minnesota, in 1894. There he continued his Native American apostolates. Exhausted from his years in the mission fields, Bishop Marty died in St. Cloud on September 19, 1896.

Enemond Massé

A Jesuit missionary taken prisoner by the English in Maine, he was born in Lyons, France, in 1574. Father Massé arrived in the American colonies with Jesuit Pierre Biard, and established a Native American mission at Bar Harbor, Maine. The English sent a military unit to destroy the chapel and arrested Father Massé, putting him in an open boat on the Atlantic Ocean to die of exposure or in a storm. He was saved by a French ship sailing in the region, and was taken to France, then returned to Canada in 1625. There he labored until his death on May 12, 1646, at Sillery.

Venerable Samuel Mazzuchelli

This Dominican missionary to the Woodland Native Americans was born in Milan, Italy, in 1806. Educated in Milan and Switzerland, he entered the Order of Preachers in 1823, in Faenza, volunteering for the American missions in response to an appeal by Bishop Edward Dominic Fenwick, a Dominican pioneer in Ohio. Venerable Mazzuchelli was ordained in Cincinnati on September 5, 1830, and was then assigned to Mackinaw Island, then part of the diocese of Cincinnati.

At age twenty-four, Venerable Father Mazzuchelli was the only priest in Upper Michigan and Wisconsin. He cared for settlers, fur trappers, and above all, the local Indian tribes, the Ojibwa, Ottawa, Menóminee, and Winnebago. Venerable Father Mazzuchelli used canoes, snowshoes, and sleds to traverse the frozen wastes of his "parish." Learning the local languages of the tribes, he wrote a prayer book for the Winnebago and a calendar for the Menóminee. He also opened schools for the local Native American children.

Serving the white settlements as well, Venerable Father Mazzuchelli founded the Sinsinawa Dominican Sisters in 1848, a Dominican center, and Sinsinawa Mound College. He was a hero to people of all faiths during the cholera epidemic of 1849-1850.

Venerable Father Mazzuchelli died of pneumonia on February 23, 1864, while on a call in his mission territory. His cause was opened in 1965, and he was declared venerable by Pope John Paul II in 1993.

Zenobius Membré

A Recollect Franciscan in the early Catholic Indian missions, he was born in Mapaume, Pas-de-Calais, France, in 1645.

Father Membré arrived in Canada in 1675, and four years later accompanied René-Robert Cavelier, Sieur de La Salle, on an expedition to Illinois. He wrote a historical account of this journey. In 1681, Father Membré descended the Mississippi River, going to the Arkansas Indian village that Jesuit Father Marquette had visited. Father Membré planted a cross there and also visited the Taensa and Natchez tribes.

In 1684, with two Franciscans and three Sulpicians, Father Membré went with La Salle to Texas, where a fort was erected in the following year. Father Membré, Father Maxime LeClerq, and others died at this fort, which was attacked by Cenis Indians at Espíritu Santo Bay.

René Menard

A French Jesuit missionary believed slain by the Sioux, he was born in Paris, France, 1604. Educated and ordained in the Society of Jesus, Father Menard went to Canada in 1640. He ministered to the Hurons, Ottawas, and Ojibwa (Chippewa), and he lived with the Cayugas in the area around the Great Lakes. It is believed that Father Menard was at Keweenaw, when he received a message from the Christian Hurons who had fled to Wisconsin to escape the Iroquois.

Asked by others to stay at his mission and to avoid dangers of an overland journey, Father Menard replied that God called him with the voice of the Hurons. He left his post with a French guide and was never seen again. His breviary and cassock were later discovered in a Sioux village. Father Menard is believed to have been martyred around August 10, 1661, in modern-day Wisconsin.

Jean-Baptiste Miège

This Jesuit missionary bishop to the Native Americans was born in La Foret,

Upper Savoy, Italy, in 1815. Educated locally, he entered the Society of Jesus and was ordained a priest in 1847. Volunteering for the American missions, Father Miège arrived in St. Louis, Missouri, in 1849. One year later he was named vicar apostolic for the Indian territory east of the Rocky Mountains. He refused the honor but was compelled to accept it and was consecrated on March 25, 1851.

He started at the Potawátomi mission of St. Mary's in Kansas and also served the local Osage settlements. In 1855, Bishop Miège moved to Leavenworth, Kansas, where he started missions and schools. He resigned his office in 1874 and served in Jesuit schools and colleges until his death, in Detroit, Michigan, on July 21, 1884.

Ignatius Mrak

A missionary bishop to the Indians of the Great Lakes, he was born in Hotovie, Austria, in 1818. He was educated in Laibach and was ordained by Prince-Bishop Anton Aloys Wolf on August 13, 1837. Eight years later, Father Mrak went to Detroit, Michigan, and was sent to aid Father Francis Pierz at L'arbre Croche (Harbor Springs) Mission, where he remained for two years. His devotion and care for the Native Americans brought about his appointment as the successor of Bishop Baraga in Marquette, Michigan, an honor he tried to avoid out of humility. He was consecrated in 1869.

A decade later, Bishop Mrak, exhausted and ill, resigned from his See and returned to the Indian missions. He served at Eagle Town, where he started a Native American school and remained there until he was eighty-one years old. He then retired to Marquette, where he died on January 2, 1901. Bishop Mrak's remains were interred in the diocesan cathedral beside Bishop Baraga.

Juan de Padilla

The protomartyr of the United States, he was born in Andalusia, Spain, around 1500, and entered the Franciscan Order there. Ordained, he was assigned in 1528 to Mexico, where he established monasteries and served as superior. Some records indicate that Father de Padilla accompanied the Franciscan Marcos de Niza on his expedition in 1539.

In 1540, he joined the expedition of Francisco de Coronado and visited the Hopi on the Rio Grande. When Coronado gave up his expedition in 1542, Father de Padilla decided to remain in the last site visited, which was in the region beyond Great Bend, Kansas. The territory in which he labored was called Quiveria, and the Wichita Indians were hospitable and kindly disposed toward him. Franciscan Juan de la Cruz and Brother Luis de Ubeda remained with him. Leaving the main party, Father de Padilla took two Franciscan Tertiaries, three Indians, and Andrés de Campo, a Portuguese soldier to establish his Kansas mission. Successful, he decided to visit the nearby tribe, the Guas, in 1542, and was slain at modern-day Herington, Kansas, where a monument was erected to his memory.

Charles Pandosy

One of the first priests ordained in the present state of Washington, this Oblate was born in Margerides, France, in 1824. Educated as an Oblate of Mary Immaculate, he arrived with three companions at Walla Walla in 1847, and was ordained there on January 2, 1848, with the famed Oblate missionary Eugene Casimir Chirouse.

Their first assignment was at Yakima, which flourished until the Yakima Indian Wars, 1855-1858, when the mission was destroyed. Father Pandosy and his Catholic

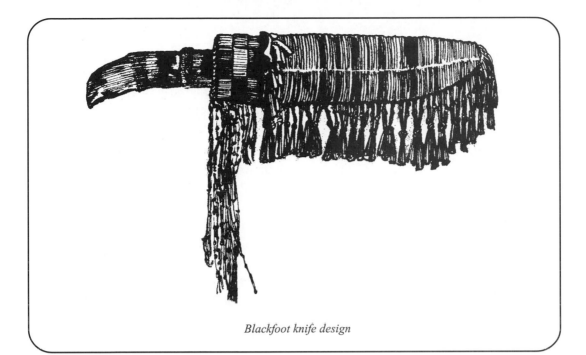

Blackfoot knife design

flock had to flee to the mountains to escape the carnage. He was assigned to British Columbia soon after, and at the Okanagon Valley labored for four decades. Father Pandosy wrote native-language dictionaries, grammars, and hymns. He died in Penticton, British Columbia, on February 6, 1891.

Francisco de Pareja

This Franciscan missionary, revered for publishing the first books in a Native American language, was born, date unknown, in Aunon, Toledo, Spain. Ordained a Franciscan, Father de Pareja arrived in St. Augustine, Florida, in 1593 or 1594. There he served in the coastal Indian missions and then became the guardian (or superior) of Immaculate Conception monastery at St. Augustine.

He was also associated with the Timucua people, and his books were written in the language of that tribe. Father Pareja returned to Mexico around 1613, and there he published six books on the Florida missions. He died in Mexico on January 25, 1628.

Jean Pierron

A Jesuit missionary to the Iroquois, he was born in Dun-sur-Meuse, France, in 1631. In 1650, he entered the Society of Jesus, was ordained, and then assigned as an instructor in various Jesuit institutions. Arriving in Canada in 1667, Father Pierron was sent to the Iroquois mission of Sainte-Marie. He studied the Iroquois language. Admiring the Iroquois tongue, he likened it to ancient Greek.

In October, 1668, Father Pierron was sent to the Mohawk settlement at Tinnontoguen. There he painted pictures and invented a catechetical game for instructions. He also visited Acadia, seeking to revive the missions there. Father Pierron returned to the Iroquois in time, serving them faithfully until 1677. He retired then and went to France, where he died.

Nicholas Point

A multitalented Jesuit missionary and companion of Father Pierre Jean De Smet, he was born in Rocroi, Ardennes, France, in 1799. He entered the Society of Jesus in

THE STORY OF THE CATHOLIC INDIAN MISSIONS

1822 and was ordained a priest in 1831. In 1836, his request to serve in the Native American missions was granted, and he was sent to conduct a college, St. Mary's, in Lebanon, Kentucky. He then opened a second college at Grand Coteau, Louisiana, becoming spiritual director to Catherine Connolly there.

In 1840, Father Point joined Father De Smet in the Flathead missions. They labored there from 1841 to 1847, also evangelizing the Coeur d'Alene and other regional tribes. He spent the winter of 1846-1847 with the Blackfeet at Fort Lewis. Then he was assigned to Canada, where he died on July 4, 1868. Father Point kept journals of his mission efforts among the Plateau Indians of Oregon, and these are respected for their historical details.

Sebastian Rale

This Jesuit, called the "Apostle to the Abenakis," a martyr of the faith, was born in Pontarlier, France, in 1652. Entering the Society of Jesus at age eighteen, he was ordained at Lyons, and set sail for Canada in 1689. Father Rale, also listed as Rasle in some histories, was sent to an Abenaki mission near Quebec for the first two years of his ministry. In 1692, he went to the Illinois Indians, serving the vast mission territory for three years. He then began his lifelong ministry on the Kennebec River, Maine, making his headquarters at Norridgewock. His church was completed by 1698.

The political unrest in the region brought English offers to the Abenaki, which they spurned. The Abenaki refused to send Father Rale out of their territory and aided him in 1721, when the English forces descended upon the area to capture him. In 1724, however, Mohawks attacked and killed him on August 23, at Norridgewock, in or-der to earn the bounty placed on his head by the English. His Abenaki dictionary, the principal source on the Canadian dialect of the eastern tribes, was taken. Some of his letters are at Harvard as well and at Cornell. Prayers and catechisms written by Father Rale were used for decades after his death by the Penobscots and Passamaquoddies. On September 23, 1941, Father Sebastian Rale was proposed for beatification by Dennis Cardinal Dougherty of Philadelphia.

Antonio Ravalli

Famed Montana Jesuit and apostle to the Native Americans, he was born in Ferrara, Italy, in 1812. At age fifteen he entered the Society of Jesus and was ordained and trained in medicine. In 1843, answering the call of Jesuit Pierre Jean De Smet, Father Ravalli sailed to America with four Jesuits and six Sisters of Notre Dame de Namur. In 1844, after learning English, he was with Jesuit Adrian Hoecken at St. Ignatius Mission among the Kalispel and Pend d'Oreille on the Columbia River in Washington. He was then laboring at Kettle Falls and in Montana's Bitter Root Valley.

There Father Ravalli served as a physician as well as priest among the Flatheads. That mission had to be abandoned in 1850 because of Blackfeet assaults, and he went to the Coeur d'Alenes in northern Idaho. He assumed the mission there, Sacred Heart (now known as Cataldo), and he started a beautiful church on the site, noted for its altar and statues, which he designed and carved.

In 1858, Father Ravalli returned to Kettle Falls, in Montana, and in 1863, after serving at the Jesuit house at Santa Clara, California, he started his labors in the Bitter Root Valley among the Flatheads. He also served the Blackfeet at St. Peter's, remaining in the Bitter Root region until his death at St. Mary's on October 2, 1884.

His medical and architectural skills served the Native Americans and then the whites drawn to the area in the later decades. Father Ravalli was called the "Good Samaritan of Western Montana." The Protestant historian Chittendon stated: "Fifty years a Jesuit and forty years a missionary, one of the noblest men that ever labored in the ranks of the Church in Montana, his fame stands very high in Montana, where a later generation knows more of him than even Father De Smet."

Augustine Ravoux

This apostle to the Santee Dakotas was born in Auvergne, France, in 1815. Studying in a seminary at Le Puy, he was recruited for the American missions by Bishop Pierre Jean Mathias Loras of Dubuque, Iowa. He completed his studies at Mount St. Mary's in Maryland and was ordained in Dubuque in 1840. After laboring in Prairie du Chien, Wisconsin, he was assigned in 1841 to the Santee Dakota, in Minnesota.

By 1843, Father Ravoux had translated into the Dakota language a catechism and a hymnal entitled *Wakantanka Ti Ki Chanku*, the "Path to the House of God." He was the only priest in Minnesota at the time, remaining alone in the territory until 1851, when the diocese of St. Paul was established. Then he served as vicar-general of the diocese for Bishop Joseph Crétin. In 1868, Pope Pius IX appointed him vicar apostolic of Montana, but Father Ravoux's health forced him to decline. He was made a domestic prelate (rank of monsignor) by Pope Leo XIII in 1887.

Retiring in 1892, Monsignor Ravoux resided at the cathedral of St. Paul, where he wrote his memoirs. He died there in 1906.

Gabriel Richard

This Sulpician missionary and United States Congressman was born in Saintes, France, in 1767. Educated locally, and at Angers, he entered the Society of St. Sulpice and was ordained in 1791. One year later, with Fathers François Ciquard and Ambrose Marechal, Father Richard fled the French Revolution and arrived in Baltimore.

He served in the Illinois missions from 1793 to 1798, and was then transferred to Detroit, Michigan, where he labored. Father Richard also visited the Lower Peninsula and Green Bay. The fire in Detroit in 1805 spurred Father Richard's activities, and he built a church, seminary, a school for Native American and French children, and a school for the blind. All of these projects failed in time, but in 1817, with the Protestant Reverend John Monteith, he founded the University of Michigan.

In 1823, Father Richard was elected to the United States Congress. He suffered calumny and lawsuits during this period and was defeated by an opponent in 1825. In June, 1833, cholera struck Detroit, and Father Richard labored heroically among the victims. He died of the disease on September 13, 1833, and was buried in a chapel of St. Anne's Church in Detroit.

Armand de la Richardie

Beloved missionary to the Hurons, he was born in Périgueux, France, in 1686. Educated locally, he entered the Jesuits in 1703, was ordained, and sent to Canada in 1725. Three years later, he established a mission for the Petun Hurons at Detroit. Father de la Richardie labored among the Hurons until 1746, when he was stricken with paralysis and taken to Quebec. The Hurons demanded his return, and only partially recovered, Father de la Richardie returned to Detroit. In

1751, he traveled to Sandusky, Ohio, to mediate a Huron dispute, and he was then recalled to Quebec, where he died as a result of his illness and labors.

Jean François de Saint-Cosmé

A Seminarist missionary serving the vast Louisiana missions, he was born in Quebec in 1667. He studied at the Seminary of the Missions in Quebec and was ordained in 1690 and subsequently sent to the Nova Scotia missions. In 1698, the bishop of Quebec assigned Father Saint-Cosmé and two others to Cahokia, Illinois, which was part of the Louisiana missions at the time.

Father Saint-Cosmé journeyed south in the following year and labored among the Natchez of Mississippi, where he founded the first mission for the tribe. He was alone in the region for many years, serving the Taensa also. In 1706, he was slain in the area by the local tribe while descending the Mississippi River. He was asleep on the banks of the river with four companions when martyred by the Shetimasha.

Juan María Salvatierra

Dedicated to the Native Americans from his youth, this Jesuit pioneer and friend of Jesuit Eusebius Kino, was born in Milan, Italy, in 1648. While in the Jesuit local college, he read a book on the missions to the Native Americans and entered the Society of Jesus. His later seminary studies were in Puebla College in Mexico, and he was ordained and began missionary work in the northern part of the territory.

In 1697, encouraged by Father Kino, Father Salvatierra was given permission to lead a company of Jesuits into Lower California, with Father Juan Ugarte. Father Salvatierra founded Our Lady of Loreto, in the area around Concepción Bay soon after landing there on October 18. Over the next years, he founded six missions and explored the region.

In 1704, he was appointed Jesuit provincial and ordered back to Mexico, but he returned again within three years. Dedicated to the California Indians and versed in their languages, Father Salvatierra also wrote records and histories in the area missions. Recalled to Mexico for a conference with the new viceroy, Father Salvatierra collapsed in Guadalajara and died on July 17, 1717. On his deathbed he instructed his companions with his vision for the missions.

Charles John Seghers

An archbishop, called the "Apostle of Alaska," he was born in Ghent, Belgium, in 1839. By the time he was twenty, his parents and four siblings had died of tuberculosis. Educated by his uncle, he was eventually ordained to the priesthood in Ghent in 1863. Father Seghers promptly volunteered for the American missions and in that same year arrived in Vancouver Island, where he labored in the diocese. He also attended the First Vatican Council with Bishop Modeste Demers and labored in Victoria.

In 1873, he was appointed the successor of Bishop Demers and was consecrated at age thirty-two. One month after becoming a bishop, he left for Alaska. He also started diocesan Indian missions and visited the local tribes. Sever years later, he was made the archbishop of Oregon City (now Portland). There he built schools, missions, and parishes and invited the Benedictines to found Mount Angel Abbey.

He wanted to go back to Alaska, however, and appealed to the Holy See and returned to Vancouver Island in 1884 after an audience with Pope Leo XIII. In 1886, accompanied by Jesuits Paschal Tosi and Louis Aloysius Robaut, Archbishop Seghers made his fifth tour of Alaska. He founded missions at Sitka and Juneau. He then started out with Francis Fuller, a layman, for Nulato. A few miles from that settlement, Fuller, who was suffering from a mental breakdown, killed Archbishop Seghers on the trail on November 28, 1886. He was buried at St. Andrew's Cathedral in Victoria.

Blessed Junípero Serra

The Franciscan founder of the California missions, he was born in Petra, Majorca, Spain, in 1713. At age sixteen he entered the Franciscans in Palma, having demonstrated an intellectual brilliance and proficiency in philosophy. Ordained and earning a doctorate in theology, Blessed Junípero held the Scotus chair of philosophy at Lullian University until 1749, when his pleas for a missionary assignment were granted. In that year he joined the Missionary College of San Fernando, in Mexico.

Landing at Vera Cruz on December 7, 1749, Blessed Junípero and a companion walked two hundred fifty miles to Mexico City, arriving there within the month. Blessed Junípero and Franciscan Francisco Palóu served the Sierra Gorda missions and, in 1758, Blessed Junípero was at San Fernando College. He held several positions there and conducted missions until 1769, when he began his California missions at San Diego. Suffering severe physical infirmities, Blessed Junípero founded nine California missions.

He was described by contemporaries as a model Franciscan, a man of prayer and profound mortification. When he died at Mission San Carlos on August 28, 1784, his missionary companions regarded him as a saintly soul. Blessed Junípero's cause was opened in 1934. He was declared venerable in 1985 by Pope John Paul II, then beatified three years later, on September 25, 1988.

Charles Felix Van Quickenborne

One of the most zealous Jesuit missionaries of his era, he was born in Petergem, Belgium, in 1788. Ordained a priest for Ghent originally, Father Van Quickenborne entered the Society of Jesus in 1815 and two years later was at Georgetown, serving as Master of Novices at the novitiate there. He desired mission work among the Native Americans, however, and asked to be sent to the Jesuit outposts in 1821.

In 1823, Father Van Quickenborne led a group of Belgian recruits to Florissant, Missouri, where he founded the first Jesuit house in the region. He also started missions for the Osage and Kickapoo, traveling endlessly in the wilderness to visit the tribes of his territory for over a decade. His health broken by the ordeals of his endless mission rounds, Father Van Quickenborne died at Portage de Sioux, Missouri, in August, 1837.

Andrew White

An English Jesuit in exile, called the "Apostle of Maryland," he was born in London in 1579. Educated at St. Alban's, at Valladolid, Spain, and in Seville and the Douai seminary, he was ordained a priest in 1605. He returned to England just in time for the Gunpowder Plot and was exiled by the authorities in 1606. Father White then entered the Jesuits at Louvain, Belgium, where he taught in the seminary.

In 1634, Father White, with Jesuits Father John Altham and Brother Thomas Gervase, arrived in Maryland. For the next ten years, he labored among the Patuxent, Potomac, Piscataway, and Anacostan Indians.

He also converted Chitomachon, the "Emperor of the Piscataway," on July 5, 1640, with Governor Calvert attending the ceremony.

Father White compiled grammars as well as a dictionary and catechism in the Algonquin language. When the Catholic government of Maryland was overthrown in 1645, Fathers White and Thomas Copley were arrested and sent to England in chains. There they were acquitted of all charges and freed. He remained in the southern part of England and worked as a missionary under an assumed name. Father White died near London on December 27, 1656.

Mountain Chief, a Blackfoot warrior

List of Kateri Circles

- Nizhoni, Immaculate Heart of Mary Parish, Page
- Phoenix Kateri Circle, Diocese of Phoenix, Phoenix
- Poston Indian Mission, Blessed Kateri Circle, Parker
- St. Anthony's Kateri Circle, Cedar Creek
- St. Catherine's Kateri Circle, Cibeque
- St. Charles Kateri Circle, San Carlos
- St. Francis Kateri Circle, Scottsdale
- Tohono O'odham Kateri, Circle Group, Sells
- Tse Ho Tso Kateri Circle, Fort Defiance
- Ts'O'Hootso Kateri Circle, St. Michael
- Tucson Kateri Circle, Tucson

California
- Blessed Kateri Tekakwitha Circle of St. Michael's Chapel, Pechanga Reservation, Temecula
- City of the Angels Kateri Circle, Northridge
- Juan Diego Intertribal Circle, Victorville
- Kateri Kids — One Nation Kateri Circle, Baldwin Park
- Kateri Tekakwitha Circle, Mission San Antonio, Pala
- Our Lady of Refuge Church, Kateri Circle, Castorville

The following list is of the Kateri Circles throughout the United States, Canada, and Europe. (This information, provided by Monsignor Paul Lenz, was current as of October, 1999.)

Alabama
- Kateri Circle Birmingham, Birmingham
- Union Springs Kateri Circle, Union Springs

Arizona
- Akimel O'otham Kateri Circle, Sacaton
- Kateri Circle Lukachukai, Lukachukai
- Komatke Kateri Circle, Laveen

- St. Joseph's Catholic Church Kateri Circle, Soboha Indian Mission, San Jacinto
- Santa Clarita Kateri Circle, Saugus
- Soboba Kateri Youth Group, St. Joseph's Catholic Soboba Indian Mission, San Jacinto
- The Peoples Kateri Circle of the High Desert, Phelan
- Two Rivers Kateri Circle, Ventura

Colorado
- Denver Kateri Circle, Denver
- Kateri Indian Parish of Denver Kateri Circle, Littleton
- Tekakwitha Circle Denver, Denver

Florida
- Sacred Circle: Kateri Tekakwitha Circle, Diocese of St. Petersburg, St. Petersburg
- St. Augustine Kateri Circle, Diocese of St. Augustine, Jacksonville

Idaho
- Nez Percé Kateri Prayer Circle, Lapwai

Illinois
- Anawim Kateri Circle, Chicago
- Peoria-Illinois Kateri Circle, Peoria

Kansas
- Our Lady of the Snows Kateri Circle, Mayetta

Louisiana
- Blessed Kateri Tekakwitha Circle, Marrero
- Holy Family's Kateri Circle, Houma
- St. Joseph Kateri Circle, Zwolle

Massachusetts
- International Kateri Tekakwitha Circle Princess, Randolph

Maine
- Burnurwurbskek Kateri Circle, St. Ann's Church, Indian Island
- The St. Ann's Sipayik Kateri Circle, St. Ann's Church, Perry

Michigan
- Archdiocese of Detroit Kateri Circle, Dearborn Heights
- Blessed Kateri Circle, Blessed Kateri Tekakwitha Parish, Bay Mills
- Dowagiac Silver Creek Kateri Circle, Dowagiac
- Four Seasons Kateri Circle, St. Michael's Parish, Muskegon
- Lansing Kateri Circle, Lansing
- Morningstar Kateri Prayer Circle, Grand Rapids
- St. Joseph-Elbridge Kateri Circle, Hart
- Tekakwitha Circle of Marquette County, Negaunee
- On Eagle Wings Kateri Circle, Grand Rapids
- The Grand Rapids Kateri Circle, Grand Rapids

Minnesota
- Cloquet/Duluth Kateri Circle, Diocese of Duluth
- Kateri Circle, Little Flower Mission, Onamia
- St. Charles Kateri Circle, St. Charles Parish, Cass Lake
- St. Mary's Kateri Circle, Red Lake Mission Church, Red Lake
- White Earth Area Kateri Circle, St. Benedict's Parish, White Earth

Mississippi
- Chahta Okla Kateri Circle, St. Therese Mission, Philadelphia

Montana

- Angels of Kateri Immaculate Conception, Wolf Point
- Blackfeet Tekakwitha Youth Runners, Heart Butte
- Fort Belknap Kateri Tekakwitha Circle, Harlem
- Heart Butte Tekakwitha Circle, St. Anne Parish, Heart Butte
- Helena Kateri Circle, St. Helena Cathedral, Helena
- Jocko-Arlee Montana Tekakwitha Circle, Sacred Head and St. John Berchmans, Arlee
- Kateri Tekakwitha Youth Group, Wyola and Lodge Grass
- Kateri Youth Organization Jr. High, St. Dennis Parish, Crow Agency
- Morningstar Circle, Lame Deer
- St. Ignatius Tekakwitha Circle, St. Ignatius
- St. Labré Kateri Circle, Ashland

North Carolina

- Eastern Cherokee Kateri Circle, Cherokee

North Dakota

- Fort Berthold Tekakwitha Circle, St. Anthony, Mandoree Indian Mission
- Kateri Family Circle, Tolna
- Plains Village Kateri Circle, Diocese of Bismarck, Bismarck
- St. Anthony's Kateri Circle, Belcourt
- Seven Dolors Kateri Circle, Fort Totten

Nebraska

- St. Augustine's Kateri Circle, Winnebago

New Mexico

- Blessed Kateri Circle, San Juan Parish, San Juan Pueblo
- Gallup Kateri Circle, Gallup
- Iselta Pueblo Kateri Circle, Isleta Pueblo
- Kateri Tekakwitha, Jemez Pueblo

- Kateri (Tsiitnuuzi Niiti) Circle, St. Joseph Mission, Mescalero
- Laguna Tekakwitha Chapter, Kateri Circle, Casa Blanca
- Nataani Nez Kateri Circle, Shiprock
- Pueblo de Cochiti Tekakwitha Group, Cochiti
- Queen of Angels Kateri Circle, Albuquerque
- Sandia Pueblo Kateri Circle, St. Anthony's Mission, Sandia Pueblo
- Tesuque Pueblo Kateri Circle, Tesuque Pueblo
- Walatowa Kateri Circle, San Diego Mission, Jemez Pueblo

Nevada

- Kateri of Las Vegas Circle, Our Lady of Las Vegas, Las Vegas

New York

- A Kateri Prayer Circle, Syracuse
- Akwesasne Mohawk Reserve, Kateri Circle, Bombay
- Kateri Tekakwitha Committee, St. Lucy's Parish, Syracuse
- St. Lawrence Kateri Circle, Rochester

Oklahoma

- Kateri Circle — Sacred Heart Church, Miami
- Osage Kateri Tekakwitha Circle, Hominy, Pawhuska, Fairfax
- St. Brigid's Kateri Circle, Tahlequah
- St. Mary's Kateri Circle, Ponca City
- St. Patrick's Kateri Circle, Anadarko
- Shawnee Oklahoma Kateri Circle, Shawnee

Oregon

- City of Roses Kateri Circle, Portland
- Kateri Friendship Circle, St. Andrew's Mission, Pendleton

Pennsylvania
• Lily of the Mohawks Circle, Philadelphia

South Dakota
• Blue Dog Lake Kateri Circle, Waubay
• Kateri Circle, Kyle
• Kateri Okolakiciye Kateri Circle, St. Charles Parish, St. Francis
• Kateri Youth Group, Mission
• Marty Kateri Circle, Marty
• Mission Antelope Kateri Circle, St. Thomas Parish, Mission
• St. Agnes Kateri Circle, Manderson
• St. Bridget's Kateri Circle, Rosebud
• St. Isaac Jogues Hi Sapa (Blessed), Kateri Circle, Rapid City
• St. Joseph and St. Mary, St. Joseph Church, Fort Thompson
• St. Thomas Kateri Youth Group, St. Thomas Parish, Mission
• Wiconi Kateri Circle, Holy Family Center, Sioux Falls

Tennessee
• The Tekakwitha Circle of the River, Memphis

Texas
• Tiguas' Kateri Circle, Our Lady of Mount Carmel, El Paso

Utah
• Fort Duchesne Kateri Circle, St. Helen Parish, Roosevelt
• Wasatch Front Kateri Circle, Salt Lake City

Washington
• Kateri Tekakwitha, Catholic Guild of Yakima Indian Reservation, Yakima

• Pacific Northwest Kateri, Tekakwitha Circle, Tacoma
• St. Michael Kateri Circle, Keshena

Wisconsin
• Kateri Circle, Stone Lake
• Kateri Circle of the Great Spirit, Milwaukee
• Kateri Circle St. Francis Solanus, Stone Lake
• La Crosse Kateri Circle, La Crosse
• St. Anthony's Menominee Indian Kateri Circle, Neopit

Wyoming
• St. Stephen's Kateri Circle, St. Stephen's Mission

Canada
• St. Mary's Kateri Prayer Circle, Enderby, British Columbia
• RC First Nation Circle, North Battleford, Saskatchewan

Spain
• Associación Benaurada, Kateri Tekakwitha, Barcelona

Inactive
• Holy Name Blessed Kateri Circle, Most Holy Name of Jesus Parish, Baraga, Michigan
• The Grand Rapids Diocese Kateri Circle, Grand Rapids, Michigan
• The Twelve-Step Kateri Circle, Grand Rapids, Michigan
• Mission Valley Tekakwitha Youth Group, St. Ignatius, Montana
• Oneida Kateri Circle, Oneida, Wisconsin

Keokuk, chief of the Sauk-Fox Indians

APPENDIX 4

Statement on the Native Americans

religious and lay persons, past and present, who have sought to share with the Indian people the Good News of Jesus Christ. They learned the Indian languages, and, insofar as they were able within their own cultural limits, they adapted themselves to Indian cultures. In the name of the Church, these missionaries also offered to the Indian communities their talents and knowledge of medicine and education.

4. Some who have worked with American Indians, however, recognize that efforts of the Church to promote the Gospel among Indian communities have at times been attempted in ways that actually failed to respect Indian cultures. We come to this statement with a keen awareness of our not infrequent failures to respect the inherent rights and cultural heritage of our American Indian brothers and sisters. We offer this reflection on our attitudes and actions in the spirit of reconciliation and with a stronger commitment to be more sensitive and just in our relationships with American Indians.

Faith and Culture

5. The Church, by its very nature, must always and everywhere proclaim and give witness to God's saving love revealed by

The following statement was issued by the U.S. Catholic bishops on May 4, 1977, concerning Native Americans.

1. In this statement, we wish to share our reflections on the relationship of the Catholic Church in the United States with the American Indian peoples.

2. As American Catholics, we have learned only gradually and with difficulty that the building of one community can only be authentic if it is based upon respect for the distinctive traditions, customs, institutions and ways of life of its peoples. Indeed, we are only now beginning to understand that unity which grows through dialogue and respect for diversity is far stronger and deeper than conformity forged by dominance.

3. We recall with gratitude the great dedication and sacrifice of the many priests,

245

Jesus Christ in the Holy Spirit. This is the center and foundation of the Church's mission to proclaim that in Jesus Christ, the incarnate Word, who died and rose from the dead, salvation is offered to all people as a gift of God's grace and mercy.[1]

6. This Good News of salvation is not bound by time or human structures. Christ's Gospel of love and redemption, addressed to all people, transcends national boundaries, cultural differences and divisions among peoples. It cannot be considered foreign anywhere on earth; nor can it be considered identical with any particular culture or heritage.[2] It is the common blessing of all.

7. But persons are vitally dependent upon the institutions of family and community that have been passed down to them. These institutions — political, social, economic and religious — shape their self-understanding and are necessary to their full development as persons. Indeed, the Second Vatican Council affirmed that persons can come to an authentic and full humanity only through those distinct cultures which form the basis and heritage of each human community.[3]

8. The Christian faith should celebrate and strengthen the many diverse cultures which are the product of human hope and aspiration. The Gospel message must take root and grow within each culture and each community. Faith finds expression in and through the particular values, customs and institutions of the people who hear it. It seeks to take flesh within each culture, within each nation, within each race, while remaining the prisoner of none. Pope Paul VI, in his recent statement on evangelization, stressed these themes in calling for "fidelity both to a message whose servants we are and to the people to whom we must transmit it."[4]

The Church and Justice

9. The Church is also required by the Gospel and by its tradition to promote and defend human rights and human dignity. Pope Paul VI has underscored the fact that "between evangelization and human advancement — development and liberation — there are in fact profound links. . . . The necessity of ensuring fundamental human rights cannot be separated from this just liberation which is bound up with evangelization and which endeavors to secure structures safeguarding human freedoms." The Church, Pope Paul continued, "has the duty to proclaim the liberation of millions of human beings — the duty of assisting the birth of this liberation, of giving witness to it, of ensuring that it is complete. This is not foreign to evangelization."[5]

10. In all its activities the Church must seek to preach and act in ways that lead to greater justice for all people. Its ministry cannot neglect the violations of human rights resulting from racism, poverty, poor housing, inadequate education and health care, widespread apathy and indifference and a lack of freedom. These realities are fundamentally incompatible with our faith and the Church is required to oppose them. Pope Paul VI stressed the profound link between the Church's mission to preach the Gospel and action on behalf of justice: "How in fact can one proclaim the new commandment without promoting justice?"[6]

The American Experience

11. We, as American Catholics, should be especially sensitive to these aspects of the Church's mission. Over the centuries, peoples from every continent and heritage have joined in the formation of the United States. Each group to come has constructed its communities and established its institu-

tions. Gradually, all Americans learned the lesson that to build a nation free and independent, a people must be prepared to engage in a never ending process of change and dialogue. Each group has experienced the tensions that arise between the legitimate cultural independence that people claim for themselves and the pressing need for true and fruitful dialogue with other groups.

12. Today, we Americans are called to reflect upon past injustices and to consider again the need for both unity and diversity, to become one nation built upon respect for the distinctive traditions and values of many peoples and cultures. Both respect for cultural diversity and dialogue between cultures are indispensable if the legitimate quest for cultural identity is to lead to human development and social progress and not simply perpetuate the bitter divisions of the past. The challenge of this effort is placed before the nation by black Americans, by Spanish-speaking Americans, by the heirs of Europe's migrations and by the persevering voice of the oldest Americans, the American Indians.

American Indians

13. The American Indian peoples had developed rich and diverse cultures long before the first Europeans came to the American continent. Migrating across this great continent, they dispersed over thousands of years, from the coasts of the Pacific Northwest to the mesas of the Southwest, the vast grasslands of mid-America and the mountains and woodlands of the East. Adapting themselves to changing environments as they went, they developed over two hundred distinct languages and a variety of carefully developed social, economic, and political institutions to meet their needs.

14. But the arrival of later immigrants created conflicts not yet resolved. Indian ways of life were challenged; their very existence was continually threatened by newcomers who were their superiors in the arts of war. For the Indians, the saga of nation building in America has been a story filled with sorrow and death.

15. American Indians in the United States today comprise less than one percent of our total population. In all, they belong to more than 250 distinct tribes and bands.

16. Many tribes have retained a special trust status with the United States and continue to live on reservation lands held in trust for them by the federal government. Over the long years, however, many tribes have been deprived of their communal lands, and with them have partially or entirely lost the traditional vestiges of their culture, their languages, customs and ways of living.

17. During recent decades, increasing numbers of American Indians, especially the young people, have migrated to cities in search of jobs, shelter and social services which are sorely lacking on many reservations. Those who have chosen or been forced to migrate to cities in response to promises of employment and a better life have too often found only new frustrations and broken dreams. Many contend with a deep sense of uprootedness, trying to maintain ties with their families and tribes while coping with the economic hardships and social prejudices, even racism, of urban society.

18. American Indians today are struggling against great obstacles to renew the special values of their unique heritage and to revitalize the ways of their ancestors. They are striving to achieve economic development and social justice without compromising their unique cultural identity. For some American Indian peoples the struggle is to retain rights to their land and resources; for

some it is to gain employment and economic security; and for others, it is to obtain political power in order to set their own goals and to make decisions affecting their own futures. These goals, to be achieved within the framework of Indian culture and traditions, test the strength of the American ideal of liberty and justice for all. America must respond, not to atone for the wrongs of the past, for that in a sense is beyond our power, but to be faithful to our national commitment and to contribute to a truly human future for all.

The Role of the Church

19. As American Catholics, we have a special responsibility to examine our attitudes and actions in light of Jesus' command to love our neighbor and to proclaim the Gospel message and its implications for society. The Church is compelled, both through its institutions and through its individual members, to promote and defend the human rights and dignity of all people.

20. Accordingly, we recognize our own responsibility to join with our American Indian sisters and brothers in their ongoing struggle to secure justice. We realize that there is much that we can and must do within our Church and in society to make our support real. We must first of all increase our understanding of the present needs, aspirations and values of the American Indian peoples. This responsibility can only be carried out effectively in dialogue with American Indians.

21. We are encouraged in our efforts by the many hopeful initiatives that Catholic communities in various parts of the country have undertaken on behalf of American Indians. From the national level, the Campaign for Human Development, the National Conference of Catholic Charities and the Commission for Catholic Missions Among the Colored People and the Indians have provided support to many constructive local efforts.

22. For over 90 years, the Commission for Catholic Missions Among the Colored People and the Indians, together with the Bureau of Catholic Indian Missions, has had a particular responsibility to support efforts to advance the life of the Church among American Indian communities. The historical success of this work reflects the generosity of Catholics in the United States. We are particularly encouraged by the recent revitalization of these organizations and hope to see their efforts renewed and redoubled in the coming years. We would also support efforts to broaden the involvement of Indian peoples in the work of the Bureau of Catholic Indian Missions.

23. We note also the serious and sustained efforts in several dioceses to improve the Church's ministry among American Indians. In particular, the bishops of Minnesota have offered their own reflection on the Church's relationship with American Indians in their statement, A New Beginning.

24. We recommend that other dioceses and Catholic organizations make similar efforts to improve their ministry with American Indians and we pledge our own efforts to cooperate with the American Indian people and the local Catholic churches in these endeavors.

25. One area which deserves our special attention is that of government policy and legislation. Perhaps no other group of people in the United States is so vitally affected by government policies and programs as are American Indians. We have a responsibility to examine these systems and policies in light of the Gospel and the Church's social teachings and to urge the adoption of more just

policies and legislation affecting American Indians. It seems to us that such efforts must include advocacy of: the speedy and equitable resolution of treaty and statute questions; protection of Indian land and resource rights; more adequate housing and delivery of social, education and health care services; and increased levels of funding and technical assistance necessary to aid American Indians in achieving political and economic self-determination and full employment.

26. We understand that such efforts will mean little if they are not accompanied by honest reflection on the entire ministry of the Church with American Indians. We must examine the Church's liturgical expressions and social and educational services within Indian communities to ask if they indeed reflect an appreciation of Indian heritage and cultural values. We would encourage national and diocesan liturgical offices to provide assistance to Indian communities to incorporate their languages and prayer forms in the liturgy and other worship services. We urge Catholic educational institutions to examine their textbooks and curriculums and to promote programs and activities that will enable students at all levels to appreciate American Indian history, cultures and spirituality.

27. We also urge that Church property and facilities adjacent to Indian lands or located in the midst of urban Indian neighborhoods be made more available for use by Indian communities for such activities as religious celebrations, group meetings, programs for the elderly, day care centers and educational programs.

28. Perhaps the most important task before us is the development of Indian leadership — clerical, religious and lay — within the Church. This is necessary if the Church is to prosper in Indian communities. We are especially encouraged by the efforts of several dioceses to include American Indians in their permanent diaconate programs and hope that this effort is expanded. In addition, efforts should be made to ensure that American Indians have representation and a voice in all decisions made by Church agencies and organizations affecting their communities.

29. Drawing on the two themes of faith and culture, and the Church and justice, and working with all others of good will, we hope to fashion a renewed commitment to serve Indian peoples. In turn, their participation in and challenge to our Christian community will strengthen our common witness to Jesus and the Gospel message.

Notes

1. Pope Paul VI, *Exhortation on Evangelization in the Modern World*, Nos. 5, 14-16, 26-27; Vatican II, *Decree on the Missionary Activity of the Church*, Nos. 2-4.
2. Pope Paul VI, op. cit. Nos. 20, 28; Vatican II, *Dogmatic Constitution on the Church*, No. 48; *Decree on the Missionary Activity of the Church*, No. 8.
3. Vatican Council II, *The Church in the Modern World*, No. 53.
4. Pope Paul VI, op. cit. No. 4.
5. Pope Paul VI, op. cit. Nos. 31; 39; 30.
6. Pope Paul VI, op. cit. Nos. 29-36; Vatican Council II, *The Church in the Modern World*, No. 41.

Index

The Story of the Catholic Indian Missions

The Story of the Catholic Indian Missions

Crétin, Joseph, 84, 85, 190, 196, 219, 237
Crimont, Joseph, 182
Criodo, Dominic, 187
Cristo Crucificado College, 230
Croix, Charles de, 76, 82, 190, 197, 219, 220
Crooked Tree, 37
Crookston, 110, 196
Croquet, Adrian, 110, 204, 208, 220
Crow(s), 19, 94, 110, 158, 160, 198, 221, 224
Crow Creek, 126, 205
Crow Wing, 196
Cruz, Diego de, 44, 206
Cruz, Juan de la, 42, 46, 52, 234
Crystal Falls, 53
Cuba, 26, 27, 120, 187, 201, 230
Cuban Missile Crisis, 161
Cuellar, Miguel de, 191
Cuipa, Amador, 187
Cumberland Island, 26, 52, 188, 219, 232
Cuny, Genevieve, 166
Cupeño, 18
Curé of Ars, 219
Curtis, Charles, 149
Cusabo, 21
Custer, George Armstrong, 107, 108
Czolgosz, Leon, 134

D

D-Day, 155
D'Eschambault, Alexis, 192
Dablon, Claude, 33, 37, 39, 194, 201, 209, 217, 220, 221
Daillon — see under La Roche Daillon
Dakota Sioux — see under Sioux
Dakotas, 77, 81, 99, 114, 118, 132, 176, 177, 196, 229, 232
Dana's Point, 109, 193
Dandia, 74, 200
Daran, Adrian, 194
Darnall, 66
Davenport, 190
Davion, Antoine, 41, 181, 191, 196
Davis, Mary Anne, 32
Dawes, Henry L., 121
Dawes Act, 121
Dawes Commission, 121

Dawes General Allotment Act, 120, 121, 132, 138, 142
Dawes Severalty Act, 121
De Bry, Theodore, 28
De Monts Island, 192
De Pere, 39, 53, 208, 209
De Smet, Pierre Jean — see under Smet, Pierre Jean de
De Soto, Hernando — see under Soto, Hernando de
Death Cabin, 124
Declaration of Independence, 66, 69, 71
Deguerre, Jean, 53
Dejean, Peter, 82, 194
Dekanawidah, 58
Delaware, State of, 35, 60, 186
Delaware Indians, 21, 74, 131, 191, 204
Delaware River, 36
Delgado, Marcos, 54, 187
Delhalle, Nicholas Constantin, 54, 194
Demers, Modeste, 83, 100, 203, 208, 215, 221, 238
Demillier, 193
Denver, 39, 70, 151, 155, 166, 172
DEW (Distant Early Warning) Line, 176
Díaz, Juan Marcello, 54, 185
Díaz de León, Antonio, 54
Díaz de Velasco, Francisco Martínez de la Tejadu, 187
Dicppc, 33, 220, 229
Diequeño, 18
Diez, John Joseph, 50, 184
Distinguished Service Cross, 141
Dogrib, 17
Dole, William, 107
Dollier, François, 37, 194
Domínguez, Atanasio, 69, 199, 207
Dominican(s), 25, 26, 36, 44, 52, 71, 73, 80, 93, 181, 186, 188, 190, 193, 203, 205, 206, 207, 209, 216, 233
Dongan, Thomas, 60, 201, 226
Dorchester, Daniel, 122
Douay, Anastase, 36, 41, 44, 181, 191, 196, 206
Dougherty, Dennis, 151, 236
Doutreleau, Stephen, 38, 42, 190, 191
Dover, 60
Drake, Sir Francis, 187
Drexel, Francis Martin, 125, 222

Drexel, St. Katharine Marie, 120, 125, 126, 127, 131, 132, 178, 184, 201, 203, 204, 222, 223
Dried Salmon, 129, 217
Druillettes, Gabriel, 30, 35, 37, 39, 186, 192, 193, 194, 205, 208, 212, 220, 223
Du Tissenet, 190
Dubourg, Louis, 72, 76, 81, 184, 190, 197, 220, 223
Dubuque, 81, 82, 190, 219, 228, 237
Duchesne, St. Rose Philippine, 80, 81, 84, 190, 197, 223
Duffy, Patrick, 141
Dumoulin, Joseph Sévère, 74, 77, 82, 202
Dunne, Mary Amadeus, 137, 224
Dun-sur-Meuse, 235
Dunwoodie, 145
Durán, Roderic, 47
Durham, 35, 199
Dust Bowl, 149
Duwamish, 18, 208

E

Eagle Town, 234
East Bloomfield, 34, 201
Eastern Eskimo — see under Eskimo
Eastern Woodlands, 20, 21
Eberschweiler, Frederick, 110, 126, 198
Ebner, Claude, 110, 202
Echo Lake, 34
Echon, 216
Edesto, 205
Edmonton, 229
Edmund Campion — see under Campion, St. Edmund
Egan, Michael, 73
Egypt, 42, 121
Einsiedeln, Maria, 232
Eisenhower, Dwight D., 160
El Paso, 44, 47, 200, 206
Elbowoods, 202
Eliot, John, 35
Elizabeth Seton — see under Seton, St. Elizabeth
Ellis Island, 160
Ellsworth, 89
Emmons, Glenn, 160
Engelhardt, Zephyrin, 209, 224
Enixa, Anthony, 187
Enjahan, Jean, 37, 194

Heiltsuk, 18
Helena, 104, 110, 198
Hemauer, Gilbert, 166
Hemes, 47
Hennepin, Louis, 37, 38, 40, 43, 189, 190, 195, 201, 226
Henry, Patrick, 64
Henryville, St. Georges d', 106
Herington, 234
Hernández, Francisco, 186
Heynen, William, 182
Hidalgo, Francisco, 44, 206
Hidatsa, 19, 145
Hin-mah-too-yah-lat-kekht, 110
Hindus, 180
Hiroshima, 156
Hitchcock, Ethan Allen, 133
Hitchiti, 21
Hoecken, Adrian, 205, 208, 226, 236
Hoecken, Christian, 40, 50, 76, 80, 84, 190, 196, 202, 205, 209, 226
Hofbauer, St. Clement Mary, 79, 213
Hohenlode, Prince Chlodwig K. Victor von, 118
Holocaust, 156
Holy Angels College, 215
Holy Cross, 91, 125, 182, 190, 195, 218
Holy Family, 189, 198, 217
Holy Heart of Mary, 197
Holy Rosary, 110, 117, 127, 134, 205
Holy See, 59, 91, 137, 141, 158, 238; *see also* Vatican
Holy Spirit, 170, 246
Holyoke, 215
Homestead Act, 91
Hong Kong, 219
Honolulu, 124
Hoorbeke-St.-Corneille, 219
Hoover, Herbert, 149
Hoover Report, 159
Hopi, 19, 47, 48, 155, 183, 234
Horcasitas, 207
Horse Creek Valley, 222
Horseshoe Bend, 75
Horvath, Tibor, 171
Hotovie, 234
Houma, 21
Howard, Oliver, 111
Hualapai, 19
Hubert, Jean François, 194

Hughes, John, 86, 90
Hughes, William McDermott, 144, 145, 146, 150
Huichol, 19
Huma, 41
Hungary; *also* Hungarian, 140, 195
Hunkpapa, 19
Hunt, Jerome, 82, 202
Hupa, 18
Huron(s), 21, 29, 32, 34, 37, 38, 39, 194, 201, 203, 211, 216, 217, 218, 224, 226, 230, 233, 237, 238
Huronia, 38

I

Ibarra, Francisco de, 46, 199
Iberville, Pierre Le Moyne d', 41, 181
Icaful, 21
Idaho, 43, 84, 94, 109, 111, 112, 126, 188, 189, 198, 236, 242
Igulik, 17
Ihonateria, 227
Illinois, State of, 38, 189
Illinois Indians, 21, 37, 39, 74, 209, 217, 231, 236
Immaculate Conception Mission, 34, 38, 126, 189, 201, 205
Incas, 24, 25
India, 33, 219
Indian Appropriations Act, 124, 134
Indian Civil Rights Act, 162
Indian Claims Commission, 157, 158
Indian Education Act, 165
Indian New Deal, 149, 151, 152, 157
Indian Removal Act, 77, 92
Indian Reorganization Act, 149, 152
Indian Rights Association, 119, 137
Indian Rights Movement, 162
Indian Self-Determination Act, 165
Indiana, 189, 190
Indies, 15
Ingalik, 17, 125, 182
Innocent XI, Pope, 33
Interior Lowlands, 16
International Eucharistic Congress, 149

Inuit(s); *also* Inupiat *and* Inupiat Inuit, 17, 120, 129, 137, 174, 182, 229
Iowa, State of, 43, 81, 82, 84, 94, 121, 130, 190, 219, 221, 227, 228, 237
Iowa Indians, 19
Ireland; *also* Irish, 31, 59, 60, 79, 90, 145, 161, 218
Iron Horse, 98
Iroquois; *also* Iroquoian, 20, 21, 33, 34, 35, 38, 39, 50, 57, 58, 65, 73, 74, 168, 188, 189, 194, 197, 201, 202, 211, 216, 226, 227, 229, 230, 233, 235
Isaac Jogues — *see under* Jogues, St. Isaac
Isle La Motte, 35, 207, 224
Isle Massacre, 54
Isleta, 19, 47, 74, 177, 200, 201, 206
Isleta Pueblo, 176
Issati Sioux — *see under* Sioux
Italy; *also* Italian, 24, 49, 80, 122, 140, 216, 225, 233, 234, 236, 238

J

Jackson, Andrew, 75, 77
James II, 60
Jamestown, 25, 29, 36, 207, 214
Janssens, Francis, 110, 196
Japan; *also* Japanese, 89, 153, 155, 156
Jayme, Luis, 54, 185
Jeaga, 21
Jean, Ignatius, 102
Jean de Brébeuf — *see under* Brébeuf, St. Jean de
Jean Lalande — *see under* Lalande, St. Jean
Jemez, 19, 53, 212
Jerome of Westphalia, 134
Jerusalem, 67
Jesuits, 26, 29, 31, 33, 34, 35, 36, 37, 38, 39, 40, 43, 47, 48, 50, 60, 67, 75, 76, 80, 82, 86, 93, 94, 104, 109, 110, 120, 121, 125, 126, 127, 171, 178, 182, 183, 184, 185, 186, 187, 188, 189, 190, 191, 192, 193, 194, 195, 196, 197, 198, 199, 200, 201, 202, 203, 204, 205, 207, 208, 209, 214, 220, 221, 223, 225, 232, 236, 237, 238, 239

Maricopa, 19, 126, 184
Mariposa, 18, 86
Marlborough, 73, 66
Marquette, Jacques, 23, 33, 36, 37, 38, 39, 41, 43, 184, 189, 190, 194, 197, 199, 205, 206, 209, 211, 220, 221, 231, 232, 233
Marquette University, 179
Martínez, Alonso, 47, 200
Martínez, Francisco de la Tejadu Díaz de Velasco, 187
Martínez, Pedro, 26, 52, 188, 232
Marty, Martin, 102, 109, 110, 118, 119, 129, 196, 202, 205, 232
Martyrs Shrine, 171
Marvville, 132
Mascouten(s), 20, 21, 189, 231
Masonic Lodge of Oregon, 147
Masons, 147
Massachuset, 21
Massachusetts, 31, 32, 59, 61, 121, 130, 162, 193, 194, 215, 242
Massé, Enemond, 192, 232
Massenet, Damian, 44, 206
Massey, Masseus, 37, 193
Mather, Cotton, 31
Matheson, Lucille, 84
Matignon, François, 218
Mattapony, 21, 193
Matthew, John, 196
Mattole, 18
Maumee, 38, 203
Maxwell, James, 197
Maya, 230
Mayflower, 162
Mazaitzashanawi, 205
Mazella, Andrew, 199
Mazzuchelli, Venerable Samuel, 80, 82, 190, 195, 209, 233
McCloskey, John, 107
McCorkell, Patrick, 171
McDermott, Catherine Ellen, 145
McElroy, John, 86
McKinley, William, 133, 134
McLaughlin, James, 122, 123, 179
McLaughlin, Marie, 179
McMaster, James, 112
McMeel, Bernard Francis "Barney," 176
Mdewakanton, 21
Meductic, 192

Meerschaert, Theophile, 126, 130, 131, 132, 134, 137, 203
Memberton, Chief, 192
Membré, Zenobius, 36, 38, 41, 44, 53, 184, 189, 191, 196, 206, 233
Memphis, 206
Menard, René, 33, 34, 37, 39, 53, 194, 201, 208, 233
Menchero, John, 47, 200
Méndez, Hernando, 44, 206
Méndez, Juan, 36, 52, 207
Mengarini, Gregorio, 197, 209, 217
Menóminee, 21, 80, 85, 195, 209, 224, 233
Meriam Report, 149
Merton, Thomas, 158
Mescalero, 19, 47
Mesoamerican, 25, 46
Messaiger, Charles, 40, 195
Metis, 174
Mettapony, 36
Meurin, Sebastian, 43, 77, 184, 196, 197
Mexico; *also* Mexico City, Mexican(s), 19, 25, 42, 43, 44, 46, 47, 49, 72, 74, 81, 85, 86, 93, 113, 114, 145, 183, 185, 206, 207, 208, 217, 228, 230, 231, 234, 235, 238, 239
Meyer, Dillon S., 159, 160
Miami, 172
Miami Indians, 21, 38, 39, 72, 74, 81, 84, 86, 172, 187, 189, 190, 191, 209, 211, 226, 231
Michigamea, 21, 191
Michigan, 37, 39, 40, 43, 54, 74, 75, 79, 80, 82, 85, 109, 130, 137, 149, 157, 177, 178, 190, 194, 195, 212, 213, 216, 217, 221, 223, 224, 225, 226, 230, 231, 233, 234, 237, 242, 244
Michigan City, 190
Michilimackinac, 194, 225
Michipicoton, 195
Micmac(s), 21, 29, 192, 193, 215
Middlendorf, Gottfried, 49
Miège, Jean-Baptiste, 191, 199, 209, 233
Milan, 80, 233, 238
Mile Bluff, 181
Miles, Nelson A., 111
Miles City, 224
Military Chaplains Association, 147

Millet, Pierre, 34, 201, 202
Milwaukee, 179, 209
Mina, Juan de, 44, 206
Mingo(s), 21, 36, 204
Mingües, Juan, 43, 54, 199
Miniconjou, 19, 123
Minneapolis, 40, 161, 226
Minnesota, 195, 196
Miranda, Antonio, 44, 206
Mirvelo, 186
Mishawaka, 190
Mishóngnovi, 19, 48, 183
Mission la Candelaria, 54
Missionary College of San Fernando, 239
Mississippi, River *and* State, 16, 19, 23, 25, 33, 38, 40, 41, 42, 43, 44, 54, 58, 61, 77, 85, 110, 127, 143, 177, 180, 181, 189, 191, 196, 205, 221, 225, 226, 231, 233, 238, 242
Missouri, State of, 191, 196, 197, 219, 220, 221, 222, 223, 224, 225, 226, 234, 239
Missouri Indians, 20
Miwok, 86
Moapa, 19
Mobile, 21, 181, 182
Mobridge, 123
Mococo, 21
Modoc(s), 18, 101, 131
Mohan, Robert Paul, 162
Mohave, 19
Mohawk(s), 21, 30, 31, 32, 33, 57, 58, 65, 117, 167, 168, 171, 185, 201, 202, 207, 216, 224, 225, 227, 229, 230, 235, 236
Mohegan, 21, 31
Mohican, 21, 186
Molala, 18
Molin, Laurent, 192
Molokai, 219
Molyneux, Richard, 36, 204
Monacan, 21
Monaco, José María, 29, 188
Monge, Ildefonso, 44, 206
Mono, 18, 19
Monroe, James, 76
Montagnais, 17, 29
Montana, 197, 198
Montana Territorial Legislature, 225
Montauban, 218
Montauk, 21
Monteith, John, 237

Nuestra Señora del Pilar, 50, 185, 206, 231

Nuestra Señora del Pilar de los Adayes, 46, 206

Nuestra Señora del Refugio, 46, 207

Nulato, 125, 182, 239

Nun-da-wa-o-ne — see under Seneca(s)

O

O-na-yoté-ka — see under Oneida(s)

O-nun-da-ga-o-no — see under Onondaga(s)

O'Connor, John J., 9

O'odham, 19

O'Rourke, Patricia, 180

Oakland, 145

Ocale, 21

Occaneechi, 21

Ocejo, Martínez de, 81, 183

Och, Joseph, 49

Odermatt, Adelhelm, 132, 133

Odin, John M., 184

Ofo, 21

Ogdensburg, 34, 202

Oglala, 19, 135, 136, 137, 165

Oglethorpe, James, 60, 188

Ohio, 203

Ohio Valley, 65

Ojibwa(s); *also* Cree-Ojibwa, 17, 196

Oka, 74

Okanagon(s), 18, 110, 126, 197, 198

Okanagon Valley, 235

Okinawa, 155

Oklahoma, 203

Oklahoma City, 130, 137

Oklahoma Territory, 122, 130, 203

Oklahoma Tuberculosis Association, 140

Old Gabe, 78

Old Hickory, 75

Old Ignace, 43, 50, 188

Old Mines, 43, 197

Old Town, 85, 89, 192, 193

Old World, 15, 93

Olives, 44

Olmos, Andrés de, 44, 52, 206

Olympia, 86, 208, 218

Omaha, 199

Omaha Indians, 20

Oñate, Don Juan de, 47, 200

Onathesqua, 21

One Who Yawns, 113, 114

Oneida(s), 21, 32, 33, 57, 64, 65, 155, 201

Onondaga(s), 21, 57, 202, 220, 229, 230

Ontario, 32, 34, 57

Opata, 19

Oraibi, 19, 48

Order of Preachers, 80, 216, 233; *see also* Dominicans

Order of St. Gregory, 103

Oregon, 18, 49, 50, 78, 83, 88, 89, 94, 95, 99, 100, 101, 106, 107, 111, 112, 121, 125, 126, 133, 147, 148, 159, 203, 204, 215, 218, 219, 220, 221, 236, 238, 243

Oregon City, 94, 100, 215, 221, 238

Oregon Compulsory Education Act, 147, 148

Oregon Country, 49

Oregon Territory, 49, 83, 88, 106, 107, 215

Oregon Trail, 78, 106, 218

Orista, 26, 205

Orléans, 225, 226

Orono, Chief, 193

Osage, 20, 43, 76, 80, 81, 82, 86, 131, 153, 184, 190, 197, 203, 219, 220, 226, 234, 239

Osceola, Chief, 20

Oshkosh, 53

Osorio, Tiburcio de, 187

Ospa, 27

Osuna, Luciano, 126, 185

Oswegatchié, 34, 202

Oswego, 201

Ota, 20

Otoe, 199

Ottawa, 20, 37, 40, 74, 80, 82, 131, 194, 195, 197, 209, 211, 212, 213, 217, 224, 233

Oumamik, 208

Our Lady of Good Hope, 182

Our Lady of Hope, 192

Our Lady of Loreto, 238

Our Lady of Sorrows, 126, 202

Ouray, Chief, 70

Outagami, 211

P

Pacelli, Eugenio, 153

Padanniapapi, Chief, 205

Padilla, Juan de, 42, 52, 234

Padoucas, 190

Paine, Thomas, 64

Paiute, 19, 90, 112, 123

Pakawá, 44, 206

Palatka, 187

Palma, 239

Palos, Juan de, 25

Palóu, Francisco, 239

Palouse, 90

Palus, 18

Pamlico, 21

Pamunkey, 21

Pan-American Exposition, 134

Panama Canal, 135, 140

Panawaniske, 85, 192

Pandosy, Charles, 208, 234, 235

Papago, 19, 126, 140, 142, 183, 184, 228

Papal Line of Demarcation, 24

Paraguay, 164

Pareja, Francisco de, 187, 235

Paret, John J., 171

Parga, Juan de, 187

Paris, 41, 101, 216, 219, 225, 229, 233

Pariseau, Mother Joseph, 90

Parker, Ely, 98

Parliament, 69

Parra, Francisco de, 48

Parris Island, 219

Pas-de-Calais, 233

Pasadena, 145

Pascagoula, 21

Passamaquoddy(ies), 21, 74, 192, 193, 236

Patoli, 54

Patuxent, 21, 36, 193, 239

Patwin, 18

Paul III, Pope, 25, 46

Paul VI, Pope, 246, 251

Paviotso, 19

Pawhuska, 126, 131, 203

Pawnee, 20

Payaya, 206

Pearl Harbor, 121, 153

Pechillo, Jerome, 164

Pecos, 19, 52, 74, 173, 200

Pedee, 21

Pedrosa, Juan de la, 53

Peinada, Alonso, 200

Pelotte, Donald E., 11, 171, 172

Pembina, 74, 82, 202

Peña Blanca, 120, 201

Penal Period, 37, 55, 60, 90

Peñalosa, Diego de, 52
Pend d'Oreille(s), 18, 84, 86, 94, 188, 197, 221, 236
Pendleton, 204
Penn, William, 60
Pennacook, 21
Pennsylvania, 35, 36, 60, 74, 86, 127, 134, 149, 163, 177, 204, 244
Pennsylvania Avenue, 149
Penobscot(s), 21, 29, 74, 192, 193, 236
Pensacola, 21
Pentaquet, 192
Penticton, 235
Peoria(s), 21, 38, 43, 53, 81, 131, 189, 190, 225, 226
Pequot, 21, 31, 186
Pereira, Antonio, 44, 206
Perez, Juan, 50, 203
Pericú, 18
Périgueux, 237
Perris, 145
Perry, Matthew, 89
Perryman, Chief, 131
Pershing, John J., 140
Persons, Robert, 67
Petit, Benjamin Marie, 84, 190
Petitot, Emil, 108, 182
Petra, 239
Petun Hurons — see under Huron(s)
Pfefferhorn, Ignatz, 49
Phoenix, 172
Piankashaw, 21, 39, 74, 81, 84, 189, 190, 226
Picos, 200
Picquet, François, 34, 191, 202
Picuris, 19, 53, 212
Piegan, 20, 100, 126, 198, 228
Pierce, Franklin, 90
Pierron, Jean, 34, 35, 186, 201, 202, 235
Pierz, Francis, 82, 85, 195, 196, 234
Pijart, Claude, 194
Pilabo, 47
Pilgrim Springs, 129, 143, 229
Pima, 19, 172, 183
Pimería Alta, 49, 228
Pine Bluff, 184
Pine Ridge, 110, 123, 162, 165, 205
Pineville, 192
Pio, Juan Bautista, 53

Pious Fund, 184
Piros, 200
Piscataway, 9, 21, 36, 193, 239, 240
Pita, José, 46, 54, 206
Pitahauret, 20
Pittsburgh, 63
Pius V, Pope St., 26, 232
Pius VI, Pope, 67
Pius VII, Pope, 73, 218
Pius IX, Pope, 97, 103, 143, 237
Pius X, Pope St., 135, 137, 181
Pius XI, Pope, 148, 227
Pius XII, Pope, 153, 155, 159, 168
Plains Cree — see under Cree
Plains Indians, 123, 145
Plainview, 171
Platte, 43, 198, 199
Pleasant Point, 109, 193
Plunket, Christopher, 36, 208
Plymouth Colony, 130, 131
Pocomtuc, 21
Podunk, 186
Pohoy, 21
Point, Nicholas, 84, 188, 197, 235, 236
Poisson, Paul du, 41, 42, 54, 184, 191, 196
Pojoaque, 19
Pokagon Bay, 195
Poland, 153
Polar Eskimo — see under Eskimo
Pomo, 18
Ponca, 20, 197, 199
Ponce de León, Augustín, 187
Ponce de León, Juan, 23, 25, 186
Poncet, Joseph, 33, 194, 201
Pondichery, 219
Pontarlier, 236
Ponziglione, Paul Mary, 37, 84, 110, 191, 197, 209
Popay, Chief, 47
Pope Day, 64
Popes — see under given names
Porra, Francisco de, 53, 183
Port Huron, 178
Port Royal, 26, 188, 205, 214
Port Toco, 193
Portage, 30, 43, 80, 82, 195, 239
Portier, Michael, 81, 182
Portugal; also Portuguese, 24, 234
Potano, 21
Potawátomi, 13, 21, 39, 43, 76,

77, 79, 80, 82, 84, 86, 94, 110, 131, 172, 190, 191, 195, 197, 199, 203, 205, 213, 221, 223, 224, 226, 234
Potier, Pierre, 37, 203
Potomac, 21, 36, 193, 239
Potopaco, 36, 193
Poullain, Guillaume, 194
Powhatan, 21, 26
Poynaque, 74, 200
Prairie du Chien, 84, 190, 205, 237
Prando, Peter, 126, 198
Presidents of the United States — see under given names
Priest's Point, 208, 218
Prince, John Charles, 106
Prince Gallitzin Chapel, 163
Prince of Wales Island, 177
Promontory Point, 98
Propaganda Fide — see under Congregation of the Propagation of the Faith
Prouix, Jean B., 195
Provencher, Joseph, 82, 202
Puarray, 52
Pueblo(s), 19, 47, 48, 49, 74, 126, 137, 148, 173, 176, 183, 184, 200, 201
Puerto de San Sebastian, 212
Puget Sound, 18, 83, 89, 90, 110, 203, 208
Purcell, John Baptist, 118
Puritan(s), 30, 31, 32, 59, 60, 130
Puyallup, 18, 50

Q

Quadii magni nobis, 122
Quakers, 59, 60
Quanah Parker, Chief, 105
Quapaw, 20, 21, 41, 126, 131, 137, 184, 197, 203
Quebec Act, 59, 64, 67
Queen Anne's War, 27, 55, 56
Queen of Angels Monastery, 133
Queres — see under Keres
Querétaro, 43, 44
Quick Bear v. Leupp, 137
Quileute-Chimakum, 18
Quino, 227
Quintana, Andrés, 54, 81, 185
Quintanilla, Luis de, 192
Quiros, Luis de, 26, 36, 52
Quiveria, 42, 190, 234

United States Census, 149, 173
United States Congress, 82, 112, 129, 138, 140, 194, 237
United States Senate, 104
University of Freiburg, 118
University of Michigan, 237
University of Oregon Medical School, 219
University of Paris, 219
Upper Kalispel — *see under* Kalispel
Ury, John, 60
Utah, 207
Utah Lake, 69
Ute, 19, 126, 172, 186
Utica, 38, 189
Utina, 21

V

Vaillant de Gueslis, François, 225, 226
Valdez, 182, 224
Valentine, Robert, 138
Van Buren, Martin, 82
Van Quickenborne, Charles Felix, 76, 82, 190, 197, 203, 239
Vancouver, 83, 90, 94, 106, 203, 204, 215, 217, 221, 222, 238
Vargas, Francisco, 47, 200
Vásquez de Ayllón, Lucas, 23, 24, 36, 186, 188, 202, 205, 207
Vásquez de Coronado, Francisco, 42, 183, 185, 190, 199, 203, 206
Vatican, 22, 112, 113, 124, 153, 158, 159, 172, 173, 180, 246
Vatican Council I (First Vatican Council), 221, 238
Vatican Council II (Second Vatican Council) 13, 97, 161, 246
Velasco, Fernando, 53
Velden, 126, 198
Vélez, Silvestre de Escalante, 69, 186, 199, 207
Vera Cruz, 239
Veráscola — *see under* Beráscola
Verendrye, François *and* Pierre, 197, 202, 205
Vermont, 35, 207, 215, 224
Verrazano, Giovanni da, 23
Verreydt, Felix, 80, 84, 190, 199
Vespucci, Amerigo, 23
Vest, George, 104

Veteran's Memorial Coliseum, 172
Vetromile, Eugene, 85, 193
Vianney, St. John, 219
Vicksburg, 54
Victoria, 221, 238, 239
Vietnam War, 160
Villabilla, 219
Villareal, Francisco de, 187
Villasur, Pedro de, 199
Vincennes, 26, 38, 39, 72, 189, 190, 225, 230
Vinita, 126, 131, 203
Virginia, 207, 208
Virginia City, 225
Virot, Claude François, 36, 193, 204
Viszoczky, Andrew, 195
Vizcaino, Sebastian, 23, 50, 203, 212

W

Wabash, 191
Waccamaw, 21
Wachter, Bernardine, 132, 133, 204
Wahpekute, 21
Wahpeton, 21
Wakantanka Ti Ki Chanku, 237
Wales, 58, 129, 177, 229
Walhalla, 82, 202
Walker, Thomas, 191
Wall Street, 60
Walla Walla, 18, 87, 89, 106, 204, 208, 214, 218, 234
Wallowa Valley, 111
Walpi, 19, 48, 183
Wambli Wakiata, 127, 129, 144
Wampanoag(s), 21, 61
Wappinger, 21, 186
Warmspring, 50
Wasco, 50
Washington, George, 31, 42, 64, 65, 66, 71, 73
Washington State, 208
Washington Territory, 74
Washo, 19
Watching Eagle, 127, 129, 144
Wateree, 21
Watergate, 165
Waterville, 171
Waxhau, 21
Weampemeoc, 21
Wenatchee, 18
Wenrohronon, 21

Wesel, 219
West Virginia, 36, 208
Western Eskimo — *see under* Eskimo
Wheeler Howard Act, 149
Wheelright, Esther, 31
Whidbey Island, 83, 203, 208
Whig Party, 86
Whiskey Ring, 98
White, Andrew, 9, 36, 193, 212, 239, 240
White, Emmett, 172
White Earth, 102, 176, 196
White House, 11, 76, 77, 82, 89, 90, 92, 98, 113, 119, 137, 147, 156, 165, 224
White Mountain, 19
Whitemarsh, 221
Whitman Massacre, 89, 90, 106, 204, 208, 214, 215, 218
Whitman, Marcus *and* Narcissa, 88
Wichita, 20, 42, 43, 44, 190, 234
Wild Oats, 231
Wild West Show, 123
Willamette Valley, 203, 220
William III of England, 55
William of Orange, 60
Williams, Eunice, 31
Williams, John, 31
Wills Point, 130
Wilson, Woodrow, 139, 140, 141
Winnebago(s), 21, 39, 80, 84, 86, 134, 190, 208, 219, 233
Wintun, 18
Winyaw, 21
Wisconsin, 208, 209
Wishram, 18
Wiyot, 18
Woccon, 21
Wolf, Anton Aloys, 234
Wolf Robe, Chief, 19
Woman Who Always Prays, 80, 223
Woodbridge, 34
Woodridge, 199
Work, Hubert, 148
World War I, 140, 142, 147, 149
World War II, 153, 156, 157
World's Columbian Exposition, 124
Wounded Knee Massacre, 135
Wovoka, 123

About the Authors

An internationally known writer and artist, Margaret Bunson began her writing career as a journalist for Catholic newspapers. In addition to her book *Father Damien: The Man and His Era (Revised and Updated)*, Margaret is the author of the *Encyclopedia of Ancient Egypt, Faith in Paradise,* and *Kateri Tekakwitha* and coauthor of the *Encyclopedia of Ancient Mesoamerica.*

An archaeologist and French-language translator, Stephen Bunson is the award-winning translator of *Larousse's Prehistory* and coauthor of the *Encyclopedia of Ancient Mesoamerica, Our Sunday Visitor's Encyclopedia of Saints,* and *John Paul II's Book of Saints.*

Our Sunday Visitor. . .
Your Source for Discovering the Riches of the Catholic Faith

Our Sunday Visitor has an extensive line of materials for young children, teens, and adults. Our books, Bibles, booklets, CD-ROMs, audios, and videos are available in bookstores worldwide.

To receive a FREE full-line catalog or for more information, call **Our Sunday Visitor** at **1-800-348-2440**. Or write, **Our Sunday Visitor** / 200 Noll Plaza / Huntington, IN 46750.

- -

Please send me: ___A catalog
Please send me materials on:
___Apologetics and catechetics   ___Reference works
___Prayer books   ___Heritage and the saints
___The family   ___The parish
Name_____
Address_____Apt._____
City_____State_____Zip_____
Telephone (   ) _____

                                                        A09BBABP

- -

Please send a friend: ___A catalog
Please send a friend materials on:
___Apologetics and catechetics   ___Reference works
___Prayer books   ___Heritage and the saints
___The family   ___The parish
Name_____
Address_____Apt._____
City_____State_____Zip_____
Telephone (   ) _____

                                                        A09BBABP

- -

Our Sunday Visitor
200 Noll Plaza
Huntington, IN 46750
Toll free: 1-800-348-2440
E-mail: osvbooks@osv.com
Website: www.osv.com

Your Source for Discovering the Riches of the Catholic Faith